SODA BREAD, JALAPEÑO CORN MUFFINS, WATERCRESS ... ABY

BOK CHOY WITH GINGER AND GARLIC, PANZANELLA, CANNELLINI BEANS WITH

PANCETTA, FRIED SAGE, AND GRILLED SAUSAGES, BA ... HICKEN,

HERB FRITTATA WITH ZUCCHINI AND YELLOW SQ ... KOREAN

barbecued ribs WITH PICKLED GREENS, NEW ORLEANS-STYLE

SHRIMP AND RICE, HAZELNUT-ORANGE SHORTBREAD, CHOCOLATE-CARAMEL

PECAN CLUSTERS, MELON BALLS WITH MOSCATO, MARINATED OLIVES WITH

OREGANO AND FENNEL SEEDS, *coffee-cake muffins,* YOGURT

PARFAITS WITH BLUEBERRIES AND LEMON, BREAD PUDDING WITH HAM, LEEKS,

AND CHEESE, GOAT CHEESE AND PISTACHIO STUFFED DATES, PITA CRISPS WITH

FETA-RADISH SPREAD, POPOVERS WITH WILD-MUSHROOM SAUCE, ASPARAGUS

SALAD WITH TENDER GREENS AND MINT, WATERCRESS AND GREEN BEAN SALAD,

lamb chops with artichoke hearts, CITRUS-

ROASTED SALMON WITH SPRING-PEA SAUCE, GOAT CHEESE AND RADICCHIO

PANINO, BACON AND GORGONZOLA PANINO, WILTED BABY SPINACH WITH CRISPY

SHALLOTS, CHOCOLATE-HAZELNUT SPREAD AND PEAR PANINO, RICOTTA AND

FIG PANINO, ALMOND CUSTARD CAKE, CHOCOLATE-PISTACHIO PHYLLO ROLLS,

CARAMEL CRUNCH, *grasshopper pie,* NUT BRITTLE, CHICKEN

SOUP WITH PARSLEY DUMPLINGS, CHILLED PEA AND PEA-SHOOT SOUP WITH

SHRIMP, GARLIC BREAD SOUP, TABBOULEH, MASHED PLANTAINS, SEARED STEAK

WITH OLIVE RELISH, CHINESE-STYLE *steamed sea bass* WITH

VEGETABLES, FETTUCCINE WITH ASPARAGUS RIBBONS, POACHED SALMON

STEAKS WITH CREAMY DILL SAUCE, *grilled pizzas* WITH CLAMS
PEA SHOOT AND VEGETABLE STIR-FRY, RISOTTO WITH PEA SHOOTS, GRILLED
PIZZAS WITH CANADIAN BACON AND PINEAPPLE, ROASTED TILEFISH OVER
POTATOES, NEW YORK–STYLE CHEESECAKE, COCONUT CREAM BARS, ORANGE
LIME MOUSSE, *frozen espresso cheesecake,* CHOCOLATE
CHEESECAKE, CITRUS-RICOTTA CHEESECAKE, PEA-SHOOT PESTO, BEET SOUP
WITH INDIAN SPICES, GRILLED-VEGETABLE GAZPACHO WITH SHRIMP, GRILLED
VEGETABLES WITH HERB VINAIGRETTE, VIETNAMESE SUMMER ROLLS, AVOCADO
AND ORANGE SALAD, WARM GOAT-CHEESE TOASTS, PROSCIUTTO CROSTINI AND
FRESH FIGS WITH GORGONZOLA, GINGER PICKLED BEETS, CABBAGE AND RADISH
SLAW WITH PEANUT DRESSING, *classic creamy coleslaw,*
CARROT SLAW WITH GOLDEN RAISINS, ITALIAN POTATO SALAD, FENNEL, RED
ONION, AND PARSLEY SALAD, GRILLED ASPARAGUS WITH BEET AND CUCUMBER
RELISH, TOASTED-BULGHUR PILAF, RED AND GREEN CABBAGE SLAW WITH
BACON, BEET AND BROWN RICE SALAD WITH GOAT CHEESE, GRILLED LEMON
CHICKEN, *shrimp po'boys,* NIÇOISE SALAD, PORK KABOBS WITH
ORANGE AND THYME, ROASTED SHRIMP AND CHORIZO, CARAMELIZED ONION
AND GORGONZOLA QUICHE, RICOTTA, LEMON, AND ARUGULA QUICHE, QUICHE
LORRAINE, APRICOT-WALNUT BISCOTTI, LEMON-BLACKBERRY PUDDING CAKES
PATTI'S NECTARINE-BLUEBERRY PIE, VANILLA ICE CREAM WITH PLUM COMPOTE
STRAWBERRY SPONGE PUDDING, PATTI'S LEMON MERINGUE PIE, CHOCOLATE
MALT SANDWICH COOKIES, ROSÉ SANGRIA, *rose-petal gin fizz*

MARTHA STEWART LIVING

Annual Recipes

2005

MARTHA STEWART LIVING

Annual Recipes

2005

from the editors of **MARTHA STEWART LIVING**

Originally published in book form by Martha Stewart Living Omnimedia, Inc. in 2004.
Published simultaneously by Oxmoor House, Inc.
These recipes were previously published by Martha Stewart Living Omnimedia, Inc.

Printed in the United States of America.

ISBN 0-8487-2822-X
ISSN 1541-9541

Acknowledgments

It takes the collaboration of many individuals to publish a collection of more than five hundred inspired recipes every year. A very special thank you to deputy food editors Lucinda Scala Quinn and Susan Sugarman for leading a team of wonderful, inventive cooks, including senior food editors Jennifer Aaronson, John Barricelli, Tara Bench, Sarah Carey, and Heidi Johannsen. Thanks to all the members of the food department, including Shelly Kaldunski, Anna Kovel, and Melissa Perry, for their tireless development of outstanding recipes, and for the support of Lillian Kang, Darlene Sepiol-Schrack, Yolanda Florez, Aida Ibarra, and Gertrude Porter. Thank you to recipes editor Miranda Van Gelder and assistant recipes editor Amanda Genge, whose combined efforts ensure that every recipe is written just so. Thanks to books editor Ellen Morrissey for overseeing the creation of this book from start to finish, and to Robert Bowe and Natalie Ermann for their keen attention to detail. Thanks as well to Mary Jane Callister, James Dunlinson, and Amber Blakesley for art directing and designing the pages of this book, and to the production team of Duane Stapp and Denise Clappi. And many thanks to everyone who contributed their time and energy to the creation of this book, among them Elizabeth Alsop, Roger Astudillo, Marc I. Bailes, Dora Braschi Cardinale, Elizabeth Brownfield, Peter Colen, Eric Hutton, Jennifer J. Jarett, Shelley Jefferson, Martin Kearton, Matthew Landfield, Stacie McCormick, Jim McKeever, Christine Moller, Elizabeth Parson, Meg Peterson, Eric A. Pike, George D. Planding, Debra Puchalla, Madhu Puri, Margaret Roach, Lauren Podlach Stanich, Gael Towey, Beverly Utt, and Alison Vanek, and to everyone at Oxmoor House, AGT.seven, and R.R. Donnelley and Sons. Finally, a big thank you to Martha, for always encouraging us to create the most delicious, creative, and easy-to-follow recipes for our readers.

Contents

Introduction

Here at MARTHA STEWART LIVING, we aim to create recipes and food stories that are classic and unique. When we set out to publish a piece on guacamole, for example, we start by considering where the dish originated and which techniques and ingredients make it authentic. Then we begin developing our own version, testing, tasting, fine-tuning, and retesting. Once we've decided on the recipe we like best, we go further, preparing variations that are true to the original yet unmistakably their own.

So if you look for a guacamole recipe, you'll find in our January section not only Classic Mexican Guacamole, with the most basic ingredients (avocado, white onion, cilantro, chile pepper, tomato, and salt), but three other versions as well: mango and pear; tomatillo; and cumin-garlic. The same is true of the bread pudding in our October section. We start with a recipe featuring an old-fashioned egg custard with raisins, cinnamon, and nutmeg, then offer a wide range of add-ins, including bananas, coconut, and rum; cranberries, orange, and pecan; chocolate; and even chai-tea spices.

Our goal is twofold: First, to teach you a basic method so you can successfully re-create a favorite dish; and second, to encourage you to try flavor combinations you may never have imagined.

We hope that you enjoy all of the recipes in this book—from the most traditional to the most inventive, and the hundreds of others that fall somewhere in between.

—THE FOOD EDITORS OF
MARTHA STEWART LIVING

Winter

BAKING IS A YEAR-ROUND PLEASURE, but warm biscuits and breads from the oven seem to beckon more than ever during the winter months. Among the recipes that follow are several that provide the joys of old-fashioned baking—starting from scratch and sinking your hands into big bowls of flour and dough. No modern equipment required.

January

mushroom soup with poached eggs and Parmesan cheese

SERVES 4

½ ounce dried mushrooms, such as porcini (about ½ cup)

2 cups boiling water

4½ teaspoons extra-virgin olive oil

1 medium onion, halved and thinly sliced into half-moons

3 garlic cloves, minced

1 celery stalk, finely chopped (about ½ cup)

1 pound cremini or white mushrooms, caps and stems thinly sliced lengthwise (about 6 cups)

½ teaspoon coarse salt

½ cup dry white wine

2 cups homemade or low-sodium store-bought chicken or vegetable stock

1 tablespoon finely chopped fresh tarragon, plus 4 sprigs for garnish

4 large eggs

1 ounce Parmesan cheese, thinly shaved with a vegetable peeler

Freshly ground pepper

1 Soak dried mushrooms in boiling water, covered, until soft, about 20 minutes. Lift out mushrooms; squeeze over liquid. Finely chop; set aside. Pour liquid through a fine sieve into a bowl; reserve liquid.

2 Heat oil in a medium saucepan over medium heat until hot but not smoking. Add onion, garlic, and celery; cook, stirring occasionally, until soft, about 8 minutes. Add fresh mushrooms and salt; cook, stirring occasionally, until most liquid has evaporated and mushrooms are soft, about 12 minutes. Raise heat to high. Add wine, reserved mushrooms and liquid, stock, and 1½ cups water; bring to a simmer. Reduce heat to medium-low; cook 30 minutes. Add tarragon.

3 Fill another medium saucepan three-quarters full with water; bring to a bare simmer over medium heat. Crack eggs into pan; cook until whites are set but yolks are slightly runny, 3 to 4 minutes.

4 Divide soup among four bowls. Transfer one egg to each bowl; divide cheese among bowls, sprinkling over eggs. Season with pepper, and garnish with tarragon sprigs.

PER SERVING: 239 CALORIES, 12 G FAT, 219 MG CHOLESTEROL, 12 G CARBOHYDRATE, 694 MG SODIUM, 14 G PROTEIN, 2 G FIBER

from Fit to Eat: Light Main Courses

classic Mexican guacamole

MAKES 1½ CUPS

1½ tablespoons finely chopped white onion

1 tablespoon plus 2 teaspoons finely chopped fresh cilantro

1¼ teaspoons finely chopped, seeded fresh jalapeño chile

Coarse salt

1 ripe Hass avocado, pitted, peeled, and coarsely chopped

3 tablespoons finely chopped, seeded tomato

With a large mortar and pestle, mash onion, 1 tablespoon cilantro, jalapeño, and ½ teaspoon salt until smooth and juicy. Add avocado, and mash slightly (avocado should remain somewhat chunky). Stir in tomato and remaining 2 teaspoons cilantro. Season with salt if desired. Serve immediately.

from Guacamole

cumin-garlic guacamole

MAKES 3 CUPS

2 ripe Hass avocados, pitted, peeled, and cut into ¾-inch chunks

1 garlic clove, minced

⅔ cup finely chopped seeded tomato (about 1 small)

¼ cup finely chopped red onion

1½ tablespoons fresh lime juice

1 teaspoon coarse salt

¼ teaspoon ground cumin

Mix all ingredients together in a medium bowl with a fork, mashing avocado slightly (avocado should remain somewhat chunky). Serve immediately.

from Guacamole

mango and pear guacamole

MAKES 1½ CUPS

4½ teaspoons finely chopped white onion

1¼ teaspoons finely chopped, seeded fresh jalapeño chile

¼ teaspoon coarse salt

1 ripe Hass avocado, pitted, peeled, and coarsely chopped

⅓ cup peeled, cubed mango (½ inch cubes)

¼ cup peeled, cubed Anjou pear (½ inch cubes)

With a large mortar and pestle, mash onion, jalapeño, and salt until smooth and juicy. Add avocado, and mash slightly (avocado should remain somewhat chunky). Stir in mango and pear. Serve immediately.

from Guacamole

tomatillo guacamole

MAKES 1 CUP

6 tomatillos (about 13 ounces), husked and halved
½ fresh jalapeño chile with seeds (about ¼ ounce)
¼ cup finely chopped white onion
2 tablespoons finely chopped fresh cilantro
¾ teaspoon coarse salt
1 ripe Hass avocado, pitted, peeled, and coarsely chopped

Purée the tomatillos, jalapeño, onion, cilantro, and salt in a food processor or blender until smooth. Purée ½ cup salsa and the avocado until smooth. The remaining cup salsa can be served separately.

from Guacamole

little "drumsticks"

MAKES 6 DOZEN | PHOTO ON PAGE 69

5 tablespoons olive oil
1 cup finely chopped onion
2 garlic cloves, minced
1 whole chicken breast on the bone (1¾ pounds), skinned
  Coarse salt and freshly ground pepper
1 tomato, coarsely chopped (about 1 cup)
⅓ cup finely chopped fresh flat-leaf parsley
⅛ teaspoon cayenne pepper
1¾ cups milk
6 tablespoons unsalted butter
3 cups all-purpose flour
1½ quarts canola oil
4 large eggs
2½ cups plain breadcrumbs

1 Make filling: Heat 3 tablespoons olive oil in a large saucepan over medium heat until hot but not smoking. Add half the onion and garlic, and cook, stirring, until onion is translucent, about 3 minutes. Add chicken, 2 teaspoons salt, and ¼ teaspoon pepper; cook 2 minutes more. Cover with water (about 4 cups), and bring to a boil. Reduce heat; simmer until chicken is cooked through, about 30 minutes.

2 Transfer chicken to a plate; set aside. Pour stock through a fine sieve into a bowl; discard solids. Set aside. When chicken is cool enough to handle, finely shred meat; discard bones.

3 Heat remaining 2 tablespoons oil in a large skillet over medium-low heat until hot but not smoking. Add the remaining onion and garlic, and cook, stirring, until onion is translucent, about 3 minutes. Add the tomato, parsley, and

reserved chicken. Stir in cayenne and ½ cup reserved stock, and simmer 3 minutes. Season with salt and pepper. Transfer to a bowl to cool.

4 Make dough: Bring 1½ cups milk, the butter, salt, and 2¼ cups stock to a boil in a large saucepan. Remove from heat, and add all of the flour at once. Stir with a wooden spoon until mixture forms a slightly sticky mass. Transfer to a bowl.

5 Roll a generous tablespoon of dough into a ball, then flatten into a 3-inch round about ⅛ inch thick. Put 1 teaspoon filling in center; bring edges up to form a 1½- to 2-inch high teardrop shape. Repeat with remaining dough and filling.

6 Fry drumsticks: Heat canola oil in a large saucepan until it registers 360°F on a deep-fry thermometer. Line baking sheets with paper towels. Beat eggs and remaining ¼ cup milk in a shallow bowl. Working with one at a time, dip drumsticks in egg mixture, then roll in breadcrumbs.

7 Working in batches to avoid crowding, fry drumsticks, turning occasionally, until golden brown, about 1 minute. With a slotted spoon, transfer drumsticks to lined baking sheets to drain. (Adjust heat between batches as necessary to keep oil at a steady temperature.) If not serving drumsticks immediately, keep warm in a 275°F oven up to 30 minutes.

from Cocktail Hour in South Beach

mini crab cakes on seashells

MAKES 2 DOZEN | PHOTO ON PAGE 69

3 slices white bread, crusts removed
½ cup milk
3 tablespoons olive oil
1 cup finely chopped onion
1 pound jumbo lump crabmeat, cartilage removed, crabmeat squeezed dry
1 tablespoon rum
1 teaspoon tomato paste
1 teaspoon fresh lemon juice
1 large egg yolk
2 tablespoons finely chopped fresh cilantro
  Coarse salt and freshly ground pepper
  Hot sauce, such as Tabasco
24 clam or scallop shells (2 to 2½ inches), rinsed and dried
½ cup fresh fine breadcrumbs
2 tablespoons unsalted butter, melted

1 Preheat oven to 375°F. Soak bread in milk until almost all milk is absorbed. Squeeze out milk; discard. Set bread aside.

2 Heat oil in a large skillet over medium heat until hot but not smoking. Add onion; cook, stirring occasionally, until

translucent, 4 to 5 minutes. Reduce heat to low; add two-thirds of crabmeat, the soaked bread, rum, tomato paste, lemon juice, and egg yolk; cook, stirring, 4 minutes. Add cilantro; season with salt, pepper, and hot sauce.

3   Continue to cook mixture, stirring, until combined and crabmeat is broken up, about 5 minutes more. Remove from heat; add remaining crabmeat.

4   Mound the crab mixture onto shells; transfer to rimmed baking sheets. Stir breadcrumbs into butter in a small bowl; sprinkle mixture on tops of crab cakes. Bake until heated through and brown, 15 to 18 minutes. Serve warm.

from Cocktail Hour in South Beach

salt-cod croquettes

MAKES ABOUT 4 DOZEN | **PHOTO ON PAGE 69**

1   pound salt cod
1   pound Yukon gold potatoes, peeled
     and cut into 1-inch chunks
     Coarse salt
5   tablespoons olive oil
1   cup finely chopped onion
2   garlic cloves, minced
¼   cup finely chopped fresh flat-leaf parsley
     Freshly ground pepper
2   large eggs, lightly beaten
1   cup plain dried breadcrumbs
1½ quarts canola oil

1   Cover cod with cold water in a large bowl, and cover with plastic wrap. Refrigerate at least 12 hours or overnight, changing the water twice.

2   Drain and rinse cod. Transfer to a large saucepan; cover with cold water. Bring to a boil. Reduce heat; simmer 5 minutes. Drain and rinse cod. Wrap in a clean kitchen towel, and roll back and forth until cod is dry and finely shredded. Shake out into a small bowl; set aside.

3   Cover potatoes with cold water in a clean large saucepan; season with salt. Bring to a boil; reduce heat, and simmer until tender, about 15 minutes. Drain potatoes, then mash in saucepan; set aside.

4   Heat olive oil in a large skillet over medium heat until hot but not smoking. Add onion and garlic; cook, stirring occasionally, until onion is translucent, about 3 minutes. Reduce heat to medium-low, and stir in cod. Cook until it looks dry, about 3 minutes. Stir in parsley. Season with salt and pepper. Transfer to a bowl; let cool.

5   Stir eggs and reserved potatoes into cod mixture, mashing ingredients to combine. Mold about 1 tablespoon mixture into a 2-inch-long log (slightly taper ends). Repeat with remaining cod mixture. Roll logs in breadcrumbs.

6   Heat canola oil in a large saucepan over medium-high heat until it registers 360°F on a deep-fry thermometer. Line a baking sheet with paper towels. Working in batches to avoid crowding, fry logs, turning occasionally, until just golden brown, about 1 minute. With a slotted spoon, transfer to lined sheet to drain. (Adjust heat between batches as necessary to keep oil at a steady temperature.) If not serving immediately, keep warm in a 275°F oven up to 30 minutes.

from Cocktail Hour in South Beach

shrimp empanadas

MAKES 5 DOZEN | **PHOTO ON PAGE 69**

Empanadas can be made through step six, wrapped in plastic, and frozen for up to three weeks. Bake in a 400 degree oven for ten minutes.

4   cups plus 1 tablespoon all-purpose flour
1   tablespoon olive oil
½   cup finely chopped onion
1   small garlic clove, minced
½   pound medium shrimp (about 15), peeled,
     deveined, and finely chopped
2   teaspoons tomato paste
     Coarse salt and freshly ground pepper
⅛   teaspoon cayenne pepper
2   tablespoons finely chopped fresh flat-leaf parsley
4   green olives, pitted and chopped
4   tablespoons unsalted butter, softened
1   cup mayonnaise
2   large eggs, plus 1 large egg beaten with
     a pinch of coarse salt for glaze
¼   cup milk

1   Stir together 1 tablespoon flour and ¼ cup water in a small bowl until flour is dissolved; set aside.

2   Heat oil in a large skillet over medium heat until hot but not smoking. Add onion and garlic; cook, stirring occasionally, until onion is soft but not brown, about 2 minutes. Add shrimp and tomato paste; season with salt and pepper. Cook, stirring occasionally, until shrimp are cooked through and opaque, about 3 minutes. Stir in cayenne and parsley. Stir in flour mixture; simmer 2 minutes. Turn off heat; stir in olives. Season again with salt and pepper. Set aside.

3 Preheat oven to 375°F. Place remaining 4 cups flour in a large bowl; make a well in the center. Place butter, mayonnaise, eggs, milk, and 2 teaspoons salt in well. Squeeze wet ingredients between fingers of one hand to combine. Gradually work in flour, squeezing to form a soft dough.

4 Pinch off 60 cherry-size balls of dough; reserve leftover dough. Set aside 15 dough balls. Transfer remaining 45 dough balls to baking sheets. Wrap in plastic, and refrigerate. Divide reserved dough into 4 pieces; set aside 1 piece. Wrap remaining 3 pieces in plastic, and refrigerate.

5 Transfer reserved dough balls to fifteen round tartlet molds (each 1½ inches in diameter and ½ inch high). Press dough into molds; it should reach just over tops. Mound 1 teaspoon filling into each mold.

6 Roll out reserved dough piece to ⅛ inch thick. With a 2-inch round cookie cutter, cut out 15 tops. Place over filling, pressing edges of dough to seal; trim excess. Transfer empanadas to a baking sheet.

7 Brush tops with egg glaze. Bake empanadas until cooked through and golden brown, 25 to 30 minutes. Let cool slightly on a wire rack; unmold. Serve warm or at room temperature. Repeat process with remaining dough balls, filling, and divided dough pieces.

from Cocktail Hour in South Beach

shrimp stew with kabocha squash and okra

SERVES 6

If you can't find whole shrimp (with heads intact), use regular medium unpeeled shrimp.

1½ pounds medium whole shrimp, heads intact (do not peel)

2 teaspoons grated peeled fresh ginger

½ teaspoon paprika

Coarse salt and freshly ground pepper

¼ cup olive oil, plus more if needed

2 large shallots, coarsely chopped (about ⅓ cup)

2 garlic cloves, minced

1 fresh serrano chile, thinly sliced

1 teaspoon ground cumin

1 medium kabocha squash (about 3 pounds), peeled, seeded, and cut into 1-inch cubes

1 can (14 ounces) coconut milk

12 okra (about 5 ounces), cut into ½-inch-thick rounds

¼ cup finely chopped fresh cilantro, plus leaves for garnish (optional)

1 Toss shrimp, ginger, and paprika in a large bowl; season with salt and pepper.

2 Heat 3 tablespoons oil in a large sauté pan over medium-high heat until hot but not smoking. Working in batches, and adding more oil as needed, cook shrimp, turning once, until browned on both sides, about 4 minutes total. With a slotted spoon, transfer shrimp to a plate to cool; keep pan on stove with heat turned off.

3 Set aside 6 shrimp. Shell remaining shrimp, transferring shells and heads to a large square of cheesecloth as you work. Set aside shrimp; tie cheesecloth into a secure bundle.

4 Add remaining tablespoon oil to pan, along with shallots, garlic, chile, and cumin. Cook over medium heat, stirring, 1 minute. Stir in squash; add cheesecloth bundle and 1 cup water. Reduce heat to medium-low. Cover; simmer until squash begins to soften, about 15 minutes.

5 Stir in coconut milk and okra. Simmer, covered, until squash is cooked through and soft and the sauce is thick, about 30 minutes. Transfer cheesecloth bundle to a sieve set over the pan; squeeze liquid into sauce, and discard bundle. Stir in reserved shelled shrimp and cilantro. Season with salt and pepper.

6 Divide stew among small serving bowls. Garnish with reserved shell-on shrimp, and, if desired, cilantro leaves.

from Cocktail Hour in South Beach

SALADS AND SIDE DISHES

frisée and radicchio salad

SERVES 4

1 large head frisée, trimmed

1 small head radicchio, halved and cut crosswise into ¼-inch-thick slices

2 tablespoons red-wine vinegar

1 tablespoon Dijon mustard

Coarse salt and freshly ground pepper

¼ cup extra-virgin olive oil

1 Tear the frisée into bite-size pieces, and place in a large bowl with the radicchio; set aside.

2 Whisk together vinegar and mustard in a small bowl. Season with salt and pepper. Whisking constantly, pour in oil in a slow, steady stream; whisk until emulsified. Just before serving, drizzle vinaigrette over salad; toss gently.

from What's for Dinner?

chayote squash salad with parsley

SERVES 6

Chayote squash is known as mirliton in some areas.

4 chayote squash (about 2¼ pounds)
2 tablespoons extra-virgin olive oil
¼ cup coarsely chopped fresh flat-leaf parsley,
  plus leaves for garnish (optional)
  Coarse salt and freshly ground pepper

1 Quarter squash, and remove and discard inner membranes. Cut each squash quarter lengthwise into four pieces, and transfer to a steamer basket.

2 Bring 2 cups water to a boil in a large saucepan. Place basket in saucepan; reduce heat to a simmer. Cover; steam squash until tender and translucent, about 30 minutes. Transfer to a medium bowl to cool. Toss with oil and parsley; season with salt and pepper. Refrigerate until cold, 1 to 2 hours. Serve salad garnished with parsley leaves, if desired.

from Cocktail Hour in South Beach

roasted carrots and parsnips

SERVES 4 | PHOTO ON PAGE 81

2 pounds carrots, peeled and halved lengthwise
1½ pounds parsnips, peeled and halved lengthwise
  (quartered if large)
2 tablespoons olive oil
  Coarse salt and freshly ground pepper
1 tablespoon chopped fresh thyme

1 Preheat oven to 475°F. Arrange carrots and parsnips in a single layer on a rimmed baking sheet. Drizzle oil over vegetables; lightly toss to coat. Season with salt and pepper; sprinkle with thyme.

2 Roast vegetables, turning occasionally, until they start to brown and are tender, about 30 minutes. Remove from oven; transfer vegetables to a serving platter.

from What's for Dinner?

MAIN COURSES

chicken with onions and garlic

SERVES 4 | PHOTO ON PAGE 76

For crispier skin, panfry the chicken before roasting it.

1 whole roaster chicken (about 4 pounds), cut into 8 pieces
1 tablespoon unsalted butter, softened
  Coarse salt and freshly ground pepper
2 onions, quartered lengthwise
10 garlic cloves, peeled
6 sprigs thyme, plus more for garnish

1 Preheat oven to 475°F. Rinse chicken pieces; pat dry. Brush chicken with butter, and season with 2 teaspoons salt and 1 teaspoon pepper.

2 Place chicken in a small roasting pan. Arrange onions, garlic, and thyme sprigs over and under chicken. Roast, basting with pan drippings halfway through, until chicken is golden and cooked through, 35 to 40 minutes. Transfer the chicken to a platter, and set aside.

3 Pour pan drippings through a sieve into a small bowl; discard solids. Arrange onions and all but three garlic cloves around chicken on platter. Whisk remaining garlic cloves with pan juices. Strain juices again; discard solids. Pour sauce over chicken; serve garnished with thyme sprigs.

from What's for Dinner?

crisp salmon with braised red cabbage and mustard sauce

SERVES 4

2 teaspoons olive oil
⅓ cup finely chopped onion
½ pound red cabbage (about ½ small head), thinly sliced
  (about 4 cups)
¾ teaspoon coarse salt
3 tablespoons balsamic vinegar
  Vegetable-oil cooking spray
4 salmon fillets with skin (5 ounces each)
  Freshly ground pepper
2 teaspoons Dijon mustard

1 Heat oil in a medium sauté pan over medium heat until hot but not smoking. Add onion, and cook, stirring occasionally, until soft, about 4 minutes. Add cabbage, ½ teaspoon salt, the vinegar, and ½ cup water to pan; raise heat to medium-high. Cook, stirring, until cabbage begins to wilt and liquid

has evaporated, about 8 minutes. Transfer cabbage to a bowl; cover with foil to keep warm.

2 Lightly coat a large nonstick skillet with cooking spray; place over medium heat. Season skinless sides of fillets with pepper and remaining ¼ teaspoon salt. Place fillets, skin sides down, in hot skillet. Cook, without turning, until skin is very crisp and golden brown, 5 to 6 minutes. Turn fillets; cook until flesh is opaque, about 3 minutes. Transfer fillets to a plate; loosely cover with foil.

3 Wipe skillet clean with a paper towel; place over medium-high heat. Add mustard and ½ cup water to skillet; when the water begins to bubble, whisk until smooth. Cook mixture until thickened, about 2 minutes.

4 Divide cabbage among four plates, and top with fillets. Drizzle mustard sauce over fillets. Season with pepper, and serve immediately.

PER SERVING: 243 CALORIES, 11 G FAT, 78 MG CHOLESTEROL, 5 G CARBOHYDRATE, 457 MG SODIUM, 29 G PROTEIN, 1 G FIBER

from Fit to Eat: Light Main Courses

cumin-dusted shrimp with black-eyed peas and collard greens

SERVES 4 | PHOTO ON PAGE 79

1   cup dried black-eyed peas (6 ounces)
1   small onion, finely chopped (about 1 cup)
1   celery stalk, cut into ¼-inch dice
1   red bell pepper, cut into ¼-inch dice
3   garlic cloves, minced
1   bay leaf
1½ teaspoons dried thyme
1½ teaspoons ground cumin
    Coarse salt
    Pinch of crushed red-pepper flakes
2   teaspoons cider vinegar
20 large shrimp (about 1 pound), peeled and deveined
    Vegetable-oil cooking spray
2   teaspoons olive oil
¾   pound collard greens, stemmed and cut crosswise into ½-inch strips (about 6 cups)

1 Cover black-eyed peas with cold water in a medium bowl. Let soak 1 hour or overnight; drain.

2 Bring peas, onion, celery, bell pepper, one-third of garlic, bay leaf, 1 teaspoon thyme, and 1½ quarts cold water to a boil in a medium saucepan. Reduce heat to medium; cook until beans are soft, about 40 minutes. Drain in a colander over a bowl; reserve ¼ cup cooking liquid. Discard bay leaf.

3 Transfer beans to a medium bowl. Stir in ½ teaspoon cumin, 1 teaspoon salt, and the red-pepper flakes. Stir in vinegar and reserved cooking liquid. Cover to keep warm.

4 Toss shrimp with remaining ½ teaspoon thyme, 1 teaspoon cumin, and ¼ teaspoon salt in a medium bowl. Lightly coat a large nonstick skillet with cooking spray; place over medium-high heat. Place shrimp in skillet in a single layer; cook, without turning, until shrimp are pink on one side, 2 to 3 minutes. Turn, and cook until shrimp are opaque, about 2 minutes. Transfer shrimp to a plate, and loosely cover with foil.

5 Wipe skillet clean with a paper towel. Add oil and remaining garlic to skillet. Cook over medium-high heat until fragrant, about 30 seconds. Add collard greens, a pinch of salt, and 2 tablespoons water. Cook, stirring occasionally, until collard greens are bright and crisp-tender, 2 to 3 minutes.

6 Divide beans and collard greens among four plates, and top each serving with 5 shrimp.

PER SERVING: 333 CALORIES, 5 G FAT, 172 MG CHOLESTEROL, 37 G CARBOHYDRATE, 863 MG SODIUM, 36 G PROTEIN, 9 G FIBER

from Fit to Eat: Light Main Courses

lasagna Bolognese

MAKES ONE 9-BY-13-INCH LASAGNA | PHOTO ON PAGE 76

If using fresh lasagna noodles, cook them in four batches.

    Coarse salt
1   pound fresh or dried lasagna noodles
    Unsalted butter, for baking dish
    Ragu Bolognese (recipe follows)
    Béchamel Sauce (recipe follows)
1⅓ cups finely grated Parmigiano-Reggiano cheese
    Freshly ground pepper
    Olive oil, for drizzling

1 Preheat oven to 425°F, with rack in upper third. Bring a large pot of water to a boil; add a generous amount of salt. Add pasta; cook, stirring occasionally, until barely tender, 1 to 2 minutes for fresh pasta or 6 to 8 minutes for dried. With tongs, transfer noodles to a bowl of very cold water to stop the cooking. Separate any noodles that are stuck together. Lay noodles flat on baking sheets lined with clean kitchen towels, and pat dry.

2 Butter a 9-by-13-by-2-inch ceramic or glass baking dish; cover bottom with a layer of noodles. They should fit snugly but not overlap. Trim noodles to fit dish. Spread 1¼ cups Bolognese sauce over the noodles. Drop ⅔ cup béchamel in dollops over Bolognese. Gently spread béchamel with a rubber spatula. Sprinkle with ¼ cup cheese. Repeat layers three

times. Top with a layer of noodles. Spread ⅓ cup béchamel on top, and sprinkle with ⅓ cup cheese. Season with pepper, and drizzle with oil.

3 Bake until golden brown and bubbling, about 25 minutes. Let stand 10 minutes before cutting with a serrated knife.

from Lasagna Bolognese 101

ragu Bolognese

MAKES ABOUT 5 CUPS

This sauce can be made two days ahead and stored in an airtight container in the refrigerator. Reheat before using.

- 2½ tablespoons unsalted butter
- 1 tablespoon plus 1 teaspoon extra-virgin olive oil
- 1¼ cups finely chopped onion (about 1 large onion)
- ¾ cup finely chopped celery (about 1¼ stalks)
- ¾ cup finely chopped carrot (about 1 large carrot)
- 1¼ pounds ground chuck
- 10 ounces ground pork
- 2¼ teaspoons coarse salt
- 2½ cups milk
- ⅛ to ¼ teaspoon freshly grated nutmeg
- 1¼ cups dry white wine
- 2¼ cups homemade or low-sodium store-bought chicken stock
- 2½ cups canned diced plum tomatoes, with juice
  Freshly ground pepper

1 Heat butter and oil in a large Dutch oven or heavy-bottom 6-quart pot over medium heat until butter is melted. Add onion, celery, and carrot; cook, stirring frequently, until vegetables are soft and pale golden brown, 8 to 11 minutes.

2 Add chuck and pork to pot; stir, breaking up meat with a fork. Add salt; cook, stirring occasionally, until meat is cooked through but not browned, about 5 minutes more.

3 Gradually add milk; bring mixture to a simmer. Reduce heat to medium-low; add nutmeg to taste, and gently simmer until milk has evaporated, about 20 minutes.

4 Add wine; simmer until liquid is reduced by half, about 15 minutes. Stir in stock; simmer until liquid is reduced by half, about 30 minutes. Add tomatoes and juice; simmer, stirring occasionally, until fat has risen to the top and sauce is thick and meaty, 60 to 70 minutes. Season with pepper. Let sauce cool slightly before using.

béchamel sauce

MAKES ABOUT 3 CUPS

This sauce is best used fresh, but it can be made a day ahead and stored in an airtight container in the refrigerator. Reheat gently in a heatproof bowl over a pan of simmering water.

- 7 tablespoons unsalted butter
- 6 tablespoons all-purpose flour
- 3½ cups milk, heated just until steaming
  Pinch of freshly grated nutmeg
- ½ teaspoon coarse salt
  Freshly ground pepper

1 Melt butter in a medium heavy-bottom saucepan over medium-low heat. Add flour to make a roux, whisking constantly. Cook, whisking occasionally, 2 to 3 minutes; do not let roux brown.

2 Whisking constantly, add about 2 tablespoons hot milk to saucepan. Pour half of the remaining hot milk into the saucepan in small increments, whisking the mixture constantly, until a smooth paste forms.

3 Whisk remaining milk into pan; add nutmeg and salt. Cook, stirring with a wooden spoon and scraping bottom and sides, until sauce is thick and creamy, about 15 minutes; if any lumps form, whisk sauce rapidly. Season with pepper; remove from heat. Let sauce stand until lukewarm, stirring occasionally, about 30 minutes.

poached beef with leeks

SERVES 6

- 1 pound Yukon gold potatoes, peeled and quartered
  Coarse salt
- 3 tablespoons finely grated peeled fresh horseradish
- 2 teaspoons white-wine vinegar
- ½ cup coarsely chopped fresh flat-leaf parsley
- 1 teaspoon extra-virgin olive oil
- 1 quart homemade or low-sodium store-bought chicken or vegetable stock
- 1 cup dry white wine
- 2 celery stalks, cut on the diagonal into 2½-inch lengths
- 1 garlic clove, lightly smashed
- 3 medium leeks (white and pale-green parts only), halved lengthwise, cut into 2-inch lengths, and rinsed well
- 3 sprigs thyme, plus more for garnish
- 1 piece beef tenderloin (1¾ pounds), trimmed of excess fat and tied
- 4 whole black peppercorns

1 Cover potatoes with cold water in a saucepan, and add ¼ teaspoon salt. Bring to a boil. Reduce heat, and simmer until tender, 10 to 15 minutes; drain. Return to pot; cover.

2 Stir together horseradish, vinegar, parsley, oil, and a pinch of salt; set sauce aside.

3 Bring stock, wine, celery, and garlic to a boil in a tall, narrow 6-quart pot. Reduce heat to medium-low; add leeks and 3 sprigs thyme. Simmer until vegetables are tender, 5 to 10 minutes. With a slotted spoon, transfer vegetables to a large bowl; cover. Place beef and peppercorns in pot; add water just to cover, if necessary. Partially cover pot, and cook at a bare simmer until an instant-read thermometer registers 130°F when inserted into center of beef, 20 to 25 minutes. Remove beef, and let rest 10 minutes.

4 Carve beef into 18 thin slices; add any juices to broth. Pour broth through a fine sieve into bowl with vegetables; discard solids. Divide soup, potatoes, and beef among six bowls; garnish with thyme. Serve sauce on the side.

PER SERVING: 462 CALORIES, 29 G FAT, 93 MG CHOLESTEROL, 12 G CARBOHYDRATE, 559 MG SODIUM, 28 G PROTEIN, 3 G FIBER

from Fit to Eat: Light Main Courses

DESSERTS

almond macaroons

MAKES 1 DOZEN

Cookies can be stored in an airtight container at room temperature for up to five days.

 4 ounces almond paste (about 5½ tablespoons)
½ cup confectioners' sugar, plus more for dusting
   Pinch of salt
 1 large egg white
¼ teaspoon pure vanilla extract
¼ cup sliced almonds

1 Preheat oven to 300°F. Line a baking sheet with parchment paper, and set aside. Place almond paste, sugar, and salt in the bowl of an electric mixer fitted with the paddle attachment; beat on medium speed until mixture looks crumbly, about 3 minutes. Add egg white and vanilla. Continue beating until mixture is smooth and thick, about 3 minutes more.

2 Drop 12 even tablespoons of batter about 2 inches apart on lined baking sheet; place 2 almond slices on each mound of dough. Bake cookies, rotating baking sheet halfway through, until golden brown, 20 to 25 minutes. Transfer cookies to a wire rack; let cool completely. Just before serving, lightly dust cookies with confectioners' sugar.

from What's for Dinner?

caramel flan

MAKES ONE 8-INCH FLAN; SERVES 8

 1 cup sugar
 1 can (14 ounces) sweetened condensed milk
1⅓ cups milk
 3 large eggs

1 Fill a roasting pan with 2 inches of water. Transfer to oven; preheat to 325°F. Prepare an ice-water bath; set aside.

2 Cook sugar in a small saucepan over medium-high heat, stirring constantly and washing down sides with a wet pastry brush to prevent crystals from forming, until sugar dissolves. Continue cooking, without stirring, until sugar turns a deep caramel color. Immediately dip bottom of pan in ice-water bath, then pour caramel into an 8-inch round cake pan.

3 Blend condensed milk, milk, and eggs in a blender until smooth. Pour into cake pan. Transfer to roasting pan, placing it in the water. Bake flan until just set and golden brown on top, about 1 hour.

4 Transfer flan to a wire rack to cool. Refrigerate at least 6 hours or preferably overnight. Just before serving, run a knife around edge of flan; invert flan onto a plate. Spoon sauce from pan over top.

from Cocktail Hour in South Beach

coconut bars

MAKES 4 DOZEN

Stirring will prevent the candy from burning. These bars can be stored in an airtight container for up to one week.

   Vegetable-oil cooking spray
 1 pound finely grated fresh coconut or unsweetened shredded coconut
2¾ cups sugar
 1 can (14 ounces) sweetened condensed milk
 1 can (12 ounces) evaporated milk

1 Coat a rimmed baking sheet with cooking spray. Stir together remaining ingredients in a large saucepan. Cook over medium-low heat, stirring almost constantly, until mixture thickens and forms a cohesive mass, about 30 minutes.

2 Pour mixture onto prepared sheet. With an offset spatula, spread ½ inch thick; shape into a 12-by-13-inch rectangle. Let cool completely, then cut into 1½-by-2-inch rectangles.

from Cocktail Hour in South Beach

Key-lime bars

MAKES 16

This recipe is based on the famous Key-lime pie from Joe's Stone Crab restaurant in Miami Beach. If you can't find Key limes, use regular fresh lime juice. Store ungarnished bars, wrapped in plastic, in the refrigerator for up to three days.

5¾ ounces graham crackers (about one-third of a 1-pound box), ground to fine crumbs in a food processor (1 cup plus 2½ tablespoons)

⅓ cup sugar

5 tablespoons unsalted butter, melted

3 large egg yolks

1½ teaspoons finely grated lime zest (about 2 limes)

1 can (14 ounces) sweetened condensed milk

⅔ cup fresh Key-lime juice (about 20 Key limes), plus 2 Key limes thinly sliced into half-moons for garnish

¼ cup heavy cream

1 Preheat oven to 350°F. Stir together crumbs, sugar, and butter in a small bowl. Press evenly onto bottom of an 8-inch square glass pan. Bake until dry and golden brown, about 10 minutes. Let cool in pan on a wire rack. Leave oven on.

2 Place egg yolks and zest in the bowl of an electric mixer fitted with the whisk attachment; beat on high speed until mixture is very thick, about 5 minutes. On medium speed, pour in condensed milk in a steady stream, scraping down sides of bowl. Beat on high speed until thick, about 3 minutes. On low speed, add lime juice; mix until just combined.

3 Pour filling over crust; spread evenly with an offset spatula. Bake until just set, about 10 minutes. Let cool completely on a wire rack. Refrigerate at least 4 hours or overnight.

4 Beat cream in a medium bowl until stiff peaks just form. Cut dessert into 1½-by-2-inch rectangles. Garnish each with a dollop of whipped cream and a slice of Key lime.

from Cocktail Hour in South Beach

peanut butter buttercream

MAKES ABOUT 1 CUP

⅔ cup natural, creamy peanut butter, preferably salted

8 tablespoons (1 stick) unsalted butter, softened

¾ cup confectioners' sugar

Salt (optional)

Cream peanut butter and butter in the bowl of an electric mixer fitted with the paddle attachment on high speed. On low speed, mix in sugar until combined, then mix on high speed until fluffy and smooth, about 3 minutes. Add salt to taste, if desired. Use immediately.

peanut butter whoopie pies

MAKES 18 COOKIE SANDWICHES

These whoopie pies are best eaten the day they are made.

1¾ cups all-purpose flour

¾ cup unsweetened cocoa powder (not Dutch process)

1½ teaspoons baking soda

½ teaspoon salt

4 tablespoons unsalted butter, softened

¼ cup vegetable shortening

½ cup granulated sugar

½ cup packed dark-brown sugar

1 large egg

1 cup whole milk

1 teaspoon pure vanilla extract

Peanut Butter Buttercream (recipe above)

2 ounces bittersweet chocolate, finely chopped

1 Preheat oven to 375°F. Line two large baking sheets with parchment paper; set aside. Sift together flour, cocoa, baking soda, and salt into a small bowl; set aside.

2 Add butter, shortening, and sugars to the bowl of an electric mixer fitted with the paddle attachment; cream on high speed until smooth, about 3 minutes. Add egg; mix until pale and fluffy, about 2 minutes. Add half the flour mixture, then the milk and vanilla; mix until combined. Add the remaining flour mixture. Mix, scraping down sides of bowl with a rubber spatula as needed.

3 Drop 12 slightly rounded tablespoons of batter 2 inches apart on each baking sheet. Bake the cookies in the upper and lower thirds of oven 10 minutes; switch the positions of the baking sheets, and rotate each. Continue baking until the cookies spring to the touch, 2 to 4 minutes more.

4 Remove from oven; let cookies cool on baking sheets, 10 minutes. Transfer with a spatula to a wire rack; let cool completely. Meanwhile, line a cooled baking sheet with a new piece of parchment; repeat process with remaining batter.

5 Spread 1 scant tablespoon buttercream on flat sides of half the cookies. Top each with one of the remaining cookies, flat side down, and gently press together. Transfer pies to a tray.

6 Melt half the chocolate in a saucepan over low heat, stirring until smooth. Remove from heat; add remaining chocolate, and stir until melted and smooth. Transfer to a pastry bag fitted with a plain round tip (Ateco #2 or #3) or a small parchment cone. Pipe chocolate in a spiral pattern on top of each pie. Let chocolate set before serving, about 1 hour.

from Dessert of the Month

buttermilk biscuits

MAKES 1 DOZEN | PHOTO ON PAGE 65

Once baked, the biscuits can be frozen in an airtight container for up to one month.

2¼ cups all-purpose flour, plus more for dusting
2¼ teaspoons baking powder
1 teaspoon sugar
¾ teaspoon salt
½ teaspoon baking soda
6 tablespoons cold unsalted butter, cut into small pieces
1 cup buttermilk

1 Preheat oven to 450°F. Sift flour, baking powder, sugar, salt, and baking soda into a bowl. Work in butter with your finger-tips or a pastry blender until mixture resembles coarse meal. Mix in buttermilk with your hands until just combined.

2 Turn out mixture onto a lightly floured work surface. Quickly bring dough together, and pat into a 7-inch circle about 1 inch thick. Cut out 12 rounds with a floured 2-inch biscuit cutter, gathering and patting out scraps as necessary.

3 Arrange rounds on a parchment-lined baking sheet. Bake until cooked through and golden brown, 10 to 15 minutes.

from Baking by Hand

challah

MAKES 1 LARGE LOAF | PHOTO ON PAGE 66

All ingredients except the milk and water should be at room temperature. If you keep a kosher kitchen, substitute canola or vegetable oil for the butter, and soy milk or water for the whole milk.

2 tablespoons unsalted butter, softened, plus more for bowl, plus 2 tablespoons, melted and cooled for brushing
3½ cups unbleached bread flour, plus more for dusting
½ cup water, warmed to 100°F
⅓ cup sugar
¼ cup whole milk, warmed to 100°F
2 large eggs, lightly beaten, plus 1 large egg, lightly beaten
3 large egg yolks, lightly beaten
2 teaspoons coarse salt
2 teaspoons active dry yeast

1 Butter a large bowl; set aside. Stir softened butter, flour, water, sugar, milk, 2 eggs, egg yolks, salt, and yeast in a large bowl until well combined. Turn out dough onto a lightly

floured work surface; knead dough until smooth and pliable, adding flour if needed, about 15 minutes.

2 Transfer dough to buttered bowl; brush top with 1 table-spoon melted butter. Loosely cover with plastic wrap. Let dough rise in a warm, draft-free spot until almost doubled in bulk, about 1½ hours.

3 Turn out dough onto a lightly floured work surface; knead 5 minutes, then return to bowl. Brush top with remaining tablespoon melted butter, and loosely cover with plastic wrap. Let dough rise again until doubled in bulk, about 1 hour more.

4 Preheat oven to 375°F. Divide dough into three equal pieces. Roll each piece into a ball, and loosely cover each ball with buttered plastic wrap. Let rest 20 minutes.

5 Roll each ball into a 12-inch log, leaving middles thicker than the ends. Lay logs side by side lengthwise; pinch together ends farthest from you. Tightly braid strands, pulling them as you go. Tuck ends of braid underneath loaf. Transfer to a buttered baking sheet; loosely cover with buttered plastic wrap. Let rise until almost doubled in bulk, about 45 minutes.

6 Brush dough lightly with egg wash. Bake until golden brown and firm and an instant-read thermometer inserted into bottom registers 180°F and comes out clean, 35 to 40 minutes. If challah browns too quickly, loosely tent with foil. Transfer to a wire rack; let cool at least 45 minutes.

from Baking by Hand

cranberry bran muffins

MAKES 1 DOZEN | PHOTO ON PAGE 67

Store muffins in an airtight container at room temperature for up to three days, or freeze for up to one month.

2 cups all-purpose flour
1½ cups wheat bran
1½ teaspoons baking powder
¾ teaspoon salt
¼ teaspoon baking soda
1½ cups packed dark-brown sugar
1¼ cups plus 2 tablespoons buttermilk
11 tablespoons (1⅜ sticks) unsalted butter, melted and cooled
2 large eggs
1 tablespoon finely grated orange zest
2 teaspoons pure vanilla extract
1½ cups fresh or frozen cranberries

1 Preheat oven to 350°F. Line a 12-cup standard muffin tin with paper liners. Put flour, bran, baking powder, salt, and baking soda in a large bowl. Stir in sugar, and set aside.

2 Whisk buttermilk, butter, eggs, zest, and vanilla in a bowl. Add flour mixture; stir until just combined. Stir in berries.

3 Divide batter among lined muffin cups. Bake until cooked through and golden brown, about 30 minutes. Transfer to a wire rack to cool slightly before turning out.

from Baking by Hand

dried-apricot and sage scones

MAKES 8

2 cups all-purpose flour, plus more for dusting

¼ cup granulated sugar

1 tablespoon baking powder

¾ teaspoon salt

5 tablespoons cold unsalted butter, cut into small pieces

1 cup chopped dried apricots (about 4 ounces)

2 tablespoons plus 1 teaspoon finely chopped fresh sage

1 cup heavy cream, plus more for brushing

Sanding sugar, for sprinkling

1 Preheat oven to 375°F. Put flour, granulated sugar, baking powder, and salt in a large bowl. Work in butter with your fingertips or a pastry blender until mixture resembles coarse meal. Stir in dried apricots and sage. Add cream; gather mixture together with your hands until it starts to hold together.

2 Turn out mixture onto a floured work surface. Quickly bring dough together; pat into an 8-inch circle 1 inch thick. Smooth top with a rolling pin. Cut into 8 wedges with a bench scraper.

3 Transfer to a parchment-lined baking sheet. Brush tops with cream; sprinkle with sanding sugar. Bake until cooked through and golden brown, about 30 minutes. Transfer scones to a wire rack; let cool 10 minutes before serving.

from Baking by Hand

walnut-fig bread

MAKES 1 LOAF

1¼ cups water, warmed to 110°F

1 tablespoon sugar

1 tablespoon active dry yeast

Olive oil, for brushing

3 cups all-purpose flour, plus more for dusting

1 cup rye flour

2 cups chopped dried Calimyrna figs (about 10 ounces)

2 tablespoons fennel seeds

2 tablespoons coarse salt

1 cup toasted and chopped walnuts (about 4 ounces)

1 Stir together warm water, sugar, and yeast in a small bowl until yeast is dissolved. Let mixture stand until foamy, about 5 minutes. Brush a large bowl with oil; set aside.

2 Put flours, 1 cup figs, fennel seeds, and salt in another bowl. Add yeast mixture; bring mixture together with your hands. Turn out dough onto a lightly floured work surface; knead until smooth and elastic, about 5 minutes.

3 Transfer dough to oiled bowl, and cover loosely with a piece of lightly oiled plastic wrap. Let dough rise in a warm place until almost doubled in bulk, about 1 hour.

4 Preheat oven to 375°F. Turn out dough onto a lightly floured work surface, and knead in walnuts and remaining 1 cup figs (be aggressive with the dough to work in nuts and figs). Shape dough into a ball; pull seams in toward bottom to stretch and smooth top.

5 Transfer dough to an oiled baking sheet. Loosely cover with a piece of lightly oiled plastic wrap. Let rise in a warm place until almost doubled in bulk, about 40 minutes.

6 Bake until pale golden brown, about 30 minutes. Tent with foil; bake until an instant-read thermometer inserted in the bottom of loaf registers 180°F and comes out clean, about 30 minutes. Transfer to a wire rack; let cool completely.

from Baking by Hand

triple citrus coffee cake

MAKES TWO 16-INCH-LONG LOAVES | PHOTO ON PAGE 67

13 tablespoons (1⅝ sticks) unsalted butter, melted and cooled, plus more for bowl

½ cup water, warmed to 110°F

2 envelopes active dry yeast (2 scant tablespoons)

⅔ cup plus 1 teaspoon granulated sugar

1 cup fresh orange juice

2 large eggs, lightly beaten, plus 1 large egg, lightly beaten for egg wash

Finely grated zest of 1 lemon, 1 lime, and 1 orange

1 teaspoon salt

5 to 6 cups all-purpose flour, plus more for dusting

1 pound cream cheese (two 8-ounce bars), room temperature

1 cup confectioners' sugar

2 large egg yolks

2 teaspoons pure vanilla extract

1 cup dried cranberries (4¼ ounces)

⅔ cup poppy seeds

1 Butter a large bowl; set aside. Stir warm water, yeast, and 1 teaspoon granulated sugar in another large bowl until yeast dissolves. Let stand until foamy, about 5 minutes. Whisk in orange juice, 2 eggs, remaining ⅔ cup granulated sugar, ½ cup butter, citrus zests, and salt. Stir in 5 cups flour, 1 cup at a time (add up to 1 cup additional flour if needed), until dough pulls away from sides of bowl and forms a ball.

2 Turn out dough onto a lightly floured work surface; knead until smooth and slightly sticky, about 5 minutes. Transfer to buttered bowl; brush dough with 1 tablespoon butter. Loosely cover with plastic wrap; let dough rise until doubled in bulk, about 1½ hours.

3 Meanwhile, stir together cream cheese, confectioners' sugar, egg yolks, and vanilla in a small bowl until smooth. Stir in dried cranberries and poppy seeds; set aside.

4 Butter two baking sheets; set aside. Punch down dough, and divide in half. Roll out one half into an 11-by-15-inch rectangle. Brush with 2 tablespoons butter, leaving a ½-inch border. Spread 1½ cups filling evenly over butter. Beginning at one long side, tightly roll dough into a log, encasing filling. Pinch seam to seal.

5 Transfer log to a prepared baking sheet. With a sharp knife, make 6 cuts, about 2 inches apart, along one long side of log, cutting three-quarters of the way across. Lift the first segment, turn it cut side up, and lay it flat on sheet. Repeat with next segment, twisting so it sits on the opposite side of roll. Continue down log, alternating sides. Repeat with remaining dough, butter, and filling on second baking sheet.

6 Preheat oven to 350°F, with racks in upper and lower thirds. Loosely cover dough with buttered pieces of plastic wrap, and let rise until almost doubled in bulk, about 30 minutes. Brush dough with egg wash, avoiding filling. Bake, switching positions of sheets halfway through, until cooked through and golden brown, about 30 minutes. Carefully slide cakes onto wire racks; let cool completely before slicing.

from Baking by Hand

....

DRINKS
....

lemonade Caipirinhas
SERVES 4 TO 6

2 limes, each cut into 16 small wedges

½ cup sugar

2 cups cachaça (Brazilian brandy)

6 cups crushed ice

1 cup lemonade

   Lime-peel twists, for garnish (optional)

   Lemon slices, for garnish (optional)

With a wooden pestle or spoon, crush lime wedges and sugar in a large glass until juices are released. Stir in cachaça. Fill a pitcher with ice; add cachaça mixture, and stir. Stir in lemonade; divide among serving glasses. Garnish with lime-peel twists and lemon slices, if desired.

from Cocktail Hour in South Beach

pineapple-mint juice
SERVES 5 OR 6

1 pineapple, peeled, cored, and coarsely chopped (about 6 cups)

5 cups ice, plus more for glasses

¼ cup sugar

½ cup loosely packed fresh mint leaves, plus sprigs for garnish (optional)

Blend the pineapple in a blender until smooth. Pour purée through a fine sieve into a bowl; discard solids. Return half the juice to blender; blend with half the ice and sugar. Add half the mint; pulse to combine. Transfer to a pitcher; repeat with remaining ingredients. Stir just before serving; pour into ice-filled glasses. Garnish with mint sprigs, if desired.

from Cocktail Hour in South Beach

....

MISCELLANEOUS
....

mustard sauce for stone-crab claws
MAKES ABOUT 2½ CUPS (ENOUGH FOR 3 DOZEN CLAWS)

2 cups mayonnaise

1 tablespoon Worcestershire sauce

2 tablespoons dry mustard

½ cup heavy cream

   Coarse salt

Whisk together mayonnaise, Worcestershire sauce, and mustard in a medium bowl. Add cream; whisk until smooth. Season with salt. If not serving immediately, refrigerate, covered, up to 1 day; whisk briefly before serving.

from Cocktail Hour in South Beach

February

hoecakes

MAKES ABOUT 10 PANCAKES

1½ cups yellow cornmeal

1 cup all-purpose flour

⅓ cup sugar

1 teaspoon salt

1 teaspoon baking soda

1½ cups buttermilk

2 large eggs

5 tablespoons corn oil, plus more if needed

Unsalted butter, for serving

Honey, for serving

1 Stir together cornmeal, flour, sugar, salt, and baking soda in a medium bowl. Add buttermilk, eggs, and ¼ cup oil; whisk until smooth.

2 Heat a large skillet over medium heat until hot. Add remaining tablespoon oil; swirl to coat, and heat until a drop of batter sizzles upon contact. Working in batches, pour ⅓ cup batter into skillet for each hoecake. Cook, turning once, until golden and cooked through, about 4 minutes total.

3 Repeat with remaining batter (add more oil if needed, and reduce heat if sides brown too quickly). Serve immediately, topped with butter and honey.

from Celebrating Presidents' Day

pear-stuffed French toast

SERVES 6 | **PHOTO ON PAGE 67**

It's best to use pears that are ripe but not too soft.

4 tablespoons unsalted butter, plus more if needed

3 firm-ripe Bosc pears, cored, peeled, and cut into ¼-inch-thick slices

3 tablespoons sugar

4 large eggs

1 cup whole milk

¼ cup fresh orange juice

2½ tablespoons pear eau de vie, such as Poire William (optional)

1½ tablespoons fresh lemon juice

Pinch of coarse salt

1½ tablespoons finely grated orange zest

Finely grated zest of 1 lemon

1 loaf day-old brioche (1 pound), cut into ½-inch-thick slices

Pure maple syrup, for serving (optional)

Confectioners' sugar, for serving (optional)

1 Melt 1 tablespoon butter in a large skillet over medium-high heat. Add pear slices and 1 tablespoon sugar; cook, stirring occasionally, until pears are tender and caramelized, about 10 minutes.

2 Put eggs, milk, orange juice, eau de vie (if desired), lemon juice, remaining 2 tablespoons sugar, salt, and zests in a wide, deep dish. Beat well with a fork.

3 Dip brioche slices into egg mixture; transfer to a rimmed baking sheet. Divide pears among half the slices. Top with remaining bread slices.

4 Melt remaining 3 tablespoons butter in a large nonstick skillet over medium heat. Transfer 2 or 3 pear sandwiches to skillet with a spatula. Cook until deep golden brown on one side, about 2 minutes. Turn; cook until deep golden brown and slightly puffy all over, about 2 minutes more. Repeat with remaining sandwiches, adding more butter to skillet, if needed. Serve immediately with maple syrup or confectioners' sugar, if desired.

from Mother Knows Best

Polish mushroom soup

MAKES 1¼ GALLONS; SERVES 10 TO 12

6 ounces dried mushrooms, such as Polish borowik or porcini

1 ounce large dried shiitake mushrooms, stemmed

1½ quarts boiling water

3 quarts homemade or low-sodium store-bought beef or vegetable stock

5 celery stalks, cut into ¼-inch dice

2 large onions, finely chopped

5 carrots, cut into ¼-inch dice

1 pound white mushrooms, cut into ¼-inch-thick slices

1 cup orzo

2 tablespoons unsalted butter

2 tablespoons all-purpose flour

2 tablespoons finely chopped fresh flat-leaf parsley

2 tablespoons finely chopped fresh dill

1 cup sour cream

1 tablespoon coarse salt

Freshly ground pepper

1 Rinse dried mushrooms. Put in a large bowl, and cover with boiling water. Soak, stirring occasionally, 1 hour.

2 Lift out mushrooms; squeeze out any liquid. Set aside. Pour soaking liquid through a fine sieve into a large bowl.

3 Bring 1 quart soaking liquid and the stock to a simmer in a large pot over medium-high heat. Add celery, onions, and carrots. Chop reserved mushrooms into ¼-inch pieces, and add to pot along with sliced white mushrooms.

4 Cover, and reduce heat to medium-low; cook vegetables and stock 1 hour. Uncover; raise heat to high. Bring to a boil, stirring occasionally. Reduce heat to medium, and add orzo. Cook, stirring often, until al dente, 8 to 10 minutes.

5 Meanwhile, make roux: Melt butter in a small saucepan over medium heat. Add flour; cook, stirring, until smooth, about 2 minutes. Add 1 cup soup; whisk constantly until mixture is slightly thick and free of lumps. Stir roux into soup; add parsley and dill. Remove from heat.

6 Whisk together ¼ cup soup and sour cream in a small bowl. Add mixture to soup; whisk constantly until incorporated, about 3 minutes. Stir in salt; season soup with pepper.

from Mother Knows Best

roasted-carrot soup

SERVES 2

You can make this soup through step two the day before you serve it; cover it and refrigerate until you're ready to finish.

1 small onion

1 bunch carrots (about 1 pound), peeled and cut into 2-inch chunks

1 small Belgian endive, quartered lengthwise

2 tablespoons olive oil

Coarse salt and freshly ground pepper

1 bay leaf

2 cups homemade or low-sodium store-bought chicken stock, plus more for thinning

⅓ cup heavy cream or milk

¼ teaspoon grated peeled fresh ginger, or to taste

Crème fraîche, for garnish (optional)

1 Preheat oven to 450°F. Cut onion into 8 wedges (keep root end intact so layers stay together). Toss onion, carrots, endive, oil, ¼ teaspoon salt, and a pinch of pepper in a medium bowl. Transfer to a rimmed baking sheet, and spread out in a single layer. Roast vegetables, turning occasionally, until edges are deep golden brown, about 30 minutes.

2 Cut off root ends of onion pieces. Transfer all vegetables to a large saucepan, and add bay leaf. Add enough stock to just cover (about 2 cups). Bring to a simmer, and cook until carrots are very soft, about 30 minutes. Let cool slightly, and discard bay leaf. Purée vegetables and stock in a blender until smooth (work in batches to avoid filling blender more than halfway).

3 Transfer purée to a clean pan; place over low heat. Stir in cream; add stock to thin soup to desired consistency. Season with salt and pepper; stir in ginger. If desired, pipe crème fraîche onto each serving, or spoon a dollop on top.

from Easy Entertaining: Dinner for Two

endive, avocado, and red-grapefruit salad

SERVES 4

2 red grapefruit

¾ teaspoon white-wine vinegar

1 tablespoon honey

1½ tablespoons low-fat sour cream

⅛ teaspoon coarse salt

Freshly ground pepper

1½ tablespoons extra-virgin olive oil

4 Belgian endives

1 ripe Hass avocado, pitted and peeled

1   Cut peels, including pith, from grapefruit; discard. Working over a bowl to catch any juices, cut segments from membranes, letting them fall into bowl. Squeeze the remaining juice from membranes into bowl.

2   Whisk together vinegar, honey, sour cream, salt, and 3 tablespoons grapefruit juice in a small bowl. Season with pepper. Whisking constantly, add oil in a slow, steady stream; whisk until emulsified.

3   Halve endives lengthwise, and core; cut leaves into 1-inch-pieces. Toss with three-quarters of the dressing. Cut avocado into ¼-inch-thick slices. Divide endive and avocado among four plates. Drizzle each serving with one-quarter of remaining dressing. Divide grapefruit among plates.

PER SERVING: 218 CALORIES, 14 G FAT, 3 MG CHOLESTEROL, 25 G CARBOHYDRATE, 98 MG SODIUM, 3 G PROTEIN, 13 G FIBER

from Fit to Eat: Red Grapefruit

warm lentil salad with goat cheese

SERVES 4 | **PHOTO ON PAGE 81**

¾ cup green lentils (4¾ ounces)

3 tablespoons extra-virgin olive oil

3 shallots, thinly sliced crosswise and separated into rings

1 carrot, cut into ¼-inch dice

1 celery stalk, cut into ¼-inch dice

1 red bell pepper, ribs and seeds removed, flesh cut into ¼-inch dice

2 teaspoons coarsely chopped fresh flat-leaf parsley

2 tablespoons balsamic or sherry vinegar

6 ounces spinach, stemmed and coarsely chopped (about 2 cups)

Coarse salt and freshly ground pepper

4 ounces soft goat cheese

1   Bring a saucepan of water to a boil. Add lentils; simmer, stirring occasionally, until tender, about 15 minutes.

2   Meanwhile, heat 2 tablespoons oil in a large skillet over medium heat until hot but not smoking. Add shallots, and cook, stirring occasionally, until they begin to soften, about 2 minutes. Add carrot, celery, and bell pepper; continue to cook, stirring occasionally, until vegetables are tender, about 5 minutes more. Stir in parsley, vinegar, and remaining tablespoon oil. Transfer to a large bowl.

3   Drain lentils, and add to bowl with vegetables. Stir in spinach, and season with salt and black pepper. Crumble goat cheese into bowl, and toss gently to combine.

from What's for Dinner?

crimson couscous

SERVES 2 | **PHOTO ON PAGE 79**

½ cup peeled, diced (¼ inch) beet (about 1 medium beet)

Coarse salt

½ tablespoon unsalted butter

⅛ teaspoon ground coriander

⅛ teaspoon ground cumin

½ cup couscous

¼ cup dried apricots, cut into ¼-inch dice

2 tablespoons dried currants

1 teaspoon finely grated orange zest

2 tablespoons fresh orange juice

Freshly ground pepper

1   Bring ¾ cup water, the diced beet, and ½ teaspoon salt to a boil in a medium saucepan. Reduce heat; simmer beet, covered, until tender, about 15 minutes.

2 Drain beet, reserving ½ cup cooking liquid (if you don't have ½ cup liquid, add water to fill). Return beet and liquid to pan. Add butter, coriander, and cumin; bring to a boil. Stir in couscous; cover. Remove from heat; let stand 5 minutes.

3 Fluff couscous with a fork. Stir in apricots, currants, zest, and orange juice. Season with salt and pepper.

from Easy Entertaining: Dinner for Two

haricots verts with mustard vinaigrette

SERVES 2 | **PHOTO ON PAGE 79**

Blanched haricots verts can be refrigerated, in a resealable plastic bag, up to one day. Refrigerate vinaigrette separately, up to one day; bring to room temperature before serving.

Coarse salt

½ pound haricots verts or other thin green beans, trimmed

½ teaspoon finely chopped shallot

1½ teaspoons red-wine vinegar

Freshly ground pepper

½ teaspoon grainy or smooth Dijon mustard

4½ teaspoons extra-virgin olive oil

1 Bring a large saucepan of water to a boil. Prepare an ice-water bath. Add salt to boiling water, then add haricots verts; cook just until beans are bright green all over, 1 to 2 minutes.

2 Drain beans; immediately transfer to ice-water bath. When chilled completely, drain; pat dry.

3 Put shallot and vinegar in a small bowl; season with salt and pepper. Let stand 15 minutes. Whisk in mustard. Whisking constantly, pour in oil in a slow, steady stream until emulsified. Dress beans; toss to coat.

from Easy Entertaining: Dinner for Two

potato pierogi

MAKES ABOUT 70; SERVES 8 TO 10

1 large egg

2 tablespoons sour cream

1 cup milk

4½ to 5 cups all-purpose flour, plus more for dusting

8 ounces (2 sticks) unsalted butter, melted, plus more for plastic wrap

4½ pounds russet potatoes (about 8 medium), peeled and quartered

Coarse salt

6 ounces cream cheese (not whipped), room temperature

Freshly ground pepper

2 tablespoons coarse yellow cornmeal

1 Make dough: Whisk together egg and sour cream in a medium bowl until smooth. Whisk in milk and 1 cup water. Gradually stir in 3½ cups flour, ½ cup at a time, until a very sticky dough forms.

2 Turn out dough onto a well-floured surface. Knead, slowly working in 1 cup flour (use a bench scraper to lift dough, as it will stick to surface before flour is worked in). Continue to knead, working in up to ½ cup more flour, until dough is elastic and no longer sticky, 8 to 10 minutes. Put dough in a lightly floured bowl. Cover with buttered plastic wrap; let rest.

3 Make filling: Cover potatoes with cold water in a large pot. Bring to a boil; add 2 tablespoons salt. Cook potatoes until tender, about 25 minutes. Drain; return to pot. Cook over low heat, stirring, until potatoes are dry, about 2 minutes. Pass potatoes through a ricer into a large bowl, or use a potato masher. Add 4 tablespoons butter and cream cheese; mash until well incorporated. Season with salt and pepper.

4 Lay a clean linen towel on a large rimmed baking sheet, and sprinkle cornmeal evenly on top; set aside. Divide dough into 4 equal pieces. Working with 1 piece at a time, roll out dough on a well-floured surface to about ⅛ inch thick. With a 2½-inch round cookie cutter or a drinking glass, cut out as many circles as possible. Gather scraps, and roll them out again; cut out additional circles.

5 Mold filling into 1½-inch balls (1 heaping tablespoon), and place one in center of each dough circle. Holding a filled circle in your hand, gently fold dough over filling, and tightly pinch edges with forefinger and thumb to form a well-sealed half-moon. Transfer to towel-lined baking sheet. Repeat with remaining dough and filling.

6 Bring a large (8-quart) pot of water to a boil; add salt. Working in batches of 8 to 10, carefully add pierogi to boiling water. When they rise to the top (after about 5 minutes), continue to cook, stirring occasionally, 1 minute more.

7 Meanwhile, drizzle a large platter with 6 tablespoons butter. Transfer pierogi with a slotted spoon to platter; cover to keep warm. Drizzle with remaining 6 tablespoons butter.

from Mother Knows Best

roasted yam halves

SERVES 4 | **PHOTO ON PAGE 81**

Halving the yams before roasting greatly reduces the cooking time and gives them a nice golden crust.

2 yams or sweet potatoes (about 1 pound each)
2 tablespoons extra-virgin olive oil
1 tablespoon finely chopped fresh thyme
 Coarse salt and freshly ground pepper

Preheat oven to 400°F. Halve yams, and place cut sides up in a shallow baking dish just large enough to hold them in a single layer. Drizzle with oil, and sprinkle with thyme. Season with salt and pepper. Bake until golden brown and very tender, 35 to 45 minutes.

from What's for Dinner?

. . . .

MAIN COURSES

. . . .

baked gnocchi with cheese

SERVES 4 TO 6 | **PHOTO ON PAGE 75**

1 cup heavy cream
6 ounces Italian fontina or Taleggio cheese, grated (about 1½ cups)
 Pinch of freshly grated nutmeg
 Coarse salt and freshly ground pepper
 Unsalted butter, for baking dish
 Basic Potato Gnocchi (recipe follows)

1 Heat cream in a small saucepan over medium heat until just simmering. Add two-thirds of the cheese; stir until melted. Stir in nutmeg and ¼ teaspoon pepper. Remove from heat; cover pan to keep warm.

2 Preheat oven to 400°F. Butter an 8-inch square baking dish; set aside. Bring a large pot of water to a boil; add 1 tablespoon salt. Add half the gnocchi; when they rise to the top (after about 2 minutes), continue to cook until tender, about 15 seconds more. Transfer gnocchi with a slotted spoon to buttered dish. Repeat process with remaining gnocchi.

3 Pour cheese sauce over gnocchi, and gently toss. Sprinkle the remaining cheese on top. Bake gnocchi until golden brown, about 25 minutes.

from Gnocchi 101

basic potato gnocchi

SERVES 4 TO 6

To make spinach gnocchi, thaw a ten-ounce package of frozen spinach. Very finely chop leaves, and squeeze out moisture. Add spinach to potatoes in bowl; sprinkle with an additional two tablespoons flour. Formed gnocchi can be refrigerated on a floured baking sheet, uncovered, for up to twelve hours.

2 cups all-purpose flour, plus more for dusting
2 pounds Yukon gold or russet potatoes
 Coarse salt and freshly ground pepper
2 large eggs

1 Lightly flour a baking sheet; set aside. Put potatoes in a large saucepan, and cover with cold water by 2 inches. Bring to a boil, and add 1 tablespoon salt. Reduce to a simmer; cook until potatoes are very tender, about 25 minutes.

2 Drain potatoes. When they are cool enough to handle, peel them, then pass them through a ricer or food mill into a medium bowl. Sprinkle with the flour, and add the eggs. Add 2½ teaspoons salt and ¼ teaspoon pepper. Stir mixture with a fork to combine well.

3 Turn out dough onto a lightly floured surface. Gently knead dough, adding a small amount of flour if it is too sticky, until dough is soft and smooth, about 3 minutes. Do not overwork. With a bench scraper, divide dough into 4 to 6 pieces. With fingertips, roll each piece into a long rope about ¾ inch thick. Cut ropes crosswise into 1-inch gnocchi.

4 Roll a cut side of each dumpling against the tines of a fork with your thumb (each piece will have ridges on one side and an indentation on the other). Set aside on the floured baking sheet until ready to cook.

gnocchi with mushrooms and Gorgonzola sauce

SERVES 4 TO 6

3 tablespoons extra-virgin olive oil, plus more for brushing

Coarse salt and freshly ground pepper

Basic Potato Gnocchi (page 33)

1 cup heavy cream

1 cup homemade or low-sodium store-bought chicken stock

4 ounces Gorgonzola cheese

Pinch of freshly grated nutmeg

Pinch of cayenne pepper

12 ounces assorted mushrooms, such as chanterelle, cremini, and portobello, stemmed and coarsely chopped

1 Lightly brush a rimmed baking sheet with oil; set aside. Bring a large pot of water to a boil; add 1 tablespoon salt. Add half the gnocchi; when they rise to the top (after about 2 minutes), continue to cook until tender, about 15 seconds more. Transfer gnocchi with a slotted spoon to the oiled baking sheet. Repeat process with remaining gnocchi.

2 Bring cream and stock to a boil in a large saucepan over medium-high heat. Reduce heat, and let mixture simmer until slightly thickened and reduced by one-third, about 10 minutes. Add cheese, and stir until melted. Stir in nutmeg and cayenne. Season with salt and pepper. Remove from heat; cover pan to keep warm.

3 Heat oil in a large skillet over medium heat until hot but not smoking. Add mushrooms, and cook, stirring occasionally, until they are tender and any released liquid has evaporated, about 4 minutes. Add gnocchi; cook, stirring occasionally, until heated through. Pour Gorgonzola sauce over gnocchi, and gently toss.

from Gnocchi 101

gnocchi with sage and brown butter

SERVES 4 TO 6 | PHOTO ON PAGE 72

8 tablespoons (1 stick) unsalted butter

16 sage leaves

Extra-virgin olive oil, for brushing

Coarse salt and freshly ground pepper

Basic Potato Gnocchi (page 33)

1 Heat butter in a large heavy-bottom skillet over medium-high heat until foam subsides and butter begins to brown. Add sage; cook, stirring, until leaves are crisp and butter is golden brown. Transfer sage leaves to a paper-towel-lined plate to drain. Reserve brown butter in skillet with heat off.

2 Lightly brush a rimmed baking sheet with oil; set aside. Bring a large pot of water to a boil; add 1 tablespoon salt. Add half the gnocchi; when they rise to the top (after about 2 minutes), continue to cook until tender, about 15 seconds more. Transfer gnocchi with a slotted spoon to oiled baking sheet. Repeat process with remaining gnocchi.

3 Reheat reserved brown butter over medium heat. Add gnocchi; cook, stirring occasionally, until heated through. Season with salt and pepper. Add reserved sage leaves, and gently toss.

from Gnocchi 101

spinach gnocchi with tomato sauce

SERVES 4 TO 6 | **PHOTO ON PAGE 75**

1 tablespoon extra-virgin olive oil

1 small onion, finely chopped

3 garlic cloves, minced

¼ cup dry white wine

1 can (28 ounces) whole plum tomatoes with juice, coarsely chopped

1 can (14½ ounces) tomato sauce

2 sprigs basil

¼ teaspoon crushed red-pepper flakes

Coarse salt and freshly ground pepper

Basic Potato Gnocchi with spinach (page 33)

Thinly shaved Parmesan cheese, for serving

1 Heat oil in a large saucepan over medium heat until hot but not smoking. Add onion and garlic; cook, stirring occasionally, until onion is translucent, 5 to 7 minutes. Add wine; cook until most liquid has evaporated. Add tomatoes and juice, tomato sauce, basil, and red-pepper flakes. Reduce heat to medium-low; simmer until slightly thick, about 30 minutes. Season with salt and pepper. Remove from heat; cover pan to keep warm.

2 Bring a large pot of water to a boil; add 1 tablespoon salt. Add half the gnocchi; when they rise to the top (after about 2 minutes), continue to cook until tender, about 15 seconds more. Transfer gnocchi with a slotted spoon to pan with sauce. Repeat process with remaining gnocchi.

3 Reheat gnocchi and sauce, gently tossing over low heat. Serve with cheese shavings.

from Gnocchi 101

pork chops with red-wine sauce

SERVES 4

⅓ cup all-purpose flour
  Coarse salt and freshly ground pepper
½ teaspoon ground cinnamon
4 rib pork chops (about 8 ounces each)
3 tablespoons olive oil
1 cup dry red wine, such as Cabernet or Merlot
1¾ cups homemade or low-sodium store-bought
  chicken stock
1½ cups assorted dried fruits, such as pitted prunes,
  apricots, and cherries

1 Preheat oven to 400°F. Whisk together flour, 1½ teaspoons salt, ½ teaspoon pepper, and the cinnamon in a small bowl; set aside 2 tablespoons. Sprinkle remaining flour mixture over pork chops, turning to coat; shake off excess.

2 Heat oil in a large ovenproof skillet over medium heat until hot but not smoking. Add pork chops, and brown well, 3 to 4 minutes per side. Transfer skillet to oven; roast pork chops until they are cooked through, about 5 minutes more.

3 Transfer pork chops to a plate; cover to keep warm. Place skillet over high heat; add wine, and deglaze, scraping up browned bits from bottom of pan. Whisk reserved flour mixture into stock; pour into skillet while whisking mixture in pan. Stir in dried fruits. Continue to cook, stirring occasionally, until sauce has thickened and fruits are tender, about 15 minutes more. Season with salt and pepper; serve sauce over pork chops.

from What's for Dinner?

red-grapefruit risotto with red onions and thyme

SERVES 4

3 medium red onions
  Vegetable-oil cooking spray
⅛ teaspoon coarse salt
  Freshly ground pepper
1 red grapefruit
1 quart homemade or low-sodium store-bought
  chicken stock
1 tablespoon olive oil
1½ cups Arborio rice
½ cup dry white wine
1 tablespoon chopped fresh thyme, plus 4 sprigs for garnish
1 teaspoon unsalted butter
½ cup finely grated Parmesan cheese (1 ounce)

1 Cut 2 onions crosswise into ½-inch-thick slices. Coat a medium nonstick skillet with cooking spray; place over medium heat. Place onion slices in skillet in a single layer; sprinkle with the salt, and season with pepper. Cook, without turning, until undersides are deep golden brown, about 3 minutes. Turn, and cook until soft, about 4 minutes more. Reserve slices in skillet with heat off.

2 Bring a small pot of water to a boil. Meanwhile, finely zest half of the grapefruit. Add zest to pot, and boil 3 minutes. Remove zest with a fine sieve, and set aside. Zest remaining half of grapefruit into long strips; cover strips with a damp paper towel, and set aside for garnish.

3 Cut pith from grapefruit, and discard. Working over a bowl to catch the juices, cut segments from membranes, letting them fall into bowl. Squeeze the remaining juice from membranes into bowl.

4 Bring 1½ cups water, the stock, and ¼ cup grapefruit juice to a bare simmer in a medium saucepan over medium heat.

5 Meanwhile, finely chop remaining onion. Heat oil in a large heavy-bottom pot over medium heat until hot but not smoking. Add chopped onion; cook, stirring occasionally, until soft and golden brown, 4 to 5 minutes. Add rice, and stir until coated with oil, 1 to 2 minutes. Add wine; stir until completely absorbed.

6 Stirring constantly, add simmering stock, ½ cup at a time, letting rice absorb each addition before adding the next. Stir until all stock has been absorbed and rice is creamy but al dente, about 20 minutes. Stir in grapefruit segments and reserved boiled zest; cook 3 minutes more. Season with pepper. Stir in chopped thyme, butter, and cheese.

7 Meanwhile, reheat the reserved onions over medium-low heat. Divide risotto among four bowls. Top each serving with onions, then garnish with reserved zest and a sprig of thyme.

PER SERVING: 439 CALORIES, 7 G FAT, 9 MG CHOLESTEROL, 72 G CARBOHYDRATE, 677 MG SODIUM, 11 G PROTEIN, 6 G FIBER

from Fit to Eat: Red Grapefruit

roasted-garlic risotto with mushrooms

SERVES 4 | **PHOTO ON PAGE 75**

You might not need to use all of the stock. Just-right risotto should be creamy—not too soupy, not too dry.

Whole Roasted Garlic (recipe follows)

 2 **quarts homemade or low-sodium store-bought chicken stock, skimmed of fat**

12 **ounces assorted mushrooms, such as chanterelle, cremini, and portobello**

 3 **tablespoons extra-virgin olive oil**

 5 **tablespoons unsalted butter**

 2 **shallots, finely chopped**

 1 **cup Arborio rice**

½ **cup dry white wine**

½ **cup finely grated Parmigiano-Reggiano cheese, plus more for garnish**

¼ **cup finely chopped fresh chives, plus more for garnish**

Coarse salt and freshly ground pepper

1 With a fork, mash garlic cloves in a medium bowl to form a smooth paste; set aside. Bring stock to a simmer in a medium saucepan over medium heat. Reduce heat to low; whisk in 1 tablespoon garlic paste, and continue to simmer.

2 Remove stems from mushrooms, and finely chop. Cut mushroom caps into ¼-inch-thick slices. Heat 1 tablespoon oil in a large saucepan over medium heat until hot but not smoking. Add caps, and cook, stirring occasionally, until golden, 5 to 7 minutes; transfer to a bowl.

3 Add remaining 2 tablespoons oil and 1 tablespoon butter to pan. Add shallots and mushroom stems, and cook, stirring, until shallots are soft, about 2 minutes. Add rice; cook, stirring, until coated with oil and butter, 3 to 4 minutes. Add wine; stir until completely absorbed.

4 Stirring constantly, add the simmering stock, ¾ cup at a time, letting rice absorb each addition before adding the next. Continue to add stock until rice is creamy but al dente, 17 to 20 minutes.

5 Stir in the remaining 3 tablespoons garlic paste and 4 tablespoons butter, along with the cheese, chives, and reserved cooked mushrooms. Season with salt and pepper. Garnish risotto with additional cheese and chives.

from Roasted Garlic

whole roasted garlic

MAKES 2 BULBS | **PHOTO ON PAGE 81**

You can cut off the tops of the garlic bulbs to expose the cloves—or not. Squeeze the cloves out of the papery pockets for an instant appetizer; spread cloves on crusty bread or crackers, and top with a drizzle of olive oil, if desired. If you roast the bulbs intact, they can be saved overnight (wrapped in foil and placed in the refrigerator) to mix into butter, a vinaigrette, or a sauce or gravy.

 2 **garlic bulbs, papery outer skins discarded**

 4 **sprigs thyme**

 2 **tablespoons extra-virgin olive oil**

Preheat oven to 425°F. Cut a thin (¼-inch) slice from the top of each bulb, if desired; discard. Place bulbs and thyme in a baking dish. Drizzle with oil. Cover with foil; roast bulbs until soft and golden, about 1 hour and 15 minutes.

roasted-garlic chicken

SERVES 4 | **PHOTO ON PAGE 77**

Whole roasted garlic bulbs are a delicious garnish for this dish; you can roast them at the same time you roast the chicken. And you can refrigerate the roasted-garlic butter, covered with plastic wrap, for up to one week.

 1 **roasting chicken (3 to 4 pounds)**

Coarse salt and freshly ground pepper

 8 **sprigs flat-leaf parsley**

 4 **sprigs rosemary, plus more for garnish**

 2 **lemons, halved**

10 **Roasted Garlic Cloves (recipe follows)**

 8 **tablespoons (1 stick) unsalted butter, softened**

 2 **recipes (4 bulbs) Whole Roasted Garlic (recipe above), for garnish (optional)**

1 Let chicken stand at room temperature 30 minutes. Preheat oven to 425°F. Remove giblets and any excess fat from chicken cavity. Rinse chicken inside and out with cold water; pat dry with paper towels. Tuck wing tips under body. Season cavity with salt and pepper; stuff with parsley, rosemary, and 2 lemon halves.

2 Squeeze garlic cloves from their skins into a small bowl. Add the butter, and stir together until smooth. Gently separate skin from chicken with your hands. Spread garlic butter over entire surface of chicken and under skin. Generously season with salt and pepper. Cross chicken legs; tie ends together with kitchen twine. Transfer chicken to a roasting pan. Arrange remaining 2 lemon halves around bird.

3 Roast chicken, basting occasionally with accumulated pan juices, until skin is crisp and deep golden brown, and an instant-read thermometer inserted into thickest part of thigh registers 175°F, about 1 hour and 10 minutes.

4 Transfer chicken and lemon halves to a platter. Let chicken stand 10 to 15 minutes. Garnish with rosemary and whole roasted garlic, if desired.

from Roasted Garlic

roasted garlic cloves

MAKES ABOUT 28

2 **garlic bulbs, papery outer skins discarded**
2 **sprigs thyme**
1 **tablespoon extra-virgin olive oil**

1 Preheat oven to 425°F. Separate garlic cloves (do not peel); arrange with thyme in a single layer on a piece of foil. Drizzle with oil. Seal garlic in foil to form a packet.

2 Roast garlic until soft and golden, about 1 hour. Remove garlic from foil, and let cool slightly before using.

sauerbraten

SERVES 10 TO 12 | **PHOTO ON PAGE 76**

You can refrigerate the sauerbraten, covered, for up to two days. In fact, the flavors develop nicely when the dish is made ahead of time.

1 **bottom round of beef (4 to 5 pounds)**
   Coarse salt and freshly ground pepper
¼ **cup vegetable oil**
4 **garlic cloves, coarsely chopped**
2 **large onions, thinly sliced**
2 **bay leaves**
¼ **cup tomato paste**
¼ **cup ketchup**
1 **cup red-wine vinegar**
2 **cups dry red wine, such as Burgundy**
¼ **cup sour cream**

1 Season beef with salt and pepper. Tie kitchen twine around beef at 2-inch intervals and once from end to end. Heat 2 tablespoons oil in a large (8-quart) heavy-bottom pot over medium heat until hot but not smoking. Brown meat all over, including ends, about 3 minutes per side; transfer to a plate. Keep pot on stove, and reduce heat to medium-low.

2 Add remaining 2 tablespoons oil and the garlic and onions to pot. Cook, stirring often, until onions are soft, 5 to 7 min-

utes. Add bay leaves, tomato paste, ketchup, vinegar, and wine. Raise heat to medium-high; bring mixture to a boil.

3 Return beef to pot; add 2 cups water. Cover pot with a tight-fitting lid. Reduce heat to medium-low; simmer 2 hours. Turn beef; continue to simmer until tender, 1½ to 2 hours more. Let cool slightly.

4 Transfer beef to a cutting board. Remove twine; let beef stand 15 minutes. Skim fat from sauce. Bring sauce to a simmer over medium heat; cook until liquid is reduced by one-quarter, about 7 minutes. Season with salt and pepper. Remove from heat; whisk in sour cream.

5 Cut beef across the grain into ¼-inch-thick slices. Return slices to pot to immerse in sauce, then transfer to a large serving platter. Ladle more sauce on top.

from Mother Knows Best

sesame chicken with cabbage and red-grapefruit sauce

SERVES 4

⅓ **cup sesame seeds**
4 **boneless, skinless chicken breast halves (5 ounces each)**
   Coarse salt and freshly ground pepper
2 **red grapefruit, plus 1½ cups freshly squeezed red-grapefruit juice (from about 3 red grapefruit)**
2 **teaspoons olive oil**
2 **tablespoons finely chopped shallots**
¼ **cup dry white wine**
1 **teaspoon minced peeled fresh ginger**
½ **pound napa cabbage (about ½ small head), cut into 4 wedges, core intact**
¼ **teaspoon toasted sesame oil**
   Vegetable-oil cooking spray
6 **scallions, cut on the diagonal into 2-inch pieces**

1 Preheat oven to 375°F. Toast sesame seeds in a medium nonstick skillet over medium heat, shaking skillet, until seeds are golden, about 2 minutes; transfer to a plate. Sprinkle chicken with ½ teaspoon salt; season with pepper. Dredge chicken in seeds, and set aside.

2 Cut peels, including pith, from grapefruit; discard. Working over a bowl to catch the juices, cut segments from membranes, letting them fall into bowl.

3 Heat olive oil in a small saucepan over medium heat until warm. Add shallot, and cook, stirring occasionally, until soft, about 2 minutes. Add wine and grapefruit juice; bring to a simmer. Reduce heat to medium-low; cook until liquid is reduced by half, about 20 minutes.

4 Bring ¼ cup water, ½ cup grapefruit sauce, and ginger to a simmer in a large sauté pan over medium-high heat. Place cabbage in pan in a single layer; sprinkle with ½ teaspoon salt. Cover; cook until tender, about 15 minutes. Add sesame oil; remove from heat.

5 Meanwhile, coat an ovenproof nonstick skillet with cooking spray; place over medium heat. Add chicken; cook until undersides are golden, about 3 minutes. Turn; transfer skillet to oven. Bake until cooked through, 8 to 10 minutes.

6 Transfer cabbage to a plate; cover to keep warm. Add ¼ cup grapefruit sauce, scallions, and grapefruit segments to pan. Cook over medium-low heat, 2 minutes. Divide chicken, cabbage, grapefruit, and sauce among four plates.

PER SERVING: 277 CALORIES, 9 G FAT, 41 MG CHOLESTEROL, 28 G CARBOHYDRATE, 606 MG SODIUM, 21 G PROTEIN, 9 G FIBER

from Fit to Eat: Red Grapefruit

spice-crusted rack of lamb

SERVES 2 | **PHOTO ON PAGE 79**

Rack of lamb is truly a special-occasion treat. Usually you need to order it from a butcher, at the supermarket or in a butcher shop. Ask him to "french" the bones, which means removing excess meat and fat from the bones so it will look nice and so it will be neat to eat. Be sure to let the meat rest for ten minutes before serving (during this time, it will finish cooking and reabsorb juices).

1 rack of lamb (8 ribs, about 1¼ pounds), frenched
 Coarse salt and freshly ground pepper
¼ cup yellow mustard seeds
2 teaspoons fennel seeds
1 tablespoon olive oil
 Herb Oil (recipe follows), for serving

1 Preheat oven to 375°F. Cut the rack into two 4-rib pieces, and season the meat generously with salt and pepper.

2 Toast the mustard and fennel seeds in a large cast-iron (or ovenproof) skillet over medium heat, stirring constantly, until fragrant, 1 to 2 minutes. Transfer to a plate to cool slightly.

3 Heat oil in skillet until hot but not smoking. Place 1 piece of lamb in skillet, bone side down, and brown all over, 1 to 2 minutes per side. Transfer to a plate; repeat with remaining piece of lamb. Roll meat in spices to coat (do not coat the cut sides on either end).

4 Return meat to skillet, and transfer to oven. Roast meat until an instant-read thermometer inserted into center (avoiding the bones) registers 135°F, for medium-rare, 18 to 24 minutes.

5 Remove meat from skillet, and let stand at least 10 minutes. Cut meat into individual or double chops, and cross the bones, if desired. Serve with herb oil.

from Easy Entertaining: Dinner for Two

herb oil

MAKES ABOUT 1 CUP

Herb oil can be refrigerated for up to two days before using; bring to room temperature before serving.

1 cup fresh mint leaves
½ cup fresh flat-leaf parsley leaves
½ cup extra-virgin olive oil
¼ teaspoon coarse salt

1 Bring a small saucepan of water to a boil. Prepare an ice-water bath. Add mint and parsley to boiling water; cook 30 seconds. Drain; immediately plunge herbs into ice water.

2 Wrap herbs in paper towels; squeeze out as much liquid as possible. Purée herbs with oil in a blender until well blended, about 3 minutes. Stir in the salt.

....

DESSERTS
....

butterscotch blondies

MAKES 9 LARGE OR 16 SMALL SQUARES | **PHOTO ON PAGE 88**

Store blondies in airtight containers at room temperature for up to three days.

9 tablespoons (1⅛ sticks) unsalted butter, softened, plus more for pan
1⅔ cups all-purpose flour
1 teaspoon baking powder
¾ teaspoon salt
1 cup packed light-brown sugar
2 large eggs
1 teaspoon pure vanilla extract
⅓ cup butterscotch chips
½ cup unsalted cashews, coarsely chopped (3 ounces)
¼ cup toffee bits

1 Preheat oven to 350°F. Butter an 8-inch square baking pan; line with foil or parchment paper, allowing 2 inches to hang over sides. Butter lining (excluding overhang); set pan aside.

2 Whisk together flour, baking powder, and salt in a medium bowl, and set aside.

3 Put butter and sugar in the bowl of an electric mixer fitted with the paddle attachment; cream on medium speed until

pale and fluffy, about 3 minutes. Add eggs and vanilla; beat until combined. Add flour mixture, and mix on low speed, scraping down sides of bowl, until well incorporated. Mix in butterscotch chips, cashews, and toffee bits.

4 Pour batter into prepared pan; spread with a rubber spatula. Bake until golden brown and a cake tester inserted into blondies (avoid center and edges) comes out with a few crumbs but is not wet, 42 to 45 minutes.

5 Let cool slightly in pan, about 15 minutes. Lift out, and let cool completely on a wire rack before cutting into squares.

from Brownies and Blondies

cream-cheese swirl blondies

MAKES 9 LARGE OR 16 SMALL SQUARES | **PHOTO ON PAGE 87**

Ingredients for Butterscotch Blondies (page 38), omitting butterscotch, cashews, and toffee

6 ounces cream cheese (not whipped), room temperature

¼ cup sugar

2 tablespoons unsalted butter, softened

2 tablespoons all-purpose flour

1 large egg

½ teaspoon pure vanilla extract

1 Follow the recipe for Butterscotch Blondies, preheating oven to 325°F. Proceed with recipe until the flour mixture is added (end of step 3).

2 Put cream cheese, sugar, butter, flour, egg, and vanilla in the bowl of an electric mixer fitted with the paddle attachment; mix on medium speed just until smooth.

3 Pour half the batter into prepared pan; spread evenly with an offset spatula. Spoon two-thirds of cream-cheese mixture on top; spread evenly. Place dollops of remaining batter on top; spread. Place dollops of remaining cream-cheese mixture about 1 inch apart on top.

4 With a butter knife, gently swirl filling into batter, running knife lengthwise and crosswise through layers three times each, and reaching to bottom of pan. Bake until golden brown and a cake tester inserted into center comes out with a few crumbs but is not wet, 45 to 47 minutes.

from Brownies and Blondies

magic blondies

MAKES 1 DOZEN | **PHOTO ON PAGE 87**

⅔ cup sweetened flaked coconut

⅔ cup semisweet chocolate chips

⅔ cup chopped walnuts (2½ ounces)

⅔ cup dried cherries or cranberries

Ingredients for Butterscotch Blondies (page 38), omitting butterscotch, cashews, and toffee

1 Stir together coconut, chocolate, walnuts, and cherries in a medium bowl; set aside. Place cupcake liners in a standard 12-cup muffin tin; set aside.

2 Follow the recipe for Butterscotch Blondies. After the flour mixture is added (at the end of step 3), mix 1 cup coconut mixture into batter.

3 Divide batter among muffin cups, filling each three-quarters full. Sprinkle remaining coconut mixture over tops. Bake until a cake tester inserted into centers comes out with a few crumbs but is not wet, about 25 minutes.

from Brownies and Blondies

pear, pistachio, and ginger blondies

MAKES ABOUT 1 DOZEN | **PHOTO ON PAGE 87**

You can also make these blondies in an eight-inch square baking pan (follow step one of Butterscotch Blondies, page 38).

Ingredients for Butterscotch Blondies (page 38), omitting butterscotch, cashews, and toffee

¾ cup coarsely chopped dried pear

¾ cup shelled pistachios, coarsely chopped (3¼ ounces)

¼ cup chopped candied ginger

1 Follow the recipe for Butterscotch Blondies, buttering a 9-inch springform pan in step 1. Proceed with recipe.

2 At the end of step 3, mix in dried pear, pistachios, and candied ginger. Bake until a cake tester inserted into blondies (avoid center and edges) comes out with a few crumbs but is not wet, 33 to 35 minutes. Cut into wedges.

from Brownies and Blondies

raspberry-almond blondies

MAKES 9 LARGE OR 16 SMALL SQUARES | PHOTO ON PAGE 87

Ingredients for Butterscotch Blondies (page 38), omitting butterscotch, cashews, and toffee

1 cup sliced almonds (3 ounces), toasted

1 pint raspberries

Confectioners' sugar, for dusting

Follow recipe for Butterscotch Blondies, preheating oven to 325°F. At the end of step 3, mix in ¾ cup almonds. Scatter berries and remaining ¼ cup nuts over batter in pan. Bake until a cake tester inserted into blondies (avoid center and edges) comes out with a few crumbs but is not wet, 55 to 60 minutes. Dust with sugar before cutting into squares.

from Brownies and Blondies

double-chocolate brownies

MAKES 9 LARGE OR 16 SMALL SQUARES | PHOTO ON PAGE 88

Store brownies in an airtight container at room temperature for up to three days.

6 tablespoons unsalted butter, plus more for pan

6 ounces good-quality semisweet chocolate, coarsely chopped

¼ cup unsweetened cocoa powder (not Dutch-process)

¾ cup all-purpose flour

¼ teaspoon baking powder

¼ teaspoon salt

1 cup sugar

2 large eggs

2 teaspoons pure vanilla extract

1 Preheat oven to 350°F. Butter an 8-inch square baking pan; line with foil or parchment, allowing 2 inches to hang over sides. Butter lining (excluding overhang); set aside.

2 Put butter, chocolate, and cocoa in a heatproof medium bowl set over a pan of simmering water; stir until butter and chocolate are melted. Let cool slightly.

3 Whisk together flour, baking powder, and salt in a separate bowl; set aside.

4 Put sugar, eggs, and vanilla in the bowl of an electric mixer fitted with the whisk attachment, and beat on medium speed until pale, about 4 minutes. Add chocolate mixture; beat until combined. Add flour mixture; beat, scraping down sides of bowl, until well incorporated.

5 Pour batter into prepared pan; smooth top with a rubber spatula. Bake until a cake tester inserted into brownies (avoid center and edges) comes out with a few crumbs but is not wet, about 35 minutes. Let cool slightly in pan, about 15 minutes. Lift out brownies; let cool completely on a wire rack before cutting into squares.

from Brownies and Blondies

peanut-butter swirl brownies

MAKES 9 LARGE OR 16 SMALL SQUARES | PHOTO ON PAGE 87

FOR THE FILLING:

4 tablespoons unsalted butter, melted

½ cup confectioners' sugar

¾ cup smooth peanut butter

¼ teaspoon salt

½ teaspoon pure vanilla extract

FOR THE BATTER:

8 tablespoons (1 stick) unsalted butter, cut into small pieces, plus more for pan

2 ounces good-quality unsweetened chocolate, coarsely chopped

4 ounces good-quality semisweet chocolate, coarsely chopped

⅔ cup all-purpose flour

½ teaspoon baking powder

¼ teaspoon salt

¾ cup granulated sugar

3 large eggs

2 teaspoons pure vanilla extract

1 Make filling: Stir together butter, confectioners' sugar, peanut butter, salt, and vanilla in a bowl until smooth. Set aside.

2 Preheat oven to 325°F. Butter an 8-inch square baking pan; line with foil or parchment, allowing 2 inches to hang over sides. Butter lining (excluding overhang); set aside.

3 Make batter: Put butter and chocolates in a heatproof medium bowl set over a pan of simmering water; stir until melted. Let cool slightly.

4 Whisk together flour, baking powder, and salt in a separate bowl, and set aside.

5 Whisk granulated sugar into chocolate mixture. Add eggs, and whisk until mixture is smooth. Stir in vanilla. Add flour mixture; stir until well incorporated.

6 Pour one-third of batter into prepared pan, and spread evenly with a rubber spatula. Place dollops of filling (about 1 tablespoon each) about 1 inch apart on top of batter. Drizzle remaining batter on top, and gently spread to fill pan. Place dollops of remaining filling on top.

7 With a butter knife, gently swirl filling into batter, running knife lengthwise and crosswise through layers three times each, and reaching to bottom of pan. Bake until a cake tester inserted into brownies (avoid center and edges) comes out with a few crumbs but is not wet, about 45 minutes. Let cool slightly in pan, about 15 minutes. Lift out brownies; let cool completely on a wire rack before cutting into squares.

from Brownies and Blondies

coconut swirl brownies variation

MAKES 9 LARGE OR 16 SMALL SQUARES | **PHOTO ON PAGE 87**

FOR THE FILLING:

2 tablespoons granulated sugar

⅔ cup sweetened condensed milk

1¼ cups unsweetened shredded coconut

1 large egg

½ teaspoon pure vanilla extract

FOR THE BATTER:

Ingredients for Peanut-Butter Swirl Brownies batter (page 40)

1 Make filling: Stir together sugar, condensed milk, coconut, egg, and vanilla in a medium bowl; set aside.

2 Make batter and bake brownies, following steps 2 through 7 of the Peanut-Butter Swirl Brownies recipe.

truffle brownies

MAKES ABOUT 1 DOZEN

Refrigerate brownies, covered, for up to two days. Bring to room temperature before serving. You can also make the brownies in an eight-inch square baking pan (prepare pan as directed in step one of Double-Chocolate Brownies, page 40).

FOR THE BATTER:

4 tablespoons unsalted butter, plus more for pan

3 ounces good-quality unsweetened chocolate, coarsely chopped

½ cup all-purpose flour

¼ teaspoon baking powder

½ teaspoon salt

1 cup sugar

2 large eggs

¼ cup milk

1 teaspoon pure vanilla extract

FOR THE GANACHE TOPPING:

4 ounces good-quality semisweet chocolate, coarsely chopped

⅔ cup heavy cream

Heart-shaped sprinkles, for garnish (optional)

1 Preheat oven to 325°F. Butter a 9-inch springform pan.

2 Make batter: Melt butter and chocolate in a heatproof medium bowl set over a pan of simmering water, stirring. Let cool. Whisk flour, baking powder, and salt in a separate bowl.

3 Put sugar and eggs in the bowl of an electric mixer fitted with the whisk attachment, and beat on medium speed until pale and fluffy, about 4 minutes. Add chocolate mixture, milk, and vanilla; beat until combined. Add flour mixture; beat, scraping down sides of bowl, until well incorporated.

4 Pour batter into pan. Bake until a cake tester inserted into brownies (avoid center and edges) comes out with a few crumbs but is not wet, 27 to 30 minutes. Let cool in pan.

5 Make topping when brownies are cool: Put chocolate in a medium bowl. Heat cream in a small saucepan over medium-high heat until just simmering. Pour over chocolate; let stand 5 minutes. Gently stir until smooth. Let cool, stirring every 10 minutes, until slightly thickened, 25 to 30 minutes.

6 Pour ganache over brownies in pan; let set, about 20 minutes. Refrigerate until cold, 30 minutes to 1 hour. Let stand at room temperature 15 minutes before serving. Lift out brownies; cut into wedges, wiping knife with a hot, damp cloth between cuts. Scatter sprinkles on top, if desired.

from Brownies and Blondies

turtle brownies

MAKES 8 | **PHOTO ON PAGE 87**

FOR THE BATTER:

Ingredients for Truffle Brownies batter (page 41)

FOR THE TOPPING:

1 cup sugar

⅓ cup heavy cream

1 teaspoon pure vanilla extract

½ teaspoon salt

1 cup coarsely chopped toasted pecans (4 ounces)

1 Preheat oven to 325°F. Butter an 8-inch square baking pan; line with foil or parchment paper, allowing 2 inches to hang over sides. Butter lining (excluding overhang); set pan aside.

2 Make brownies: Follow steps 2 through 4 of the Truffle Brownies recipe.

3 Make caramel topping when brownies are cool: Bring ⅓ cup water and the sugar to a boil in a medium saucepan over medium-high heat, stirring until sugar has dissolved. When syrup comes to a boil, stop stirring, and wash down sides of pan with a wet pastry brush to prevent crystals from forming. Continue to cook, swirling pan occasionally, until mixture is medium amber, 5 to 7 minutes.

4 Remove from heat; immediately add cream, vanilla, and salt (mixture will steam). Gently stir with a clean wooden spoon or heatproof spatula until smooth. Add pecans; stir until caramel begins to cool and thickens slightly, about 1 minute.

5 Pour caramel over brownies; spread with an offset spatula. Refrigerate until cold, 30 minutes to 1 hour.

6 Let brownies stand at room temperature 15 minutes before serving. Lift out brownies; cut into 8 rectangles (2 by 4 inches each), wiping knife with a hot, damp cloth between cuts.

from Brownies and Blondies

chocolate pots de crème

MAKES 4 | **PHOTO ON PAGE 83**

Pots de crème can be made two days ahead. Keep refrigerated until ready to serve.

1¼ cups half-and-half

3 ounces bittersweet chocolate, finely chopped

¼ cup sugar

3 large egg yolks

½ teaspoon pure vanilla extract

1 tablespoon unsweetened cocoa powder

Pinch of salt

1 tablespoon hazelnut-flavored liqueur, such as Frangelico (optional)

Freshly whipped cream, for serving (optional)

1 Preheat oven to 300°F. Bring a kettle of water to a boil, and set aside.

2 Heat half-and-half in a small saucepan over medium heat until it just begins to simmer. Remove from heat, and add chocolate and sugar. Let stand 5 minutes.

3 Stir together yolks, vanilla, cocoa, salt, and liqueur, if desired, in a large bowl.

4 With a fork, stir chocolate mixture until smooth. Gradually stir chocolate mixture into egg mixture. Pour through a fine sieve into a glass measuring cup.

5 Place four ramekins or pudding molds (3 to 4 ounces each) in a shallow roasting pan, and divide the chocolate mixture among them. Pour the hot water into the pan so that it reaches halfway up the sides of the ramekins.

6 Bake until custards are not quite set in centers, about 30 minutes (custards will firm up as they cool). Carefully remove ramekins from water bath, and let custards cool slightly.

7 Cover with plastic wrap; refrigerate until ready to serve. Just before serving, dollop with whipped cream, if desired.

from Easy Entertaining: Dinner for Two

chrusciki (bow-tie cookies)

MAKES 6 DOZEN

You can store chrusciki (pronounced *khroost-CHEE-kee*) in waxed-paper-lined airtight containers at room temperature for up to one week. Wait until just before serving to dust them with confectioners' sugar.

- 1 tablespoon unsalted butter, melted
- 2 large eggs plus 5 large egg yolks
- ¼ cup granulated sugar
- 3 tablespoons sour cream
- 2 teaspoons salt
- 1 teaspoon pure orange extract
- 1 teaspoon pure lemon extract
- 1 teaspoon pure vanilla extract
- 1 teaspoon distilled white vinegar
- 1 tablespoon rum
- 1 tablespoon finely grated lemon zest
- 1 tablespoon finely grated orange zest
- 2 to 3 cups all-purpose flour, plus more for dusting
- 7 cups vegetable shortening (3 pounds)
  Confectioners' sugar, for dusting

1 Put butter, eggs, yolks, granulated sugar, sour cream, salt, extracts, vinegar, and rum in the bowl of a standing mixer fitted with the paddle attachment. Beat on medium-high speed until mixture is pale, about 3 minutes. With mixer running, add zests. Reduce speed to low; gradually add up to 3 cups flour, ½ cup at a time, until a fairly stiff dough forms.

2 Turn out dough onto a lightly floured surface, and knead, dusting with flour if it seems sticky, until dough becomes smooth, soft, and elastic, about 10 minutes. Halve dough, and wrap each piece in plastic wrap. Let dough rest at room temperature, 30 minutes.

3 Working with 1 piece at a time, roll out dough on a lightly floured surface until very thin (about ¹⁄₁₆ inch thick). Using a straightedge as a guide, cut the dough into 5-by-1¼-inch strips. Trim ends on the diagonal.

4 Lay dough strips vertically in front of you, and cut a 1¼-inch-long opening through the middle of each strip. Working with one strip at a time, push one end through the cut, then pull through to make a bow-tie shape. Transfer formed chrusciki to a large parchment-lined baking sheet, and cover with a clean, slightly damp kitchen towel. Repeat process with remaining dough.

5 Heat shortening in a large (6-quart) pot over medium-high heat until it registers 375°F on a deep-fry thermometer.

6 Working in batches of about 7, fry chrusciki, turning once with a slotted spoon, until lightly browned, about 1 minute. Transfer fried chrusciki with slotted spoon to two paper-towel-lined baking sheets to drain. (Adjust heat between batches as necessary to keep oil at a steady temperature.)

7 Before serving, dust chrusciki with confectioners' sugar.

from Mother Knows Best

hazelnut kisses

MAKES 18

You can store leftover kisses in an airtight container at room temperature for up to three days.

- 6 ounces hazelnuts (about 1⅓ cups)
- ¾ cup sugar
- 2 large egg whites
- ¼ teaspoon salt
- ½ cup all-purpose flour
- ½ teaspoon pure vanilla extract

1 Preheat oven to 375°F. Spread hazelnuts in a single layer on a rimmed baking sheet; toast in oven until skins split and flesh turns deep golden brown, 10 to 12 minutes. When cool enough to handle, rub nuts vigorously with a clean kitchen towel to remove as much of the papery skins as will come off easily. Let cool completely.

2 Process nuts in a food processor with ¼ cup sugar until very fine.

3 Beat egg whites with the salt in the bowl of an electric mixer (or by hand) until soft peaks form. Add remaining ½ cup sugar, and beat until egg whites hold stiff (but not dry) peaks.

4 Add nut mixture, flour, and vanilla to egg whites; beat until just combined. Refrigerate, covered, until cold, at least 1 hour or up to 1 day.

5 Line a baking sheet with parchment paper or a Silpat baking mat. With cool, dampened hands, mold heaping tablespoons of dough into kisslike (pyramid) shapes, each about 1½ inches wide and 1¼ inches high. Transfer to lined sheet.

6 Bake cookies until edges and bottoms begin to brown, 15 to 18 minutes.

from Easy Entertaining: Dinner for Two

ice cream with butterscotch sauce

SERVES 4

1 cup heavy cream

1 cup hard, dark butterscotch candies, finely chopped, plus more for garnish (optional)

1 pint vanilla ice cream, for serving

1 Heat cream in a medium saucepan over medium-high heat until almost boiling. Stir in chopped candies, and reduce heat to medium. Continue to cook, stirring constantly, until candies have melted, about 5 minutes. Let sauce cool slightly.

2 Divide ice cream among four serving bowls, and top with sauce. Garnish with additional crushed candies, if desired.

from What's for Dinner?

Mrs. Kostyra's babkas

MAKES THREE 8-INCH BABKAS | PHOTO ON PAGE 67

8 ounces (2 sticks) unsalted butter, softened, plus more for molds and bowl

2 cups whole milk

3 envelopes active dry yeast (3 scant tablespoons), or 1⅓ ounces compressed fresh yeast, crumbled

1 cup plus a pinch of sugar

½ cup warm water (about 110°F)

5 large eggs plus 4 large egg yolks

1 teaspoon salt

1 teaspoon pure vanilla extract

1 tablespoon orange-flavored liqueur, such as Grand Marnier
Finely grated zest of 1 orange
Finely grated zest of 1 lemon

9 to 10 cups sifted all-purpose flour, plus more for dusting

1 cup dried currants

1½ cups golden raisins

1 cup dark raisins

1 cup blanched almonds, coarsely chopped

1 tablespoon heavy cream

1 Butter three kugelhopf molds (each 1½ quarts and 8 inches in diameter); set aside. Butter a large bowl; set aside. Heat milk and butter in a saucepan over medium-low, stirring, until butter is melted.

2 Sprinkle yeast and a pinch of sugar over the warm water in a small bowl. Let stand until foamy, 7 to 10 minutes.

3 Whisk together 4 eggs, the egg yolks, sugar, and salt in a large bowl until thick, about 3 minutes. Add vanilla, liqueur, zests, yeast mixture, and milk mixture; whisk 1 minute more. With a wooden spoon, gradually stir in up to 10 cups flour,

1 cup at a time, until a sticky dough forms. Stir in dried fruits and almonds.

4 Turn out dough onto a lightly floured surface; knead, dusting with flour if it seems sticky, until smooth and soft, about 10 minutes. Transfer to buttered bowl. Loosely cover with buttered plastic wrap; let rise in a warm place until doubled in bulk, about 2 hours. Punch down dough. Loosely cover with buttered wrap; let rise until doubled in bulk, 1½ to 2 hours more.

5 Punch down dough, and turn it out onto a lightly floured surface; knead 1 minute. Divide dough into 3 equal pieces. With lightly floured hands, roll each piece into an 18-inch-long rope. Fit each rope into a buttered mold; press end of rope into dough to seal. Loosely cover with buttered wrap. Let rise until doubled in bulk, about 45 minutes.

6 Preheat oven to 350°F. Whisk together remaining egg and the cream in a small bowl. Brush dough with egg wash. Bake until golden, about 35 minutes. Let cool slightly in molds on a wire rack, about 10 minutes. Unmold onto rack, and let cool completely, larger sides down.

from Mother Knows Best

red grapefruit with brûléed meringue

SERVES 4

2 large egg whites

⅛ teaspoon salt

¼ cup packed dark-brown sugar

2 red grapefruit, halved crosswise

1 Preheat broiler, with rack in lowest position. Put egg whites and salt in the bowl of an electric mixer fitted with the whisk attachment; beat on medium speed until frothy, about 30 seconds. Raise speed to high, and add sugar 1 tablespoon at a time, beating until incorporated. Continue to beat until egg whites hold stiff (but not dry) peaks, about 3 minutes.

2 Place grapefruit halves, cut sides down, on a plate; let drain 2 minutes. Invert; carefully cut between membranes to loosen segments completely. Spoon one-quarter of meringue onto each half, using the spoon to create swirls and peaks. Transfer to a baking pan. Broil, checking frequently, until meringues are browned, about 30 seconds. Serve.

Note: The eggs in this dish are not fully cooked, so it should not be prepared for pregnant women, babies, young children, the elderly, or anyone whose health is compromised.

PER SERVING: 88 CALORIES, 0 G FAT, 0 MG CHOLESTEROL, 21 G CARBOHYDRATE, 105 MG SODIUM, 2 G PROTEIN, 6 G FIBER

from Fit to Eat: Red Grapefruit

spice cake

SERVES 8 TO 10

8 tablespoons (1 stick) unsalted butter, softened,
  plus more for pan
4 cups cake flour (not self-rising), plus more for dusting
4 teaspoons baking powder
2 teaspoons ground cinnamon
1 teaspoon ground allspice
½ teaspoon salt
½ teaspoon freshly grated nutmeg
½ teaspoon ground mace
  Pinch of ground cloves
1½ cups packed dark-brown sugar
4 large eggs
1½ cups whole milk
  Orange Glaze (recipe follows)
  Confectioners' sugar, for dusting (optional)
  Freshly whipped cream, for serving (optional)

1 Preheat oven to 350°F. Butter and flour a 9-inch round
baking pan or an 8-inch square baking pan; tap out excess
flour. Sift flour, baking powder, cinnamon, allspice, salt, nutmeg, mace, and cloves three times into a large bowl.

2 Put butter in the bowl of an electric mixer fitted with the
paddle attachment, and crumble brown sugar into bowl.
Cream butter and sugar on medium-high speed until pale
and fluffy, about 2 minutes. Add eggs one at a time, mixing
well after each addition and scraping down sides of bowl.
Reduce speed to low. Add flour mixture and milk in two alternating additions, beginning with flour mixture.

3 Pour batter into prepared pan. Bake until golden brown
and a cake tester inserted into center comes out clean,
about 1 hour. Let cake cool slightly in pan on a wire rack set
over a sheet of waxed paper, about 20 minutes. Invert cake
to unmold, and reinvert onto rack.

4 Poke holes all over top of cake with a toothpick. Brush top
and sides of cake with about half the glaze; let cool. Just
before serving, brush with remaining glaze. Dust with confectioners' sugar, and serve with whipped cream, if desired.

from Mother Knows Best

orange glaze

MAKES ABOUT ⅓ CUP

⅓ cup fresh orange juice
2 tablespoons sugar
1 tablespoon unsalted butter

Cook all ingredients in a small saucepan over medium-low
heat, stirring, until butter is melted and mixture is smooth,
about 2 minutes.

tapioca passion-fruit parfaits

MAKES 6

Passion fruits are easy to work with. They are ripe when
wrinkled; if the skin is smooth, let them sit at room
temperature for a few days.

2 cups canned unsweetened coconut milk (16 ounces)
1 cup heavy cream
1 piece peeled fresh ginger (1½ inches), cut into
  ⅛-inch-thick slices
1¾ teaspoons unflavored gelatin
¾ cup plus 1 teaspoon sugar
1 cup passion-fruit juice or nectar
5 green cardamom pods
10 whole black peppercorns
1 fresh bay leaf
3½ cups whole milk, plus ½ cup if needed
½ cup large pearl tapioca (3¼ ounces)
3 ripe passion fruits

1 Make panna cotta: Bring 1 cup coconut milk and the
cream to a simmer in a medium saucepan over medium-low
heat. Remove from heat, and add ginger. Cover, and let steep
30 minutes. Pour mixture through a fine sieve into a clean
medium saucepan; discard ginger.

2 Sprinkle 1 teaspoon gelatin over 1½ tablespoons cold water
in a small bowl, and let stand 2 minutes to soften. Whisk
gelatin mixture and ¼ cup sugar into coconut-milk mixture.
Cook over medium heat, stirring, until sugar and gelatin have
dissolved. Pour ½ cup panna cotta into each of six glasses.
Refrigerate until firm, about 2½ hours.

3 Make gelée: Sprinkle remaining ¾ teaspoon gelatin over
passion-fruit juice in a small saucepan; let stand 2 minutes to
soften. Whisk in 1 teaspoon sugar. Cook over medium-low
heat, stirring, until gelatin and sugar have dissolved. Pour
through a fine sieve into a glass measuring cup; let cool,
about 10 minutes. Pour 3 tablespoons gelée into each glass.
Refrigerate until firm, about 1½ hours.

4 Meanwhile, make tapioca: Tie cardamom, peppercorns, and bay leaf in a square of cheesecloth. Bring whole milk and remaining cup coconut milk to a simmer in a medium saucepan over medium-low heat. Add bouquet garni, remaining ½ cup sugar, and the tapioca; bring to a simmer over medium heat, stirring. Cook, stirring often, until tapioca pearls are tender, 35 to 40 minutes (consistency will be loose). Discard bouquet garni. Cover tapioca; let cool to room temperature, or refrigerate until ready to serve.

5 Just before serving, if you prefer a thinner tapioca, stir in up to ½ cup milk. Divide tapioca among glasses over gelée. Halve passion fruits; spoon pulp and seeds over each parfait.

from Dessert of the Month

....

MISCELLANEOUS
....

lemon-sage breadcrumbs

MAKES 2¼ CUPS

1 loaf (8 ounces) day-old bread, crusts removed and bread cut into 1-inch cubes (about 5 cups)
3 tablespoons finely grated lemon zest (about 2 lemons)
5 tablespoons finely chopped fresh sage
4½ teaspoons coarse salt
Freshly ground pepper

Working in two batches, pulse bread cubes in a food processor until fine crumbs form. Stir together breadcrumbs, zest, sage, and salt; season breadcrumbs with pepper. Freeze in resealable plastic bags up to 1 month.

from Good Things

almond and garam masala variation
Follow recipe for Lemon-Sage Breadcrumbs, using ½ cup chopped, toasted sliced almonds and 2 teaspoons garam masala in place of lemon zest and sage.

coconut-lime variation
Follow recipe for Lemon-Sage Breadcrumbs, using ½ cup toasted, unsweetened shredded coconut, 2½ tablespoons finely grated lime zest (2 to 3 limes), and ¾ teaspoon cayenne pepper in place of lemon zest and sage.

Parmesan-oregano variation
Follow recipe for Lemon-Sage Breadcrumbs, using 3½ tablespoons finely chopped fresh oregano (or 1 teaspoon dried) and ¾ cup finely grated Parmesan cheese in place of lemon zest and sage. Decrease salt to 1 tablespoon.

roasted-garlic aïoli

MAKES ABOUT 1 CUP

You can make this garlic mayonnaise with a mortar and pestle or a food processor. Store in an airtight container in the refrigerator for up to three days.

1 bulb Whole Roasted Garlic (page 36), cloves peeled
½ teaspoon coarse salt
3 large egg yolks
½ teaspoon Dijon mustard
¾ cup olive oil
1 tablespoon fresh lemon juice

WITH A MORTAR AND PESTLE:

In a large mortar, mash garlic cloves and salt with pestle until combined. Add egg yolks; stir until combined. Stir in mustard. Pour in oil a few drops at a time, stirring until emulsified. Stir in lemon juice.

WITH A FOOD PROCESSOR:

Process garlic cloves, salt, egg yolks, and mustard until combined, about 5 seconds. With machine running, pour in ¼ cup oil in a slow, steady stream; process until mixture is slightly thickened, about 10 seconds. With machine still running, pour in remaining ½ cup oil in a slow, steady stream; process until mixture is thick. Pulse in lemon juice.

Note: Raw eggs should not be used in food prepared for pregnant women, babies, young children, the elderly, or anyone whose health is compromised.

from Roasted Garlic

roasted-garlic vinaigrette

MAKES ¾ CUP

10 Roasted Garlic Cloves (page 37)
3 tablespoons sherry vinegar
1 tablespoon honey
1 teaspoon Dijon mustard
¾ teaspoon coarse salt
½ cup extra-virgin olive oil
Freshly ground pepper

Squeeze garlic cloves from skins into a blender. Add vinegar, honey, mustard, and salt; blend until smooth, about 10 seconds. With machine running, pour in oil in a slow, steady stream; blend until emulsified. Season with pepper. Refrigerate vinaigrette in an airtight container up to three days.

from Roasted Garlic

March

whole-wheat buttermilk pancakes
MAKES ABOUT 16; SERVES 4

- 1 cup whole-wheat flour
- ⅔ cup all-purpose flour
- ⅓ cup toasted wheat germ
- 1 tablespoon packed light-brown sugar
- 1 teaspoon baking powder
- ½ teaspoon baking soda
- ¼ teaspoon salt
- 3 tablespoons unsalted butter, melted
- 2¾ cups low-fat buttermilk
- 2 large eggs, lightly beaten
- Vegetable-oil cooking spray
- Pure maple syrup, for serving (optional)
- Raspberries, for serving (optional)

1 Preheat oven to 200°F. Whisk together both flours, the wheat germ, sugar, baking powder, baking soda, and salt in a medium bowl; set aside.

2 Heat a griddle or seasoned cast-iron skillet over medium heat. Stir together melted butter, buttermilk, and eggs in a medium bowl. Stir the flour mixture into the buttermilk mixture until just combined (batter will be slightly lumpy).

3 Generously coat griddle with cooking spray. Working in batches, pour ¼ cup batter onto griddle for each pancake. Cook until surface is bubbling and edges are slightly dry, 3 to 4 minutes. Turn pancakes; cook until undersides are golden brown, about 3 minutes more. Transfer to a baking sheet, and keep warm in oven. Divide pancakes among four plates. Serve with syrup and berries, if desired.

PER SERVING: 396 CALORIES, 14 G FAT, 124 MG CHOLESTEROL, 53 G CARBOHYDRATE, 873 MG SODIUM, 17 G PROTEIN, 5 G FIBER

from Fit to Eat: Buttermilk

Irish soda bread
SERVES 4 TO 6

Graham flour is coarser than regular whole-wheat flour, which would also work in this recipe. If using the latter, substitute one-half cup wheat bran for one-half cup of the all-purpose flour.

- 3 cups all-purpose flour, plus more for dusting
- 1 cup whole-wheat graham flour
- 2½ teaspoons coarse salt
- 1 teaspoon baking soda
- 1 teaspoon baking powder
- 4 tablespoons cold unsalted butter, cut into small pieces
- 1⅔ cups buttermilk

1 Preheat oven to 350°F. Line a baking sheet with parchment paper, and set aside. Whisk together both flours, the salt, baking soda, and baking powder in a large bowl. With a pastry blender or your fingertips, blend in butter until it resembles small peas. Add buttermilk all at once; stir with a fork until mixture holds together.

2 In the bowl, pat the dough into a dome-shaped loaf about 7 inches in diameter. Lift out dough; transfer to lined sheet.

3 Lightly dust top of loaf with flour. Cut a ¾-inch-deep cross in top, reaching almost all the way to edge of loaf. Bake, rotating sheet halfway through, until deep golden brown and a cake tester inserted into the center comes out clean, about 1 hour and 20 minutes. Let cool on a wire rack.

from Irish Dinner

jalapeño corn muffins

MAKES 1 DOZEN

8 tablespoons (1 stick) unsalted butter, plus more for tin, melted

¾ cup nonfat buttermilk

2 large eggs

½ cup sour cream

1 cup yellow cornmeal

1 cup all-purpose flour

½ cup packed light-brown sugar

2 tablespoons baking powder

1 teaspoon coarse salt

2 jalapeño chiles, seeded and finely chopped

¼ cup plus 2 tablespoons fresh or frozen (thawed) corn kernels

Unsalted butter, for serving

1 Preheat oven to 375°F. Brush the cups of a standard 12-cup muffin tin with melted butter. Whisk together buttermilk, eggs, and sour cream in a medium bowl until combined, and set aside. Whisk together cornmeal, flour, sugar, baking powder, salt, jalapeños, and corn in a large bowl until combined.

2 With a rubber spatula, fold buttermilk mixture into cornmeal mixture until well combined. Fold in melted butter. Divide batter among muffin cups, filling each three-quarters full. Bake until a cake tester inserted into centers comes out clean, about 25 minutes. Let muffins cool in tin 5 minutes. Turn out into a basket or bowl lined with a clean kitchen towel; cover to keep warm. Serve with butter.

from What's for Dinner?

SOUPS

buttermilk squash soup

MAKES 7 CUPS; SERVES 7

4 slices (each about ½ inch thick) sourdough bread (about 7 ounces), crusts removed

1 tablespoon extra-virgin olive oil

Coarse salt and freshly ground pepper

2 tablespoons unsalted butter

1 medium onion, coarsely chopped

3 garlic cloves, minced

2 pounds yellow summer squash, cut into ½-inch-thick rounds

1 russet potato (about ¾ pound), peeled and cut into ½-inch cubes

3½ cups homemade or low-sodium store-bought chicken stock, skimmed of fat

½ cup low-fat buttermilk

Finely chopped fresh chives, for garnish

1 Preheat oven to 350°F. Tear bread into ½-inch pieces (to measure about 1 cup). Transfer to a medium bowl; drizzle with oil. Season with ¼ teaspoon salt and pepper to taste, and toss to combine. Transfer to a rimmed baking sheet; toast bread in oven until crisp and golden brown, about 13 minutes. Let cool.

2 Melt butter in a large saucepan over medium heat. Add onion, garlic, squash, and potato; cook, stirring often, until vegetables begin to soften, about 5 minutes. Add 3 cups stock, and bring to a boil. Reduce heat; simmer, stirring occasionally, until potato is tender, 20 to 25 minutes.

3 Let soup cool slightly. Carefully ladle soup into a blender (work in batches to avoid filling blender more than halfway); purée until smooth. Pour soup through a fine sieve into a clean large saucepan.

4 Place pan over medium-low heat. Add ½ teaspoon salt, then stir in remaining ½ cup stock; while stirring, slowly pour in buttermilk. Heat until warm, about 5 minutes. Divide soup and reserved croutons among bowls, and garnish with chives.

PER SERVING: 185 CALORIES, 7 G FAT, 10 MG CHOLESTEROL, 24 G CARBOHYDRATE, 637 MG SODIUM, 6 G PROTEIN, 4 G FIBER

from Fit to Eat: Buttermilk

watercress and leek soup

SERVES 4

4½ cups homemade or low-sodium store-bought
　 chicken stock

3 medium leeks (about 12 ounces), white and pale-green
　 parts only, cut into ½-inch-thick rounds and rinsed well

1 russet potato (8 ounces), peeled and cut into
　 ¼-inch-thick rounds

1 garlic clove, thinly sliced

1 bunch watercress, largest stems discarded, remainder
　 coarsely chopped, plus more for garnish (optional)

　 Coarse salt and freshly ground pepper

　 Sour cream, for serving

1　Bring stock, leeks, potato, and garlic to a boil in a medium
pot. Reduce heat to medium; cook until leeks are tender and
potato is soft, about 15 minutes. Add chopped watercress;
cook until beginning to soften, about 2 minutes.

2　Blend the stock and vegetables in a blender until smooth
(work in batches, if necessary, to avoid filling blender more
than halfway). Season with salt and pepper. Top each serving
with sour cream, and garnish with watercress, if desired.

from Asian Greens

....

SALADS AND SIDE DISHES
....

arugula and radicchio with
Parmesan shavings

SERVES 6 | PHOTO ON PAGE 71

9 ounces fresh arugula (about 8 cups), stemmed

4 ounces radicchio, halved crosswise and cut into
　 thin strips (about 1½ cups)

8 ounces Parmesan cheese, shaved with a vegetable
　 peeler (about ½ cup)

4½ teaspoons balsamic vinegar

　 Coarse salt and freshly ground pepper

3 tablespoons extra-virgin olive oil

1　Put arugula, radicchio, and Parmesan in a serving bowl,
and set aside.

2　Whisk vinegar with salt and pepper, to taste, in a medium
bowl. Whisking constantly, pour in oil in a slow, steady
stream, and whisk until emulsified. Toss salad with just
enough vinaigrette to coat.

from A Tuscan Dinner on a California Hillside

Asian salad greens with pine nuts
and pancetta

SERVES 4

4 ounces assorted delicate salad greens, such as baby
　 mizuna, baby tatsoi, and chrysanthemum greens
　 (about 8 cups)

8 very thin slices pancetta

2 tablespoons extra-virgin olive oil

2 medium shallots, thinly sliced

3 tablespoons pine nuts

3 tablespoons sherry vinegar

　 Coarse salt and freshly ground pepper

1　Put greens in a serving bowl; set aside. Place a medium
skillet over medium heat; arrange pancetta in a single layer
in skillet. Cook, turning once, until crisp, 2 to 4 minutes per
side. Transfer with tongs to paper towels to drain.

2　Pour off half of fat from skillet. Add oil to skillet; place over
medium-low heat. When fat is hot but not smoking, add shallots and pine nuts. Cook, stirring, until pine nuts are golden
brown, about 2 minutes. With a slotted spoon, transfer pine
nuts and shallots to serving bowl. Remove skillet from heat.

3　Immediately add vinegar to skillet; scrape up browned
bits from bottom with a wooden spoon. Drizzle warm dressing over salad. Season with salt and pepper; toss well. Add
reserved pancetta, and toss again.

from Asian Greens

baby bok choy with ginger and garlic

SERVES 4 TO 6 | PHOTO ON PAGE 80

2 pounds baby bok choy (8 to 10), halved lengthwise
　 and soaked in cold water to remove any dirt

2 teaspoons minced peeled fresh ginger

2 garlic cloves, thinly sliced

1 tablespoon plus 1 teaspoon toasted sesame oil

¼ cup tamari soy sauce

2 tablespoons oyster sauce

1　Bring a large pot of water to a boil. Add bok choy (in batches,
if necessary); cook until tender, 5 to 7 minutes. Drain in a
colander; let stand 5 minutes, then transfer to a serving dish.

2　Meanwhile, cook ginger and garlic in oil in a small saucepan over medium-low heat, stirring, until ginger and garlic
are soft, about 8 minutes. Add tamari and oyster sauce; cook,
stirring, until heated through, about 30 seconds more. Pour
sauce over bok choy, and toss to coat.

from Asian Greens

panzanella

SERVES 6 | **PHOTO ON PAGE 70**

- 9 tablespoons extra-virgin olive oil
- ½ pound crusty Italian country bread, cut into ½-inch-thick slices
- 3 garlic cloves, 1 halved and 2 minced
- 1 pound cherry tomatoes (3 cups), halved
- ½ cup thinly sliced red onion
- 1 cup bocconcini (mini mozzarella balls), halved
- 10 to 15 fresh basil leaves, thinly sliced, plus whole leaves for garnish
- 2 tablespoons red-wine vinegar
- Coarse salt and freshly ground pepper

1 Preheat a grill to medium-high. (Alternatively, heat a grill pan over medium-high heat until hot.) Using 3 tablespoons of oil, brush bread slices on both sides.

2 Grill bread slices, turning once, until toasted on both sides, about 5 minutes total. Rub both sides of each with halved garlic. Tear bread into bite-size pieces.

3 Toss bread, tomatoes, onion, bocconcini, and sliced basil in a serving bowl.

4 Whisk together vinegar and minced garlic in a small bowl. Whisking constantly, pour in remaining 6 tablespoons oil in a slow, steady stream, and whisk until emulsified. Pour dressing over salad. Season with salt and pepper. Let stand at room temperature, tossing occasionally, 1 hour. Garnish with whole basil leaves.

from A Tuscan Dinner on a California Hillside

....

MAIN COURSES

....

baked buttermilk chicken

SERVES 4 | **PHOTO ON PAGE 75**

- Olive-oil cooking spray
- 4 chicken drumsticks (about 1 pound), skins removed
- 2 whole boneless, skinless chicken breasts (about 1¾ pounds), halved
- 2½ cups low-fat buttermilk
- 4 cups cornflakes, finely crushed
- ¾ teaspoon Old Bay seasoning
- ½ teaspoon dried thyme
- ½ teaspoon dried basil
- ¼ teaspoon cayenne pepper
- Lemon wedges, for garnish (optional)
- Flat-leaf parsley sprigs, for garnish (optional)

1 Preheat oven to 400°F. Generously coat a rimmed baking sheet with cooking spray; set aside. Rinse chicken, and pat dry. Transfer to a medium bowl. Pour buttermilk over chicken. Cover, and marinate 1 hour in refrigerator.

2 Toss cornflakes, Old Bay seasoning, thyme, basil, and cayenne in a large bowl. Remove 1 piece of chicken at a time from buttermilk, letting excess drip back into bowl, and dredge in cornflake mixture.

3 Transfer pieces to oiled baking sheet; lightly coat each one with cooking spray. Bake, turning pieces halfway through, until crisp and cooked through, about 40 minutes. Transfer to a platter; garnish with lemon wedges and parsley, if desired.

PER SERVING: 362 CALORIES, 5 G FAT, 119 MG CHOLESTEROL, 32 G CARBOHYDRATE, 586 MG SODIUM, 46 G PROTEIN, 1 G FIBER

from Fit to Eat: Buttermilk

cannellini beans with pancetta, fried sage, and grilled sausages

SERVES 6 | **PHOTO ON PAGE 71**

For this recipe, we used precooked chicken and turkey sausages, but just about any kind of sausage—precooked or not—can be used in this dish. You can substitute the dried cannellini beans with canned ones (use three 15½-ounce cans). Rinse and drain the beans, then begin with step three. Truffle oil, which has a garlicky aroma and earthy taste, can be found at specialty-food stores.

- 2 cups dried cannellini beans (12 ounces)
- Coarse salt
- Vegetable oil, for frying
- ⅓ cup packed fresh sage leaves
- 6 thin slices pancetta or bacon
- 12 sausage links, such as chicken, turkey, or pork, halved lengthwise
- 3 tablespoons extra-virgin olive oil
- ½ teaspoon crushed red-pepper flakes, or to taste
- 2 teaspoons white truffle oil (optional)
- Freshly ground pepper

1 Put beans in a large bowl; cover with cold water by 2 inches. Loosely cover; let soak overnight at room temperature.

2 Drain beans; transfer to a large saucepan. Cover with cold water by 2 inches, and bring to a boil. Reduce heat, and simmer until beans are tender (add 1 teaspoon salt after 45 minutes), about 1 hour, adding more water if necessary to keep beans covered. Drain beans; set aside.

3 Heat 1 inch vegetable oil in a 4-quart heavy-bottom saucepan until it registers 365°F on a deep-fry thermometer.

Working in small batches, fry sage leaves, turning them occasionally, until crisp, about 10 seconds. Transfer with a slotted spoon to paper towels to drain. Immediately season with salt. (Adjust heat between batches as necessary to keep oil at a steady temperature.) Coarsely crumble two-thirds of the sage leaves; set aside. Set aside remaining whole leaves.

4 Cook pancetta in a 12-inch nonstick skillet over medium-high heat, turning once, until crisp, 1 to 2 minutes per side. Transfer with tongs to paper towels to drain. Reserve fat in skillet with heat off. Coarsely crumble pancetta; set aside.

5 Preheat grill to medium. (Alternatively, heat a grill pan over medium heat until hot.) Grill sausages, turning occasionally, until cooked through, 3 to 6 minutes (cooking time will depend on size of links and whether sausages are precooked). Transfer to a serving platter; cover to keep warm.

6 Add 1 tablespoon olive oil to reserved fat in skillet, and heat over medium heat until hot but not smoking. Add reserved beans and the red-pepper flakes; cook, stirring, until warm, about 2 minutes.

7 Put beans in a large serving bowl, and add reserved crumbled pancetta and crumbled sage leaves, the truffle oil, if desired, and ¾ teaspoon salt. Season with pepper.

8 Just before serving, drizzle beans with remaining 2 tablespoons olive oil, and garnish with reserved whole sage leaves. Serve with sausages.

from A Tuscan Dinner on a California Hillside

herb frittata with zucchini and yellow squash

SERVES 6 | **PHOTO ON PAGE 68**

1 tablespoon unsalted butter
2½ tablespoons olive oil
7 large eggs
¼ cup heavy cream or milk
¼ cup coarsely chopped fresh chives, plus whole chives for garnish
¼ cup coarsely chopped fresh flat-leaf parsley
½ teaspoon coarsely chopped fresh thyme
¼ teaspoon finely chopped fresh marjoram
½ teaspoon coarse salt
  Freshly ground pepper
1 small zucchini, cut into thin rounds
1 small yellow summer squash, cut into thin rounds

1 Heat butter with 1½ tablespoons oil in a 10-inch ovenproof nonstick skillet over medium-low heat until melted.

2 Preheat broiler, with the rack about 7 inches from heat source. Meanwhile, whisk together eggs, cream, and herbs until well blended. Stir in the salt, and season with pepper.

3 Add egg mixture to skillet; cook until bottom is set and golden, about 4 minutes. Continue to cook, gently shaking pan occasionally, until 1 inch of the edges is almost set, about 4 minutes more. Remove from heat. Gently press zucchini and squash on top, overlapping slightly in concentric circles.

4 Broil (checking often) until golden and just cooked through in center, 1 to 2 minutes. Gently slide frittata onto a plate with a spatula; drizzle with remaining tablespoon oil. Garnish with whole chives, and serve.

from A Tuscan Dinner on a California Hillside

Irish stew

SERVES 4 TO 6 | **PHOTO ON PAGE 76**

Irish stew is traditionally served with buttered boiled carrots.

3 pounds small Yukon gold potatoes, peeled
2 medium onions (about 1 pound), halved lengthwise and cut into thin half-moons
2½ pounds lamb shoulder, cut into 1-inch cubes
2½ teaspoons coarse salt
  Freshly ground pepper
2 teaspoons coarsely chopped fresh thyme
3 cups Lamb Stock (page 54), or homemade or low-sodium store-bought chicken stock
2 tablespoons finely chopped fresh curly- or flat-leaf parsley

1 Preheat oven to 325°F. Cut 1 pound of the potatoes into ¼-inch-thick rounds; spread them out in a large (5- to 6-quart) heavy-bottom pot or Dutch oven. Layer half the onions on top of the potatoes.

2 Place lamb cubes on top of onions. Sprinkle with 1½ teaspoons salt; season with pepper. Add the thyme. Place the remaining onions on top of lamb. Add stock and 1 cup water.

3 Place whole potatoes on top of onions. Sprinkle with the remaining teaspoon salt, and season with pepper. Cover pot with a tight-fitting lid; bring to a boil over medium-high heat. Transfer to oven; cook, without stirring, 2 hours. Sprinkle stew with parsley.

from Irish Dinner

lamb stock

MAKES 3 CUPS

You can ask your butcher for lamb bones. Alternatively, when you purchase lamb for the stew recipe, buy shoulder-blade-bone chops or shoulder-round-bone chops (add about 2 pounds to the total weight of your meat order). Remove the bones from the chops, and cut the meat into cubes for the stew (if you have a little extra, add it to the pot for a meatier stew or save for another use). This stock can be refrigerated in an airtight container for up to two days.

2 pounds lamb bones

1 medium onion, quartered

1 medium carrot, quartered crosswise

2 large garlic cloves

6 sprigs thyme

1 bay leaf

6 whole black peppercorns

Pinch of coarse salt

1 Preheat oven to 400°F. Spread out bones in a roasting pan, and roast 20 minutes. Turn bones, and add onion, carrot, and garlic to pan. Continue roasting until bones are browned, about 25 minutes.

2 With tongs or a spatula, transfer bones and vegetables to a large pot (leave fat in pan behind, and discard). Add thyme, bay leaf, peppercorns, and 2½ quarts cold water to pot; bring to a boil. Skim any froth from surface. Reduce heat to low, and simmer 1 hour. Pour stock through a fine sieve into a large bowl; discard solids. Stir in the salt.

Korean barbecued ribs with pickled greens

SERVES 4 TO 6 | **PHOTO ON PAGE 79**

Both the ribs and the greens need to marinate overnight, so plan accordingly.

2½ pounds flanken-style short ribs, cut ½ inch thick

FOR THE MARINADE:

4 garlic cloves, minced

3 scallions, white and pale-green parts only, very finely chopped

¼ cup packed dark-brown sugar

2 tablespoons granulated sugar

Pinch of coarse salt

¼ cup fresh lime juice (2 to 3 limes)

½ cup soy sauce

⅓ cup mirin (Japanese sweet rice wine)

2 tablespoons toasted sesame oil

3 tablespoons sesame seeds, toasted

1 teaspoon Asian chili sauce or ½ teaspoon crushed red-pepper flakes (optional)

FOR THE PICKLED GREENS:

1 pound Taiwan bok choy or napa cabbage, cut into ½-inch strips (8 cups)

1 bunch scallions, white and pale-green parts only, cut into ½-inch pieces

3 garlic cloves, halved lengthwise

2 small dried hot red chiles or a pinch of crushed red-pepper flakes (optional)

2 teaspoons toasted sesame oil

1 piece peeled fresh ginger (about 1 inch), cut into thin matchsticks

¼ cup rice-wine vinegar (not seasoned)

¼ cup mirin (Japanese sweet rice wine)

1 teaspoon coarse salt

Vegetable oil, for brushing

1 Cut each short rib crosswise into 3 pieces, cutting between the bones. Soak ribs in a large bowl of ice water for at least 20 minutes, or up to 2 hours.

2 Make marinade: Stir together marinade ingredients in a medium bowl until sugar is dissolved. Drain ribs, and pat dry. Put ribs and marinade in a 9-by-13-inch glass baking dish; turn each rib to coat. Cover, and refrigerate overnight.

3 Make pickled greens: Put greens and scallions in a medium bowl, and set aside. Cook garlic and chiles in sesame oil

in a small saucepan over medium heat until garlic is pale golden, 2 to 3 minutes. Add ginger, and cook, stirring, until fragrant, about 2 minutes.

4 Remove from heat; stir in vinegar, mirin, and the salt. Immediately pour contents of pan over greens, and toss to coat. Let cool to room temperature. Cover with plastic wrap, and refrigerate overnight.

5 Preheat broiler, with the rack about 6 inches from heat source. Line a rimmed baking sheet with foil, and very lightly brush with vegetable oil. Lift ribs from marinade, and arrange in a single layer on sheet (discard marinade).

6 Broil ribs (checking often) until well browned on top, about 5 minutes. Turn, and continue to cook until well browned on other side, about 4 minutes more. Serve ribs with chilled pickled greens.

from Asian Greens

mussels and wrapped-heart mustard cabbage with green-curry broth

SERVES 4 | **PHOTO ON PAGE 78**

You can make this dish with bok choy in place of the wrapped-heart mustard cabbage.

Coarse salt

1 pound wrapped-heart mustard cabbage (also called dai gai choy), trimmed, small leaves left whole, and large leaves halved lengthwise

1 quart homemade or low-sodium store-bought chicken stock

2 pounds mussels, scrubbed well and beards removed

6 tablespoons Thai green-curry paste, or to taste

1 quart unsweetened canned coconut milk, stirred

4 lime wedges, for serving

Garlic chives (also called ku chai) or fresh cilantro, for garnish (optional)

1 Bring a medium pot of water to a boil. Add salt to water, then add cabbage; cook until crisp-tender, about 2 minutes. With a slotted spoon, transfer greens to a colander to drain.

2 Bring stock to a simmer in a large saucepan over medium-high heat, and add mussels. Cover pan, and cook until mussels open (check pan frequently after 2 minutes). With a slotted spoon, transfer mussels as they open to four large soup bowls, dividing evenly. (Discard any mussels that remain unopened after 5 minutes.) Divide reserved greens among the soup bowls.

3 Pour broth from pan through a fine sieve into a bowl, and rinse pan. Return broth to pan, and stir in green-curry paste. Bring to a simmer over high heat. Add coconut milk, whisking until incorporated. Bring to a bare simmer.

4 Divide broth among bowls, pouring over mussels and greens to reheat. Serve with lime wedges. Garnish with garlic chives, if desired.

from Asian Greens

New Orleans–style shrimp and rice

SERVES 4 | **PHOTO ON PAGE 74**

8 tablespoons (1 stick) unsalted butter

1 tablespoon plus 1 teaspoon all-purpose flour

2 green bell peppers, cut lengthwise into ¼-inch-thick slices

1 large onion, halved lengthwise and cut into ¼-inch-thick slices

2 celery stalks, cut into ½-inch-thick pieces

6 canned whole plum tomatoes (from one 28-ounce can), crushed

1 can (14½ ounces) low-sodium chicken broth

2 teaspoons chopped fresh flat-leaf parsley, plus more for garnish

1½ teaspoons Cajun seasoning

½ teaspoon paprika

½ teaspoon coarse salt

½ teaspoon hot sauce, such as Tabasco, or to taste

1 pound large shrimp (21 to 30), peeled and deveined

2 cups cooked white rice, for serving

1 Melt butter in a large Dutch oven over medium heat. Add flour, and stir until light brown, 3 to 4 minutes. Add bell peppers, onion, and celery; cook, stirring occasionally, until softened, about 7 minutes. Add tomatoes, broth, parsley, spices, salt, and hot sauce.

2 Bring mixture to a boil, then reduce heat, and simmer until vegetables are soft and mixture is slightly thickened, about 30 minutes. Stir in shrimp, and cook until pink and cooked through, 3 to 5 minutes.

3 Sprinkle shrimp with parsley, and serve over rice.

from What's for Dinner?

rice noodles with Chinese broccoli and shiitake mushrooms

SERVES 4 | PHOTO ON PAGE 79

Similar greens—such as yow choy, also known as choy sum (which looks almost identical to bok choy but bears small yellow flowers), broccolini, or even regular broccoli—will work well in this dish if you can't find Chinese broccoli. You can buy wide rice noodles at Asian grocery stores, or use the narrow rice noodles (often labeled "pad thai noodles"), which many supermarkets carry.

- 8 ounces wide (about ⅜ inch) or other rice noodles
- 12 ounces Chinese broccoli (also called gai lan), cut into 2-inch pieces
- 3 tablespoons low-sodium tamari soy sauce
- 1 tablespoon plus 1 teaspoon Thai fish sauce (also called nam pla)
- 1 tablespoon plus 1 teaspoon rice-wine vinegar (not seasoned)
- 1 teaspoon sugar
- ¾ cup homemade or low-sodium store-bought chicken stock
- 1 tablespoon canola oil
- 1 tablespoon minced peeled fresh ginger, or more to taste
- 2 garlic cloves, minced
- 8 shiitake mushrooms, stemmed, caps quartered
- 2 teaspoons cornstarch mixed with 2 tablespoons cold water
- 4 scallions, white and pale-green parts only, cut on the diagonal into 1-inch pieces
- 2 teaspoons toasted sesame oil
  Crushed red-pepper flakes, for sprinkling (optional)
  Sesame seeds, for sprinkling (optional)
  Coarse salt, for sprinkling (optional)

1 Cover noodles with very hot water in a large bowl, and let soak 30 minutes. Drain noodles, and set aside.

2 Meanwhile, bring a large pot of water to a boil. Add broccoli; cook until crisp-tender, about 1 minute. Drain; set aside.

3 Stir together tamari, fish sauce, vinegar, sugar, and stock in a small bowl; set aside. Heat canola oil in a large nonstick skillet or a wok over medium heat until hot but not smoking. Add ginger, garlic, and mushroom caps; cook, stirring, until mushrooms are soft, about 2 minutes.

4 Add tamari mixture to skillet; bring to a simmer over high heat. Stir in cornstarch mixture; simmer 2 minutes. Add reserved noodles and broccoli, along with scallions; toss to coat. Drizzle with sesame oil; toss again. Serve with red-pepper flakes, sesame seeds, and salt for sprinkling, if desired.

from Asian Greens

DESSERTS

chrysanthemum cupcakes

MAKES 26 | PHOTOS ON PAGES 84 AND 85

FOR THE CUPCAKES:

Butter Cake I (follow directions for cupcakes; recipe follows)

Meringue Buttercream (recipe follows)

FOR DECORATING:

Gel-paste food coloring in assorted colors (forest green, lemon yellow, egg yellow, orange, leaf green)

Pastry tips, such as Ateco #68 leaf tip, #80 fluted tip, #3 round tip, and #12 round tip (optional)

1 Tint 1 cup of frosting forest green (for leaves and dots); set aside. Divide remaining frosting into three batches. Tint each batch a base-coat shade (for cupcake tops): chartreuse (mix leaf green, lemon yellow, and a touch of egg yellow), lemon yellow, and orange.

2 Alternating among the three base colors, frost cupcakes with a small offset spatula or butter knife, using about 3 tablespoons frosting per cupcake. (Reserve leftover frosting for piping flowers.)

3 Decorate cupcakes: Make the leaves: Fit a pastry bag with a coupler, and fill with forest-green frosting. With the #68 leaf tip, hold the bag at a 45-degree angle to the cake with the tip's flat side up. Squeeze bag, and pull out from the base of the leaf, releasing pressure and lifting to form the end. If desired, repeat to make a second leaf. With the coupler alone (or the #12 round tip) and frosting in the flower color, make a raised ½-inch-wide dot in the center of the cupcake to anchor the petals. Change to the #80 fluted tip; hold bag at a 45 degree angle against the edge of the dot, the tip forming a U. Gently squeeze the bag while pulling out in a quick stroke. Repeat all around the dot; form two or more petal layers over the first, making petals shorter and pulling bag upward with each layer. With the #3 tip and green frosting, pipe three dots in the center.

4 Refrigerate cupcakes in airtight containers until ready to serve, up to 4 hours. Let stand at room temperature 20 minutes before serving.

from Buttercream in Bloom

butter cake I

MAKES 26 CUPCAKES OR TWO 9-BY-13-INCH CAKE LAYERS

Refrigerate undecorated cupcakes or cake layers, wrapped in plastic wrap, up to two days.

- 8 ounces (2 sticks) unsalted butter, softened, plus more for pans
- 3 cups all-purpose flour, plus more for dusting
- 1 tablespoon baking powder
- ½ teaspoon salt
- 2 cups sugar
- 4 large eggs
- 1 teaspoon pure vanilla extract
- 1 cup whole milk

1 Preheat oven to 350°F. For cupcakes: Line a standard muffin tin with paper liners. Set aside. For cake layers: Cut a long sheet of parchment or waxed paper into two 9-by-13-inch rectangles to line the bottom of two 9-by-13-inch baking pans. Butter and line pans. Butter linings, then flour pans, tapping out excess. Set aside. (Alternatively, if you have only one pan, set aside second piece of parchment paper to bake one layer at a time.)

2 Whisk together flour, baking powder, and salt in a medium bowl; set aside. Put butter and sugar in the bowl of an electric mixer fitted with the paddle attachment; cream on medium-high speed until pale, 2 to 3 minutes. On medium speed, add eggs one at a time, mixing well after each addition. Add vanilla, and mix, scraping down sides of bowl. With the mixer on low speed, add the flour mixture in three batches, alternating with two batches of milk. Stir with a rubber spatula until the batter is evenly blended.

3 For cupcakes: Pour batter into lined cups, filling each two-thirds full. (You will have batter left over for additional batches.) For cake layers: Pour 2¾ cups batter into each prepared pan. Smooth the top of each layer with a small offset spatula.

4 Bake until a cake tester inserted into centers comes out clean, 15 to 18 minutes for the cupcakes and 20 to 25 minutes for the cake layers.

5 Let layers or cupcakes cool in pans on wire racks, 20 minutes. Run a knife around edges of cakes to loosen. Invert cake layers or cupcakes to remove from pans (peel off parchment from cake layers). Reinvert, and let cool completely on racks. Wrap in plastic wrap, and refrigerate until ready to decorate.

6 For cupcakes (or cake layers if baking in two batches): Repeat with remaining batter, lining muffin tin (or baking pan) when cooled.

meringue buttercream

MAKES ABOUT 10 CUPS

THE EQUIPMENT This recipe is best made using an electric mixer with at least a five-quart bowl. You can also make it with a handheld electric mixer in a large heatproof bowl, but the mixing times will likely be longer than those listed here. Disposable pastry bags are quite helpful: They are inexpensive enough to buy in quantity, and having many makes it possible to use one for each shade of frosting, so you can switch from color to color. There's no need to buy an entire set of pastry tips; at a dollar or less per tip at cookware stores, you can buy just the ones you need. Fitting the bags with couplers allows you to change pastry tips without emptying the bag. Use a rotating cake stand so you can turn the cake as you decorate and take the pressure off your wrists.

THE BUTTERCREAM Having plenty of frosting on hand allows you to practice mixing colors and piping flowers before you begin decorating. To blend colors, first tint a small amount of buttercream by adding gel-paste food coloring a dab at a time. Blend after each addition, until the color is darker than you would like. (You can use a single shade of food coloring or experiment by mixing two or more.) Gradually mix the tinted frosting into more buttercream until you get the right shade. Pipe flowers onto parchment or waxed paper until you're comfortable enough to try them on the actual cake. You can refrigerate the buttercream in an airtight container up to one week, or freeze it up to one month. Before using, bring it to room temperature and stir with a rubber spatula.

- 3 cups granulated sugar
- 12 large egg whites
- 2 pounds (8 sticks) unsalted butter, softened and cut into tablespoon-size pieces
- 2 teaspoons pure vanilla extract

1 Whisk sugar and egg whites in a large heatproof bowl set over a pan of simmering water until sugar is dissolved and mixture registers 140°F on an instant-read thermometer, 2 to 3 minutes.

2 Fit an electric mixer with the whisk attachment, and beat the egg-white mixture on high speed until it holds stiff (not dry) peaks and mixture is fluffy and cooled, about 10 minutes.

3 Reduce speed to medium-low, and add butter several tablespoons at a time, beating well after each addition (meringue will deflate slightly as butter is added). Add vanilla; beat until frosting comes together, 3 to 5 minutes. Beat on lowest speed until air bubbles diminish, about 2 minutes. Stir with a rubber spatula until frosting is smooth.

daisy cake

MAKES ONE TWO-LAYER 9-INCH
ROUND CAKE | **PHOTO ON PAGE 85**

This cake can be refrigerated for up to four hours.

FOR THE CAKE:

Butter Cake II (recipe follows)
Meringue Buttercream (page 57)

FOR DECORATING:

Gel-paste food coloring in assorted colors (leaf green, lemon yellow, forest green, egg yellow)
Pastry tips, such as Ateco #3 round tip and #352 leaf tip

1   Trim the top of the cake with a long serrated knife to make the surface level. Using a ruler as a guide, insert toothpicks or wooden skewers around the outside of the cake at 2-inch intervals to mark two equal layers. Rest the serrated knife on the toothpicks, and halve the cake horizontally using a sawing motion. Carefully slide the top cake layer onto a cardboard round, and set it aside.

2   With a small offset spatula, spread top of bottom layer with 1¼ cups frosting; carefully slide the second cake layer back on top of the first.

3   Fit a pastry bag with a coupler, and fill with frosting (for petals); set aside. Tint ¾ cup of remaining frosting dark green (for leaves and stems) and ⅓ cup of frosting bright yellow (for dots); set aside. Tint 4 cups frosting chartreuse (for base coat) by mixing leaf green, lemon yellow, and a touch of egg yellow.

4   Gently brush away loose crumbs from top and sides of cake with a pastry brush. With the offset spatula, spread about 1½ cups chartreuse frosting over top and sides of cake to form a crumb coat. Refrigerate cake until frosting is firm, about 15 minutes.

5   With a large offset spatula, spread about 2 more cups chartreuse frosting over top and sides of cake to form a second coat. Smooth top and remove excess frosting with the spatula. Smooth sides with a bench scraper. Return cake to refrigerator; chill until second coat is firm, about 15 minutes.

6   Lightly score surface of cake with a knife or bench scraper to mark 8 wedges, wiping knife clean after making each mark. (You will pipe a daisy within each section of the cake.)

7   Decorate cake: Make the stems: Using forest-green frosting and the #3 tip, pipe a slightly curved line for the stem down the middle of a cake section, starting about 1 inch from center of cake and ending about 2 inches from edge. Make petals using the #352 leaf tip: Using white frosting and holding the bag with the tip's pointed end facing up, apply pressure and pull out straight from the stem; release pressure

and pull upward to finish each petal. Repeat for twelve or more petals, wiping off the tip between strokes if necessary. Switch to yellow frosting and the #3 tip. Holding the bag at a 90-degree angle to the cake, make a mound of tiny dots in the center of the flower. Finally, with forest-green frosting and the #352 leaf tip, pipe a small leaf originating at the base of the stem (using the same technique described for the petals). Repeat to make one flower in each wedge.

8   Refrigerate cake until ready to serve. Let stand at room temperature 20 minutes before serving. Slice into wedges: To avoid crumbs on surface, make each cut with one downward motion, pulling knife back toward you (not upward) and wiping knife clean after each cut.

from Buttercream in Bloom

cherry blossom cake variation

FOR THE CAKE:

Butter Cake II (recipe follows)
Meringue Buttercream (page 57; use packed light-brown sugar instead of granulated sugar)

FOR DECORATING:

Gel-paste food coloring in assorted colors (leaf green, lemon yellow, deep pink, chocolate brown)
Pastry tips, such as Ateco #2 round tip, #102 petal tip, #3 round tip, and #349 leaf tip

1   Follow recipe for Daisy Cake through step 5, skipping step 3 (do not tint buttercream before frosting cake). Tint 1½ cups frosting pale pink (for flowers and buds). Tint ½ cup frosting a darker pink (for more flowers and buds). Tint ½ cup chocolate brown (for branches), and ½ cup green (for leaves). Tint ¼ cup yellow (for dots). Set aside. Using a toothpick or wooden skewer, mark a pattern on the frosting to serve as a guideline for piping branches.

2   Decorate cake: Pipe thin branches using brown frosting and the #2 tip. With one of the pink frostings and the #102 petal tip, make basic petals: Hold the bag at a 45 degree angle to the cake, with the tip's wide end down and narrow end pointed away and slightly to the left. Move the tip forward ⅛ inch and back again while you pivot the narrow end to the right. Make five or six petals, turning the cake as you go. Switch to yellow frosting and the #2 tip to pipe dots in the bloom's center. With the other pink frosting and the #102 petal tip, pipe two small overlapping petals on the branch for a closed blossom. With green frosting and the #3 round tip, pipe a dot, pulling upward, to make a bud; connect to branch with brown frosting. With the #349 tip, pipe tiny green leaves. Repeat to make more cherry blossoms.

3 Refrigerate cake until ready to serve. Let stand at room temperature 20 minutes before serving. Slice into wedges: To avoid crumbs on surface, make each cut with one downward motion, pulling knife back toward you (not upward) and wiping knife clean after each cut.

butter cake II

MAKES ONE 9-INCH ROUND CAKE

Refrigerate undecorated cake, wrapped in plastic wrap, for up to two days.

- 12 tablespoons (1½ sticks) unsalted butter, softened, plus more for pans
- 2¼ cups all-purpose flour, plus more for dusting
- 2¼ teaspoons baking powder
- ¼ teaspoon salt
- 1½ cups sugar
- 3 large eggs
- ½ teaspoon pure vanilla extract
- ¾ cup whole milk

1 Preheat oven to 350°F. Cut a 9-inch round of parchment or waxed paper to line the bottom of a 9-by-2-inch round cake pan. Butter and line pan. Butter lining, then flour pan, tapping out excess. Set aside.

2 Whisk together flour, baking powder, and salt in a medium bowl; set aside. Put butter and sugar in the bowl of an electric mixer fitted with the paddle attachment; cream on medium-high speed until pale, 2 to 3 minutes. On medium speed, add eggs one at a time, mixing well after each. Add vanilla, and mix, scraping down sides of bowl. On low speed, add the flour mixture in three batches, alternating with two batches of milk. Stir batter with a rubber spatula until evenly blended.

3 Pour batter into prepared pan, and smooth top with a small offset spatula. Tap pan on work surface several times to release air pockets.

4 Bake until a cake tester inserted into center comes out clean, 45 to 50 minutes. Let cake cool in pan on a wire rack, 20 minutes. Run a knife around edge of cake to loosen. Invert cake to remove from pan, and peel off parchment. Reinvert, and let cool completely on rack. Wrap in plastic wrap, and refrigerate until ready to decorate.

rose cake

MAKES ONE TWO-LAYER 9-INCH ROUND CAKE

FOR THE CAKE:

2 recipes Butter Cake II (recipe above)

Meringue Buttercream (page 57; use packed dark-brown sugar instead of granulated sugar)

FOR DECORATING:

Pastry tips, such as Ateco #12 round tip, #103 petal tip, #3 round tip, #352 leaf tip, #70 leaf tip, and #5 round tip
Flower nail #7, available in baking-supply stores

1 Trim the tops of the cakes with a long serrated knife to make the surfaces level. With a small offset spatula, spread top of one cake layer with 1¼ cups frosting. Place the second cake layer, cut side down, on top of the first cake layer.

2 Gently brush away loose crumbs from top and sides of cake with a pastry brush. With the offset spatula, spread about 2 cups frosting over top and sides of cake to form a crumb coat. Refrigerate cake until frosting is firm, about 15 minutes.

3 With a large offset spatula, spread about 2 more cups frosting over top and sides to form a second coat. Smooth top and remove excess frosting with the large offset spatula. Smooth sides with a bench scraper. Return cake to refrigerator, and chill until second coat is firm, about 15 minutes.

4 Using a toothpick or wooden skewer, mark a pattern on the frosting to serve as a guideline for piping stems.

5 Decorate cake: Pipe stems, using the #3 round tip, on the cake. For rosebuds, first make one basic petal with the #103 petal tip: Hold the bag at a 45 degree angle to the cake, with the tip's wide end down and narrow end pointed away and slightly to the left. Move the tip forward ⅛ inch and back again while you pivot the narrow end to the right. Make a second, smaller petal on top of the first. Pipe a strip of frosting from left to right over the base of the two petals. Repeat, from right to left, angling the tip slightly away from the bud, releasing pressure at the end. With the #352 leaf tip, make leaves at the bud's base: Starting at the base of the bloom with the tip's pointed end facing up, pipe small leaves, pulling tip toward flower. Switch to the #3 tip to fill in under the leaves and connect to stems. Pipe dots against the stem, pulling off at an angle for thorns. To make leaves for large roses, switch to the #70 leaf tip. To make a rose, you'll need a "flower nail" (when you need both hands to switch tips or colors, anchor the nail in a block of floral foam or in a potato with a flat-cut bottom). Dab frosting on the top of the nail to secure a small square of parchment paper on top. Using the #12 round tip, squeeze bag gently and pull up slowly to make an acorn shape on top of the parchment. Switch to the #103 petal tip. Holding tip against the point of the acorn, wide end down and the narrow end angled in toward the acorn's center, pipe a wide strip as you turn the nail, enrobing the top completely. Turning the nail as you go, make two slightly arched petals that each reach around half of the circumference of the acorn. Continue turning the nail, making longer petals that overlap, until you reach the edge of the nail. Gently slide the parchment with the rose off the nail and onto a baking sheet, and refrigerate about 20 minutes.

6 Transfer cake to a serving platter; use a small offset spatula to transfer roses to the top of the cake. Fit a pastry bag with the #5 round tip, and fill with frosting. Make a border at bottom of cake: Pipe overlapping teardrop shapes (to resemble thorns) by applying pressure quickly and releasing as you pull away.

7 Refrigerate cake until ready to serve. Let stand at room temperature 20 minutes before serving. Slice into wedges: To avoid crumbs on surface, make each cut with one downward motion, pulling knife back toward you (not upward) and wiping knife clean after each cut.

from Buttercream in Bloom

pansy cake

MAKES ONE TWO-LAYER 9-INCH SQUARE CAKE | **PHOTOS ON PAGES 85 AND 86**

Cake can be refrigerated for up to two hours.

FOR THE CAKE:

Butter Cake II (page 59; use a 9-inch square baking pan, and bake as directed)

Meringue Buttercream (page 57)

Ganache Glaze (recipe follows)

FOR DECORATING:

Gel-paste food coloring in assorted colors (violet, super red, royal blue, lemon yellow, leaf green)

Pastry tips, such as Ateco #2 round tip, #103 petal tip, and #102 petal tip

1 Trim the top of the cake with a long serrated knife to make the surface level: Using a ruler as a guide, insert toothpicks or wooden skewers horizontally into the sides of the cake at 2-inch intervals to mark two equal layers. Rest the serrated knife on the toothpicks, and halve the cake horizontally using a sawing motion. Carefully slide the top cake layer onto a cardboard round, and set it aside.

2 Gently brush away loose crumbs from top and sides of cake with a pastry brush. With a small offset spatula, spread

top of one cake layer with 1¼ cups frosting; carefully slide the second cake layer back on top of the first layer. With the offset spatula, spread about 1½ cups frosting over top and sides of cake to form a crumb coat. Refrigerate cake until frosting is firm, about 15 minutes.

3 With a large offset spatula, spread about 2 more cups frosting over top and sides to form a second coat. Smooth sides with a bench scraper. Return cake to refrigerator, and chill until second coat is firm, about 15 minutes.

4 Transfer cake to a wire rack set over a rimmed baking sheet. Starting at center, slowly drizzle ganache in a circular, outward motion, letting it run over sides. Fill in bare spots by continuing to drizzle. If necessary, smooth cake with a small offset spatula to cover completely. Refrigerate until set, about 20 minutes.

5 Meanwhile, tint 1½ cups frosting each violet, pale lavender, and lavender (for flowers). Tint 1 cup pale green (for stems and leaves) and ½ cup yellow (for dots). Set aside.

6 Using a toothpick or wooden skewer, mark a pattern on the ganache to serve as a guideline for piping stems.

7 Decorate cake: With green frosting and the #2 round tip, pipe stems. Using violet frosting and the #103 petal tip, pipe a large, basic petal: Hold the bag at a 45 degree angle to the cake, with the tip's wide end down and narrow end pointed away and slightly to the left. Move the tip forward ⅛ inch and back again while you pivot the narrow end to the right. Make a second petal to the side of the first. Then make two smaller petals, one on top of each of the first ones by using the same petal technique; apply less pressure on the bag and make a smaller arc than you did for the larger petals. Turn cake and change to one of the lavender frostings; using a pivoting motion as with petals, pipe a ruffle for the flower's base, turning the cake and connecting the petals. To finish the ruffle neatly, pull bag toward the center of the flower as you release pressure. Repeat to make more flowers, using alternate shades of lavender for the flower bases. Pipe a yellow circle in the center of each blossom with the #2 tip; pipe a leaf with the #102 tip, using the petal technique but moving the arc farther forward before turning it back, and allowing frosting to ruffle.

8 Refrigerate cake until ready to serve. Let stand at room temperature 20 minutes before serving. Slice into squares: To avoid crumbs on surface, make each cut with one downward motion, pulling knife back toward you (not upward) and wiping knife clean after each cut.

from Buttercream in Bloom

ganache glaze

MAKES 3 CUPS

12 ounces best-quality semisweet chocolate, finely chopped

1¾ cups heavy cream

1 Put chocolate in a medium bowl, and set aside. Heat cream in a small saucepan over medium heat, stirring occasionally, until it just begins to simmer.

2 Pour cream over chocolate; let stand 5 minutes. Stir until smooth and glossy. Let cool, stirring occasionally, until thickened, about 15 minutes. Use immediately.

sweet pea cake

MAKES ONE TWO-LAYER 8-BY-11-INCH RECTANGULAR CAKE

Cake can be refrigerated for up to four hours.

FOR THE CAKE:

Butter Cake I (page 57; follow directions for cake layers)
Meringue Buttercream (page 57)

FOR DECORATING:

Gel-paste food coloring in assorted colors (deep pink, egg yellow, orange, leaf green, lemon yellow)
Pastry tips, such as Ateco #2 round tip, #103 petal tip, #352 leaf tip, #1 round tip, and #5 round tip

1 Tint 5¼ cups frosting pale pink (for filling and base coat). With a small offset spatula, spread top of one cake layer with 1¼ cups pale-pink frosting; carefully slide the second cake layer on top of the first.

2 With a serrated knife, trim cake to measure 8 by 11 inches. Gently brush away loose crumbs from top and sides of cake with a pastry brush. With the spatula, spread about 1½ cups pale-pink frosting over top and sides of cake to form a crumb coat. Refrigerate cake until frosting is firm, about 15 minutes.

3 With a large offset spatula, spread about 2 more cups pale-pink frosting over top and sides to form a second coat. Smooth top and remove excess frosting with the large spatula. Smooth sides with a bench scraper. Return cake to refrigerator, and chill until second coat is firm, about 15 minutes.

4 Tint 1½ cups frosting each pale pink and dark pink (for flowers). Tint ¾ cup each pale peach and peach (for more flowers). Tint ¾ cup green (for leaves, stems, and calyxes).

5 Using a toothpick or wooden skewer, mark a pattern on the frosting to serve as a guideline for piping stems.

6 Decorate cake: Pipe stems using green frosting and the #2 tip. Then, using dark pink or peach frosting and the #103 petal tip, pipe a basic petal: Hold the bag at a 45-degree angle

to the cake, with the tip's wide end down and narrow end pointed away and slightly to the left. Move the tip forward ⅛ inch and back again while you pivot the narrow end to the right. Make a second petal to the side of the first. Pipe two smaller petals overlapping each other on top of the first two. Switch to one of the lighter-color frostings; hold bag at a 90-degree angle to the flower with wide end facing forward, and pipe a center, pulling down slightly. Repeat to make more flowers, alternating between dark and pale shades. Switch to green frosting and the #352 leaf tip: Starting at the base of the bloom with the tip's pointed end facing up, pipe small leaves, pulling tip toward flower. For small blooms and buds, make fewer petals. Add curlicues with the #1 tip.

7 Fit a pastry bag with the #5 round tip, and fill with pale pink frosting. Make a dotted border: Using a toothpick or wooden skewer, mark a rectangle on frosting around flowers (½ to 1 inch from edge of cake) to serve as a guideline. Applying a small amount of pressure each time, pipe dots close together in straight lines to form a rectangular border.

8 Refrigerate cake until ready to serve. Let stand at room temperature 20 minutes before serving. Slice into squares: To avoid crumbs on surface, make each cut with one downward motion, pulling knife back toward you (not upward) and wiping knife clean after each cut.

from Buttercream in Bloom

flowerpot cakes

MAKES 6

We used unglazed, untreated terra-cotta flowerpots (each with a six-ounce capacity, about 2¾ inches tall and 2¾ inches across the top). Wash pots in hot water before using. You can also bake eighteen of these cakes in standard muffin tins: Place a paper liner in each cup, and fill halfway with batter.

⅓ cup vegetable oil, plus more for pots
¾ cup unsweetened cocoa powder, plus more for dusting
1½ cups all-purpose flour
1½ cups sugar
1½ teaspoons baking soda
¾ teaspoon baking powder
¾ teaspoon salt
1 large egg plus 1 large egg yolk
¾ cup buttermilk
¾ teaspoon pure vanilla extract
Quick Chocolate Frosting (recipe follows)
½ cup crushed chocolate wafer cookies (about 10)
Multicolored pebble-shaped chocolate candies, for garnish
Mint sprigs, for garnish

1 Preheat oven to 350°F. Brush the inside of each flowerpot with oil, and line with parchment paper or foil. Brush lining with oil, and lightly dust with cocoa.

2 Sift the cocoa, flour, sugar, baking soda and powder, and salt together into the bowl of an electric mixer fitted with the paddle attachment. Add egg and yolk, ¾ cup warm water, buttermilk, oil, and vanilla; mix on low speed until smooth, about 3 minutes.

3 Divide batter among prepared pots, filling each about two-thirds full. Transfer to a rimmed baking sheet. Bake, rotating sheet halfway through, until a cake tester inserted into centers comes out clean, 20 to 30 minutes. Let cakes cool completely on sheet on a wire rack.

4 Frost cakes with an offset spatula; sprinkle with crushed cookies. Top with candies; "plant" 1 mint sprig in each cake.

from Dessert of the Month

quick chocolate frosting

MAKES ABOUT 3 CUPS

3½ cups confectioners' sugar
1 cup unsweetened cocoa powder
12 tablespoons (1½ sticks) unsalted butter, softened
½ cup milk, room temperature
2 teaspoons pure vanilla extract

Sift sugar and cocoa together into a medium bowl. Whisk in butter, milk, and vanilla until smooth. Use immediately.

chocolate-caramel pecan clusters

MAKES 1 DOZEN | **PHOTO ON PAGE 82**

1 cup pecan halves (3¼ ounces)
12 soft caramel-candy cubes
1½ ounces bittersweet chocolate, broken into 12 pieces (½ inch each)

1 Preheat oven to 350°F. Arrange pecans in a single layer on a rimmed baking sheet; toast in oven until fragrant, about 10 minutes. Remove from oven (leave oven on); set aside 36 pecans on baking sheet. Finely chop remaining pecans (for about ¼ cup); set aside.

2 When pecans are cool enough to handle, make 12 clusters by arranging 2 pecans vertically, side by side, below 1 pecan placed horizontally. Gently flatten each caramel; place 1 on top of each cluster. Bake clusters 5 minutes. Remove from oven (leave oven on).

3 Place 1 piece of chocolate on top of each cluster. Return to oven; bake until chocolate begins to melt, 1 to 2 minutes. Remove from oven. With the back of a spoon, gently spread chocolate over caramel without completely covering it.

4 Sprinkle clusters with reserved chopped pecans. Refrigerate until set, about 15 minutes. Bring to room temperature before serving.

from What's for Dinner?

hazelnut-orange shortbread

MAKES 2 DOZEN WEDGES

1½ cups hazelnuts (6 ounces)

1¼ cups all-purpose flour, plus more for dusting

½ cup plus 2 tablespoons granulated sugar

10 tablespoons (1¼ sticks) unsalted butter, melted and cooled

1½ teaspoons freshly grated orange zest

¼ teaspoon salt

2 tablespoons sanding sugar

1 Preheat oven to 350°F, with racks in upper and lower thirds. Place the hazelnuts on a rimmed baking sheet in a single layer; toast in upper rack of oven, shaking occasionally, until skins begin to split, about 15 minutes. Remove from oven (leave oven on); immediately rub hazelnuts vigorously in a clean kitchen towel to remove skins (as much as will come off easily). Let cool.

2 Finely chop hazelnuts in a food processor (do not overprocess), about 20 seconds. Transfer chopped nuts to a large bowl, and add flour, granulated sugar, melted butter, zest, and the salt. Mix with hands until dough just comes together and forms a ball.

3 Line two rimmed baking sheets with parchment paper. Divide dough in half. Shape each piece into a disk; transfer each disk to a lined baking sheet. With lightly floured hands, flatten one piece into a 7-inch round.

4 Score round (do not cut all the way through) to divide into 12 equal wedges. Sprinkle round with 1 tablespoon sanding sugar. Repeat with remaining disk.

5 Bake shortbread in upper and lower thirds of oven, switching positions of sheets and rotating about halfway through, until rounds are golden brown, 15 to 20 minutes. While shortbread is still warm, cut wedges to fully separate. Let wedges cool slightly on sheets, then transfer to a wire rack to cool completely.

from A Tuscan Dinner on a California Hillside

shamrock cookies

MAKES 50

You will need three- or four-leaf clover stencils for these cookies. To make a stencil, draw a clover shape (slightly smaller than the 2½-inch cookies) onto parchment paper, and cut out, leaving parchment around clover intact. You can freeze the dough, wrapped in plastic wrap, for up to one month. Store the baked cookies in an airtight container for up to five days.

4 cups sifted all-purpose flour (sifted, then measured), plus more for dusting

½ teaspoon salt

1 teaspoon baking powder

8 ounces (2 sticks) unsalted butter, softened

2 cups granulated sugar

2 large eggs

2 teaspoons pure vanilla extract

⅓ cup confectioners' sugar

1 teaspoon green powdered food coloring

1 Sift flour, salt, and baking powder into a large bowl, and set aside. Put butter and granulated sugar in the bowl of an electric mixer fitted with the paddle attachment; cream on high speed until fluffy. Beat in eggs.

2 Reduce speed to low. Add flour mixture in two additions, and mix until well combined. Mix in vanilla. Divide the dough in half, and wrap in plastic wrap; refrigerate 30 minutes.

3 Preheat oven to 350°F, with rack in upper and lower thirds. Sift confectioners' sugar and food coloring together into a small bowl, and set aside.

4 Line baking sheets with parchment paper. Roll out 1 piece of dough on a lightly floured work surface to ⅛ inch thick. With a 2½-inch cookie cutter, cut out 25 rounds. Arrange rounds on lined baking sheets, spacing them 2 inches apart.

5 Working with one round at a time, place clover stencil on top; using a small sieve, sprinkle surface with green sugar. Refrigerate until firm, about 15 minutes, or until ready to bake. Repeat process with remaining dough.

6 Bake in upper and lower thirds of oven, switching positions of sheets and rotating about halfway through, until edges just start to brown, 10 to 12 minutes. Let cool completely on sheets on wire racks.

from Good Things

melon balls with Moscato
SERVES 6

2 honeydew melons (6 pounds each), halved and seeded

2 tablespoons small tarragon leaves

1½ cups chilled Moscato or other sweet sparkling wine

With a melon baller, scoop out enough melon to measure 6 cups. Divide melon among six dessert bowls. Sprinkle with tarragon, and pour ¼ cup Moscato over each serving.

from A Tuscan Dinner on a California Hillside

DRINKS

buttermilk banana smoothies
SERVES 2

1 cup low-fat buttermilk

2 ripe bananas, cut into 2-inch-thick rounds

11 dried pitted dates

1 teaspoon honey

Pinch of salt

1 cup ice

Blend all ingredients in a blender on high speed until mixture is smooth and ice is finely ground. Pour into two glasses.

PER SERVING: 294 CALORIES, 2 G FAT, 5 MG CHOLESTEROL, 70 G CARBOHYDRATE, 277 MG SODIUM, 6 G PROTEIN, 6 G FIBER

from Fit to Eat: Buttermilk

French Quarter cocktails
SERVES 4

This rum-and-juice cocktail is our take on the Hurricane—the classic New Orleans drink.

¼ cup spiced light rum

¼ cup dark rum

1 cup orange juice

1 cup pineapple juice

Splash of grenadine

4 maraschino cherries, for garnish

Fill a cocktail shaker and four tall glasses with ice. Pour the rums and the orange and pineapple juices into shaker; add the grenadine. Shake well. Pour through a fine sieve into each glass. Garnish each cocktail with a maraschino cherry.

from What's for Dinner?

lemon sparkler
SERVES 1

Look for lemon balm and lemon verbena at your local farmers' market.

1 tablespoon Galliano (Italian herb liqueur)

1 tablespoon fresh lemon juice

1 tablespoon orange-flavored liqueur, such as Cointreau

½ cup club soda

½ teaspoon chopped fresh lemon balm or lemon verbena (optional), plus leaves for garnish

1 lemon slice, for garnish

Fill a tumbler with ice. Pour all ingredients into tumbler, and stir until combined. Garnish with lemon-balm leaves, if desired, and the lemon slice.

from A Tuscan Dinner on a California Hillside

Portofino cocktail
SERVES 1

1 tablespoon Campari

¼ cup fresh red-grapefruit juice

6 tablespoons tonic water

1 red grapefruit slice, for garnish

Fill a tumbler with ice. Shake Campari, grapefruit juice, and tonic in a cocktail shaker. Pour into tumbler, and garnish with the grapefruit slice.

from A Tuscan Dinner on a California Hillside

MISCELLANEOUS

marinated olives with oregano and fennel seeds
MAKES 3 CUPS

The olives can be prepared three days ahead and refrigerated, covered. Bring to room temperature before serving.

1¼ pounds assorted brine-cured olives (3 cups), such as Alfonso, Gaeta, and Sicilian, rinsed and drained well

3 tablespoons extra-virgin olive oil

1 teaspoon fennel seeds, crushed

2½ tablespoons fresh oregano, chopped

1 garlic clove, thinly sliced

Stir together ingredients in a medium bowl. Cover, and let stand at room temperature, stirring occasionally, 1 hour.

from A Tuscan Dinner on a California Hillside

BUTTERMILK BISCUITS | PAGE 24

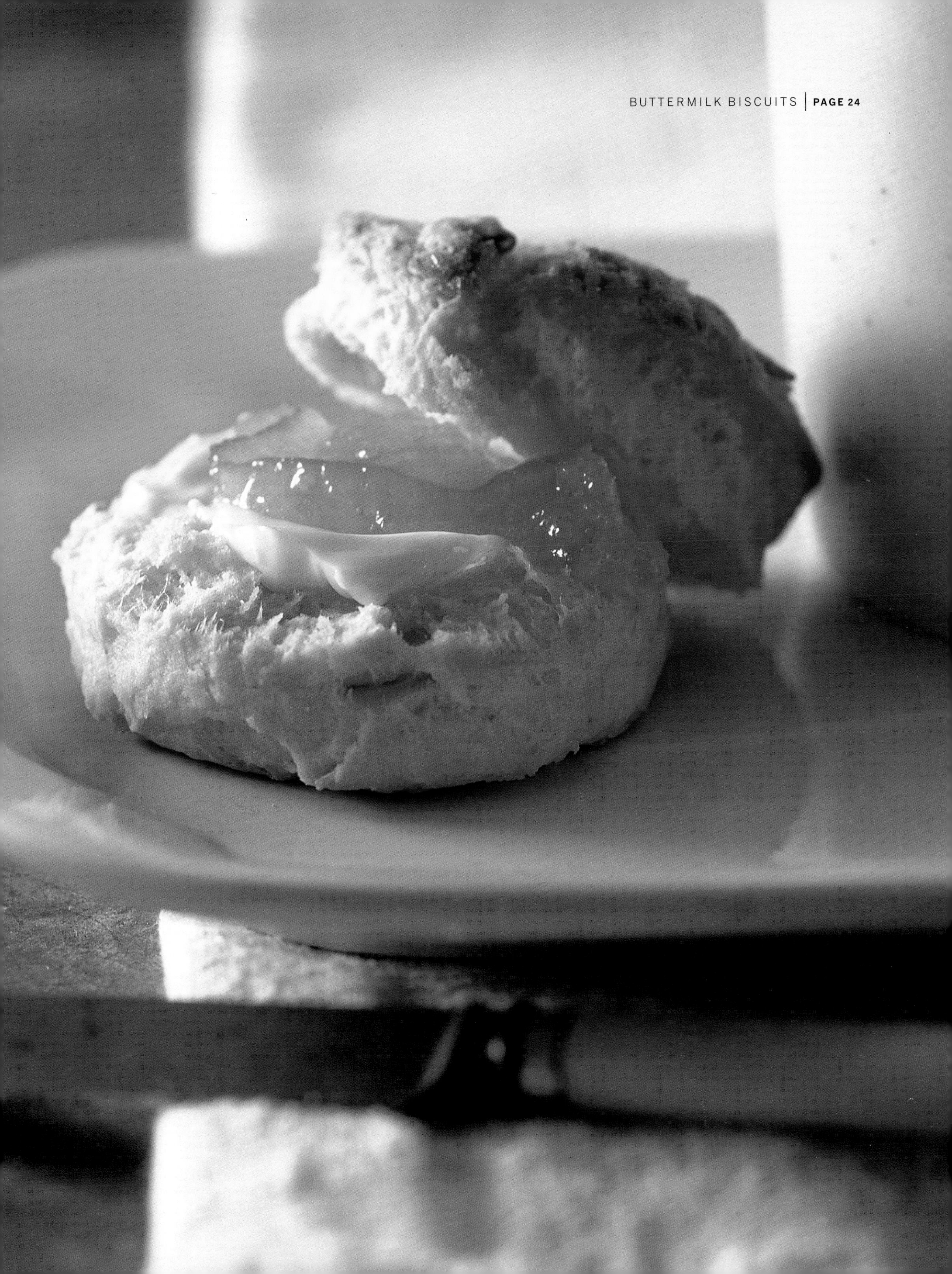

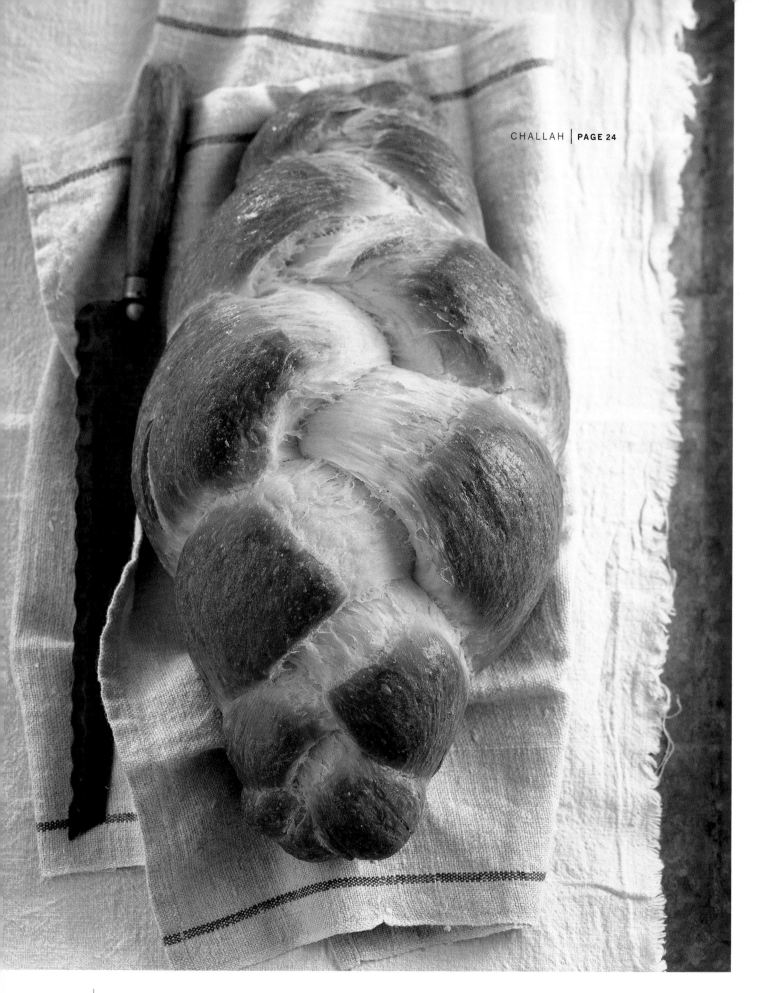

CHALLAH | **PAGE 24**

MRS. KOSTYRA'S BABKAS | **PAGE 44**

CRANBERRY BRAN MUFFINS | **PAGE 24**

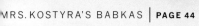

PEAR-STUFFED FRENCH TOAST | **PAGE 29**

TRIPLE CITRUS COFFEE CAKE | **PAGE 25**

HERB FRITTATA WITH ZUCCHINI
AND YELLOW SQUASH | **PAGE 53**

SHRIMP EMPANADAS | **PAGE 17**

SALT-COD CROQUETTES | **PAGE 17**

LITTLE "DRUMSTICKS" | **PAGE 16**

MINI CRAB CAKES ON SEASHELLS | **PAGE 16**

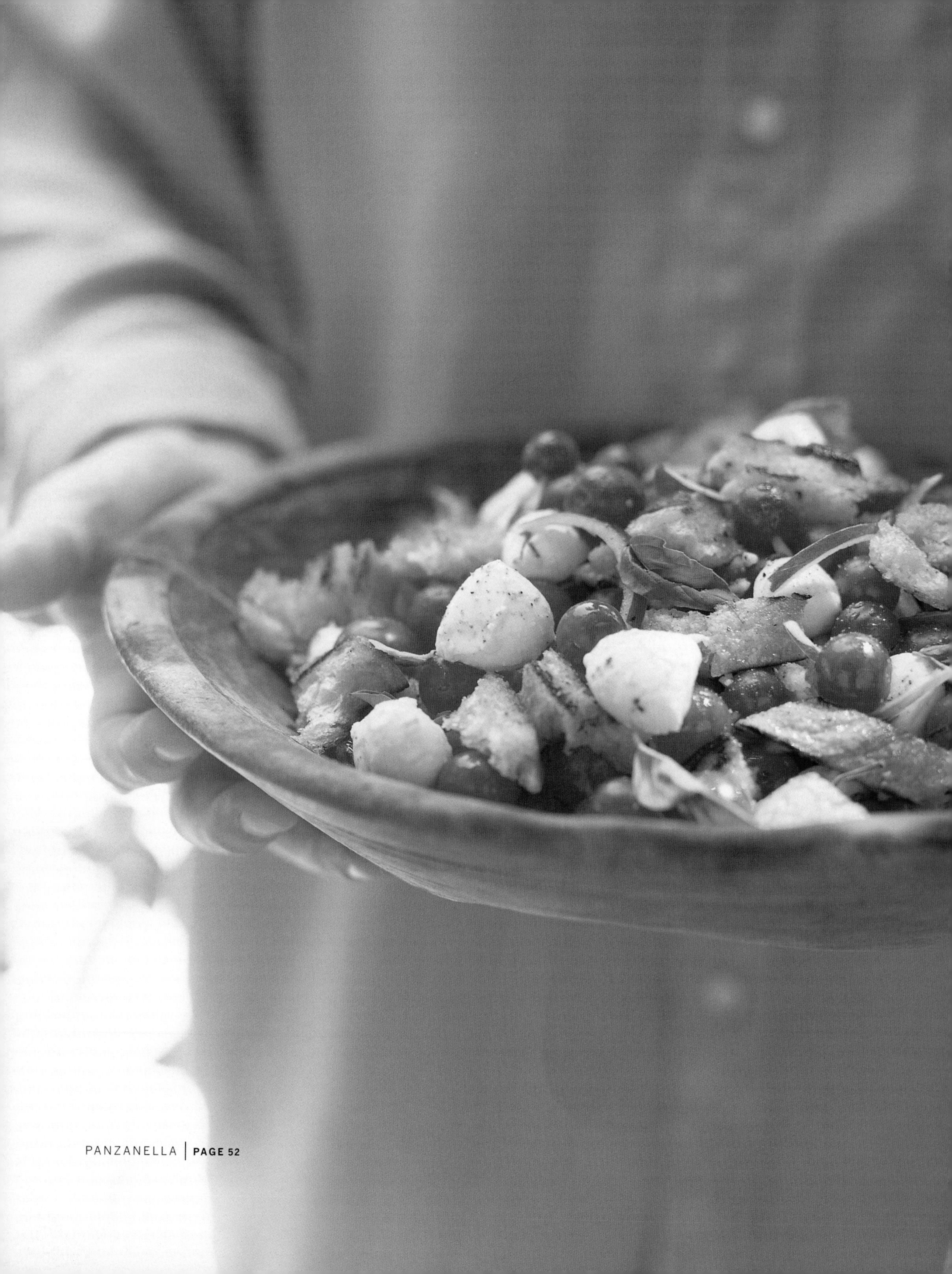

PANZANELLA | PAGE 52

CANNELLINI BEANS WITH PANCETTA,
FRIED SAGE, AND GRILLED SAUSAGES | **PAGE 52**

ARUGULA AND RADICCHIO
WITH PARMESAN SHAVINGS | **PAGE 51**

GNOCCHI WITH SAGE AND BROWN BUTTER | **PAGE 34**

MAKING GNOCCHI

1. Pass the cooked potatoes through a ricer or a food mill—a ricer will yield a finer texture. **2.** As you gently knead the dough, add a small amount of flour if it is too sticky. Be careful not to overwork the dough. **3.** A bench scraper is handy for dividing the dough. **4.** Use your fingertips to roll each piece into a rope. **5.** Roll each dumpling over the tines of a fork to create grooves that will trap the sauce. **6.** Use a slotted spoon to remove the gnocchi from the boiling water; they may fall apart if you pour them into a colander.

NEW ORLEANS–STYLE SHRIMP AND RICE | **PAGE 55**

ROASTED-GARLIC RISOTTO WITH MUSHROOMS | **PAGE 36**

BAKED GNOCCHI WITH CHEESE | **PAGE 33**

BAKED BUTTERMILK CHICKEN | **PAGE 52**

SPINACH GNOCCHI WITH TOMATO SAUCE | **PAGE 34**

SAUERBRATEN | **PAGE 37**

CHICKEN WITH ONIONS AND GARLIC | **PAGE 19**

LASAGNA BOLOGNESE | **PAGE 20**

IRISH STEW | **PAGE 53**

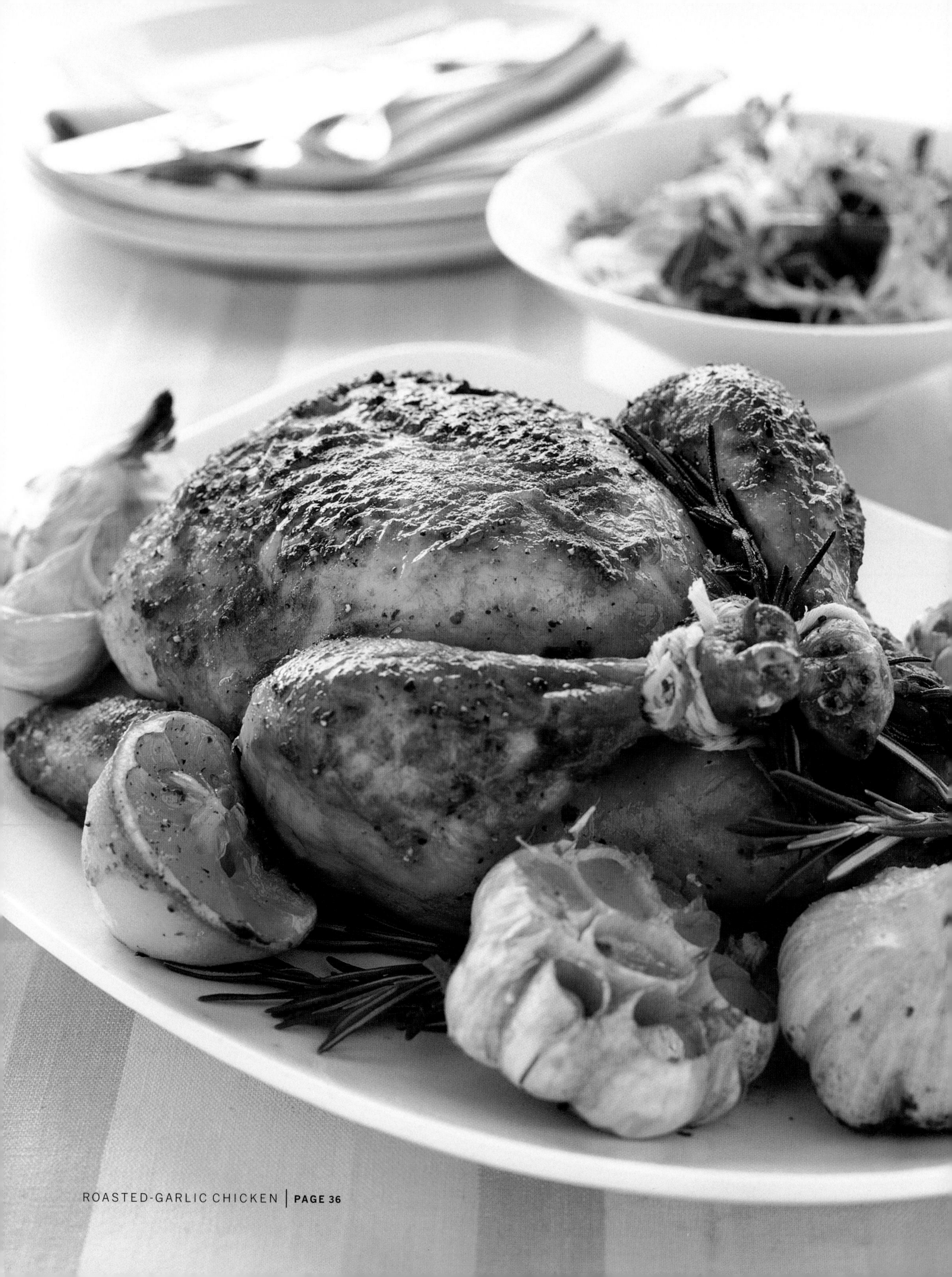

ROASTED-GARLIC CHICKEN | **PAGE 36**

MUSSELS AND WRAPPED-HEART
MUSTARD CABBAGE WITH GREEN-CURRY BROTH | **PAGE 55**

KOREAN BARBECUED RIBS WITH PICKLED GREENS | PAGE 54

CUMIN-DUSTED SHRIMP WITH BLACK-EYED PEAS
AND COLLARD GREENS | PAGE 20

SPICE-CRUSTED RACK OF LAMB | PAGE 38
HARICOTS VERTS WITH MUSTARD VINAIGRETTE | PAGE 32
CRIMSON COUSCOUS | PAGE 31

RICE NOODLES WITH CHINESE
BROCCOLI AND SHIITAKE MUSHROOMS | PAGE 56

BABY BOK CHOY WITH
GINGER AND GARLIC | PAGE 51

ROASTED CARROTS AND PARSNIPS | **PAGE** 19

WHOLE ROASTED GARLIC | **PAGE** 36

WARM LENTIL SALAD WITH GOAT CHEESE | **PAGE** 31

ROASTED YAM HALVES | **PAGE** 33

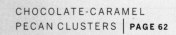

CHOCOLATE-CARAMEL
PECAN CLUSTERS | **PAGE 62**

CHOCOLATE POTS DE CREME | **PAGE 42**

FORMING BUTTERCREAM FLOWERS

DAISY FLOWERS

DAISY CAKE | **PAGE 58**

CHRYSANTHEMUM FLOWERS

PANSY FLOWERS

DAISY Using green frosting and a #3 tip, pipe a slightly curved line for the stem. Switch to white frosting and a leaf tip; hold bag with tip's pointed end facing up. Apply pressure and pull out straight from stem; release pressure, pulling upward to finish petal. Make about twelve petals; switch to yellow frosting and #3 tip. Hold bag at a 90-degree angle to cake; make a mound of dots in center. With green frosting and leaf tip, pipe a small leaf originating at base of stem.

CHRYSANTHEMUM Make leaves: With a leaf tip and green frosting, hold bag at a 45-degree angle to cake, with tip's flat side up. Squeeze bag, and pull out from base of leaf, releasing pressure and lifting to form the end. With the coupler alone and the frosting in the flower color, make a raised dot to anchor petals. Change to a fluted tip; hold bag at a 45-degree angle against edge of dot, the tip forming a U. Gently squeeze bag while pulling out in a quick stroke. Repeat all around dot; form two or more petal layers over the first, making petals shorter and pulling bag upward with each layer. With #3 tip and green frosting, pipe three dots in center.

PANSY Pipe stem. Using violet frosting and a petal tip, pipe a petal: Hold bag at a 45-degree angle to cake, with tip's wide end down. Move tip forward ⅛ inch and back again while pivoting narrow end to the right. Pipe a second petal beside first. Make two smaller petals on top using the same technique; apply less pressure on bag and make smaller arc. Change to lavender frosting; pipe a ruffle for the flower's base, turning cake and connecting petals. To finish ruffle neatly, pull bag toward center of flower as you release pressure. With a #2 tip, pipe a yellow circle in center of blossom; pipe a leaf with a #102 tip using petal technique but moving arc farther forward before turning it back, and allowing frosting to ruffle.

BUTTERSCOTCH BLONDIES | **PAGE 38**

DOUBLE-CHOCOLATE BROWNIES | **PAGE 40**

Spring

THE ARRIVAL OF ARTICHOKES, ALONG WITH OTHER BELOVED harbingers of spring, offers an occasion to celebrate the end of another winter as well as the first signs of new growth. Peel back the tough outer layers and savor what's inside—because after the season is over, it'll be another year before these springtime favorites are at their peak again.

April

banana bread with walnuts and flaxseed

MAKES 1 LOAF; SERVES 8 | **PHOTO ON PAGE 138**

You can store the banana bread, wrapped well in plastic wrap, at room temperature for up to four days.

2 tablespoons unsalted butter, melted,
   plus 1 teaspoon unsalted butter, softened, for pan

½ cup whole-wheat flour

¾ cup all-purpose flour

¼ cup ground golden flaxseed (from about 2 tablespoons whole)

¾ teaspoon coarse salt

½ teaspoon baking powder

½ teaspoon baking soda

1 large egg, plus 1 large egg white

½ cup packed light-brown sugar

1½ teaspoons pure vanilla extract

¾ cup mashed very ripe bananas (about 2 medium)

½ cup walnuts (about 1¾ ounces), toasted and coarsely chopped

1 Preheat oven to 350°F. Butter a 9-by-5-by-3-inch loaf pan, and set aside. Whisk together the flours, flaxseed, salt, baking powder, and baking soda in a medium bowl, and set aside.

2 Put egg and egg white in the bowl of an electric mixer fitted with the paddle attachment, and mix on medium-low speed until well combined, about 2 minutes. Add melted butter, sugar, vanilla, and bananas, and mix until combined. Add the reserved flour mixture, and mix on low speed until well incorporated, about 10 seconds. Stir in walnuts.

3 Pour batter into buttered pan. Bake until golden brown and a cake tester inserted into the center comes out clean, about 35 minutes. Let cool slightly in pan on a wire rack. Invert bread to unmold; reinvert, and let cool completely on rack.

PER SERVING: 236 CALORIES, 10 G FAT, 36 MG CHOLESTEROL, 33 G CARBOHYDRATE, 459 MG SODIUM, 6 G PROTEIN, 4 G FIBER

from Fit to Eat: Flaxseed

bread pudding with ham, leeks, and cheese

SERVES 6 TO 8

Using both Gruyère and fontina gives this savory dish complex flavor—and they melt beautifully. If you use only Gruyère, just double the amount. You can assemble most of this dish up to one day ahead and refrigerate, covered; then add the batter, and bake.

2 tablespoons unsalted butter, plus more for dish

1 bunch leeks (4 to 6), white and pale-green parts only, halved lengthwise, cut into ¼-inch-thick half-moons, and rinsed well (about 3 heaping cups)

Coarse salt and freshly ground pepper

8 large eggs

1 quart milk

8 slices (each ½ inch thick) challah or brioche

6 ounces thinly sliced ham

2 tablespoons thyme leaves

1 cup grated Gruyère cheese (4 ounces)

1 cup grated fontina cheese (4 ounces)

1 Preheat oven to 325°F. Butter a 9-by-13-inch casserole dish. Heat the butter in a medium skillet over medium heat. Cook leeks, covered, until softened, about 5 minutes. Season with salt and pepper, and transfer to a small bowl.

2 Whisk together eggs and milk. Whisk in 1 teaspoon salt and ¼ teaspoon pepper. Set batter aside.

3 Layer bread and ham shingle-style in buttered dish, scattering leeks, thyme, and cheeses on top. Pour batter over top; press down gently so bread absorbs liquid.

4 Bake until puffed and golden brown (tent with foil if edges brown too much before center is set), about 1 hour.

from Easy Entertaining: Buffet Brunch

coffee-cake muffins

MAKES 10 | **PHOTO ON PAGE 138**

You can bake the muffins up to a week ahead. Let them cool completely, then wrap in plastic wrap and freeze in resealable plastic bags. Warm thawed muffins, wrapped in foil, in a 300 degree oven, for eight to ten minutes. Or make the streusel and mix together the wet ingredients up to two days in advance, and refrigerate separately. The mixed dry ingredients and cinnamon sugar can be stored at room temperature.

FOR THE CINNAMON SUGAR:

2 tablespoons granulated sugar

½ teaspoon ground cinnamon

FOR THE STREUSEL:

¼ cup pecan halves (about 1 ounce)

3 tablespoons packed light- or dark-brown sugar

¼ teaspoon ground cinnamon

Pinch of salt

1½ teaspoons all-purpose flour

½ tablespoon cold unsalted butter

FOR THE DRY INGREDIENTS:

2 cups all-purpose flour

1 tablespoon baking powder

½ teaspoon salt

¾ cup granulated sugar

1 teaspoon ground cinnamon

A few gratings of whole nutmeg

FOR THE WET INGREDIENTS:

2 large eggs, room temperature

1 teaspoon pure vanilla extract

¾ cup milk

8 tablespoons (1 stick) unsalted butter, melted, plus more for muffin tin

1 Preheat oven to 350°F. Stir together the sugar and cinnamon in a small bowl; set aside. Butter 10 cups of a standard nonstick muffin tin; set aside.

2 Make streusel: Spread out pecans on a baking sheet. Toast in oven, shaking every few minutes, until crisp and fragrant, 8 to 10 minutes. Let cool completely.

3 Raise oven temperature to 375°F. Put brown sugar, cinnamon, salt, and flour in a medium bowl. Blend in butter with your fingertips until well combined. Crumble pecans into small pieces; work into butter mixture with fingertips until just combined. Cover, and refrigerate.

4 Combine dry ingredients: Sift flour, baking powder, salt, granulated sugar, and spices into a large bowl; set aside.

5 Combine wet ingredients: Whisk together eggs, vanilla, and milk in a separate large bowl. Whisk in melted butter.

6 Fold wet ingredients into dry ingredients with a rubber spatula. Spoon enough batter into buttered cups to fill each less than one-third full. Gently spread batter in each cup with the back of a spoon to level.

7 Divide streusel among cups, then top with remaining batter. Sprinkle with cinnamon sugar. Fill any empty cups in the tin halfway with water to evenly distribute heat in tin. Bake muffins until puffed and golden brown, about 18 minutes.

8 Let cool slightly in tin, 5 to 10 minutes. Turn out onto a wire rack; let cool a few minutes more before serving warm.

from Easy Entertaining: Buffet Brunch

granola with flaxseed

MAKES 5½ CUPS | **PHOTO ON PAGE 138**

Store granola in an airtight container at room temperature for up to one week.

2 cups old-fashioned rolled oats

1 cup sweetened shredded coconut

¾ cup sliced blanched almonds (about 2½ ounces)

¼ cup vegetable oil

¼ cup honey

1 tablespoon flaxseed oil

½ cup dried cranberries

½ cup golden raisins

¼ cup unsalted hulled sunflower seeds

1 tablespoon ground golden flaxseed (from about 1½ teaspoons whole)

1 Preheat oven to 350°F. Toss together oats, coconut, and almonds in a medium bowl; set aside. Whisk together vegetable oil and honey in a small bowl; stir into oats mixture. Spread out oats mixture on a rimmed baking sheet.

2 Bake, stirring occasionally, until golden brown, 17 to 20 minutes. Let cool 10 minutes, then toss with flaxseed oil. Let cool completely. Transfer to a large bowl; stir in dried cranberries, raisins, sunflower seeds, and ground flaxseed.

PER SERVING (½ CUP): 271 CALORIES, 15 G FAT, 0 MG CHOLESTEROL, 32 G CARBOHYDRATE, 25 MG SODIUM, 5 G PROTEIN, 4 G FIBER

from Fit to Eat: Flaxseed

yogurt parfaits with blueberries and lemon

SERVES 6 | **PHOTO ON PAGE 138**

3 containers blueberries (4.4 ounces each; about 3 cups)

½ cup confectioners' sugar

1 quart whole-milk plain yogurt, preferably Greek yogurt

1 teaspoon fresh lemon juice

2 teaspoons freshly grated lemon zest

1 Set aside ½ cup blueberries for garnish. Stir together remaining blueberries and ¼ cup sugar in a medium sauce-pan. Cover; cook over medium heat 5 minutes. Uncover; cook, tossing occasionally, until berries begin to darken, 2 to 3 min-utes. Bring to a boil; cook 1 minute more. Pour into a medium nonreactive (glass or ceramic) bowl; let sauce cool completely.

2 Put yogurt, remaining ¼ cup sugar, and the lemon juice in a medium bowl. Set aside ½ teaspoon lemon zest for gar-nish. Very finely chop remaining 1½ teaspoons lemon zest, then stir into yogurt mixture. Set yogurt mixture aside.

3 Divide blueberry sauce among six drinking glasses. Divide yogurt among glasses, spooning it over the sauce. Sprinkle parfaits with reserved berries and zest. If not serving immedi-ately, refrigerate, covered with plastic wrap, up to 3 hours.

from Easy Entertaining: Buffet Brunch

....

STARTERS

....

goat cheese and pistachio stuffed dates

MAKES 16; SERVES 8

You can make the goat-cheese filling one day ahead and refrigerate it. These hors d'oeuvres can be assembled several hours before serving; loosely cover them with plastic wrap, and refrigerate for up to three hours. Bring to room temperature before serving.

4 ounces soft goat cheese

3 tablespoons shelled salted pistachios, toasted and coarsely chopped

1 tablespoon finely chopped fresh chives, plus more for garnish

Freshly ground pepper

8 plump, soft dried dates (preferably Medjool), pitted and halved lengthwise

1 Stir together goat cheese, 2 tablespoons pistachios, and chives in a small bowl until smooth. Season with pepper.

2 Arrange the dates, cut sides up, on a platter. Fit a pastry bag with a large round tip, and fill with goat-cheese mixture. Pipe mixture onto each date half to cover. (Alternatively, pipe goat-cheese mixture using a resealable plastic bag with 1 inch cut off of one corner, or simply spread mixture on dates with a butter knife.) Garnish dates with remaining tablespoon pistachios and more chives.

from Celebrating Spring

pita crisps with feta-radish spread

SERVES 4

The thick consistency of Greek yogurt is ideal for this spread. If your grocer doesn't sell it, use another whole-milk yogurt, and drain it for thirty minutes in a fine sieve set over a bowl. You can make the spread one day ahead and refrigerate it (covered with plastic wrap); wait until just before serving to stir in the parsley and radishes.

5 tablespoons extra-virgin olive oil

2 pocket pitas, split open

8 ounces sheep's-milk feta cheese, coarsely chopped

¼ cup plain whole-milk yogurt, preferably Greek yogurt

2 tablespoons fresh lemon juice

3 tablespoons coarsely chopped fresh flat-leaf parsley

4 radishes, quartered lengthwise and thinly sliced (about ½ cup)

1 Preheat oven to 350°F. Using 2 tablespoons oil, brush in-sides of pita rounds. Cut each round into 6 wedges. Arrange wedges in a single layer on a baking sheet, oiled sides up; toast until golden brown and crisp, 7 to 10 minutes.

2 Meanwhile, pulse feta, yogurt, lemon juice, and remaining 3 tablespoons oil in a food processor just until mixture is thick and spreadable, about 10 pulses. Transfer to a medium bowl, and stir in parsley and radishes. Serve with pita crisps.

from What's for Dinner?

popovers with wild-mushroom sauce

MAKES 1 DOZEN | **PHOTO ON PAGE 141**

You can prepare the popover batter up to one day ahead, and refrigerate it. Let it stand at room temperature for twenty minutes before baking. The sauce can also be made one day in advance. Let it cool completely, then refrigerate. Reheat over medium-low heat; add heavy cream to thin, if necessary.

2 cups whole milk

4 large eggs

2 tablespoons unsalted butter, melted,
   plus 8 tablespoons (1 stick) unsalted butter

2 cups all-purpose flour
   Coarse salt

½ cup vegetable oil or vegetable shortening

4 shallots, finely chopped

2 pounds fresh mushrooms, preferably wild ones
   such as morels, halved, or quartered if large

¾ cup medium-dry sherry

3 cups heavy cream

2 tablespoons finely chopped fresh tarragon
   Freshly ground pepper

1 Whisk together milk, eggs, and melted butter in a medium bowl; set aside. Whisk together flour and 2 teaspoons salt in a separate medium bowl. Pour milk mixture into flour mixture, and whisk until blended. Cover; let batter stand 1 hour.

2 Preheat oven to 450°F. Put 2 teaspoons oil into each cup of two standard 6-cup popover pans or a large (each cup having a 1-cup capacity) 12-cup muffin tin. Place pans on a rimmed baking sheet. Transfer to oven; heat oil in pans 20 minutes.

3 Pour batter into popover cups, filling each two-thirds full. Bake 15 minutes (do not open oven while popovers cook). Reduce oven temperature to 350°F; continue to bake popovers until well browned and crusty, about 20 minutes more. Invert popovers to unmold. Transfer to a bowl lined with a clean kitchen towel; cover to keep warm.

4 Meanwhile, heat remaining 8 tablespoons butter in a large skillet over medium heat. Add shallots; cook, stirring occasionally, until fragrant, about 2 minutes. Add mushrooms; cook, stirring occasionally, until golden, about 5 minutes. Add sherry; cook until liquid is reduced by half, about 2 minutes. Raise heat to medium-high; add cream, and heat until just about to simmer, stirring. Reduce heat to low, and simmer 1 minute. Stir in tarragon, and season with salt and pepper. To serve, place popovers on plates, and spoon mushroom sauce over top.

from Celebrating Spring

asparagus salad with tender greens and mint

SERVES 8 | **PHOTO ON PAGE 142**

Speck, a flavorful smoked ham, is a specialty of the South Tyrolean region of Italy. You can use prosciutto instead. Spring onions are a more mature version of the scallion; they are available at specialty-food stores and farmers' markets.

¼ cup champagne vinegar

1 spring onion (bulb only) or shallot, finely chopped
   Coarse salt

1 pound green asparagus

1 pound white asparagus

1 tablespoon grainy Dijon mustard

1 teaspoon fresh lemon juice

¾ cup extra-virgin olive oil
   Freshly ground pepper

4 ounces mixed tender salad greens, such as
   mâche and baby arugula

¾ cup loosely packed mint leaves

8 thin slices speck (about 4 ounces)

1 Bring vinegar and spring onion to a boil in a small saucepan over medium heat. Cook until liquid is reduced by half, about 2 minutes. Set aside.

2 Bring a medium saucepan of water to a boil; add salt. Prepare an ice-water bath, and set aside. Peel bottom 2 inches of asparagus, reserving peels. Blanch asparagus peels 2 minutes; immediately transfer with tongs to ice-water bath to stop the cooking. (Keep water at a boil.) Remove peels with a slotted spoon; set aside. (Reserve ice-water bath.) Blanch asparagus until crisp-tender, about 4 minutes. Immediately transfer with tongs to ice-water bath. Drain.

3 Cut lower third from each asparagus spear, and transfer pieces to a food processor. Set remaining asparagus aside. Add reserved peels, the vinegar mixture, and mustard to processor; process until smooth. With processor running, pour in lemon juice and then oil in a slow, steady stream. Pass mixture through a fine sieve into a small bowl; discard solids. Season vinaigrette with salt and pepper.

4 Put salad greens and mint in a large nonreactive bowl (glass or ceramic). Drizzle with vinaigrette, and gently toss. Divide asparagus among serving plates. Top each serving with dressed salad greens and a slice of speck.

from Celebrating Spring

watercress and green bean salad

SERVES 4 | **PHOTO ON PAGE 143**

To keep watercress fresh, wrap it in damp paper towels and place it in a resealable plastic bag. Stored this way, it can be refrigerated for up to four days. Just before making the salad, "crisp" the watercress by soaking it in a bowl of ice water for a few minutes, then gently pat dry.

Coarse salt

8 ounces green beans, trimmed and cut into 1-inch pieces

2 tablespoons finely chopped shallot

2 tablespoons fresh lemon juice

Freshly ground pepper

2 tablespoons extra-virgin olive oil

1 kirby cucumber, peeled, halved lengthwise, and thinly sliced

1 bunch watercress, thick stems discarded

¼ cup packed mint leaves (large leaves torn in half)

1 Prepare an ice-water bath; set aside. Bring a medium pot of water to a boil; add salt. Blanch green beans until crisp-tender, 4 to 5 minutes. Immediately transfer with a slotted spoon to ice-water bath to stop the cooking. Drain.

2 Whisk together shallot, lemon juice, and ½ teaspoon salt in a serving bowl; season with pepper. Whisking constantly, pour in oil in a slow, steady stream; whisk until emulsified.

3 Add cucumber and reserved beans to bowl; toss to coat. Add watercress and mint; toss. Season with salt and pepper.

from What's for Dinner?

wilted baby spinach with crispy shallots

SERVES 6

Vegetable or light olive oil, for frying

All-purpose flour, for dredging

Coarse salt and freshly ground pepper

1 large shallot, cut crosswise and separated into rings (about ⅓ cup)

2 tablespoons extra-virgin olive oil

1 pound baby spinach

1 Heat ½ inch vegetable oil in a small skillet over medium heat. Meanwhile, put flour in a bowl, and season with salt and pepper. Dredge shallot rings in flour all at once. When oil is hot (a shallot ring will sizzle on contact), fry rings in batches, shaking off excess flour before transferring them to skillet. Fry until golden brown and crisp, 1 to 3 minutes. Transfer rings with a slotted spoon or tongs to paper towels to drain.

2 Heat the extra-virgin olive oil in a Dutch oven or shallow stockpot over medium heat until hot but not smoking. Add spinach (if it doesn't fit all at once, wait until some of it cooks down to add more, or cook in two batches). Season with salt and pepper. Cover; cook, uncovering occasionally to toss, until spinach is wilted, 2 to 3 minutes.

3 Transfer spinach to a serving bowl with tongs or a slotted spoon, leaving excess liquid in pot. Sprinkle with shallot rings, and serve immediately.

from Easy Entertaining: Buffet Brunch

MAIN COURSES

citrus-roasted salmon with spring-pea sauce

SERVES 8 | **PHOTO ON PAGE 153**

1 side of salmon (about 3 pounds), trimmed of fat and excess skin, and small pin bones removed with tweezers

Freshly grated zest of 1 orange, plus 2 oranges, cut into ¼-inch-thick rounds

Freshly grated zest of 1 lemon, plus 2 lemons, cut into ¼-inch-thick rounds

Freshly grated zest of 1 lime

2 teaspoons coarse salt

2 teaspoons sugar

1½ teaspoons freshly ground white pepper

1 teaspoon coriander seeds, crushed

2 tablespoons extra-virgin olive oil

Spring-Pea Sauce (recipe follows)

Pea shoots or watercress, for garnish

1 Place salmon, skin side down, in a nonreactive baking dish (glass or ceramic) large enough for it to lay flat.

2 Stir together zests, salt, sugar, pepper, and coriander in a small bowl. Rub spice blend all over salmon flesh. Wrap salmon in plastic wrap. Refrigerate 2 hours.

3 Preheat oven to 400°F. Wipe spice blend from salmon with paper towels. Let fish stand at room temperature 20 minutes.

4 Arrange half of the orange and lemon slices in a single layer in a large roasting pan; place salmon, skin side down, on top. Rub oil all over salmon flesh. Roast until cooked through, about 17 minutes.

5 Cut salmon crosswise into 8 pieces. Divide pea sauce among plates. Place a piece of salmon on each plate; garnish with pea shoots and remaining orange and lemon slices.

from Celebrating Spring

spring-pea sauce

MAKES ¾ CUP

You can make this sauce with thawed frozen peas instead of fresh, in which case they don't need to be blanched. The sauce can be made up to one day ahead and refrigerated in an airtight container. Reheat over medium-low heat, adding water to thin, if necessary.

Coarse salt

1⅓ pounds fresh garden peas, shelled (1⅓ cups)

1 cup loosely packed watercress (1 ounce)

4 teaspoons cold unsalted butter

1 Prepare an ice-water bath; set aside. Bring a medium pot of water to a boil; add salt. Blanch peas and watercress until bright green, about 45 seconds. Immediately transfer with a slotted spoon to ice-water bath to stop the cooking.

2 Drain peas and watercress, then purée in a blender until smooth, adding 4 to 5 tablespoons water to thin, until the mixture is the consistency of heavy cream. Pass purée through a fine sieve into a small saucepan; discard solids. Place over low heat, and whisk in butter, 1 teaspoon at a time; whisk until emulsified. Season sauce with salt.

fried rice with tofu and flaxseed

SERVES 4

½ package firm tofu (7 ounces), drained and cut into ¼-inch dice

3 tablespoons low-sodium soy sauce

1 cup jasmine rice

1 tablespoon extra-virgin olive oil

1 tablespoon unsalted butter

3 large eggs, beaten

1 medium carrot, peeled and finely grated

¾ cup shelled fresh or thawed frozen peas

6 scallions, white and pale-green parts only, thinly sliced on the diagonal

1 tablespoon whole brown flaxseed, plus 2 teaspoons ground brown flaxseed (from about 1 teaspoon whole)

¾ teaspoon toasted sesame oil

Freshly ground pepper

1 Gently toss tofu with 1 tablespoon soy sauce in a medium bowl; set aside.

2 Bring rice and 1½ cups water to a boil in a medium sauce-pan. Cover; reduce heat to medium-low, and simmer until rice is tender and water has been absorbed, about 10 minutes. Set aside.

3 Heat olive oil and butter in a large skillet over medium heat. Add eggs, and cook, stirring, until just starting to set, about 30 seconds. Add rice; stir to coat and break up any lumps. Reduce heat to medium-low, and add carrot, peas, and scallions. Cook until heated through, about 4 minutes. Add whole and ground flaxseed, remaining 2 tablespoons soy sauce, and the sesame oil and tofu; cook 5 minutes more. Season with pepper.

PER SERVING: 432 CALORIES, 17 G FAT, 167 MG CHOLESTEROL, 51 G CARBOHYDRATE, 546 MG SODIUM, 19 G PROTEIN, 6 G FIBER

from Fit to Eat: Flaxseed

lamb chops with artichoke hearts

SERVES 4 | PHOTO ON PAGE 153

4 shoulder lamb chops (½ inch thick each)

Coarse salt and freshly ground pepper

1 to 2 tablespoons extra-virgin olive oil

1 medium onion, halved crosswise and cut into ¼-inch-thick slices

4 artichoke hearts (water-packed, from one 14-ounce can), rinsed, drained, and each cut into six wedges

¼ cup fruity white wine, such as a New Zealand Marlborough Sauvignon Blanc

1 cup homemade or low-sodium store-bought chicken stock

½ cup cherry tomatoes, halved

½ cup pitted Kalamata olives, halved

1 tablespoon lemon-zest strips

1 Rinse chops, and pat dry. Season with salt and pepper. Heat 1 tablespoon oil in a large skillet over medium-high heat until hot but not smoking. Cook lamb in two batches, turning once, 4 to 5 minutes per side for medium-rare. Transfer to a platter, and loosely cover with foil.

2 Add onion and artichoke hearts to same skillet (add up to 1 tablespoon oil if skillet is dry). Cook over medium heat until softened and golden (do not brown), 3 to 5 minutes. Add wine; cook until almost all liquid is evaporated, about 3 minutes. Add stock and tomatoes; cover, and cook 3 minutes. Uncover; cook until sauce is reduced by half, 3 to 5 minutes. Stir in olives and zest. Season sauce with salt and pepper.

3 Spoon vegetables and sauce over lamb, and serve.

from What's for Dinner?

classic panino

MAKES 1 | **PHOTOS ON PAGES 150 AND 151**

1 ciabatta roll, split horizontally

2 teaspoons extra-virgin olive oil, plus more for pan

Coarse salt and freshly ground pepper

2¼ ounces fresh buffalo mozzarella, sliced

¾ ounce Parmesan cheese, shaved

1 ounce prosciutto di Parma, thinly sliced

8 fresh basil leaves

1 Heat a grill pan over medium-low to medium heat until almost smoking. Lightly brush cut sides of bread with the oil. Season with salt and pepper. Layer remaining ingredients on one piece of bread. Top with remaining bread.

2 Lightly brush pan with oil. Place panino on pan; cover with a cast-iron or other heavy skillet weighted with soup cans. Gently press straight down. Grill, undisturbed, until browned and crisp on the bottom, 3 to 4 minutes. With a spatula, flip panino. Grill until crisp and browned on the other side, 3 to 4 minutes more. Serve hot.

from Panini, Savory and Sweet

bacon and Gorgonzola variation

Follow recipe for Classic Panino, using ½ baguette (split horizontally), 3 slices cooked bacon, 1 ounce Gorgonzola dolce or other creamy blue cheese, and 1 cup baby spinach.

goat cheese and radicchio variation

Follow recipe for Classic Panino, using 2 slices rustic bread, 2 tablespoons soft goat cheese, 1 tablespoon finely chopped black olives, and ½ cup shredded radicchio.

sardine and Parmesan variation

Follow recipe for Classic Panino, using 2 slices rustic bread, 7 boneless whole sardines packed in oil, ¾ ounce shaved Parmesan cheese, ⅓ cup shaved fennel, ⅓ cup shaved red onion, and juice of 1 lemon.

soppressata and Taleggio variation

Follow recipe for Classic Panino, using 1 ciabatta roll (split horizontally) ¾ ounce thinly sliced soppressata, 1½ ounces sliced Taleggio cheese, and 4 paper-thin lemon slices.

two-cheese and walnut variation

Follow recipe for Classic Panino, using 1 baguette (split horizontally), 1½ ounces fontina cheese (preferably Fontina Val d'Aosta), 2¼ ounces sliced fresh buffalo mozzarella, ½ teaspoon finely chopped fresh rosemary, and 4 teaspoons chopped toasted walnuts.

butter and sugar variation

Follow recipe for Classic Panino, using unsalted butter for pan (instead of olive oil) and omitting salt and pepper. To make panino, spread 2 slices white bread with 2 tablespoons softened unsalted butter, and sprinkle buttered sides with 2 tablespoons granulated sugar. After grilling, dust top slice of bread with confectioners' sugar.

chocolate-hazelnut spread and pear variation | **PHOTO ON PAGE 137**

Follow recipe for Classic Panino, using unsalted butter for pan (instead of olive oil) and omitting salt and pepper. To make panino, spread cut sides of a split brioche roll with 2 teaspoons softened unsalted butter and 5 teaspoons chocolate-hazelnut spread. Top with thin slices from ¼ pear.

ricotta and fig variation

Follow recipe for Classic Panino, using unsalted butter for pan (instead of olive oil) and omitting salt and pepper. To make panino, spread cut sides of a split brioche roll with 2 teaspoons softened unsalted butter and 2 tablespoons fresh ricotta cheese. Top with thin slices from 2 or 3 dried Calimyrna figs. Using 2 teaspoons balsamic vinegar and 2 teaspoons honey, drizzle toppings with vinegar and honey, and drizzle outside of panino with honey before grilling.

almond custard cake

SERVES 8

Almond flour is simply ground blanched almonds—it doesn't contain any wheat flour. You can make your own by finely grinding one-half cup whole blanched almonds in a food processor. The dough can be refrigerated for up to two days or frozen for up to one month (thaw before using). The custard filling can be made up to one day ahead; press plastic wrap directly onto its surface (to prevent a skin from forming), and refrigerate in an airtight container.

12 tablespoons (1½ sticks) unsalted butter, softened, plus more for pan

2½ cups plus 1 tablespoon all-purpose flour, plus more for dusting

½ cup almond flour

1½ teaspoons baking powder

¼ teaspoon salt

1¾ cups plus 2 tablespoons granulated sugar

7 large egg yolks

3 tablespoons sweet dessert wine, such as Sauternes or Beaumes-de-Venise

1 teaspoon pure almond extract

1 vanilla bean, halved lengthwise, and seeds scraped to loosen

1¾ cups whole milk

Freshly grated zest of 1 orange

1 tablespoon heavy cream

2 tablespoons sliced blanched almonds

Confectioners' sugar, for dusting

Strawberry-Rhubarb Sauce (recipe follows)

1 Cut a 9-inch round of parchment paper to line the bottom of a 9-by-2-inch round cake pan. Butter and line pan. Butter lining, then flour pan, tapping out excess; set aside.

2 Make dough: Whisk together 2¼ cups flour, the almond flour, baking powder, and salt in a medium bowl; set aside.

3 Put butter and 1½ cups granulated sugar in the bowl of an electric mixer fitted with the paddle attachment. Mix on medium speed until pale and fluffy, about 2 minutes. Add 3 egg yolks, 1 at a time, mixing well after each addition and scraping down sides of bowl. Add wine, almond extract, and half the vanilla seeds; mix until combined, about 15 seconds. Add flour mixture in two additions, mixing until just combined (do not overmix).

4 Divide dough in half, and flatten each piece into a disk. Wrap disks in plastic wrap. Refrigerate 1 hour.

5 Make custard filling: Prepare an ice-water bath; set aside. Fit electric mixer with the whisk attachment. Put 3 egg yolks and remaining 6 tablespoons sugar in a clean mixing bowl; beat on medium speed until pale yellow and thickened. Add remaining 5 tablespoons flour; beat on low until combined.

6 Heat milk, remaining vanilla seeds, and orange zest in a medium saucepan over medium heat until just about to simmer. With mixer on medium-low, pour ½ cup hot-milk mixture into egg mixture in a slow, steady stream. Stir mixture into remaining milk in saucepan. Bring to a simmer over medium heat, stirring to reach bottom and sides of pan. Cook until thickened, 1 to 2 minutes. Set pan in ice-water bath; stir occasionally until cool, about 20 minutes.

7 Preheat oven to 375°F. Press 1 piece of dough onto bottom of prepared pan and 1½ inches up sides. Spoon custard on top, and spread into an even layer.

8 On a lightly floured surface, roll remaining dough into an 11-inch circle. Drape over pan; trim edges flush with pan. Gently press edges of top crust to meet bottom crust; crimp top edges with a fork to seal. Refrigerate cake 30 minutes.

9 Beat remaining egg yolk and the cream in a small bowl. Brush top of cake with egg wash; sprinkle with almonds. Bake until golden brown, about 35 minutes. Let cool completely in pan on a wire rack. Invert cake to unmold; peel off parchment, and reinvert. Just before serving, dust with confectioners' sugar. Serve with strawberry-rhubarb sauce.

from Celebrating Spring

strawberry-rhubarb sauce

MAKES 2½ CUPS

This sauce can be made two days ahead and refrigerated in an airtight container. Before serving, reheat over medium-low heat or bring to room temperature.

12 ounces rhubarb (6 to 8 stalks), trimmed and cut into 1-inch pieces

6 tablespoons sugar

1½ cups strawberries (8 ounces), hulled and halved

½ teaspoon pure vanilla extract

Bring rhubarb, sugar, and ¼ cup water to a simmer in a medium saucepan over medium-high heat, stirring occasionally. Cook until liquid is reduced by half, about 8 minutes. Stir in strawberries and vanilla; cook until berries are softened, about 3 minutes more. Serve warm or at room temperature.

chocolate-pistachio phyllo rolls

MAKES 2 DOZEN

- 6 ounces semisweet chocolate, coarsely ground
- ⅓ cup heavy cream
- ¼ teaspoon ground cinnamon
- 1 cup shelled salted pistachio nuts, coarsely chopped
- 6 sheets phyllo dough (12 by 17 inches), thawed if frozen
- 12 tablespoons (1½ sticks) unsalted butter, melted
- 1 tablespoon confectioners' sugar

1 Preheat oven to 350°F. Place chocolate in a medium bowl. Heat cream with cinnamon in a small saucepan over medium heat until just about to simmer. Stir into chocolate to melt. Chop 2 tablespoons nuts to a fine texture; set aside. Stir remaining nuts into chocolate. Spoon chocolate into a resealable plastic bag; cut 1 inch off of one corner.

2 Lay 1 sheet phyllo on a work surface (cover remaining sheets with a slightly damp kitchen towel). Lightly brush surface with melted butter; lay another sheet on top, and brush with more melted butter.

3 Immediately pipe chocolate along a short side of phyllo, 1½ inches from edges. Tightly roll into a log, lightly brushing with butter at each turn and tucking in ends. Brush log with butter, and cover with damp kitchen towel. Repeat process to make 2 more logs.

4 Transfer logs to a parchment-lined baking sheet; bake 15 minutes. Rotate sheet; brush logs with butter. Sprinkle with reserved nuts. Bake until golden, about 15 minutes more. Let cool completely, then dust with sugar. Cutting in a swift motion, slice each log into 8 pieces.

from What's for Dinner?

grasshopper pie

MAKES ONE 9-INCH PIE | **PHOTO ON PAGE 156**

- 6 tablespoons unsalted butter, melted, plus more for pie plate
- ¾ cup sweetened shredded coconut
- 1½ cups finely crushed chocolate wafer cookies (about 25)
- ½ cup sugar
- 2½ cups heavy cream, chilled
- 1 cup loosely packed mint leaves
- 3 tablespoons green crème de menthe
- 1 envelope (¼ ounce) unflavored gelatin
- 5 large egg yolks
  Semisweet chocolate, chilled, for shavings
  Freshly whipped cream, for serving (optional)

1 Preheat oven to 350°F. Lightly butter a 9-inch pie plate. Whisk together coconut, cookie crumbs, and ¼ cup sugar in a medium bowl. Add melted butter, and stir until well combined. Press crumb mixture onto bottom and up sides of pie plate. Bake until just set, 10 to 12 minutes. Let cool completely.

2 Meanwhile, bring 1½ cups cream and the mint just to a boil in a small saucepan. Remove from heat; cover. Let steep 15 minutes. Pour the mixture through a fine sieve into a glass measuring cup. Discard the mint, and set infused cream aside. Beat the remaining cup cream in a medium bowl until stiff peaks form; cover, and refrigerate.

3 Prepare an ice-water bath; set aside. Put crème de menthe in a medium heatproof bowl; sprinkle with gelatin. Let stand 5 minutes to soften. Whisk together egg yolks and remaining ¼ cup sugar in another medium bowl; set aside. Add infused cream to gelatin mixture, whisking until well combined.

4 Set bowl with cream mixture over a pan of simmering water. Cook, whisking constantly, until the gelatin is dissolved and mixture is hot to the touch, about 1 minute. Whisking constantly, pour hot cream mixture in a slow, steady stream into egg-yolk mixture. Return mixture to heatproof bowl; set over pan of simmering water. Cook, whisking constantly, until mixture is slightly thickened and registers 150°F on an instant-read thermometer, about 10 minutes.

5 Transfer bowl to ice-water bath; whisk until mixture thickens to the consistency of pudding, about 2 minutes. Remove bowl from bath. Add one-third of reserved whipped cream; whisk until combined. Gently fold in remaining whipped cream with a rubber spatula.

6 Spoon mixture into pie crust, and refrigerate until set, 45 minutes to 1 hour (or up to 1 day). Just before serving, scrape a chef's knife along surface of semisweet chocolate to make shavings. Spoon dollops of whipped cream onto pie, if desired, and top with chocolate shavings.

from Dessert of the Month

caramel crunch

MAKES ABOUT 4 QUARTS

½ cup water
1¼ cups sugar
6 tablespoons unsalted butter, cut into pieces, plus more for bowl
¾ teaspoon salt
3½ quarts popcorn (popped from ½ cup kernels)
1 cup salted peanuts (5½ ounces)

1 Pour water into a heavy-bottom saucepan. Add sugar. Cook over medium heat, stirring occasionally, until sugar is dissolved and syrup is clear. Continue to cook, without stirring, until syrup comes to a boil, washing down sides of pan with a wet pastry brush to prevent crystals from forming. Let syrup boil, gently swirling pan occasionally, until medium amber. (Remove from heat just before it reaches the desired shade; it will continue to cook for a few more seconds.)

2 Using a clean wooden spoon, gently stir in butter and salt (caramel will bubble); stir until smooth. Put popcorn and peanuts in a large buttered bowl. Pour caramel over popcorn, stirring to coat. Stir mixture every few minutes until cool. Store in an airtight container up to 1 week.

from Caramel

caramel sauce

MAKES ABOUT 1 CUP | **PHOTO ON PAGE 157**

1 cup sugar
½ cup water
¾ cup heavy cream
½ teaspoon pure vanilla extract or 1 tablespoon bourbon
⅛ teaspoon salt

1 Follow step 1 of Caramel Crunch (above), using 1 cup sugar and ½ cup water.

2 After removing caramel from heat, carefully pour in cream (caramel will bubble). Add vanilla and salt; stir with a wooden spoon until smooth. If not serving sauce immediately, let cool; refrigerate in an airtight container up to 3 weeks. (Reheat in a saucepan or in the microwave, stirring in another tablespoon heavy cream.)

nut brittle

MAKES ABOUT 1 POUND

2 cups toasted, sliced almonds with skins (5½ ounces)
½ cup water
2 cups sugar
¼ teaspoon salt

1 Prepare an ice-water bath, and set aside. Place almonds on a sheet of parchment paper in a rectangle (9 by 12 inches).

2 Follow step 1 of Caramel Crunch (above), using ½ cup water and 2 cups sugar, and adding the salt with the sugar.

3 After removing caramel from heat, set pan in ice-water bath. Remove pan; let cool until slightly thick (the consistency of honey). Pour over nuts to cover. Let cool until hardened. Peel off parchment, and break brittle into pieces.

flaxseed-and-onion crackers

MAKES ABOUT 5 DOZEN | **PHOTO ON PAGE 139**

¼ cup whole golden flaxseed, plus ¼ cup ground golden flaxseed (from about 2 tablespoons whole)
1½ cups all-purpose flour, plus more for dusting
½ teaspoon baking powder
½ teaspoon coarse salt, plus more for seasoning (optional)
2 tablespoons unsalted butter, softened
4 teaspoons finely grated onion
4 teaspoons finely chopped fresh flat-leaf parsley
½ cup skim milk
1 large egg white, lightly beaten
Freshly ground pepper

1 Preheat oven to 325°F. Put whole and ground flaxseed, flour, baking powder, salt, and butter in the bowl of an electric mixer fitted with the paddle attachment; mix on medium speed until mixture resembles coarse meal, about 2 minutes. Stir in onion and parsley. With mixer on low, pour in milk. Mix until dough just comes together (do not overmix).

2 Divide dough in half. Roll out each piece on a lightly floured surface to a 9-inch square (⅛ inch thick). Transfer to two baking sheets. Cut each square with a fluted pastry wheel or a knife into about 30 crackers (each 1½ inches square).

3 Brush with egg white; season with pepper, and salt, if desired. Bake until slightly firm, about 20 minutes. Switch positions of sheets; flip crackers. Bake until light brown and firm, 18 to 20 minutes more. Transfer to wire racks to cool.

PER SERVING (6 CRACKERS): 132 CALORIES, 5 G FAT, 6 MG CHOLESTEROL, 17 G CARBOHYDRATE, 374 MG SODIUM, 4 G PROTEIN, 3 G FIBER

from Fit to Eat: Flaxseed

May

chicken soup with parsley dumplings

SERVES 6 | PHOTO ON PAGE 143

- 4 boneless, skinless chicken breast halves (about 1¼ pounds total), each cut into 3 pieces
- 6 boneless, skinless chicken thighs (about 1¼ pounds total)
- 4 medium carrots (about ¾ pound), cut on the diagonal into ¼-inch-thick rounds
- 1 medium onion, thinly sliced into half-moons
- 2 celery stalks, cut into ¼-inch-thick pieces
- 1 garlic clove, thinly sliced
- 1 bay leaf
- 1½ cups homemade or low-sodium store-bought chicken stock
  Coarse salt
- 1 teaspoon coarsely chopped fresh thyme
- ¼ cup plus 2 tablespoons yellow cornmeal
- ¾ cup all-purpose flour
- 1 teaspoon baking powder
- 2 tablespoons finely chopped shallot
- 1 tablespoon freshly grated lemon zest
- ¾ cup finely chopped fresh flat-leaf parsley
- 2 tablespoons finely grated Parmesan cheese
- 1½ tablespoons cold unsalted butter, cut into small pieces
- ½ cup low-fat (1 percent) milk

1 Bring 2 quarts water, the chicken, carrots, onion, celery, garlic, bay leaf, stock, and ⅛ teaspoon salt to a boil in a medium pot; skim froth that rises to the top. Reduce heat to medium-low; gently simmer 20 minutes. Add thyme.

2 Meanwhile, whisk together cornmeal, flour, baking powder, ½ teaspoon salt, the shallot, zest, parsley, and cheese in a medium bowl. Add butter, and blend in with your fingertips until the mixture resembles coarse meal. Add milk, and stir with a fork just until a dough forms.

3 Roll dough into 1-inch balls; add all at once to simmering broth. Cover soup, and simmer, undisturbed, until the dumplings are cooked through, about 20 minutes. Divide soup among six serving bowls.

PER SERVING: 386 CALORIES, 9 G FAT, 143 MG CHOLESTEROL, 27 G CARBOHYDRATE, 816 MG SODIUM, 46 G PROTEIN, 3 G FIBER

from Fit to Eat: Parsley

chilled pea and pea-shoot soup with shrimp

MAKES 6 CUPS; SERVES 6 | PHOTO ON PAGE 143

- 8 ounces pea shoots
- ¼ cup extra-virgin olive oil
- 1 medium sweet onion, such as Vidalia or Walla Walla, finely chopped
- ¼ cup Pernod (anise-flavored liqueur)
- 1 quart homemade or low-sodium store-bought chicken or vegetable stock
- 1 pound shelled fresh peas
  Coarse salt and freshly ground pepper
- ½ pound small shrimp (18 to 22), peeled and deveined
- 1 shallot, finely chopped
- 2 tablespoons fresh lemon juice

1 Coarsely chop just under half of the pea shoots; set aside. Heat 2 tablespoons oil in a large saucepan over medium heat until hot but not smoking. Add onion, and cook, stirring occasionally, until tender, about 8 minutes. Add liqueur; cook until most of the liquid has evaporated, about 2 minutes. Add stock and peas, and cook until peas are tender but still bright green, about 12 minutes. Add chopped pea shoots, and cook until wilted, about 2 minutes.

2 Purée mixture in a blender in batches (so blender is never more than halfway full). Season with salt and pepper. Let mixture cool completely.

3 Meanwhile, bring a medium saucepan of water to a boil. Add shrimp; boil until pink and cooked through, 3 to 5 minutes. Drain. Refrigerate shrimp and the pea soup separately until cold, about 1 hour.

4 Chop remaining pea shoots into 1-inch pieces; stir together with shallot, lemon juice, and remaining 2 tablespoons oil in a large bowl. Add shrimp; season with salt and pepper, and toss to combine. Divide soup among bowls, and top each serving with shrimp mixture.

from Pea Shoots

garlic bread soup

MAKES 5 CUPS; SERVES 4

If you don't have stale bread on hand, lightly toast fresh bread and tear it into small pieces.

¼ cup high-quality extra-virgin olive oil, preferably Spanish

8 large garlic cloves, mashed to a paste
   with 1 teaspoon coarse salt

2 cups bite-size pieces stale crusty bread (4 ounces)

5 cups homemade or low-sodium store-bought chicken stock

1 bay leaf
   Coarse salt and freshly ground pepper

3 large eggs, beaten
   Fresh flat-leaf parsley leaves, for garnish

1 Heat oil in a large saucepan over medium-low heat until hot but not smoking. Add garlic paste; cook, stirring occasionally, until very fragrant but not browned, about 10 minutes. Add bread, and stir to coat. Stir in stock and bay leaf; season with salt and pepper. Bring to a boil. Reduce heat; simmer 10 minutes.

2 Discard bay leaf. Stir in eggs. Cook, stirring occasionally to break up eggs, about 10 minutes. Serve soup garnished with parsley leaves.

from What's for Dinner?

....

SALADS AND SIDE DISHES

....

parsley-leaf salad with pine nuts, olives, and orange dressing

SERVES 6

The raw onion in this recipe becomes milder the longer it stays in the orange-juice-and-vinegar mixture. For a strong onion flavor, let the onion slices soak for about ten minutes; to make them mellow, marinate for up to four hours.

¼ cup pine nuts

1 navel orange

½ teaspoon sherry vinegar or red-wine vinegar

¼ medium red onion, very thinly sliced into half-moons
   Pinch of coarse salt

1 tablespoon capers, rinsed and drained

¼ cup brine-cured black olives such as Kalamata
   or Gaeta, pitted and halved

3 cups loosely packed fresh flat-leaf parsley leaves
   (about 2 medium bunches)
   Freshly ground pepper

1 tablespoon extra-virgin olive oil

1 Preheat oven to 375°F. Spread out pine nuts on a rimmed baking sheet; toast in oven, shaking halfway through, until golden and fragrant, 10 minutes. Transfer to a plate to cool.

2 With a vegetable peeler, peel 8 long pieces of zest from the orange; cut lengthwise into very thin strips. Halve orange; squeeze 2 tablespoons juice into a medium bowl (reserve remainder for another use). Add vinegar, onion, and salt; let stand 10 minutes. Add capers, olives, parsley, pine nuts, and zest to bowl. Season with pepper; toss thoroughly with oil. Divide among six plates.

PER SERVING: 82 CALORIES, 6 G FAT, 0 MG CHOLESTEROL, 6 G CARBOHYDRATE, 128 MG SODIUM, 3 G PROTEIN, 2 G FIBER

from Fit to Eat: Parsley

pea-shoot salad with warm onion dressing

SERVES 6 | **PHOTO ON PAGE 143**

1 pound sugar snap peas, trimmed

2 ounces pea shoots (about 1⅓ cups)

2 heads Bibb or Boston lettuce, torn

1 small bunch radishes, quartered lengthwise

6 thin slices pancetta (about 3 ounces)

2 tablespoons extra-virgin olive oil, if needed

2 ounces pearl onions (about ¾ cup), peeled and halved

½ cup dry white wine

½ cup heavy cream
   Pinch of cayenne pepper (optional)
   Coarse salt and freshly ground pepper

1 Bring a small saucepan of water to a boil. Prepare an ice-water bath; set aside. Blanch snap peas until bright green and crisp-tender, about 1 minute. Immediately transfer to ice-water bath to stop the cooking. Drain. Transfer to a serving bowl. Add pea shoots, lettuce, and radishes; set aside.

2 Heat a large nonstick skillet over medium heat until hot. Arrange pancetta in skillet in a single layer; cook, turning once, until crisp, about 12 minutes. Transfer pancetta with tongs to paper towels to drain.

3 Pour off all but 2 tablespoons fat (if skillet seems dry, add enough oil to total 2 tablespoons fat). Add onions; cook over medium-high heat, stirring often, until tender, about 4 minutes. Add wine; cook until most of the liquid has evaporated, about 2 minutes. Add cream, and cayenne, if desired. Cook until liquid is reduced by half, about 4 minutes.

4 Pour warm cream dressing over greens; toss to coat. Season with salt and pepper, and top with pancetta.

from Pea Shoots

mashed plantains

SERVES 4

You will need sweet, fully ripened plantains (*plátanos maduros*, in Spanish) for this Cuban-inspired dish. They should be soft, with peels that are mostly brown or black. Plantains are available in Latin American markets and many grocery stores.

2 fully ripe plantains, peeled and halved lengthwise

½ teaspoon coarse salt

Pinch of cayenne pepper, or more to taste

1 tablespoon olive oil

Juice of ½ lime

1   Preheat oven to 375°F. Sprinkle plantains with salt and cayenne, and drizzle with oil to coat. Arrange, cut sides down, on a rimmed baking sheet. Roast until cut sides of plantains begin to caramelize, about 20 minutes. Turn plantains, and roast 10 minutes more.

2   Mash hot plantains on baking sheet with a potato masher until somewhat smooth (some large chunks should remain). Transfer to a serving bowl, and drizzle with lime juice.

from What's for Dinner?

tabbouleh

MAKES 4½ CUPS

1 cup bulghur

4 plum tomatoes, finely chopped, with their juice

1¾ cups finely chopped fresh flat-leaf parsley (about 2 medium bunches)

4 scallions, finely chopped

¼ cup fresh lemon juice (about 2 lemons)

¾ teaspoon coarse salt

¼ cup extra-virgin olive oil

Freshly ground pepper

2 tablespoons finely chopped fresh mint

1   Cover bulghur with cold water and soak 10 minutes. Drain in a sieve lined with damp cheesecloth; squeeze out all water. Transfer to a serving bowl, and fluff with a fork.

2   Stir in tomatoes with juice, parsley, and scallions. Add lemon juice, salt, and oil; season with pepper. Toss to coat. Just before serving, stir in mint.

PER SERVING (¾ CUP): 184 CALORIES, 10 G FAT, 0 MG CHOLESTEROL, 23 G CARBOHYDRATE, 311 MG SODIUM, 4 G PROTEIN, 6 G FIBER

from Fit to Eat: Parsley

Chinese-style steamed sea bass with vegetables

SERVES 2

1 whole sea bass (2 pounds), cleaned

Coarse salt and freshly ground pepper

4 thin slices peeled fresh ginger plus 2 teaspoons grated ginger

3 garlic cloves, thinly sliced

10 sprigs cilantro, plus 1 tablespoon coarsely chopped for garnish

3½ tablespoons toasted sesame oil

1½ pounds baby bok choy, white stems cut crosswise into ¾-inch-thick pieces and leaves discarded

10 small shiitake mushrooms, stemmed, caps sliced ¼ inch thick

7 scallions, thinly sliced on the diagonal

2½ tablespoons soy sauce

2½ tablespoons rice-wine vinegar

1 tablespoon mirin (Japanese sweet rice wine) or packed brown sugar

1   Rinse fish thoroughly under cold running water; remove any debris from the cavity with a spoon; pat dry. Season cavity with salt and pepper; stuff with ginger slices, 4 slices garlic, and the cilantro sprigs. Rub fish all over with 1½ tablespoons sesame oil. Season with salt and pepper.

2   Put bok choy, mushrooms, two-thirds of scallions, remaining garlic, the grated ginger, and ¼ teaspoon salt in a medium bowl. Season with pepper, and toss.

3   Transfer half of bok choy mixture to a 9-by-13-inch baking pan (not glass); place fish on top. Top with remaining bok choy mixture. Whisk together soy sauce, vinegar, mirin, and ¼ teaspoon salt; drizzle over fish. Tightly cover pan with foil.

4   Pour water to a depth of ¼ inch in another 9-by-13-inch baking pan (not glass); bring to a boil on top of stove. Reduce heat; let simmer. Set pan with fish on top; steam until cooked through, 16 to 20 minutes. Transfer to a platter; garnish with remaining scallions and chopped cilantro. Drizzle with remaining 2 tablespoons sesame oil.

from How It's Done: Great Fish

fettuccine with asparagus ribbons

SERVES 4 TO 6

Coarse salt

1 pound asparagus, trimmed

1 pound fettuccine

1 tablespoon olive oil

3 tablespoons finely chopped shallots (about 2 shallots)

¾ cup heavy cream

2 teaspoons freshly grated lemon zest plus 2 tablespoons fresh lemon juice

Freshly ground pepper

1 Bring a large pot of water to a boil; add salt. Prepare an ice-water bath; set aside. Blanch asparagus until just tender, about 3 minutes. Immediately transfer with tongs to ice-water bath to stop the cooking. (Keep water at a boil.) Drain.

2 Add pasta to pot; cook until just al dente. Reserve 1 cup cooking water; drain pasta.

3 Meanwhile, cut off tips from asparagus stalks and put them into a medium bowl. Shave stalks into long ribbons with a vegetable peeler; transfer ribbons to the same bowl as you work.

4 Heat oil in a large sauté pan over medium heat until hot but not smoking. Add shallots; cook, stirring, until translucent, about 4 minutes. Add cream, ¼ cup reserved cooking water, and asparagus tips and ribbons.

5 Bring to a boil, and add pasta. Cook, tossing, until heated through, about 2 minutes. Add more cooking water if pasta seems dry. Stir in zest and lemon juice, and season with salt and pepper.

from Good Things

pea shoot and vegetable stir-fry

SERVES 4 TO 6 | **PHOTO ON PAGE 153**

1 tablespoon finely grated peeled fresh ginger

1 tablespoon soy sauce

1 tablespoon rice-wine vinegar

1½ teaspoons toasted sesame oil

2 tablespoons vegetable oil

1 celery stalk, cut into thin half-moons

2 garlic cloves, thinly sliced

8 ounces snow peas, trimmed

6 ounces shiitake mushrooms, stemmed, caps cut into thick strips

2 heads baby bok choy, cut lengthwise into 6 wedges

1 yellow bell pepper, cut into ¼-inch-thick strips

3 scallions, cut into 2-inch matchsticks

2 ounces pea shoots (about 1⅓ cups)

Coarse salt and freshly ground pepper

Sesame seeds, toasted, for garnish

Crushed red-pepper flakes, for garnish (optional)

1 Stir together ginger, soy sauce, vinegar, and sesame oil in a bowl; set aside.

2 Heat 1½ teaspoons vegetable oil in a wok or large skillet over medium-high heat until hot but not smoking. Add celery and garlic; cook, stirring constantly, until just tender, about 4 minutes. Transfer to a rimmed baking sheet; set aside.

3 Add 1½ teaspoons vegetable oil to wok. Add snow peas and mushrooms; cook until tender, about 4 minutes. Transfer to the baking sheet; set aside.

4 Reduce heat to medium-low; add 1½ teaspoons vegetable oil to wok. Add bok choy; cook, turning frequently, until tender, 6 to 8 minutes. Transfer to the baking sheet; set aside.

5 Raise heat to medium-high. Add remaining 1½ teaspoons vegetable oil to wok. Add bell pepper, and cook until tender, about 2 minutes. Add reserved soy-sauce mixture, and cook until reduced by half, about 2 minutes. Add reserved cooked vegetables to wok, and cook, tossing frequently, until vegetables are heated through, about 3 minutes.

6 Remove wok from heat; toss in scallions and pea shoots. Season with salt and pepper. Sprinkle with sesame seeds, and with red-pepper flakes, if desired.

from Pea Shoots

poached cod with parsley sauce

SERVES 4

This dish is delicious served with boiled potatoes or rice.

2 tablespoons unsalted butter
2 tablespoons all-purpose flour
½ cup whole milk
½ cup homemade or store-bought fish or vegetable stock
Coarse salt
¾ cup finely chopped fresh flat-leaf parsley, plus sprigs for garnish
2 tablespoons finely chopped fresh chives
1 strip lemon peel (3 inches)
¼ cup plus 2 teaspoons fresh lemon juice (about 2 lemons)
4 cod fillets (5 ounces each), skinned

1 Melt butter over medium heat in a small saucepan. Add flour, and whisk until a paste forms. Reduce heat to low; cook, whisking, 2 minutes. Whisking constantly, pour in milk in a slow, steady stream; whisk until incorporated. Whisk in stock. Add ½ teaspoon salt, and cook, whisking occasionally, 10 minutes. Remove from heat; let stand 10 minutes to thicken slightly. Stir in parsley and chives.

2 Meanwhile, bring 1½ quarts water, the lemon peel, ¼ cup lemon juice, and ½ teaspoon salt to a boil in a medium sauté pan or other wide, straight-sided pan. Place fillets in liquid (do not crowd). Return to a boil, then immediately turn off the heat. Let stand until just cooked through, about 10 minutes.

3 Reheat sauce over medium-low heat, if necessary, and add remaining 2 teaspoons lemon juice. Gently lift fillets from liquid with a slotted spatula; place a fillet on each of four plates. Spoon one-quarter of sauce over each serving, and garnish with a parsley sprig.

PER SERVING: 214 CALORIES, 8 G FAT, 72 MG CHOLESTEROL, 7 G CARBOHYDRATE, 713 MG SODIUM, 28 G PROTEIN, 1 G FIBER

from Fit to Eat: Parsley

poached salmon steaks with creamy dill sauce

SERVES 4

If you don't have a very large pot, you can poach the fish in two batches; make a separate packet for each batch. If the packet starts to float, gently press on it to release trapped air.

½ cup fresh lemon juice (from 3 lemons; 2 juiced halves reserved)
Coarse salt
1½ teaspoons whole black peppercorns
4 salmon steaks (each ¾ inch thick)
1 small fennel bulb, trimmed and sliced
1 small onion, thinly sliced
½ cup finely chopped fresh dill plus 8 sprigs, plus more sprigs for garnish
8 sprigs fresh flat-leaf parsley
½ cup mayonnaise
½ cup sour cream
¾ cup snipped fresh chives
Freshly ground pepper

1 Bring 6 quarts water, 6 tablespoons lemon juice, lemon halves, 1 tablespoon salt, and the peppercorns to a boil in a large, wide pot (big enough to hold 4 steaks in one layer). Reduce heat; let simmer.

2 Season salmon steaks with salt. Place one-half each of the fennel and onion and 3 sprigs each dill and parsley on a 24-by-18-inch sheet of parchment; arrange steaks in a single layer on top, then top with remaining fennel, onion, dill, and parsley. Fold parchment to make a sealed packet.

3 With kitchen twine, tie packet to a wire rack; place in pot. Cover; poach until cooked through, about 10 minutes.

4 Use tongs and a spatula to transfer rack to a rimmed baking sheet. Carefully open packet. Remove skin and any brown fat. Transfer fish to a platter, discarding vegetables; cover. Reserve 1 tablespoon cooking liquid.

5 Whisk mayonnaise, sour cream, remaining 2 tablespoons lemon juice, and cooking liquid in a bowl. Stir in chopped dill and chives; season with salt and pepper. Garnish salmon with dill sprigs, and serve with sauce.

from How It's Done: Great Fish

risotto with pea shoots

SERVES 4 | **PHOTO ON PAGE 152**

If you don't have truffle oil, toss the pea shoots with a tablespoon of olive oil.

- 5 cups homemade or low-sodium store-bought chicken or vegetable stock
- 2 tablespoons extra-virgin olive oil
- 2 large shallots, finely chopped
- 1½ cups Arborio or other short-grain rice
- ½ cup dry white wine
- 8 ounces pea shoots
- 1 tablespoon truffle oil

  Coarse salt and freshly ground pepper
- 2 tablespoons unsalted butter
- 1 cup finely grated Parmesan cheese, plus more for serving
- ¼ cup finely chopped fresh flat-leaf parsley

1 Heat stock in a medium saucepan over medium heat, and keep at a bare simmer. Heat olive oil in a large heavy-bottom saucepan over medium heat until hot but not smoking. Add shallots; cook, stirring occasionally, until translucent, about 4 minutes. Add rice; cook, stirring, until rice makes a clicking sound (like glass beads tapping one another), 3 to 4 minutes.

2 Add wine; cook, stirring, until absorbed. Add ¾ cup stock; continue to cook, stirring at a moderate speed, until mixture is thick enough that a clear wake is left behind the spoon.

3 Continue to add stock, ¾ cup at a time (letting each addition get absorbed before adding the next), and cook, stirring, until rice is al dente but not crunchy, and liquid is creamy, 20 to 25 minutes. (There might be stock left over.) Remove risotto from heat.

4 Coarsely chop two-thirds of the pea shoots; set aside. Toss remaining pea shoots with truffle oil in a medium bowl. Season with salt and pepper; set aside. Stir butter, cheese, parsley, and chopped pea shoots into risotto; season with salt and pepper. Divide risotto among plates.

5 Top each serving with a mound of dressed pea shoots. Serve with cheese.

from Pea Shoots

roasted tilefish over potatoes

SERVES 4

If you can't find tilefish, another mild fish, such as halibut or snapper, can be used instead.

- 8 tablespoons (1 stick) unsalted butter, melted, plus more for dish

  Coarse salt and freshly ground pepper
- 16 Kalamata olives, pitted
- 2 pounds Yukon gold potatoes, peeled
- 2 medium garlic cloves, minced
- 2 tilefish fillets (12 ounces each), skinned and halved crosswise
- ¼ cup finely chopped fresh flat-leaf parsley

1 Preheat oven to 450°F. Butter a 9-by-13-inch glass or ceramic baking dish. Sprinkle bottom of dish with salt and pepper, and set aside. Finely chop 12 olives, and thinly slice remaining 4; reserve separately.

2 Slice potatoes very thin (about $\frac{1}{16}$ inch thick) with a mandoline or sharp knife. Arrange one-third of the potatoes in buttered dish, overlapping slightly. Brush with melted butter, and season with salt and pepper. Scatter one-third of the garlic and half of the chopped olives on top. Repeat process to make another layer. Top with remaining potatoes; brush with melted butter, and season with salt and pepper. Set aside remaining garlic and butter.

3 Tightly cover dish with foil. Roast until potatoes just begin to color, 16 to 18 minutes. Remove foil; roast until edges are pale golden, about 10 minutes more. Meanwhile, stir together reserved garlic and melted butter in a large dish. Dip fillets in mixture, and season with salt and pepper.

4 As soon as the potatoes come out of the oven, place fillets on top. Roast until fillets are cooked through, about 10 minutes. Scatter olive slices and parsley on top.

from How It's Done: Great Fish

seared steak with olive relish

SERVES 4 | **PHOTO ON PAGE 153**

1 tablespoon honey

3 tablespoons sherry vinegar

Coarse salt and freshly ground pepper

¼ cup olive oil, preferably Spanish, plus more for skillet

½ red onion, finely chopped (about ½ cup)

1 tablespoon minced garlic (2 medium cloves)

⅓ cup brine-cured pitted green olives, such as Picholine, cut into ¼-inch-thick rounds

1 navel orange, peel and pith cut off, flesh cut into ½-inch pieces

¼ cup coarsely chopped fresh flat-leaf parsley, plus sprigs for garnish

1 boneless sirloin steak (1½ pounds; 1 inch thick)

1 Whisk together honey and vinegar in a medium bowl; season with salt and pepper. Whisking constantly, pour in oil in a slow, steady stream; whisk until emulsified. Stir in onion, garlic, olives, orange, and parsley; set aside.

2 Season steak all over with 1 teaspoon salt and ½ teaspoon pepper. Coat a 12-inch seasoned cast-iron skillet with a thin layer of oil; heat over medium-high heat until very hot. Sear steak, turning once, 6 to 8 minutes per side for medium-rare. Transfer to a plate, and tent with foil. Let stand 10 minutes.

3 To serve, cut steak against the grain into ¼-inch-thick slices, and arrange on a platter. Spoon relish over top, and garnish with parsley sprigs.

from What's for Dinner?

....

PIZZAS

....

grilled Margherita pizzas

MAKES SIX 9-INCH PIZZAS | **PHOTO ON PAGE 149**

Pizza Dough (recipe follows)

Extra-virgin olive oil

Pizza Sauce (recipe follows)

1 pound fresh mozzarella, thinly sliced

Coarse salt and freshly ground pepper

Basil leaves, for garnish

1 Heat a grill until medium-hot. Generously brush one side of pizza dough with oil; grill, oiled side down, until underside is golden brown and top begins to bubble, 3 to 5 minutes. Quickly brush top with oil; flip crust. Top with thin layers of sauce and cheese (about one-sixth of each). Grill until cheese is just melted, sauce is hot, and crust is cooked through, 3 to 5 minutes more.

2 Slide pizza with a large spatula onto a cutting board. Season with salt and pepper. Arrange basil on top. Repeat to make more pizzas.

from Pizza, Hot off the Grill

pizza dough

MAKES ENOUGH FOR SIX 9-INCH PIZZAS

The dough is easiest to handle when it's well chilled—keep it in the refrigerator until right before it hits the grill. Depending on the size of your grill, you can make more than one pizza at a time. (Instead of making six pizzas, another option is to make four large ones; cut the dough into quarters before rolling it out.) Instead of using a grill, you could prepare the pizzas on a grill pan.

2 cups warm water (about 110°F)

½ teaspoon sugar

2 envelopes active dry yeast (2 scant tablespoons)

3 tablespoons extra-virgin olive oil, plus more for bowl

6 to 7 cups all-purpose flour, plus more for dusting

1 tablespoon salt

1 Stir warm water, sugar, and yeast in a small bowl until yeast is dissolved. Let stand until foamy, about 5 minutes. Brush a large bowl with oil, and set aside.

2 Stir together 6 cups flour and the salt in a large bowl. Pour in the yeast mixture and oil; stir mixture until all of the flour is incorporated. Continue to stir until a stiff dough forms. Turn out dough onto a lightly floured surface, and knead with floured hands (dusting with as little flour as possible if dough seems sticky) just until the ball becomes smooth, 2 to 3 minutes. Reshape the dough into a ball. (Alternatively, put 6 cups flour, the salt, yeast mixture, and oil in the bowl of an electric mixer fitted with the paddle attachment. Mix on medium speed until dough is smooth and slightly sticky to the touch, 2 to 3 minutes. If dough seems too sticky, add up to 1 cup flour, 2 tablespoons at a time, mixing after each addition. Knead 4 or 5 turns on a clean work surface to form a ball.)

3 Place dough in oiled bowl, smooth side up. Tightly cover with plastic wrap, and let rise in a warm, draft-free spot until doubled in bulk, about 40 minutes.

4 Remove plastic wrap, and punch down dough. Fold dough back onto itself 4 or 5 times; leave smooth side up. Cover with plastic wrap, and let rise again until doubled in bulk, 30 to 40 minutes.

5 Punch down dough, and transfer to a clean work surface. Cut dough with a bench scraper or knife into sixths. Knead each piece 4 or 5 turns to form a ball. Cover all but one dough ball with plastic wrap.

6 On a lightly floured work surface, flatten remaining dough ball into a disk. Loosely cover with plastic wrap; let rest 5 minutes. Using a rolling pin or your fingertips, flatten and push dough evenly out from center to form a 9-inch circle (or a 7-by-11-inch rectangle or rough oval).

7 Line a baking sheet with parchment paper, and sprinkle with flour. Place dough on top. Cover with another sheet of parchment, and sprinkle with flour. Roll out and stack remaining dough balls.

8 Wrap baking sheet with plastic wrap; refrigerate pizza dough until ready to use, up to 1 day, or freeze up to 1 month (thaw in refrigerator before using).

cornmeal pizza dough variation
MAKES ENOUGH FOR SIX 9-INCH PIZZAS

Follow the recipe for Pizza Dough (above), reducing all-purpose flour to 5 cups. Stir in 1 cup yellow cornmeal with flour. Dust with or mix in additional all-purpose flour as directed.

pizza sauce
MAKES ABOUT 4 CUPS (ENOUGH FOR SIX 9-INCH PIZZAS)

2 cans (28 ounces each) whole peeled plum tomatoes, with juice
¼ cup olive oil
3 sprigs oregano
4 teaspoons coarse salt
¼ teaspoon freshly ground pepper

1 Crush tomatoes with your hands in a large bowl. Heat oil in a large skillet over medium heat until hot but not smoking. Add crushed tomatoes, oregano, salt, and pepper, and reduce heat to medium-low. Cook, stirring occasionally, until thickened, 40 to 50 minutes.

2 Pass sauce through a food mill into a bowl; discard solids. (Alternatively, process sauce in a food processor until smooth.) If not using immediately, refrigerate sauce in an airtight container up to 1 week or freeze up to 1 month.

grilled pizzas with Canadian bacon and pineapple
MAKES SIX 9-INCH PIZZAS | **PHOTO ON PAGE 148**

1 pineapple, peeled, cored, and cut lengthwise into 1-inch-thick spears
8 ounces Canadian bacon, thickly sliced
Pizza Dough (page 111)
Extra-virgin olive oil
4 ounces fresh mozzarella, thinly sliced
Coarse salt and freshly ground pepper
Mint leaves, for garnish

1 Heat a grill until medium-hot. Grill pineapple and bacon, turning once, until browned, about 2 minutes. Cut into 1-inch pieces, and set aside.

2 Generously brush one side of pizza dough with oil; grill, oiled side down, until underside is golden brown and top begins to bubble, 3 to 5 minutes. Quickly brush top with oil; flip crust. Top with a thin layer of cheese and some of the pineapple and bacon (about one-sixth of each). Grill until cheese is just melted, toppings are hot, and crust is cooked through, 3 to 5 minutes more.

3 Slide pizza with a large spatula onto a cutting board. Season with salt and pepper. Arrange mint on top, and drizzle with oil. Repeat to make more pizzas.

from Pizza, Hot off the Grill

grilled pizzas with clams
MAKES SIX 9-INCH PIZZAS

2 cups dry white wine
2½ pounds littleneck clams (about 2 dozen), scrubbed well
5 ounces pancetta, coarsely chopped
3 garlic cloves, finely chopped
3 cups fresh corn kernels (about 3 ears)
1 tablespoon coarsely chopped fresh oregano
2 tablespoons coarsely chopped fresh flat-leaf parsley, plus more for garnish
Coarse salt and freshly ground pepper
Pizza Dough (page 111)
Extra-virgin olive oil
1 cup finely grated Parmesan cheese (4 ounces), plus more for sprinkling

1 Bring wine just to a boil in a large saucepan over medium-high heat. Add clams, and cover pan. Cook, shaking pan occasionally, until clams open (after 8 minutes, check pan often). As they open, transfer clams with a slotted spoon to a large bowl (discard any clams that remain closed after 10 minutes). When clams are cool enough to handle, remove from shells and coarsely chop; set aside.

2 Cook pancetta in a large skillet over medium-high heat, stirring occasionally, until crisp, 3 to 4 minutes. Transfer with a slotted spoon to paper towels to drain. Add garlic to skillet, and cook until fragrant, about 1 minute. Add corn kernels, and cook until tender and bright yellow, about 2 minutes.

3 Transfer corn to a large bowl. Stir in clams, pancetta, oregano, and parsley. Season with salt and pepper; set aside.

4 Heat a grill until medium-hot. Generously brush one side of pizza dough with oil; grill, oiled side down, until underside is golden brown and top begins to bubble, 3 to 5 minutes. Quickly brush top with oil; flip crust. Top with some of the cheese and some of the clam mixture (about one-sixth of each). Grill until cheese is just melted, topping is hot, and crust is cooked through, 3 to 5 minutes more.

5 Slide pizza with a large spatula onto a cutting board. Drizzle with oil; sprinkle with more cheese. Season with salt and pepper; garnish with parsley. Repeat to make more pizzas.

from Pizza, Hot off the Grill

grilled pizzas with leeks, asparagus, and mushrooms
MAKES SIX 9-INCH PIZZAS

2 tablespoons extra-virgin olive oil, plus more for brushing

2 medium leeks, halved lengthwise, cut into thin half-moons, and rinsed well

8 ounces shiitake mushrooms, stemmed, caps cut into ¼-inch-thick slices

8 ounces thin asparagus, trimmed and cut into 1½-inch pieces

¼ cup dry white wine

1 tablespoon finely chopped fresh thyme, plus more for garnish

Coarse salt and freshly ground pepper

Pizza Dough (page 111)

4 ounces Taleggio or other soft cheese (such as Camembert or Brie), sliced

Truffle oil, for drizzling (optional)

1 Heat olive oil in a large skillet over medium heat until hot but not smoking. Add leeks; cook, stirring, until they begin to soften, about 5 minutes. Add mushrooms; cook until tender and juices have evaporated, about 4 minutes. Add the

asparagus and wine; cook until asparagus is bright green and wine has evaporated, about 2 minutes. Stir in thyme; season with salt and pepper. Set aside.

2 Heat a grill until medium-hot. Generously brush one side of pizza dough with olive oil; grill, oiled side down, until underside is golden brown and top begins to bubble, 3 to 5 minutes. Quickly brush top with olive oil; flip crust. Top with a thin layer of cheese and some of the asparagus mixture (about one-sixth of each). Grill until cheese is just melted, topping is hot, and crust is cooked through, 3 to 5 minutes more.

3 Slide pizza with a large spatula onto a cutting board. Season with salt and pepper. Sprinkle with thyme, and with a small amount of truffle oil, if desired. Repeat to make more pizzas.

from Pizza, Hot off the Grill

grilled pizzas with plums, prosciutto, goat cheese, and arugula
MAKES SIX 9-INCH PIZZAS | **PHOTO ON PAGE 149**

Cornmeal Pizza Dough (page 112)

Extra-virgin olive oil

8 ounces soft goat cheese, crumbled

4 ounces prosciutto, cut into thin strips

2 large plums or apricots, pitted and cut into thin wedges

2 bunches arugula, trimmed

Coarse salt and freshly ground pepper

1 Heat a grill until medium-hot. Generously brush one side of pizza dough with oil; grill, oiled side down, until underside is golden brown and top begins to bubble, 3 to 5 minutes. Quickly brush top with oil; flip crust. Top with some of the cheese, prosciutto, and plums (about one-sixth of each). Grill until toppings are hot and crust is cooked through, 3 to 5 minutes more.

2 Slide pizza with a large spatula onto a cutting board. Place arugula in a large bowl. Drizzle with oil; toss. Drizzle pizza with oil; top with some of the arugula (or serve it on the side). Season with salt and pepper. Repeat to make more pizzas.

from Pizza, Hot off the Grill

grilled pizzas with tomatoes, avocados, and pepper-Jack cheese

MAKES SIX 9-INCH PIZZAS | **PHOTO ON PAGE 149**

½ medium red onion, finely chopped

1 pint cherry or grape tomatoes, halved or quartered

2 avocados, preferably Hass, pitted and coarsely chopped

2 tablespoons extra-virgin olive oil, plus more for brushing

⅓ cup fresh lime juice (about 3 limes), plus lime wedges for serving (optional)

Coarse salt and freshly ground pepper

Cornmeal Pizza Dough (page 112)

4 ounces coarsely grated pepper-Jack cheese (about 1⅓ cups)

Sour cream, for garnish (optional)

1 Toss onion, tomatoes, and avocados with oil and lime juice in a medium bowl. Season with salt and pepper; set aside.

2 Heat a grill until medium-hot. Generously brush one side of pizza dough with oil; grill, oiled side down, until underside is golden brown and top begins to bubble, 3 to 5 minutes. Quickly brush top with oil; flip crust. Top with a layer (about one-sixth) of cheese. Grill until cheese is just melted and crust is cooked through, 3 to 5 minutes more.

3 Slide pizza with a large spatula onto a cutting board. Season with salt and pepper. Top with about one-sixth of avocado mixture. Dot with sour cream and serve with lime wedges, if desired. Repeat to make more pizzas.

from Pizza, Hot off the Grill

grilled quattro formaggi pizzas

MAKES SIX 9-INCH PIZZAS | **PHOTO ON PAGE 149**

This Italian classic typically showcases four cheeses (*quattro formaggi*) with different characteristics. For our rendition, we topped the crust with fontina (semifirm), mozzarella (soft and fresh), Gorgonzola (blue-veined), and Pecorino Romano (hard and aged).

Pizza Dough (page 111)

Extra-virgin olive oil

4 ounces coarsely grated fontina cheese (about 1⅓ cups)

1 pound fresh mozzarella, thinly sliced

4 ounces Gorgonzola cheese, crumbled (about 1 cup)

4 ounces Pecorino Romano, thinly shaved

Coarse salt and freshly ground pepper

1 Heat a grill until medium-hot. Generously brush one side of pizza dough with oil; grill, oiled side down, until underside is golden brown and top begins to bubble, 3 to 5 minutes.

Quickly brush top with oil; flip crust. Top with a thin layer of all four cheeses (about one-sixth of each). Grill until just melted and crust is cooked through, 3 to 5 minutes more.

2 Slide pizza with a large spatula onto a cutting board. Season with salt and pepper. Repeat to make more pizzas.

from Pizza, Hot off the Grill

DESSERTS

chocolate cheesecake

SERVES 8 TO 10

This cheesecake, once set, can be wrapped in plastic and refrigerated for up to three days. Let it stand at room temperature for twenty minutes before serving.

1 cup finely ground chocolate wafer cookies (5 ounces; about 22 cookies)

4 tablespoons unsalted butter, melted

1 cup plus 3 tablespoons sugar

8 ounces bittersweet chocolate, chopped

3 packages (8 ounces each) cream cheese, room temperature

Pinch of salt

¾ cup sour cream, room temperature

3 tablespoons Dutch-process unsweetened cocoa powder

2 teaspoons pure vanilla extract

3 large eggs, room temperature

1 Preheat oven to 350°F. Stir together cookie crumbs, butter, and 3 tablespoons sugar in a medium bowl. Press crumb mixture firmly onto bottom and up 1 inch on sides of a 9-inch springform pan. Bake until set, about 10 minutes. Transfer to a wire rack; let cool. Reduce oven temperature to 300°F.

2 Melt chocolate in a medium heatproof bowl set over a pan of simmering water, stirring, about 2 minutes. Let cool.

3 Put cream cheese in the bowl of an electric mixer fitted with the paddle attachment; mix on medium speed until fluffy, about 3 minutes. With mixer on low speed, add remaining cup sugar in a slow, steady stream. Add salt, and mix until combined. Add sour cream, cocoa, vanilla, and melted chocolate; mix until combined, scraping down sides of bowl as necessary. Add eggs, one at a time, mixing each until just combined (do not overmix). Pour filling over crust.

4 Bake until cheesecake is set but still slightly wobbly in center, 50 to 60 minutes. Let cool completely in pan on rack. Refrigerate, uncovered, at least 6 hours or overnight. Before unmolding, run a knife around edge of cake.

from Cheesecake

citrus-ricotta cheesecake

SERVES 8 TO 10

Fresh ricotta cheese, which is creamier than mass-produced ricotta, is crucial to this cake's light texture. Look for it at gourmet or Italian markets. The cheesecake, once set, can be wrapped in plastic and refrigerated for up to three days. Let it stand at room temperature for twenty minutes before serving.

2 cups finely ground ladyfinger cookies (7 ounces)

8 tablespoons (1 stick) unsalted butter, melted

¾ cup sugar

1 envelope (¼ ounce; 1 tablespoon) unflavored gelatin

1 cup heavy cream, chilled

2 large eggs, separated, room temperature

½ vanilla bean, halved lengthwise

1 pound 5 ounces fresh ricotta cheese

1 tablespoon freshly grated orange zest

1 tablespoon freshly grated lemon zest plus 1 tablespoon fresh lemon juice

Pinch of salt

Citrus-Vanilla Compote (recipe follows)

1 Stir together cookie crumbs, melted butter, and ¼ cup sugar in a medium bowl. Press crumb mixture firmly onto bottom and up 1 inch on sides of an 8-inch square or 9-inch round springform pan; set aside.

2 Sprinkle gelatin over ¼ cup warm water in a small bowl. Let stand 7 minutes to soften. Stir until gelatin is dissolved, and set aside. Beat cream with an electric mixer until stiff peaks form; set aside.

3 Put egg yolks and remaining ½ cup sugar in a medium bowl. Scrape in vanilla seeds; whisk until mixture is pale and thick, about 2 minutes. Add ricotta, zests, lemon juice, salt, and gelatin mixture; gently stir until smooth. Set aside.

4 Beat egg whites in a clean mixing bowl until they hold stiff peaks. Gently fold whipped cream with a rubber spatula into ricotta mixture, and then fold in whites.

5 Pour filling over crust. Refrigerate, uncovered, at least 3 hours or overnight. Before unmolding, run a knife around edge of cake. Serve with citrus-vanilla compote.

Note: Raw eggs should not be used in food prepared for pregnant women, babies, young children, the elderly, or anyone whose health is compromised.

from Cheesecake

citrus-vanilla compote

MAKES 2 CUPS

1 red or pink grapefruit

1 navel orange

¼ cup sugar

½ vanilla bean, halved lengthwise

Pinch of salt

1 Cut peels from citrus; cut peels into very thin strips. Set aside. Cut pith from citrus. Working over a bowl to catch fruit and juices, cut fruit segments from membranes. Squeeze juice from membranes into bowl. Pour ¼ cup juice through a fine sieve into a small bowl; set aside.

2 Bring a medium saucepan of water to a boil. Add peels, and boil 1 minute. Drain; set aside. Bring sugar, ¼ cup water, and vanilla bean to a boil in a clean medium saucepan over medium-high heat, stirring until sugar is dissolved. Reduce heat to low. Add reserved juice, peels, and the salt; cook 2 minutes. Let cool completely.

3 Discard vanilla bean. Toss syrup with reserved fruit. If not serving immediately, refrigerate, covered, up to 2 days.

no-bake cheesecake

SERVES 10 TO 12

We used gingersnaps for a slightly spicy crust. Graham crackers, butter cookies, or chocolate wafer cookies would all make fine substitutes.

1½ cups finely ground cookies (8 ounces)

4 tablespoons unsalted butter, melted

1 cup plus 3 tablespoons sugar

2 packages (8 ounces each) cream cheese, room temperature

3 tablespoons fresh lemon juice

½ cup heavy cream, chilled

1 Stir together cookie crumbs, melted butter, and 3 tablespoons sugar in a medium bowl. Press crumb mixture firmly onto bottom of a 9-inch springform pan.

2 Put cream cheese in the bowl of an electric mixer fitted with the paddle attachment; mix on medium speed until fluffy, about 3 minutes. With mixer on low speed, add remaining cup sugar in a slow, steady stream. Mix in lemon juice.

3 Beat cream in a clean mixing bowl until stiff peaks form. Gently fold the whipped cream with a rubber spatula into cream cheese filling. Pour over crust. Freeze 1 hour. Refrigerate until ready to serve, at least 30 minutes.

from Cheesecake

frozen espresso cheesecake

MAKES ONE 10-BY-5-INCH CAKE; SERVES 10

Store any leftover cake in the freezer; before serving, let it soften slightly in the refrigerator for several minutes.

1½ cups finely ground chocolate wafer cookies
   (8 ounces; about 35 cookies)

 4 tablespoons unsalted butter, melted

½ cup plus 2 tablespoons sugar

 4 large egg yolks, room temperature

4½ teaspoons good-quality instant espresso powder
   (such as Medaglia d'Oro)

   Pinch of salt

1½ pounds mascarpone cheese, room temperature

1½ teaspoons pure vanilla extract

12 ounces hard torrone (Italian nougat), cut into ¼-inch pieces

½ cup heavy cream, chilled

1 Stir together cookie crumbs, melted butter, and 3 tablespoons sugar in a medium bowl; set aside.

2 Put egg yolks, ¼ cup sugar, the espresso, and salt in the heatproof bowl of an electric mixer. Set bowl over a pan of simmering water; whisk until thick, about 2 minutes. Transfer bowl to an electric mixer fitted with the whisk attachment; beat on medium speed 2 minutes. Stir in mascarpone and vanilla by hand until smooth. Stir in torrone; set aside.

3 Beat cream with remaining 3 tablespoons sugar in a clean mixing bowl until soft peaks form. Fold the whipped cream with a rubber spatula into mascarpone mixture. Refrigerate.

4 Line a 10-by-5-by-3-inch loaf pan with plastic wrap and parchment paper, leaving overhang on sides. Pour one-third of mascarpone mixture into lined pan; even layer with an offset spatula. Evenly top with half of the crumb mixture; press crumbs gently. Repeat to make a second layer of mascarpone mixture and crumbs. Top with remaining mascarpone mixture. Loosely fold over parchment and plastic wrap. Freeze at least 3 hours or overnight.

5 To serve, let cake stand at room temperature 10 minutes. Set loaf pan in a larger pan; pour cold water into pan to reach three-quarters up sides of loaf pan. Let stand 10 seconds. Holding parchment paper, lift out cake. Invert onto a plate, and peel off plastic and parchment. Let stand 10 minutes more before serving.

from Cheesecake

New York–style cheesecake

SERVES 10 TO 12 | **PHOTO ON PAGE 158**

This cheesecake, once set, can be wrapped in plastic and refrigerated for up to three days. Let it stand at room temperature for twenty minutes before serving.

½ cup all-purpose flour, plus more for dusting

   Cheesecake-Crust Dough (recipe follows)

 7 packages (8 ounces each) cream cheese, room temperature

2¼ cups sugar

 1 cup sour cream, room temperature

1½ teaspoons pure vanilla extract

 5 large eggs, room temperature

   Unsalted butter, softened, for pan

   Boiling water, for roasting pan

1 Preheat oven to 350°F. On a lightly floured surface, roll out cheesecake-crust dough slightly thicker than ⅛ inch. Place the base of a 10-inch springform pan on top as a guide, then cut out the dough. Slide dough onto the base.

2 Attach sides to pan; wrap exterior of pan (including base) in a double layer of foil. Freeze dough in pan 15 minutes.

3 Transfer pan to a baking sheet. Bake dough until golden, about 18 minutes. Transfer pan to a wire rack, and let crust cool. Leave oven on.

4 Put cream cheese in the bowl of an electric mixer fitted with the paddle attachment; mix on medium speed until fluffy, about 3 minutes.

5 Stir together sugar and flour in a large bowl. With mixer on low speed, add sugar mixture to cream-cheese mixture in a slow, steady stream; mix until smooth. Add sour cream and vanilla, and mix until smooth, scraping down sides of bowl as necessary. Add eggs, one at a time, mixing each until just combined (do not overmix).

6 Butter sides of cake pan. Pour cream cheese filling over crust. Set pan inside a large, shallow roasting pan. Transfer to oven. Carefully pour boiling water into roasting pan to reach halfway up sides of cake pan.

7 Bake 45 minutes; reduce oven temperature to 325°F. Continue to bake until cake is golden and set but still slightly wobbly in center, about 30 minutes more. Turn oven off; leave cake in oven with door slightly ajar 1 hour.

8 Transfer cake pan to rack; let cake cool completely. Refrigerate, uncovered, at least 6 hours or overnight. Before unmolding, run a knife around edge of cake.

from Cheesecake

cheesecake-crust dough

MAKES ENOUGH FOR ONE 10-INCH CRUST

8 tablespoons (1 stick) unsalted butter, room temperature
¼ cup sugar
1 large egg yolk
1 teaspoon pure vanilla extract
¾ cup all-purpose flour
  Pinch of salt

1 Put butter and sugar in the bowl of an electric mixer fitted with the paddle attachment; cream on medium speed until pale and fluffy, 3 to 4 minutes. Mix in egg yolk and vanilla. Add flour and salt; mix just until a dough forms.

2 Shape dough into a disk, and wrap in plastic wrap; refrigerate at least 30 minutes or up to 1 day.

raspberry-swirl cheesecake

SERVES 8 TO 10 | **PHOTO ON PAGE 159**

The cheesecake, once set, can be wrapped in plastic and refrigerated for up to three days. Let stand at room temperature for twenty minutes before serving.

1 cup finely ground graham crackers
  (5 ounces; about 8 sheets)
2 tablespoons unsalted butter, melted
1¾ cups sugar
6 ounces raspberries (about 1½ cups)
4 packages (8 ounces each) cream cheese,
  room temperature
  Pinch of salt
1 teaspoon pure vanilla extract
4 large eggs, room temperature
  Boiling water, for roasting pan

1 Preheat oven to 350°F. Wrap exterior of a 9-inch spring-form pan (including base) in a double layer of foil; set aside.

2 Stir together cracker crumbs, melted butter, and 2 tablespoons sugar in a medium bowl. Press crumb mixture firmly onto bottom of pan. Bake until set, about 10 minutes. Let cool in pan on a wire rack. Reduce oven temperature to 325°F.

3 Process raspberries in a food processor until smooth, about 30 seconds. Pass purée through a fine sieve into a bowl; discard solids. Whisk in 2 tablespoons sugar; set aside.

4 Put cream cheese in the bowl of an electric mixer fitted with the paddle attachment; mix on medium speed until fluffy, about 3 minutes. With mixer on low speed, add remaining 1½ cups sugar in a slow, steady stream. Add the salt

and vanilla, and mix until well combined, scraping down sides of bowl as necessary. Add eggs, one at a time, mixing each until just combined (do not overmix). Pour cream cheese filling over crust.

5 Drop raspberry sauce by the teaspoon in dots on top. With a wooden skewer or toothpick, swirl sauce into filling.

6 Set cake pan inside a large, shallow roasting pan. Transfer to oven. Carefully pour boiling water into roasting pan to reach halfway up sides of cake pan. Bake until cake is set but still slightly wobbly in center, 60 to 65 minutes.

7 Transfer cake pan to rack; let cake cool completely. Refrigerate, uncovered, at least 6 hours or overnight. Before unmolding, run a knife around edge of cake.

from Cheesecake

individual raspberry-swirl cheesecakes variation

MAKES 2 DOZEN | **PHOTO ON PAGE 159**

Use the ingredients listed for our Raspberry-Swirl Cheesecake (above), but reduce the amount of raspberries to four ounces (about one cup) and the sugar to four and a half teaspoons in step three.

1 Preheat oven to 325°F. Place paper liners in the cups of two standard 12-cup muffin tins, and set aside.

2 Follow step 2 of the Raspberry-Swirl Cheesecake recipe, pressing 1 tablespoon of the crumb mixture firmly onto the bottom of each cup in the muffin tin. Bake until set, about 5 minutes. Let cool in tins on a wire rack. Leave oven on.

3 Follow step 3 of the recipe, using 4 ounces raspberries; at the end, whisk 4½ teaspoons sugar into strained purée.

4 Follow step 4, mixing in remaining 1½ cups sugar; at the end, spoon 3 tablespoons filling into each cup.

5 Drop raspberry sauce by the ½ teaspoon in dots over cakes. With a wooden skewer or toothpick, swirl sauce into filling.

6 Bake until set, 10 to 12 minutes. Let cool completely in tins on a wire rack. Refrigerate, uncovered, at least 1 hour or overnight.

coconut cream bars

MAKES 2 DOZEN | **PHOTO ON PAGE 157**

The custard-filled crust can be refrigerated for up to two days. Wait until just before serving to cut the dessert into bars; if crumbs and filling stick to the knife, wipe the blade clean between slices. Then decorate each bar with whipped cream. If you don't have a pastry bag, use a resealable plastic bag with a corner snipped off.

2½ cups sweetened flaked coconut

3 boxes (5.3 ounces each) shortbread cookies, coarsely broken

1 cup plus 2 tablespoons granulated sugar

6 tablespoons cornstarch

½ teaspoon salt

4½ cups whole milk

6 large egg yolks

6 tablespoons cold unsalted butter, cut into small pieces

1½ cups heavy cream

3 tablespoons confectioners' sugar

1 Preheat oven to 350°F. Spread out coconut in an even layer on a rimmed baking sheet. Toast, stirring once or twice, until golden, 8 to 10 minutes. Let cool completely.

2 Process cookies and ½ cup coconut in a food processor until finely ground and mixture begins to clump together, about 2 minutes. Transfer mixture to a 9-by-13-inch rimmed baking sheet, and press into an even layer on bottom. Bake until golden and firm to the touch, 12 to 15 minutes. Let cool on sheet on a wire rack.

3 Whisk together the granulated sugar, cornstarch, and salt in a large saucepan. Whisk in milk and egg yolks. Cook over medium heat, whisking constantly, until mixture comes to a boil, 5 to 6 minutes. Continue to cook, whisking constantly, until thickened, about 3 minutes more. Remove from heat. Add butter, whisking until combined. Stir in 1½ cups coconut.

4 Spoon custard onto cooled crust; smooth top with an offset spatula. Press plastic wrap directly onto surface, to prevent a skin from forming. Refrigerate until set, about 3 hours.

5 Beat cream and confectioners' sugar in a large chilled stainless-steel bowl until stiff peaks form. Set aside.

6 Cut custard-filled crust into 24 bars (each about 3 by 1½ inches). Transfer to a platter. Spoon whipped cream into a pastry bag fitted with a medium star tip. Beginning at one corner, pipe a zigzag pattern over each bar. Sprinkle bars with remaining ½ cup coconut.

from Dessert of the Month

orange-lime mousse

SERVES 4 | **PHOTO ON PAGE 157**

4 large egg yolks, plus 1 large egg

¾ cup plus 2 tablespoons sugar

¼ cup fresh orange juice

¼ cup fresh lime juice (2 to 3 limes)

6 tablespoons unsalted butter

1 cup heavy cream, chilled

1 teaspoon ground cinnamon

1 lime, halved lengthwise and thinly sliced into half-moons

1 navel orange, halved lengthwise and thinly sliced into half-moons

1 Make citrus curd: Prepare an ice-water bath, and set aside. Heat egg yolks, egg, ¾ cup sugar, and juices in a medium saucepan over medium heat, whisking constantly (be sure to reach sides and bottom of pan) until thickened, 5 to 7 minutes. Remove from heat.

2 Whisk in butter 1 tablespoon at a time. Set pan in ice-water bath; whisk until cool, about 5 minutes. Pass curd through a sieve into a medium bowl. Press plastic wrap directly onto surface to prevent a skin from forming. Refrigerate until set, 30 to 45 minutes. Whisk cream and remaining 2 tablespoons sugar until stiff peaks form; refrigerate until ready to serve.

3 Whisk one-third of whipped cream into curd. Gently fold in remaining whipped cream. Divide among serving bowls, and refrigerate until ready to serve. Dust mousse with cinnamon, and garnish with citrus.

from What's for Dinner?

....

MISCELLANEOUS

....

pea-shoot pesto

MAKES 1¼ CUPS

1 small garlic clove, smashed

¼ cup cilantro leaves

4 ounces pea shoots, coarsely chopped

3 tablespoons fresh lime juice (about 2 limes)

¼ cup extra-virgin olive oil

¾ cup finely grated Parmesan cheese

1½ teaspoons coarse salt

¼ teaspoon freshly ground pepper

Purée all ingredients in a blender. Refrigerate in an airtight container up to 1 week.

from Pea Shoots

June

beet soup with Indian spices

MAKES ABOUT 9 CUPS; SERVES 6

Buying beets with the greens attached—as required for this recipe—is a sure way to know they're fresh. Beets are often cooked before they're peeled or cut to keep nutrients intact. Here, the prep work is done first without sacrifice: The juices that result make up the nutritious broth and give the soup its deep flavor and color.

5 or 6 medium red beets with greens (about 2½ pounds with greens), stems and greens cut off and reserved

2 teaspoons canola oil

1 medium onion, halved lengthwise and cut into thin half-moons

1 tablespoon minced garlic

1½ teaspoons ground cumin

1 teaspoon ground coriander

Pinch of cayenne pepper (or to taste)

⅛ teaspoon freshly ground pepper

3 plum tomatoes, seeded and cut into ¼-inch dice (about 1¼ cups)

¾ teaspoon coarse salt

1¾ cups homemade or low-sodium store-bought chicken stock

⅓ cup low-fat yogurt

1   Cut beet greens into thin strips, and stems into ¼-inch pieces; set both aside. Peel beets with a vegetable peeler; cut into ¼-inch-thick matchsticks. Set aside.

2   Heat oil in a large saucepan over medium heat until hot but not smoking. Add onion; cook, stirring occasionally, until softened and just browned, about 7 minutes. Add garlic; cook until fragrant, about 1 minute. Add cumin, coriander, cayenne, and pepper; cook, stirring, until fragrant, about 1 minute.

3   Add tomatoes and salt; cook, scraping up any browned bits from the bottom of the pan, until juices are released, about 2 minutes. Add stock and 4½ cups water (for a thinner consistency, add up to 5 cups water); bring to a boil. Add beets and stems. Reduce heat, and simmer until beets are tender, about 35 minutes.

4   Add greens; cook until just tender, about 5 minutes. Divide soup among six bowls; divide yogurt among servings.

PER SERVING: 147 CALORIES, 2 G FAT, 1 MG CHOLESTEROL, 24 G CARBOHYDRATE, 619 MG SODIUM, 5 G PROTEIN, 7 G FIBER

from Fit to Eat: Beets

grilled-vegetable gazpacho with shrimp

SERVES 4

If using wooden skewers, soak them in water for thirty minutes before grilling.

1 medium onion, halved crosswise

1 green bell pepper, halved lengthwise

2 yellow bell peppers, halved lengthwise

1½ pounds vine-ripened tomatoes, halved

4 garlic cloves (unpeeled)

¼ cup olive oil

Coarse salt and freshly ground pepper

1 fresh serrano chile

1 English (hothouse) cucumber, peeled and cut into ½-inch cubes

1 pound large shrimp, peeled and deveined

⅓ cup chopped cilantro

3 tablespoons fresh lime juice, plus lime wedges for garnish (3 to 4 limes total)

1   Heat a grill until medium-hot. Brush onion, bell peppers, tomatoes, and garlic with some of the oil; season with salt and pepper. Wrap garlic in foil. Grill onion, peppers, chile, and garlic, turning once, until soft and charred, 12 to 15 minutes; set aside. Grill tomatoes, turning once, until pale and skins peel, about 6 minutes. Transfer to a food processor; set aside. When cool enough to handle, peel garlic; cut peppers and onion into ½-inch pieces. Mince garlic and chile. Transfer all but tomatoes to a large bowl; add cucumber.

2   Thread shrimp onto skewers. Brush with oil, and season with salt and pepper. Grill, turning once, until shrimp are pink and cooked through, 6 to 8 minutes.

3   Pulse tomatoes until slightly chunky; stir into vegetable mixture. Stir in cilantro, lime juice, shrimp, and 1 tablespoon salt; season with pepper. Divide soup among four bowls, and garnish servings with lime wedges.

from Shrimp

grilled vegetables
with herb vinaigrette

SERVES 10

Small eggplants, often labeled "Italian" or "Asian," have fewer seeds than large eggplants and are good for grilling. We used small purple Italian eggplants and graffiti eggplants, named for their eye-catching purple-and-white striped skin. We used two kinds of radicchio: Verona, which has darker-than-usual garnet leaves, and Treviso, a variety with long, slender leaves. Grilling mellows radicchio's bitterness.

4 medium red beets (about 1 pound without greens), peeled and cut into ¼-inch-thick rounds

⅓ cup best-quality extra-virgin olive oil

Coarse salt

5 Italian or Asian eggplants, halved lengthwise or cut into thirds if large

6 baby zucchini (each about 6 inches long), some with blossoms attached (optional), halved lengthwise

6 baby yellow summer squash (each about 6 inches long), some with blossoms attached (optional), halved lengthwise

3 yellow bell peppers, sides cut off to yield about 12 slices total

1 pound assorted radicchio, such as Verona and Treviso, heads halved lengthwise or quartered if large

Herb Vinaigrette (recipe follows)

1 Heat a grill or grill pan until medium-hot. Meanwhile, bring a large saucepan of water to a boil. Add beets; boil until just tender, about 5 minutes. Drain; pat dry with paper towels.

2 Toss beets with 1 tablespoon oil in a medium bowl; season with salt, and set aside. Toss eggplants, zucchini, summer squash, bell peppers, and radicchio with remaining ¼ cup plus 1 teaspoon oil in a large bowl; season with salt.

3 Grill all vegetables, turning once, until tender and golden brown, 4 to 8 minutes (cooking time will vary among vegetables). Arrange vegetables on a large platter. Serve warm or at room temperature; just before serving, spoon vinaigrette on top, and gently toss.

from Life (and Lunch) Among the Roses

herb vinaigrette

MAKES 3 CUPS

1¼ cups plus 1 tablespoon best-quality extra-virgin olive oil

4 large shallots, finely chopped (about ½ cup)

3 garlic cloves, finely chopped

¼ cup drained capers, rinsed

6 tablespoons freshly grated lemon zest plus 3 tablespoons fresh lemon juice (about 6 lemons total)

2 cups finely chopped fresh flat-leaf parsley (about 4 ounces)

1 cup finely chopped fresh basil

¼ cup plus 2 tablespoons finely chopped fresh mint

Coarse salt and freshly ground pepper

½ cup balsamic vinegar

1 tablespoon Dijon mustard

1 Heat 3 tablespoons oil in a medium skillet over medium heat until hot but not smoking. Add shallots and garlic; cook, stirring, until softened, about 2 minutes. Transfer to a medium bowl; let cool. Stir in capers, zest, parsley, basil, and mint. Season with salt and pepper. Cover with plastic.

2 Blend vinegar, mustard, and lemon juice, plus salt and pepper to taste, in a blender until combined. With blender running, pour in remaining 1 cup plus 2 tablespoons oil in a slow, steady stream; blend until emulsified. Just before serving, stir vinaigrette into shallot mixture.

prosciutto crostini and
fresh figs with Gorgonzola

MAKES 20 OF EACH HORS D'OEUVRE | **PHOTO ON PAGE 140**

½ baguette

2 tablespoons extra-virgin olive oil

10 ounces Gorgonzola dolce, room temperature

¼ pound prosciutto, very thinly sliced

Fresh lemon thyme or small, fresh basil leaves, for garnish

10 fresh figs, halved lengthwise

Fresh tarragon, for garnish

1 Preheat broiler. Cut baguette into 20 slices (each about ¼ inch thick); transfer to a baking sheet. Brush tops with oil. Broil until golden, 1 to 2 minutes. When bread is cool enough to handle, spread 1 teaspoon cheese onto each round. Tear prosciutto into bite-size pieces, and arrange a piece next to cheese on each round; garnish with lemon thyme.

2 Spoon about 1 teaspoon cheese onto each fig half, and garnish with tarragon.

from Life (and Lunch) Among the Roses

Vietnamese summer rolls

MAKES 1 DOZEN

12 round rice-paper wrappers (8 inches in diameter)
36 large shrimp, peeled and deveined, boiled until cooked through, and split horizontally
3 ounces thin dried rice-stick noodles, prepared according to package instructions
2 medium carrots, peeled into ribbons
4 cups mâche
2 cups fresh mint leaves
2 cups cilantro leaves
   Sweet and Sour Dipping Sauce (recipe follows)

1 Soak a wrapper in warm water 30 seconds; immediately lay it flat on a work surface. Lay 6 shrimp halves, cut sides up, on bottom third, leaving a ½-inch border; top with 2 tablespoons each noodles, carrots, mâche, mint, and cilantro.

2 Fold bottom of wrapper over fillings; roll over once, tuck in sides, and roll. Cut in half; cover with a damp paper towel. Repeat to make remaining rolls. Serve with dipping sauce.

from Shrimp

sweet and sour dipping sauce

MAKES ABOUT ½ CUP

1 teaspoon crushed red-pepper flakes
¼ cup fresh lime juice (about 2 limes)
1 tablespoon minced garlic
3 tablespoons sugar
¼ cup Asian fish sauce (such as nam pla)

Soak red-pepper flakes in lime juice 4 minutes. Add the garlic, sugar, and fish sauce; stir until sugar is dissolved.

warm goat-cheese toasts

MAKES 16 | PHOTO ON PAGE 144

½ baguette, cut into 16 slices (each about ½ inch thick)
1 large log (11 ounces) soft goat cheese
   Olive oil, for drizzling
1 jar (6 ounces) best-quality store-bought pesto

1 Preheat oven to 425°F. Space baguette slices evenly on a baking sheet. Cut cheese into 16 rounds, placing them atop slices. (If cheese crumbles, press it firmly onto bread.)

2 Drizzle oil over cheese (let it drip onto crusts). Bake until undersides of bread are golden brown and cheese begins to brown, 10 to 15 minutes. Top each toast with ½ teaspoon pesto.

from Easy Entertaining: A French Lunch

SALADS AND SIDE DISHES

arugula salad

SERVES 4 | PHOTO ON PAGE 147

2 teaspoons fresh lemon juice
½ teaspoon coarse salt
   Freshly ground pepper
2 teaspoons extra-virgin olive oil
3 cups baby arugula (about 4 ounces)
1 small red onion, halved and cut into paper-thin half-moons

Put lemon juice and salt in a medium bowl; season with pepper. Whisking constantly, pour in oil in a slow, steady stream; whisk until emulsified. Add arugula and onion; toss.

from Quiche

avocado and orange salad

SERVES 10

3 firm, ripe avocados (preferably Hass)
2 heads Boston lettuce, leaves separated
4 navel oranges, peel and pith removed and flesh cut into ¼-inch-thick rounds (halve if large)
   Coarse salt
½ cup loosely packed fresh mint leaves
   Orange-Muscatel Vinaigrette (recipe follows)

Halve avocados lengthwise; pit and peel, keeping the halves intact. Cut each half lengthwise into 4 slices. Arrange lettuce, oranges, and avocados on a platter. Season with salt; garnish with mint. Serve immediately, with vinaigrette on the side.

from Life (and Lunch) Among the Roses

orange-muscatel vinaigrette

MAKES ABOUT 1 CUP

¼ cup muscatel-wine vinegar or white balsamic vinegar
2 tablespoons fresh orange juice
1 teaspoon Dijon mustard
1 garlic clove, minced
   Coarse salt and freshly ground pepper
¾ cup best-quality extra-virgin olive oil

Whisk together vinegar, orange juice, mustard, and garlic in a small bowl; season with salt and pepper. Whisking constantly, pour in oil in a slow, steady stream; whisk until emulsified. If not using immediately, refrigerate vinaigrette, covered, up to 1 day.

beet and brown rice salad
with goat cheese

SERVES 6

1 cup brown basmati or other brown rice

1 bay leaf

Coarse salt

¼ cup pine nuts

2 teaspoons olive oil

2 small onions, finely chopped

1 tablespoon minced garlic

4 medium red beets (about 1 pound without greens), peeled and cut into ½-inch cubes

Freshly ground pepper

2 teaspoons freshly grated lemon zest

¼ cup chopped fresh flat-leaf parsley, plus more for garnish

2 ounces soft goat cheese, crumbled (about ¾ cup)

1 Bring 1½ cups water to a boil in a small saucepan. Stir in rice, bay leaf, and ½ teaspoon salt; cover. Reduce heat to low; simmer 30 minutes. Remove from heat; let stand, covered.

2 Meanwhile, toast pine nuts in oil in a 10-inch skillet over medium heat. Cook, stirring, until nuts are just browned, about 5 minutes. Transfer nuts with a slotted spoon to a bowl.

3 Reduce heat to medium-low; add onions and garlic to skillet. Cook, stirring occasionally, until onions are translucent, about 8 minutes. Add beets and 1 teaspoon salt; season with pepper. Cover skillet; cook, stirring occasionally, until beets are tender, about 25 minutes (if beets stick to skillet, add up to ¼ cup water).

4 Remove bay leaf from rice. Stir rice, half of the pine nuts, the lemon zest, and parsley into beet mixture. Transfer to a platter. Top with remaining pine nuts and the goat cheese. Garnish with parsley. Serve warm or at room temperature.

PER SERVING: 230 CALORIES, 8 G FAT, 7 MG CHOLESTEROL, 33 G CARBOHYDRATE, 591 MG SODIUM, 7 G PROTEIN, 4 G FIBER

from Fit to Eat: Beets

ginger pickled beets

MAKES 4 CUPS

5 or 6 medium red or golden beets (about 1½ pounds without greens), tails and about 1 inch of stems left intact

½ cup thinly sliced, peeled fresh ginger (about 1½ ounces)

1½ cups rice-wine vinegar (not seasoned)

¼ cup plus 1 tablespoon sugar

1 teaspoon coarse salt

1 Prepare an ice-water bath; set aside. Cover beets with cold water by 2 inches in a large saucepan. Bring to a boil; reduce heat. Simmer beets until tender when pierced with the tip of a knife, about 30 minutes. Transfer beets with a slotted spoon to ice-water bath. Discard cooking liquid. Trim beets and rub off skins with paper towels, or peel beets with a paring knife. Cut beets into very thin rounds, and transfer to a large bowl.

2 Bring ginger, vinegar, sugar, and salt to a boil in a medium saucepan, stirring until sugar is dissolved. Pour liquid over beets; stir. Let stand until completely cool, at least 1 hour. Transfer to an airtight container; refrigerate up to 1 month.

PER SERVING (½ CUP): 91 CALORIES, 0 G FAT, 0 MG CHOLESTEROL, 33 G CARBOHYDRATE, 309 MG SODIUM, 1 G PROTEIN, 3 G FIBER

from Fit to Eat: Beets

cabbage and radish slaw
with peanut dressing

SERVES 8 TO 10 | **PHOTO ON PAGE 154**

The peanut dressing can be made ahead and refrigerated in an airtight container up to four days; bring it to room temperature before using. You can let this slaw stand for up to one hour after dressing it; if you do so, stir in the peanuts and red radishes just before serving so they stay crunchy.

1 tablespoon finely chopped peeled fresh ginger

¼ cup coarsely chopped shallot

¼ cup plus 1 tablespoon creamy peanut butter

½ cup rice-wine vinegar (not seasoned)

3 tablespoons soy sauce

3 tablespoons packed dark-brown sugar

¼ cup canola oil

1 small green cabbage (about 1¾ pounds), finely shredded

1 medium daikon radish, cut into ⅛-inch-thick matchsticks

16 red radishes, halved lengthwise and cut into thin half-moons

4 scallions, cut on the diagonal into long, thin slices

½ cup dry-roasted peanuts

1 Blend ginger, shallot, peanut butter, vinegar, soy sauce, sugar, and oil in a blender until smooth; set aside.

2 Put cabbage, daikon radish, red radishes, scallions, and peanuts in a large serving bowl. Pour in peanut dressing, and toss thoroughly to combine.

from Chop and Serve Slaws

carrot slaw with golden raisins

SERVES 4 TO 6 | **PHOTO ON PAGE 155**

Dress the slaw and add the cilantro just before serving.

1 teaspoon cumin seeds

1½ pounds carrots, coarsely grated (about 12 medium carrots)

¼ cup golden raisins

¼ cup fresh orange juice

4 teaspoons fresh lemon juice

¼ cup extra-virgin olive oil

Coarse salt

Pinch of cayenne pepper (optional)

½ cup loosely packed cilantro

1 Toast cumin seeds in a small skillet over medium heat, tossing occasionally, until fragrant and a shade darker, about 2 minutes. Lightly crush seeds using a mortar and pestle, or the flat side of a large knife. Set seeds aside.

2 Toss carrots, raisins, and orange and lemon juices together in a medium bowl. Add oil and cumin seeds; season with salt. Add cayenne, if desired; toss in cilantro.

from Chop and Serve Slaws

classic creamy coleslaw

SERVES 6 TO 8

1 tablespoon Dijon mustard

1 tablespoon cider vinegar

1 tablespoon fresh lemon juice

1 tablespoon sugar

1 teaspoon coarse salt

½ cup mayonnaise

¼ cup sour cream

1 small green cabbage (about 1¾ pounds), finely shredded

2 medium carrots, cut into ⅛-inch-thick matchsticks or coarsely grated

½ small onion, coarsely grated (optional)

1 Whisk together mustard, vinegar, lemon juice, sugar, salt, mayonnaise, and sour cream in a small bowl. Refrigerate dressing, covered, until ready to use, or up to 2 days.

2 Put cabbage, carrots, and onion (if desired) in a large bowl. Pour in dressing, and toss thoroughly. Refrigerate, covered, until slaw begins to soften, 1 to 2 hours. If not using immediately, refrigerate, covered, up to 2 days. Just before serving, toss coleslaw again.

from Chop and Serve Slaws

grilled asparagus with beet and cucumber relish

SERVES 4

If you use two beets of different sizes, keep in mind that their cooking times may vary. Take each out of the oven as it's ready (knife-tender).

2 medium red beets (about ½ pound without greens), tails and about 1 inch of stems left intact

1 cup diced (¼-inch pieces) peeled English (hothouse) cucumber

1 teaspoon finely chopped shallot

2 teaspoons balsamic vinegar

2 teaspoons extra-virgin olive oil

Coarse salt

1 bunch asparagus, trimmed and peeled

½ cup loosely packed fresh basil leaves

1 Preheat oven to 400°F. Wrap each beet in foil. Roast until tender when pierced with the tip of a knife, 45 to 60 minutes. When cool enough to handle, trim beets and rub off skins with paper towels, or peel beets with a paring knife.

2 Cut beets into ¼-inch dice, and transfer to a medium bowl. Stir in cucumber, shallot, vinegar, 1 teaspoon oil, and ¼ teaspoon salt. Refrigerate until ready to use, up to 2 hours.

3 Heat a grill or grill pan until hot. Toss asparagus with remaining teaspoon oil and ½ teaspoon salt in a large bowl. Grill asparagus, turning once, until tender, 4 to 8 minutes (cooking time will vary depending on thickness of spears).

4 Arrange asparagus on a platter, and let cool completely. Finely chop basil, and stir into beet relish. Using a slotted spoon, spoon beet relish over asparagus.

PER SERVING: 63 CALORIES, 3 G FAT, 0 MG CHOLESTEROL, 9 G CARBOHYDRATE, 406 MG SODIUM, 3 G PROTEIN, 3 G FIBER

from Fit to Eat: Beets

fennel, red onion, and parsley salad

SERVES 4

1 cup loosely packed fresh flat-leaf parsley leaves

1 medium fennel bulb, trimmed, halved lengthwise, and thinly sliced

1 small red onion, halved lengthwise and thinly sliced into half-moons

3 tablespoons fresh lemon juice

1 tablespoon extra-virgin olive oil

½ teaspoon celery seeds

Coarse salt and freshly ground pepper

1   Prepare a large ice-water bath. Put parsley, fennel, and onion in a colander; set in ice-water bath. Soak 10 minutes.

2   Drain, and transfer to a salad spinner. Spin until dry, and transfer to a serving bowl. Add lemon juice, oil, and celery seeds; toss to combine. Season with salt and pepper.

from What's for Dinner?

Italian potato salad

SERVES 10

8 large eggs

3 pounds small red potatoes

Coarse salt

2 to 3 tablespoons muscatel-wine vinegar or white balsamic vinegar

1 cup loosely packed fresh flat-leaf parsley leaves, coarsely chopped

1 medium red onion, coarsely chopped (about ¾ cup)

¼ cup best-quality extra-virgin olive oil

Freshly ground pepper

1   Prepare an ice-water bath; set aside. Cover eggs with water in a medium saucepan; bring to a full boil. After 1 minute, cover pan, and turn off heat. Let stand 8 minutes. Rinse eggs, and transfer to ice-water bath.

2   Cover the potatoes with water by 1 inch in a large saucepan. Bring to a boil; add salt. Simmer until just tender, about 15 minutes (do not overcook). Drain potatoes; let cool slightly. Halve lengthwise.

3   Transfer potatoes to a medium bowl. Add vinegar to taste; gently toss. Stir in parsley and onion. Gently tossing, pour in oil in a slow, steady stream; toss until incorporated. Season with salt and pepper. Just before serving, peel and quarter eggs, and arrange on top of salad.

from Life (and Lunch) Among the Roses

red and green cabbage slaw with bacon

SERVES 6 TO 8

This slaw can be made up to a day ahead and refrigerated. Chill the cooked bacon separately, wrapped in paper towels, in a resealable plastic bag; reheat it on a baking sheet in a 325 degree oven until it's warm and crisp.

½ medium red cabbage (about 1 pound), finely shredded

¼ medium green cabbage (about ½ pound), finely shredded

½ pound smoked bacon (about 8 strips), cut into ¼-inch pieces

1 teaspoon caraway seeds (optional)

3 tablespoons olive oil

1 garlic clove, minced

¼ cup plus 3 tablespoons cider vinegar

2 teaspoons sugar

2½ teaspoons coarse salt

Freshly ground pepper

1 Granny Smith apple (optional)

1   Toss the cabbages together in a large bowl; set aside. Cook bacon in a medium skillet over medium heat, stirring occasionally, until crisp, about 5 minutes. Transfer with a slotted spoon to paper towels to drain; set aside. Pour off all but about 1 tablespoon fat from skillet.

2   Add caraway seeds to skillet, if desired; cook over medium heat, shaking skillet often, until seeds begin to pop, about 1 minute. Add oil and garlic; cook, stirring, 10 seconds (do not let garlic brown). Remove from heat, and pour in vinegar. Add sugar and salt; stir until dissolved. Pour dressing over cabbage. Season with pepper. Toss thoroughly. Let stand at least 1 hour, or refrigerate, covered, overnight.

3   Just before serving, cut apple into ¼-inch-thick wedges or matchsticks, if desired. Add to dressed cabbage along with bacon, and toss again.

from Chop and Serve Slaws

toasted-bulghur pilaf

SERVES 4

1 cup bulghur

¾ cup homemade or store-bought low-sodium chicken stock

1 whole cinnamon stick

1 bay leaf

Coarse salt

½ cup salted roasted almonds, coarsely chopped

1 tablespoon extra-virgin olive oil

Freshly ground pepper

1 Heat a dry large skillet over medium-high heat until hot. Add bulghur, and toast, stirring frequently, until golden and fragrant, 4 to 5 minutes.

2 Stir together toasted bulghur, stock, ¾ cup water, cinnamon stick, bay leaf, and ½ teaspoon salt in a medium saucepan. Bring to a boil over medium-high heat; cover, and reduce heat to low. Simmer until all liquid is absorbed and bulghur is tender, 10 to 12 minutes. Discard bay leaf and cinnamon stick (or, if desired, leave in as a garnish). Stir in almonds and oil; season with salt and pepper.

from What's for Dinner?

rice salad with rock shrimp and asparagus

SERVES 4

Rock shrimp are small and slightly sweet. If they're not available, you can use small regular shrimp instead.

Coarse salt
1 bunch asparagus (about 1 pound), trimmed
1 cup jasmine rice
1½ teaspoons toasted sesame-chile oil
2 teaspoons olive oil
1 pound rock shrimp, peeled
2 tablespoons plus 1 teaspoon fresh lemon juice
Freshly ground pepper
½ cup sliced almonds, toasted
1 tablespoon freshly grated lemon zest

1 Prepare an ice-water bath, and set aside. Bring a medium pot of water to a boil; add a large pinch of salt. Blanch asparagus until bright green and tender, about 3 minutes. Immediately transfer asparagus with tongs to ice-water bath to stop the cooking. Drain well, and pat dry. Cut spears on the diagonal into thin pieces; set aside.

2 Bring rice and 1½ cups water to a boil in a medium saucepan. Cover; reduce heat to medium-low. Simmer until liquid is absorbed and rice is tender, about 10 minutes.

3 Heat sesame and olive oils in a large skillet over medium-high heat until hot but not smoking. Add shrimp, and stir to coat. Stir in lemon juice, and season with salt and pepper; cook until shrimp are pink and cooked through, about 3 minutes. Stir shrimp, rice, asparagus, and almonds in a large bowl. Garnish with lemon zest.

from Shrimp

grilled lemon chicken

SERVES 10

½ cup fresh lemon juice, plus 4 lemons, halved (about 6 lemons total)
½ cup extra-virgin olive oil
6 garlic cloves
⅓ cup loosely packed fresh rosemary leaves, plus 20 sprigs, and more sprigs for garnish
12 chicken quarters (6 to 7 pounds total)
4½ teaspoons coarse salt

1 Blend lemon juice, oil, garlic, and rosemary leaves in a blender until rosemary is finely chopped.

2 Divide chicken pieces between two large resealable plastic bags, and set in two large bowls (to catch any drippings). Divide rosemary marinade between bags. Marinate chicken in refrigerator, turning bags occasionally, 8 to 12 hours. Remove chicken pieces from bags, reserving marinade in a bowl.

3 To grill: Place rosemary sprigs on coals (if using a charcoal grill) or on lower rack (if using a gas grill); heat grill until medium-hot. Grill chicken pieces (on upper rack, if using a gas grill), skin sides up, basting with reserved marinade and sprinkling with 2¼ teaspoons salt, 15 minutes (move pieces around grill so as not to char). Turn pieces over; continue to grill, sprinkling with 2¼ teaspoons salt and squeezing juice from 2 lemon halves over chicken, until golden brown and cooked through, 15 to 30 minutes more.

To roast: Preheat oven to 425°F, with racks in upper and lower thirds. Divide the rosemary sprigs between two large rimmed baking sheets, spreading into a single layer on each. Place 6 chicken pieces on each sheet; sprinkle with 2¼ teaspoons salt. Roast in upper and lower thirds of oven, basting twice with reserved marinade, 20 minutes. Switch position of sheets. Squeeze juice from 2 lemon halves over chicken; sprinkle with 2¼ teaspoons salt. Continue to roast until golden and cooked through, 20 to 25 minutes more.

4 Discard any unused marinade. Loosely tent chicken with foil, and let stand 10 minutes. Cut chicken legs from thighs, and halve breasts crosswise.

5 Arrange chicken on a large platter; garnish with rosemary sprigs and remaining 6 lemon halves.

from Life (and Lunch) Among the Roses

niçoise salad

SERVES 6 | PHOTOS ON PAGES 144 AND 145

1 pound red fingerling or other small potatoes

Coarse salt

Garlic Vinaigrette (recipe follows)

Freshly ground pepper

4 large eggs

½ pound green beans, halved crosswise

1 head Boston lettuce

1 red or green bell pepper, cut into ¼-inch-thick rings

½ pound cherry tomatoes, halved

½ English (hothouse) cucumber, peeled and sliced

½ fennel bulb, trimmed, halved lengthwise, and thinly sliced

2 cans (6 ounces each) tuna, preferably Italian oil-packed, flaked

¾ cup niçoise or oil-cured black olives

1 scallion, chopped

2 tablespoons coarsely chopped fresh flat-leaf parsley

1 tablespoon drained capers (optional)

1 Cover potatoes with water in a large saucepan; bring to a boil. Add salt; reduce heat, and simmer until tender (do not overcook), 10 to 15 minutes. Drain; let cool slightly.

2 Cut the potatoes into bite-size pieces; peel any loose skins. Dress with enough vinaigrette to coat lightly (reserve remainder). Season with salt and pepper. Set potatoes aside.

3 Prepare an ice-water bath; set aside. Cover eggs with water in a small saucepan; bring to a full boil. After 1 minute, cover pan and turn off heat. Let stand 6 minutes. Rinse eggs with cold water, then transfer to ice-water bath.

4 Prepare another ice-water bath; set aside. Bring a medium saucepan of water to a boil; add salt. Blanch green beans until crisp-tender, 1 to 2 minutes. Drain; rinse with cold water. Let stand in ice-water bath until cool. Drain, and pat dry.

5 Peel the eggs, and halve lengthwise. Arrange lettuce, then potatoes, green beans, bell pepper, tomatoes, cucumber, fennel, tuna, eggs, and olives on a platter. (See "Composing a Niçoise Salad Platter," page 145.)

6 Sprinkle with scallion and parsley, and with capers if desired. Drizzle salad with some vinaigrette, and serve with remaining vinaigrette on the side.

from Easy Entertaining: A French Lunch

garlic vinaigrette

MAKES ABOUT 1 CUP

1 garlic clove, lightly crushed with the flat side of a knife

1 tablespoon Dijon mustard

2 tablespoons red-wine vinegar

2 tablespoons fresh lemon juice

Coarse salt and freshly ground pepper

¾ cup olive oil

Put garlic, mustard, vinegar, and lemon juice in a small bowl; season with salt and pepper, and whisk until blended. Whisking constantly, pour in oil in a slow, steady stream; whisk until emulsified. Let stand at least 30 minutes; discard garlic.

pork kabobs with orange and thyme

SERVES 4

If you are using wooden skewers, soak them in water for thirty minutes before grilling.

¼ cup fresh orange juice plus 1 tablespoon freshly grated zest, and orange wedges for garnish

5 garlic cloves, finely chopped

2 tablespoons coarsely chopped fresh thyme, plus sprigs for garnish

1 tablespoon Dijon mustard

Coarse salt and freshly ground pepper

¼ cup extra-virgin olive oil

1¼ pounds boneless pork loin, cut into 1½-inch cubes

1 Whisk together orange juice and zest, garlic, thyme, mustard, 1 teaspoon salt, and ½ teaspoon pepper in a large bowl. Whisking constantly, pour in oil in a slow, steady stream, and whisk until emulsified. Add pork, and toss to coat. Cover bowl with plastic wrap, and let pork marinate 20 minutes at room temperature.

2 Heat a grill or grill pan until medium-hot. Thread 5 or 6 cubes of pork onto each of 4 skewers; season with salt and pepper. Discard marinade. Grill pork, turning occasionally, until cooked through and slightly charred, about 12 minutes. Garnish with thyme sprigs, and serve with orange wedges.

from What's for Dinner?

roasted shrimp and chorizo

SERVES 4

2 pounds vine-ripened cherry tomatoes

3 garlic cloves, thinly sliced

1 small onion, thinly sliced

2 tablespoons fresh oregano, plus more for garnish

¼ cup plus ⅓ cup olive oil

Coarse salt and freshly ground pepper

1 pound large shrimp (18 to 22), peeled and deveined

½ pound dried, hot chorizo sausage, cut into ¼-inch-thick rounds

1 small ciabatta loaf, cut into 8 slices (each ½ inch thick)

1 Preheat oven to 400°F. Toss tomatoes, garlic, onion, and oregano with ¼ cup oil in a large bowl; season with 1 teaspoon salt, plus pepper to taste. Spread mixture out in a 12-inch ovenproof skillet. Roast in oven, stirring occasionally, until tomatoes burst, about 30 minutes.

2 Add shrimp and chorizo; stir to coat. Continue to roast until shrimp and chorizo are cooked through, 10 to 12 minutes.

3 Meanwhile, heat a grill or grill pan until medium-hot. Using remaining ⅓ cup oil, brush each side of bread with 1 teaspoon oil; season with salt and pepper. Grill bread, turning once, until golden brown, about 6 minutes. (Alternatively, toast bread under broiler.)

4 Put a bread slice in each of four serving bowls. Divide shrimp mixture among bowls; garnish with oregano. Serve remaining bread slices on the side.

from Shrimp

shrimp po' boys

MAKES 4

FOR THE SHRIMP:

1 pound large shrimp (18 to 22), peeled and deveined

Coarse salt and freshly ground pepper

¾ cup all-purpose flour

½ teaspoon cayenne pepper

1 large egg

¾ cup yellow cornmeal

7 cups peanut or vegetable oil

FOR THE REMOULADE:

2 large egg yolks

¼ cup fresh lemon juice

½ cup cornichons, finely chopped

2 tablespoons drained capers, coarsely chopped

2 tablespoons coarsely chopped fresh flat-leaf parsley

¾ teaspoon coarsely chopped fresh tarragon

1 anchovy fillet, finely chopped

Coarse salt and freshly ground pepper

1¼ cups vegetable oil

FOR THE SANDWICHES:

1 baguette, halved lengthwise and quartered

1 head Boston lettuce, leaves separated

1 Make shrimp: Season shrimp with ½ teaspoon salt and ¼ teaspoon pepper; set aside. Whisk together flour and cayenne in a small bowl; season with salt and pepper. Whisk together egg and 2 tablespoons water in a second small bowl. Put the cornmeal in a third small bowl. Set aside.

2 Pour peanut oil into a medium saucepan to a depth of about 3 inches. Heat over medium heat until a deep-fry thermometer registers 365°F. Working in small batches, dredge shrimp in flour mixture and then egg wash; lightly dip in cornmeal to cover completely.

3 In small batches, fry dredged shrimp, turning once, until golden, about 3 minutes total. Transfer with a slotted spoon to paper towels to drain. (Adjust heat between batches as necessary to keep oil at a steady temperature.)

4 Make rémoulade: Blend yolks, lemon juice, cornichons, capers, herbs, anchovy fillet, ¼ teaspoon salt, and pepper to taste in a blender until smooth. With blender running, pour in vegetable oil in a slow, steady stream; blend until emulsified.

5 Make sandwiches: Spread some of the rémoulade on the inside of baguette pieces. Line with lettuce; fill with shrimp.

Note: Raw eggs should not be used in food prepared for pregnant women, babies, young children, the elderly, or anyone whose health is compromised.

from Shrimp

quiche Lorraine

MAKES ONE 11-INCH QUICHE

All-purpose flour, for dusting
Tart Dough (recipe follows)
10 ounces slab bacon, cut into ¾-by-¼-by-¼-inch strips
3 large eggs
2 cups heavy cream
¾ teaspoon coarse salt
¼ teaspoon freshly ground pepper

1 On a lightly floured work surface, roll out dough to ¼ inch thick. Cut out a 13-inch circle from dough. Press dough onto bottom and up sides of an 11-inch tart pan with a removable bottom; trim dough flush with top edge of pan. Prick bottom all over with a fork. Transfer to a rimmed baking sheet. Freeze until firm, about 30 minutes. Preheat oven to 400°F.

2 Line tart shell with parchment paper; fill with pie weights or dried beans. Bake until dough starts to feel firm on the edges, about 20 minutes. Remove parchment and weights; continue baking until crust is pale golden brown, about 10 minutes. Let cool completely on a wire rack. Leave oven on.

3 Cook bacon in a large skillet over medium heat until browned, about 10 minutes. Transfer with a slotted spoon to paper towels to drain.

4 Whisk eggs, cream, salt, and pepper in a medium bowl. Pour mixture into tart shell, and scatter the bacon strips on top. Bake until puffed and pale golden brown, about 30 minutes. Let cool at least 30 minutes before serving.

from Quiche

tart dough

1¾ cups all-purpose flour
¼ teaspoon coarse salt
¼ cup coarsely chopped chives, rosemary, or thyme (optional)
9 tablespoons (1⅛ sticks) cold unsalted butter, cut into small pieces
1 large egg plus 1 large egg yolk, beaten
3 tablespoons ice water

Process flour, salt, and herbs (if using) in a food processor until combined. Add butter, and process just until mixture resembles coarse meal. Whisk together egg mixture and the ice water in a small bowl. With processor running, pour in egg mixture; process until dough starts to come together. Shape dough into a disk. Wrap in plastic wrap, and refrigerate at least 30 minutes.

caramelized onion and Gorgonzola quiche

MAKES ONE 8-BY-11-INCH QUICHE

All-purpose flour, for dusting
Tart Dough without herbs (recipe above)
1 tablespoon extra-virgin olive oil
1 pound onions, cut crosswise into rings
2 large eggs
½ cup milk
½ cup heavy cream
1 teaspoon coarse salt
Freshly ground pepper
2 ounces Gorgonzola dolce

1 On a lightly floured work surface, roll out dough to ¼ inch thick. Press dough onto bottom and up sides of an 8-by-11-inch rectangular tart pan with a removable bottom; trim dough flush with top edge of pan. Prick bottom all over with a fork. Transfer to a large rimmed baking sheet. Freeze until firm, about 30 minutes. Preheat oven to 400°F.

2 Line tart shell with parchment paper, and fill with pie weights or dried beans. Bake until dough starts to feel firm on edges, about 20 minutes. Remove parchment and weights; continue baking until crust is pale golden brown, about 10 minutes. Let cool completely on a wire rack. Leave oven on.

3 Heat oil in a large heavy-bottom skillet over low heat until hot but not smoking. Cook onions, stirring frequently, until golden brown, about 30 minutes. Let cool.

4 Whisk eggs, milk, cream, and salt in a medium bowl; season with pepper. Crumble in cheese, and stir in caramelized onions. Pour mixture into tart shell; bake until puffed and pale golden brown, 30 to 35 minutes. Let quiche cool at least 30 minutes before serving.

from Quiche

individual cremini and porcini quiches

MAKES SIX 4-INCH QUICHES

Tart Dough with thyme (page 130)

All-purpose flour, for dusting

½ ounce dried porcini mushrooms

1 cup boiling water

1 tablespoon unsalted butter

9 ounces cremini mushrooms, halved lengthwise

2 large eggs plus 1 large egg yolk

1½ teaspoons coarse salt

¼ teaspoon freshly ground pepper

¾ cup heavy cream

1 Set six 4-inch cake rings (with 1⅜-inch sides) on a baking sheet lined with parchment paper; set aside. Cut dough into six equal pieces. On a lightly floured surface, roll out pieces, one at a time, to ⅛ inch thick. Using a cake pan as a guide, cut an 8-inch circle from each piece. Fit circles into cake rings, trimming dough flush with tops of rings to make tart shells. Prick bottoms all over with a fork. Freeze until firm, at least 30 minutes. Preheat oven to 400°F.

2 Line tart shells with parchment paper; fill with pie weights or dried beans. Bake until dough edges start to feel firm, about 20 minutes. Remove parchment and weights; continue baking until crusts are pale golden brown, about 10 minutes. Let tart shells cool completely on a wire rack. Reduce oven temperature to 350°F.

3 Soak porcini in the boiling water; let soften 30 minutes. Melt butter in a large skillet over medium-high heat; cook cremini, cut sides down, without stirring, until deep golden brown, about 5 minutes. Set aside.

4 Lift out porcini; pour soaking liquid through a fine sieve into a blender. Add porcini, eggs and yolk, salt, and pepper; blend until smooth. Add cream, and blend.

5 Divide filling among tart shells. Arrange cremini in filling, cut sides up. Bake until set, about 40 minutes. Let cool at least 30 minutes before serving.

from Quiche

ricotta, lemon, and arugula quiche

MAKES ONE 8-INCH QUICHE | PHOTO ON PAGE 147

All-purpose flour, for dusting

Tart Dough (page 130)

12 ounces fresh ricotta cheese

1½ cups milk

2 large eggs

1½ tablespoons freshly grated lemon zest

1½ teaspoons coarse salt

¾ teaspoon freshly ground pepper

1½ cups baby arugula (about 2 ounces)

Arugula Salad (page 123)

1 Set an 8-inch cake ring (with 2-inch sides) on a rimmed baking sheet lined with parchment paper.

2 On a lightly floured work surface, roll out dough to ¼ inch thick. Cut out a 12-inch circle. Fit circle into cake ring, pressing dough onto baking sheet and up sides of ring; trim dough flush with top edge of ring. Prick bottom all over with a fork. Freeze until firm, about 30 minutes. Preheat oven to 400°F.

3 Line tart shell with parchment paper, and fill with pie weights or dried beans. Bake until dough starts to feel firm on edges, about 20 minutes. Remove parchment and weights; continue baking until crust is pale golden brown, about 15 minutes. Let cool completely on a wire rack. Leave oven on.

4 Whisk ricotta, milk, eggs, zest, salt, and pepper in a large bowl. Stir in arugula. Pour mixture into tart shell; bake until puffed and pale golden brown, about 45 minutes. Let cool at least 30 minutes before serving. Serve with arugula salad.

from Quiche

salmon, pea, and mint quiche

MAKES ONE 11½-INCH QUICHE | PHOTO ON PAGE 147

All-purpose flour, for dusting

Tart Dough with chives (page 130)

1 salmon fillet (about 1 pound), skinned

3 large eggs

1 cup milk

1 cup heavy cream

2 tablespoons Dijon mustard

1½ teaspoons coarse salt

½ teaspoon freshly ground pepper

1 cup shelled fresh peas or thawed frozen peas

⅓ cup finely shredded fresh mint

1 On a lightly floured work surface, roll out dough to ¼ inch thick. Cut out a 14-inch circle from dough. Press dough onto bottom and up sides of an 11½-inch round ceramic quiche dish; trim dough flush with top edge of dish. Prick bottom all over with a fork. Transfer to a rimmed baking sheet. Freeze until firm, about 30 minutes. Preheat oven to 400°F.

2 Line tart shell with parchment paper, and fill with pie weights or dried beans. Bake until dough starts to feel firm on edges, about 20 minutes. Remove parchment and weights; continue baking until crust is pale golden brown, about 10 minutes. Let cool completely on a wire rack. Leave oven on.

3 Fill a wide medium saucepan halfway with water; bring to a simmer over medium heat. Add salmon fillet; simmer until opaque but still pink in middle, about 11 minutes. Remove salmon, and let cool.

4 Flake salmon with a fork; set aside. Whisk eggs, milk, cream, mustard, salt, and pepper in a large bowl. Stir in salmon, peas, and mint. Pour mixture into tart shell, and bake until puffed and pale golden brown, 40 to 45 minutes. Let cool at least 30 minutes before serving.

from Quiche

zucchini and edamame quiche

MAKES ONE 8-INCH QUICHE | **PHOTO ON PAGE 146**

All-purpose flour, for dusting

Tart Dough with rosemary (page 130)

2 **tablespoons extra-virgin olive oil**

1 **tablespoon plus 1 teaspoon minced garlic**

12 **ounces zucchini (about 2 medium), trimmed and cut into ½-inch cubes**

1 **cup frozen shelled edamame, thawed**

Coarse salt and freshly ground pepper

2 **large eggs**

1 **cup heavy cream**

½ **cup milk**

1 **cup finely grated Pecorino Romano cheese (about 3 ounces)**

1 Set an 8-inch cake ring (with 1¼-inch sides) on a baking sheet lined with parchment paper; set aside. On a lightly floured surface, roll out dough to ¼ inch thick. Cut out a rough 14-inch circle from dough. Fit circle into cake ring; roughly tear edge of dough to form a ¼-inch collar above edge of cake ring. Prick bottom all over with a fork. Freeze until firm, at least 30 minutes. Preheat oven to 400°F.

2 Line tart shell with parchment paper, and fill with pie weights or dried beans. Bake until dough edges start to feel

firm, about 20 minutes. Remove paper and weights, and continue baking until crust is pale golden brown, about 10 minutes (if top edges brown too quickly, tent with foil). Let cool completely on a wire rack. Leave oven on.

3 Meanwhile, heat oil in a large skillet over medium-high heat until hot but not smoking. Add garlic, and cook, stirring, until fragrant, about 20 seconds. Add zucchini, and cook, stirring frequently, until softened, about 4 minutes. Add edamame, and cook, stirring until combined, about 1 minute. Season with ¾ teaspoon salt and ¼ teaspoon pepper. Let mixture cool completely.

4 Whisk eggs, cream, milk, and ½ teaspoon salt in a large bowl; stir in zucchini mixture, scraping the bottom of the skillet, and ¾ cup cheese. Pour into tart shell, and sprinkle with remaining ¼ cup cheese. Bake, tenting with foil after 35 minutes, until puffed and pale golden brown, about 50 minutes. Let cool at least 30 minutes before serving.

from Quiche

....
DESSERTS
....

apricot-walnut biscotti

MAKES 2 DOZEN

1 **cup walnut halves**

2 **cups all-purpose flour, plus more for dusting**

½ **teaspoon baking powder**

¼ **teaspoon salt**

5 **tablespoons unsalted butter, softened, plus more for baking sheet**

1 **cup granulated sugar**

1 **teaspoon pure vanilla extract**

2 **large eggs, lightly beaten**

¾ **cup dried apricots, cut into ¼-inch dice**

1 **large egg white, lightly beaten**

2 **tablespoons sanding sugar**

4 **ounces bittersweet chocolate, coarsely chopped**

1 Preheat oven to 375°F. Spread out nuts on a rimmed baking sheet; toast in oven, stirring occasionally, until fragrant and golden brown, about 8 minutes. Remove from oven; reduce temperature to 350°F.

2 Rub nuts between paper towels to remove loose skins; coarsely chop nuts.

3 Sift flour, baking powder, and salt together into a medium bowl; set aside. Put butter and granulated sugar in the bowl of an electric mixer fitted with the paddle attachment. Cream on medium speed until pale and fluffy. Mix in vanilla. Mix in

eggs, one at a time, mixing after each until just combined. On low speed, mix in flour mixture until just combined. Stir in walnuts and apricots by hand.

4 Butter a large baking sheet; set aside. Transfer dough to a lightly floured surface; divide in half. With floured hands, shape each half into an 8½-by-2½-by-1-inch log. Place logs at least 2 inches apart on buttered baking sheet. Bake until golden, about 30 minutes. Transfer sheet to a wire rack; let logs stand 10 minutes.

5 Transfer logs to a cutting board. Clean and butter the baking sheet again; set aside. Brush logs with egg white, and sprinkle with sanding sugar. Cut each log crosswise on the diagonal into 12 pieces (each ½ inch thick). Lay flat on buttered sheet. Bake 7 minutes; turn pieces over. Bake until golden, 7 to 9 minutes more. Transfer biscotti to a wire rack, and let cool until crisp.

6 Melt chocolate in a heatproof bowl set over a pan of simmering water, stirring occasionally, until smooth, 3 to 5 minutes. Let cool slightly.

7 Dip a flat side of 12 biscotti in melted chocolate, arranging cookies, chocolate sides up, on parchment paper as you work. Let stand until chocolate is set, about 30 minutes. Store in an airtight container, keeping chocolate-dipped biscotti in a single layer on top, up to 2 days.

from Life (and Lunch) Among the Roses

chocolate malt sandwich cookies

MAKES ABOUT 20 FILLED COOKIES | PHOTO ON PAGE 160

FOR THE COOKIES:

2 cups plus 2 tablespoons all-purpose flour

½ cup unsweetened cocoa powder

¼ cup plain malted-milk powder

1 teaspoon baking soda

½ teaspoon coarse salt

1¾ cups sugar

8 ounces (2 sticks) unsalted butter, softened

1 large egg

2 teaspoons pure vanilla extract

¼ cup crème fraîche

FOR THE FILLING:

10 ounces semisweet chocolate, coarsely chopped

4 tablespoons unsalted butter, cut into pieces

1 cup plain malted-milk powder

3 ounces cream cheese, room temperature

6 tablespoons half-and-half

1 teaspoon pure vanilla extract

1 Make cookies: Preheat oven to 350°F. Line baking sheets with Silpat nonstick baking mats or parchment paper; set aside. Sift flour, cocoa powder, malted-milk powder, baking soda, and salt together into a medium bowl; set aside.

2 Put sugar and butter in the bowl of an electric mixer fitted with the paddle attachment; cream until pale and fluffy. Mix in egg and vanilla. Mix in crème fraîche. Mix in 3 tablespoons hot water. On low speed, mix in flour mixture.

3 Drop dough onto lined sheets using a tablespoon-capacity ice-cream scoop, about 3½ inches apart (or use a tablespoon, gently shaping dough into balls). Bake until tops flatten and cookies are just firm, 10 to 12 minutes. Transfer to a wire rack, and let cool completely.

4 Make filling: Melt chocolate and butter in a heatproof bowl set over a pan of simmering water, stirring occasionally until smooth. Let cool until just warm.

5 Put malt powder and cream cheese in a clean mixing bowl; return to mixer. Mix on medium until completely smooth. Gradually mix in half-and-half; then mix in melted chocolate and the vanilla. Refrigerate until thick, about 30 minutes.

6 Return bowl to mixer, and mix on high speed until fluffy, about 3 minutes.

7 Assemble cookies: Spread a heaping tablespoon of filling on bottom of one cookie with an offset spatula. Press bottom of a second cookie onto filling. Repeat with remaining cookies and filling. Refrigerate in an airtight container up to 3 days.

from Cookie of the Month

lemon-blackberry pudding cakes

MAKES 6 INDIVIDUAL CAKES

1 pint blackberries

½ cup plus 1 tablespoon fresh lemon juice (about 3 lemons)

1 cup plus 3 tablespoons sugar

3 tablespoons unsalted butter, melted, plus more for ramekins

3 large eggs, separated

6 tablespoons cake flour (not self-rising), sifted

1 cup milk

¼ teaspoon salt

Boiling water, for pan

4 ounces crème fraîche (about ½ cup)

1 Preheat oven to 350°F. Process 2½ ounces blackberries (12 to 15 berries), 1 tablespoon lemon juice, and 3 tablespoons sugar in a food processor or blender until smooth. Pass mixture through a fine sieve into a small bowl; discard solids. Set sauce aside.

2 Butter inner top inch of six 6-ounce ramekins; set aside. Whisk together egg yolks and ¾ cup sugar in a medium bowl. Whisk in flour and milk in two batches each, beginning with the flour. Whisk in remaining ½ cup lemon juice, the salt, and the melted butter, and set aside.

3 Put egg whites in the bowl of an electric mixer fitted with the whisk attachment; beat on medium-high speed until very frothy, about 1½ minutes. With mixer running, add remaining ¼ cup sugar in a slow, steady stream; beat until whites hold stiff (but not dry) peaks, about 2 minutes. Whisk half the whites into reserved batter until combined; gently fold in remaining whites with a rubber spatula.

4 Place the ramekins in a high-sided roasting pan or baking dish, and divide the batter among ramekins, filling each almost to the top. Spoon a few drops of berry sauce in dots onto cakes, and use a toothpick or skewer to swirl sauce into batter. Transfer to oven; pour boiling water into pan, a bit more than halfway up sides of ramekins.

5 Bake until cakes are set and the tops are just starting to turn golden brown, 35 to 40 minutes. With tongs, transfer the ramekins from pan to a wire rack, and let cool 15 minutes.

6 Meanwhile, beat crème fraîche in a clean mixing bowl until it holds soft peaks. Serve cakes warm with crème fraîche and remaining blackberries.

from Dessert of the Month

Patti's lemon meringue pie

MAKES ONE 10-INCH PIE | **PHOTO ON PAGE 157**

If you prefer a buttery crust, reduce the amount of shortening by half in either of the following pie recipes, and add an equal amount of cold unsalted butter, cut into bits.

FOR THE PIECRUST:

1½ **cups all-purpose flour, plus more for dusting**

¾ **teaspoon salt**

⅔ **cup cold vegetable shortening**

⅓ **to ½ cup ice water**

FOR THE FILLING:

2 **lemons, for zesting, plus ⅔ cup fresh lemon juice (about 4 lemons total)**

2 **cups plus 1 tablespoon sugar**

½ **cup cornstarch**

4 **large egg yolks**

4 **tablespoons unsalted butter, cut into pieces**

FOR THE MERINGUE:

8 **large egg whites**

¼ **teaspoon cream of tartar**

¾ **cup sugar**

1 **teaspoon pure vanilla extract**

1 Make piecrust: Sift flour and salt together into a large bowl. Blend in shortening with a pastry blender or your fingertips until mixture resembles coarse meal. Stir in ice water a little at a time until dough comes together.

2 On a lightly floured surface, roll dough with a floured rolling pin into an 11-inch round. Transfer to a 10-inch pie plate. Trim edge to create a ½-inch overhang; tuck edge under itself. Prick bottom all over with a fork. Refrigerate 30 minutes. Preheat oven to 425°F.

3 Place pie shell on a baking sheet; line with parchment paper, and fill with pie weights or dried beans. Bake shell, rotating sheet about halfway through, until edges of crust are just browned, about 15 minutes. Remove parchment and weights; continue baking until bottom of crust is just browned, about 5 minutes more. Let cool completely on a wire rack. Reduce oven temperature to 400°F.

4 Make filling: Remove zest from 2 lemons with a vegetable peeler; finely chop zest (reserve lemons for juicing). Process zest with 1 tablespoon sugar in a food processor until finely ground.

5 Whisk together remaining 2 cups sugar and the cornstarch in a medium saucepan. Gradually whisk in 2 cups water; add zest mixture. Cook over medium heat, whisking constantly, 8 minutes (mixture will boil and thicken).

6 Lightly beat egg yolks in a large bowl. Slowly whisk half of cornstarch mixture into beaten egg yolks. Return yolk mixture to cornstarch mixture in pan, and whisk together. Bring to a boil, and whisk constantly until very thick, about 5 minutes. Remove from heat; add lemon juice and butter, and whisk until well combined. Press plastic wrap directly onto surface, to prevent a skin from forming. Refrigerate until set, about 30 minutes. (If not using immediately, you can refrigerate filling up to 3 days.)

7 Pour filling into pie shell; set aside. Make meringue: Put egg whites and cream of tartar in the bowl of an electric mixer fitted with the whisk attachment. Beat on medium-high speed until foamy. Beat in the sugar, 1 tablespoon at a time; continue beating until stiff, glossy peaks form. Beat in vanilla.

8 Heap meringue over filling, making sure it touches crust (to prevent shrinking). Bake pie until meringue is pale brown, 8 to 10 minutes. Let cool on a wire rack in a draft-free spot.

from Life (and Lunch) Among the Roses

Patti's nectarine-blueberry pie

MAKES ONE 9-INCH PIE | **PHOTO ON PAGE 157**

For tips on using butter in the piecrust, see Patti's Lemon-Meringue Pie, page 134.

FOR THE PIECRUST:

3 cups all-purpose flour, plus more for dusting

1 teaspoon salt

1 cup cold vegetable shortening

½ to ⅔ cup ice water

FOR THE FILLING:

¾ cup plus 1 teaspoon sugar

⅓ cup quick-cooking tapioca

¼ teaspoon ground cinnamon (optional)

2 cups fresh blueberries (about 10 ounces)

3 cups sliced fresh nectarines (3 to 4 nectarines)

1 tablespoon fresh lemon juice

2 tablespoons cold unsalted butter, cut into small pieces
   Freshly whipped cream (optional)

1 Make piecrust: Sift flour and salt together into a large bowl. Blend in shortening with a pastry blender or your fingertips until mixture resembles coarse meal. Stir in ice water a little at a time until dough comes together.

2 Divide dough in half. On a lightly floured sheet of parchment paper, roll each half with a floured rolling pin into an 11-inch round. Transfer one round to a 9-inch pie plate, gently pressing it in to fit. Transfer second half to a baking sheet; cover with parchment. Refrigerate both pieces 30 minutes.

3 Make filling: Preheat oven to 425°F. Stir together ¾ cup sugar, the tapioca, and the cinnamon, if desired, in a medium bowl. Put berries, nectarines, and lemon juice in a large bowl. Gently fold the sugar mixture into fruit; let stand 15 minutes.

4 Pour fruit filling into pie shell, and dot with butter. Cover with remaining dough round. Trim edge of dough flush with top edge of plate; gently press to seal. Crimp edges decoratively; cut steam vents in top crust. Cover edge with a band of foil to prevent excess browning.

5 Transfer pie to a baking sheet, and bake 35 minutes. Remove foil band, and sprinkle top of pie with remaining teaspoon sugar. Continue baking until filling is bubbling and crust is golden brown, 15 to 20 minutes more.

6 Let pie cool until warm on a wire rack. Serve with whipped cream, if desired.

from Life (and Lunch) Among the Roses

strawberry sponge pudding

SERVES 4

2 tablespoons unsalted butter, softened, plus more for pie plate

1½ cups strawberries, hulled, halved if large, plus more for garnish

1 cup milk

¼ cup all-purpose flour

½ teaspoon salt

¾ cup granulated sugar

3 large eggs, room temperature, separated

2 tablespoons fresh lemon juice

½ teaspoon pure vanilla extract
   Boiling water, for pan
   Confectioners' sugar, for dusting

1 Preheat oven to 325°F. Butter a 9-inch pie plate and place in a roasting pan; set aside. Purée berries and milk in a blender; set aside. Stir together butter, flour, salt, and ½ cup plus 2 tablespoons granulated sugar in a medium bowl. Stir in egg yolks, berry mixture, lemon juice, and vanilla.

2 Beat egg whites in the bowl of an electric mixer fitted with the whisk attachment until foamy. With mixer running, add remaining 2 tablespoons granulated sugar in a steady stream; beat until stiff (but not dry) peaks form. Gently fold whites into strawberry mixture.

3 Ladle batter into buttered pie plate. Pour boiling water into pan around plate, reaching halfway up sides. Bake until golden, about 35 minutes. (If top browns too quickly, tent with foil.) Let cool on a wire rack 10 minutes. Dust with confectioners' sugar; top with berries.

from What's for Dinner?

vanilla ice cream with plum compote

SERVES 6

Black plums will give the compote a beautiful color, but red plums can be used as well. Pay close attention to visual clues while you cook, and use the times below merely as a guideline, as some plums are juicier than others. You can serve the compote warm or cold.

½ cup sugar

6 firm, ripe black plums (about 1¾ pounds)

1½ pints vanilla ice cream

Honey, for drizzling

Fresh thyme, for garnish

1 Bring sugar and ½ cup water to a boil in a medium saucepan. Meanwhile, pit plums; cut each into 8 to 12 chunks.

2 When sugar mixture boils, add plums, and return to a boil. Cook 2 minutes. Cover; reduce heat, and simmer until plums begin to break down, about 7 minutes. Remove lid; simmer until mixture is saucy, about 10 minutes more.

3 Transfer plums to a large bowl using a slotted spoon (so excess syrup can drip back into pan). Cook syrup over high heat until it is very bubbly and has the consistency of warm jelly, about 10 minutes. Pour syrup over plums, and let cool slightly. If not serving immediately, refrigerate compote, covered, up to 3 days.

4 Divide compote among six dessert bowls. Top each serving with a large scoop of ice cream. Drizzle with honey, and sprinkle with thyme leaves or sprigs.

from Easy Entertaining: A French Lunch

- -

DRINKS

- -

orange squeeze

SERVES 1

3 tablespoons vodka

2 tablespoons orange juice

2 tablespoons fresh lime juice

1 lime slice, for garnish (optional)

Fill a tumbler with ice. Pour all ingredients but garnish into tumbler, and stir. Garnish with lime slice, if desired.

from Life (and Lunch) Among the Roses

rose-petal gin fizz

SERVES 1

¼ cup gin

¼ cup Rose-Petal Syrup (recipe follows)

2 tablespoons sparkling water

Pesticide-free rose petals, gently rinsed in cold water, for garnish (optional)

Fill a tumbler with ice. Pour in gin and syrup, and stir. Stir in sparkling water. Garnish with rose petals, if desired.

from Life (and Lunch) Among the Roses

rose-petal syrup

MAKES 6 CUPS

5 pesticide-free roses, petals removed and stems discarded

4½ cups granulated sugar

1 Gently swirl rose petals with your hands in a bowl of cold water to clean. Transfer to paper towels to drain.

2 Bring 5 cups water, the petals, and sugar to a boil in a medium saucepan. Remove from heat; let steep, covered, 1 hour. Pour syrup through a fine sieve set over a bowl; let cool. Refrigerate, covered, until ready to use, up to 1 week.

rosé sangria

SERVES 6

1 bottle (750 ml) French dry rosé wine, such as Tavel or Bandol

6 tablespoons crème de cassis (black-currant liqueur)

1 Charentais melon or ½ large cantaloupe, cut into chunks

1 peach or nectarine, pitted and cut into 8 wedges

½ pint blackberries or raspberries

1 bottle (750 ml) sparkling water

Stir together all ingredients except sparkling water in a large pitcher. Refrigerate at least 1 hour or until ready to serve, up to 3 hours. Stir in sparkling water, and serve over ice.

from Easy Entertaining: A French Lunch

CHOCOLATE-HAZELNUT SPREAD
AND PEAR PANINO | **PAGE 99**

YOGURT PARFAITS WITH BLUEBERRIES AND LEMON | **PAGE 95**

GRANOLA WITH FLAXSEED | **PAGE 94**

BANANA BREAD WITH WALNUTS AND FLAXSEED | **PAGE 93**

COFFEE-CAKE MUFFINS | **PAGE 94**

FLAXSEED-AND-ONION CRACKERS | PAGE 102

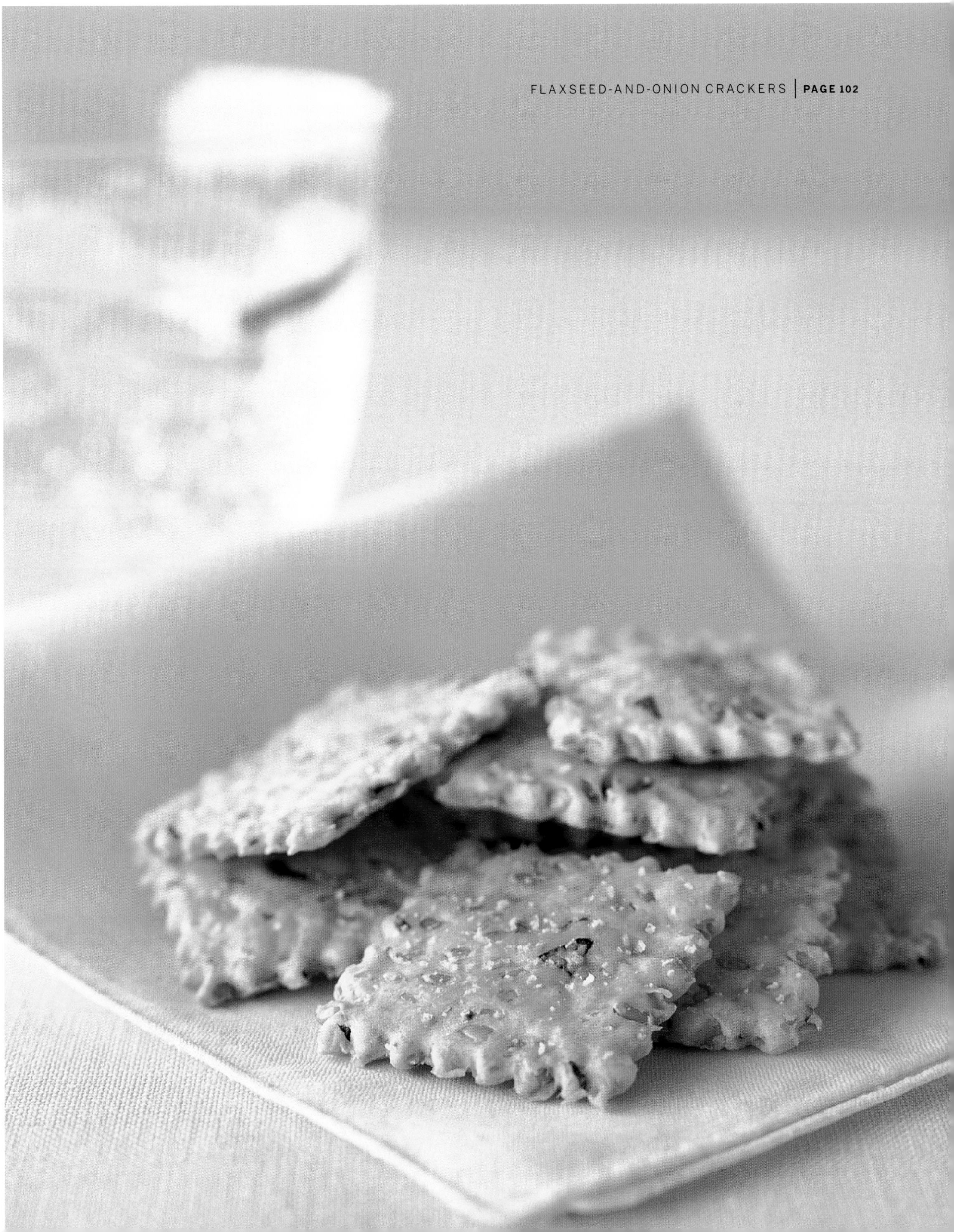

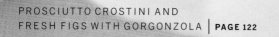

PROSCIUTTO CROSTINI AND
FRESH FIGS WITH GORGONZOLA | **PAGE 122**

POPOVERS WITH WILD-MUSHROOM SAUCE | PAGE 96

ASPARAGUS SALAD WITH TENDER GREENS AND MINT | **PAGE 96**

CHICKEN SOUP WITH PARSLEY DUMPLINGS | **PAGE 105**

WATERCRESS AND GREEN BEAN SALAD | **PAGE 97**

PEA-SHOOT SALAD WITH WARM ONION DRESSING | **PAGE 106**

CHILLED PEA AND PEA-SHOOT SOUP WITH SHRIMP | **PAGE 105**

NIÇOISE SALAD | **PAGE 128**

WARM GOAT-CHEESE TOASTS | **PAGE 123**

COMPOSING A NIÇOISE SALAD PLATTER

This classic French salad looks complicated but is mostly about layering ingredients—and being strategic: Make sure you arrange the components so each person can take a little of everything. **1.** Arrange lettuce leaves as a base on a large, deep serving platter. **2.** Place the cooked vegetables—green beans and potatoes—on top. **3.** Add the raw vegetables— bell peppers, tomatoes, cucumber, and fennel—in several piles, varying colors and textures as you go. **4.** Finish the platter by adding on tuna, eggs, olives, and the garnishes.

ZUCCHINI AND EDAMAME QUICHE | **PAGE 132**

ARUGULA SALAD | **PAGE 123**
RICOTTA, LEMON, AND ARUGULA QUICHE | **PAGE 131**
SALMON, PEA, AND MINT QUICHE | **PAGE 131**

GRILLED PIZZAS WITH CANADIAN
BACON AND PINEAPPLE | **PAGE 112**

GRILLED PIZZAS WITH TOMATOES, AVOCADOS, AND PEPPER-JACK CHEESE | **PAGE 114**

GRILLED QUATTRO FORMAGGI PIZZAS | **PAGE 114**

GRILLED MARGHERITA PIZZAS | **PAGE 111**

GRILLED PIZZAS WITH PLUMS, PROSCIUTTO, GOAT CHEESE, AND ARUGULA | **PAGE 113**

ASSORTED PANINI | **PAGE 99**

RISOTTO WITH
PEA SHOOTS | **PAGE 110**

PEA SHOOT AND VEGETABLE STIR-FRY | **PAGE 108**

CITRUS-ROASTED SALMON
WITH SPRING-PEA SAUCE | **PAGE 97**

SEARED STEAK WITH OLIVE RELISH | **PAGE 111**

LAMB CHOPS WITH ARTICHOKE HEARTS | **PAGE 98**

CABBAGE AND RADISH SLAW WITH PEANUT DRESSING | **PAGE 124**

CARAMEL SAUCE | **PAGE 102**

COCONUT CREAM BARS | **PAGE 118**

PATTI'S NECTARINE-BLUEBERRY PIE | **PAGE 135**

PATTI'S LEMON MERINGUE PIE | **PAGE 134**

ORANGE-LIME MOUSSE | **PAGE 118**

CHOCOLATE MALT SANDWICH COOKIES | PAGE 133

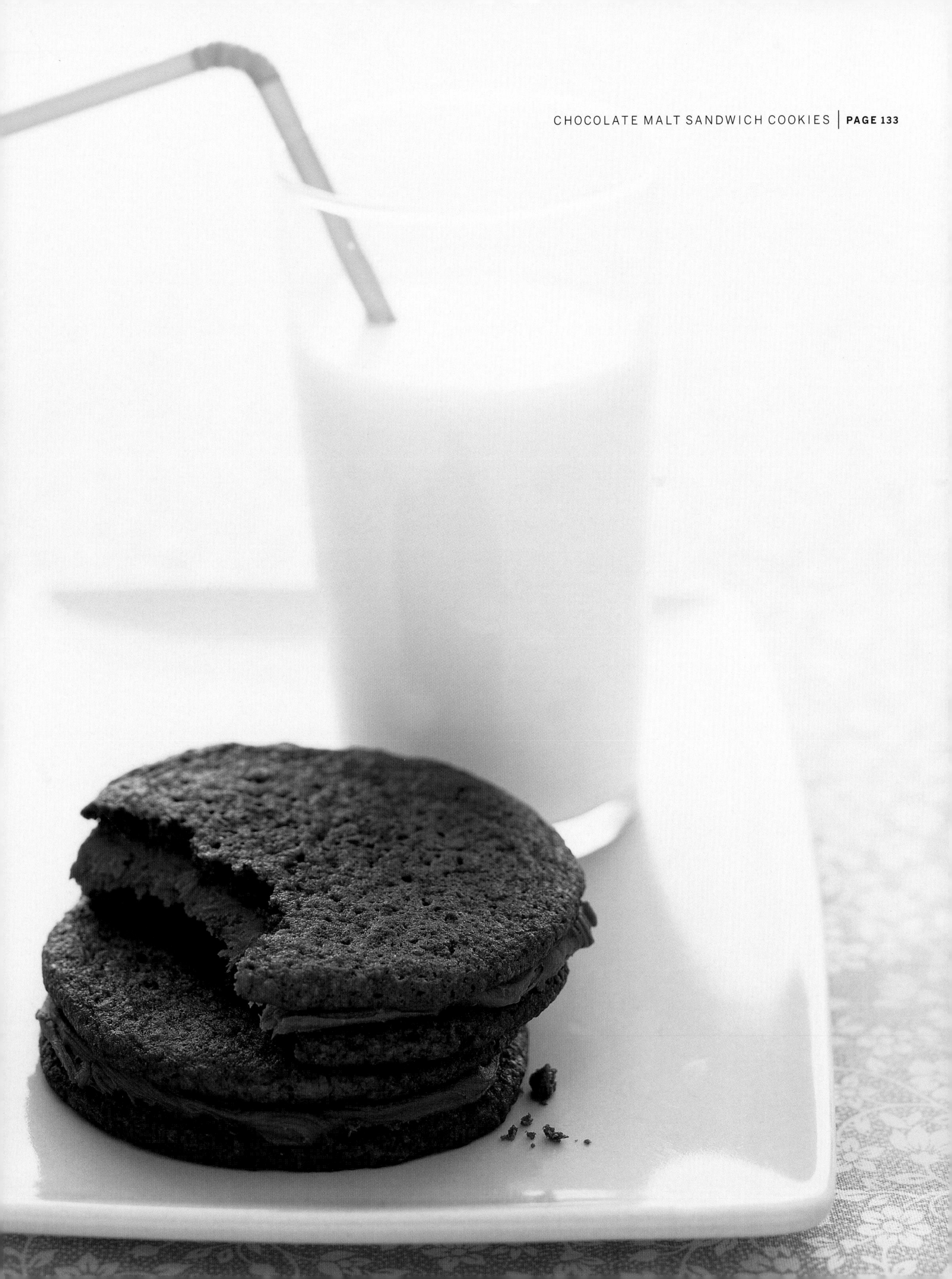

Summer

AS SEASONAL MARKERS GO, FRESH CORN ON THE COB is particularly evocative of this time of year. Ideally, it is eaten soon after picking to preserve its sweetness and prevent it from getting too starchy. We like ours steamed and brushed with herbed butter, cut off the cob and stirred into a chowder, or, in our new favorite method, wrapped in bacon and grilled.

breakfast enchiladas

SERVES 6

You can use shredded Monterey Jack cheese in place of the cotija and queso blanco. Shiitake mushrooms can be substituted for the porcini.

12 yellow corn tortillas (6 inches each)
4½ teaspoons extra-virgin olive oil
 1 cup fresh corn kernels (1 ear)
 ½ shallot, finely chopped
 ½ small zucchini, cut into ¼-inch dice
 ½ small yellow summer squash, cut into ¼-inch dice
 1 ounce fresh porcini mushrooms, cut into ¼-inch pieces
   Coarse salt and freshly ground pepper
 6 large eggs
 3 tablespoons heavy cream
 2 tablespoons unsalted butter
   Red Chile Sauce (recipe follows)
   Green Chile Sauce (page 166)
 8 ounces cotija cheese, crumbled
 2 plum tomatoes, seeded and cut into ¼-inch dice
 ¼ cup chopped cilantro
 6 ounces queso blanco, shredded

1 Wrap tortillas in a clean kitchen towel; place in a bamboo steamer basket. Fill a wok with 2 inches of water; bring to a boil. Reduce heat to medium; set steamer in wok. Steam tortillas until softened, 6 minutes. (Or wrap tortillas in a damp, clean kitchen towel, and heat until softened, 10 to 15 seconds in a microwave or 7 to 10 minutes in a 200°F oven.) Set aside.

2 Preheat oven to 375°F. Heat oil in a large nonstick skillet over medium-high heat until hot but not smoking. Cook corn, stirring, until just caramelized, about 5 minutes. Add shallot, zucchini, summer squash, and mushrooms; cook, stirring, until tender, about 4 minutes. Season with salt and pepper. Transfer mixture to a bowl.

3 Vigorously whisk eggs and cream until blended. Season with salt and pepper. Heat butter in a large nonstick skillet over medium-high heat until foamy. Add egg mixture; cook, stirring, until scrambled but not dry, about 4 minutes.

4 Pour ½ cup red chile sauce along one long side of a 9-by-13-inch baking dish; pour ½ cup green chile sauce along opposite long side (the sauces should meet in the middle).

5 Spread 1 tablespoon red chile sauce on 1 tortilla, then sprinkle 2 tablespoons cotija over entire surface. On the bottom third of the tortilla, place about 1½ tablespoons each egg and corn mixture, 1 teaspoon tomatoes, and ½ teaspoon cilantro. Firmly roll tortilla; place in baking dish, seam side down. Repeat with remaining tortillas.

6 Pour ½ cup each red and green chile sauce on top of enchiladas, mirroring the sauces on the bottom. Sprinkle with queso blanco. Bake until heated through, about 25 minutes. Garnish with remaining 2 tablespoons cilantro, and serve with remaining chile sauces.

from Brunch with Southwestern Style

red chile sauce

MAKES 3 CUPS

Be sure to wear protective gloves and to keep your kitchen ventilated when handling New Mexican and guajillo chiles (the latter are especially fiery); the vapors can be a mild irritant.

 9 dried New Mexican chiles
 6 dried guajillo chiles
 1 quart boiling water, for soaking chiles
 6 garlic cloves (do not peel)
 6 plum tomatoes
 2 tablespoons vegetable oil
 ½ large white onion, finely chopped
4½ teaspoons New Mexican chile powder
 6 chipotle chiles in adobo sauce, seeded
 1 tablespoon dried Mexican oregano
   Coarse salt

1 Toast New Mexican and guajillo chiles in a dry large cast-iron skillet over medium-high heat, turning with tongs, until warm and soft, about 30 seconds per side (do not let blacken, or chiles will be bitter). Remove chiles; reserve skillet.

2 Discard stems; cut chiles lengthwise with kitchen shears, and discard seeds. Cover chiles with boiling water. Let stand until hydrated, about 20 minutes.

3 Meanwhile, cook garlic and tomatoes in skillet over medium-high heat, turning, until charred and soft, about 10 minutes. Set tomatoes aside; peel garlic.

4 Heat oil in skillet over medium-low heat until hot but not smoking. Cook onion until translucent, about 5 minutes. Add chile powder, and cook 1 minute more. Remove from heat.

5 Drain chiles, reserving 1½ cups soaking liquid. Purée onion, hydrated chiles, chipotle chiles, tomatoes, garlic, and oregano in a blender, adding a small amount of the reserved soaking liquid if mixture seems dry. Pass chile sauce through a fine sieve into skillet.

6 Cook over medium heat, stirring, 5 minutes. Add remaining soaking liquid. Simmer until sauce is thickened, 12 to 15 minutes. Season with salt. Sauce can be refrigerated up to 2 days. Reheat over low heat, adding water if necessary.

green chile sauce

MAKES 3 CUPS

1 can (27 ounces) whole mild green chiles, drained and seeded

6 garlic cloves (do not peel)

4 tomatillos, husked

2 teaspoons extra-virgin olive oil

1 small white onion, cut into ½-inch pieces

2 teaspoons dried Mexican oregano

¾ teaspoon ground cumin

Coarse salt

1 Purée chiles in a blender, adding a little water if the purée seems dry. Cook garlic and tomatillos in a dry large cast-iron skillet over medium-high heat, turning occasionally, until golden brown and softened, about 8 minutes. Peel garlic. Coarsely chop garlic and tomatillos, and set aside.

2 Heat oil in same skillet over medium heat until hot but not smoking. Cook onion until softened and translucent, about 5 minutes. Add chile purée, garlic, tomatillos, ½ cup water, the oregano, and cumin. Bring to a boil; reduce heat. Simmer until sauce is thickened, about 15 minutes. Season with salt. If not serving immediately, refrigerate up to 2 days. Reheat over low heat, adding water if sauce seems too thick.

SOUPS AND STARTERS

summer-squash soup

MAKES 2 QUARTS | PHOTO ON PAGE 210

3 tablespoons unsalted butter

1 medium white onion, thinly sliced

½ teaspoon turmeric

Pinch of cayenne pepper

3 pounds yellow summer squash (about 6 medium), cut into thin half-moons

3½ cups homemade or low-sodium store-bought chicken stock, or water

2½ teaspoons coarse salt

¼ teaspoon freshly ground white pepper

1 tablespoon fresh lime juice

Shelled sunflower seeds, toasted, for garnish

Paprika, for garnish

1 Melt butter in a large saucepan over medium-low heat. Cook onion, stirring occasionally, until softened, about 5 minutes. Add turmeric and cayenne; cook, stirring, 30 seconds. Add summer squash and stock, and bring to a boil. Reduce heat, and simmer, stirring occasionally, until squash is very tender, about 20 minutes.

2 Let cool slightly; purée in batches in a blender (so blender is never more than halfway full). Add the salt and white pepper; stir in lime juice. Refrigerate until cold, about 6 hours, or up to 1 day. Serve chilled with seeds and paprika.

from In the Heartland

classic bruschetta

MAKES ABOUT 2 DOZEN | PHOTO ON PAGE 211

Originally devised by the Tuscans as a way to use stale bread, bruschette (the plural word for these toasts) can be served simply with a sprinkle of salt, as in this recipe, or they can support a range of ingredients, as they do in the five recipes that follow.

1 loaf rustic Italian bread, cut into ½-inch-thick slices (about 24)

4 garlic cloves, halved

Extra-virgin olive oil

Coarse salt

Heat a grill or preheat the broiler. Lightly char bread slices on grill or under broiler, turning slices halfway through. Rub bread slices with cut sides of garlic cloves, then drizzle with olive oil, and sprinkle with salt.

from Bruschetta, Six Ways

bruschetta with cannellini beans and herbs

MAKES 6 TO 8 | PHOTO ON PAGE 211

2 tablespoons extra-virgin olive oil, plus more for drizzling

1 garlic clove, minced

4 anchovy fillets, minced

1 can (19 ounces) cannellini beans, drained and rinsed

1 teaspoon each chopped fresh rosemary, sage, and thyme

6 to 8 slices Classic Bruschetta (recipe above)

Heat oil in a medium saucepan over medium heat until hot but not smoking. Add garlic and anchovy fillets, and cook until fragrant, about 1 minute. Stir in beans and herbs. Cook until beans are warm, about 3 minutes. Spoon mixture onto bruschetta slices, and drizzle with oil.

from Bruschetta, Six Ways

bruschetta with fava beans and arugula pesto

MAKES 6 TO 8 | PHOTO ON PAGE 211

- 2 cups shelled fresh fava beans (about 2½ pounds in pods)
- 1 medium bunch arugula (6 ounces)
- ¼ cup extra-virgin olive oil, plus more for drizzling
- ¼ cup grated Pecorino Romano cheese, plus shavings for garnish
- 1 tablespoon fresh lemon juice
- ½ teaspoon coarse salt
- Freshly ground pepper
- 6 to 8 slices Classic Bruschetta (page 166)

Bring a saucepan of water to a boil. Prepare an ice-water bath; set aside. Boil fava beans 2 to 3 minutes; plunge into ice-water bath. Slip off skins. Process arugula, oil, cheese, lemon juice, and salt in a food processor until smooth. Toss with beans, and season with pepper. Spoon mixture onto bruschetta slices. Top with cheese shavings, and drizzle with oil.

from Bruschetta, Six Ways

bruschetta with poached tuna

MAKES 8 | PHOTO ON PAGE 211

- ½ to ¾ cup extra-virgin olive oil
- 4 lemon slices
- Coarse salt
- 8 ounces tuna steak
- 1 tablespoon freshly grated lemon zest
- 1 tablespoon capers, drained and rinsed
- Freshly ground pepper
- 8 slices Classic Bruschetta (page 166)

Heat ½ to ¾ cup oil (enough to cover tuna) and the lemon slices in a small saucepan over very low heat until warm. Generously salt tuna steak. Poach tuna in oil, turning once, until opaque on the outside but still a bit pink in the center, about 15 minutes. Remove tuna from pan, reserving oil; flake fish with a fork. Pass poaching oil through a fine sieve into a medium bowl; stir in flaked tuna, lemon zest, and capers. Season with pepper. Spoon mixture onto bruschetta slices, and drizzle with some of the poaching oil.

from Bruschetta, Six Ways

bruschetta with roasted peppers and herbed ricotta

MAKES 8 | PHOTO ON PAGE 211

- 1 cup fresh ricotta cheese
- ½ teaspoon coarse salt
- 2 tablespoons extra-virgin olive oil, plus more for drizzling
- 2 tablespoons chopped fresh oregano
- Freshly ground pepper
- 8 slices Classic Bruschetta (page 166)
- 1 roasted red bell pepper, cut into 8 strips

Stir together ricotta, salt, oil, and oregano; season with pepper. Spread mixture onto bruschetta slices. Place a roasted pepper strip on each slice, and drizzle with oil.

from Bruschetta, Six Ways

bruschetta with tomato and basil

MAKES 6 TO 8 | PHOTO ON PAGE 211

- 2 ripe large tomatoes, seeded and chopped
- 1 tablespoon sugar
- 1 teaspoon coarse salt
- 4 fresh basil leaves, torn
- 6 to 8 slices Classic Bruschetta (page 166)
- Extra-virgin olive oil, for drizzling

Place tomatoes in a bowl. Stir in sugar and salt, and let stand until tomatoes release their juices, about 30 minutes. Toss with basil leaves. Spoon tomato mixture and juices onto bruschetta slices, and drizzle with oil.

from Bruschetta, Six Ways

green goddess dip

MAKES 2½ CUPS | PHOTO ON PAGE 210

1 cup mayonnaise

1 tablespoon tarragon vinegar or white-wine vinegar

4 anchovy fillets, finely chopped

1 small garlic clove, minced

3 scallions, chopped

3 tablespoons chopped fresh flat-leaf parsley

3 tablespoons chopped fresh chives

1 tablespoon chopped fresh tarragon

1 cup sour cream

Coarse salt and freshly ground pepper

Assorted crudités, for serving

1 Process ½ cup mayonnaise, the vinegar, anchovy fillets, garlic, scallions, and herbs in a food processor to combine.

2 Whisk with remaining ½ cup mayonnaise and the sour cream. Season with salt and pepper. Refrigerate at least 1 hour or up to 4 days. Serve with crudités.

from In the Heartland

....

SALADS AND SIDE DISHES

....

beet and mâche salad with aged goat cheese

SERVES 4 TO 6 | PHOTO ON PAGE 217

2 pounds mixed beets, such as red and Chioggia

Orange Vinaigrette (recipe follows)

¼ cup fresh chervil leaves

3 ounces mâche or other tender lettuce

Coarse salt and freshly ground pepper

6 ounces Bûcheron or other aged goat cheese, room temperature, for serving

Crackers, for serving

1 Cover beets with cold water by 2 inches in a large sauce-pan. Bring to a boil; reduce heat to medium. Simmer until tender, about 30 minutes. Let cool; peel, and halve (quarter if large). Toss with vinaigrette. Let stand 30 minutes.

2 Toss together chervil and mâche. Top with beets and 2 tablespoons vinaigrette from bowl. Season with salt and pepper. Serve with goat cheese and crackers.

from Salad Days

orange vinaigrette

MAKES 1⅓ CUPS

1 tablespoon orange zest

¾ cup fresh orange juice

2 tablespoons sherry vinegar

½ teaspoon coarse salt

½ cup extra-virgin olive oil

Freshly ground pepper

Stir together orange zest and juice, the vinegar, and salt in a medium bowl. Pour in oil in a slow, steady stream, whisking until emulsified. Season with pepper.

fingerling potato salad with sugar snap peas

SERVES 4 TO 6 | PHOTO ON PAGE 214

1½ pounds fingerling or other small potatoes, cut into ½-inch-thick rounds

Coarse salt

8 ounces sugar snap peas, plus more, split, for garnish

½ small red onion, thinly sliced

Creamy Tarragon Vinaigrette (recipe follows)

Freshly ground pepper

Fresh tarragon and tarragon flowers, for garnish (optional)

1 Cover potatoes with cold water by 2 inches in a medium saucepan. Bring to a boil; add 3 tablespoons salt. Reduce heat to medium-high; simmer potatoes until tender, about 8 minutes. Transfer to paper towels to drain.

2 Prepare an ice-water bath; set aside. Bring another medium saucepan of water to a boil; add 2 tablespoons salt. Blanch snap peas until just tender, 1 to 2 minutes. Let cool in ice-water bath. Drain, and pat dry.

3 Toss potatoes, snap peas, onion, and vinaigrette in a bowl. Season with salt and pepper. Garnish with split snap peas, tarragon, and tarragon flowers.

from Salad Days

creamy tarragon vinaigrette

MAKES ABOUT ½ CUP

2 teaspoons tarragon vinegar

¾ teaspoon Dijon mustard

Coarse salt

¼ cup extra-virgin olive oil

¼ cup sour cream

2 tablespoons finely chopped fresh tarragon

Freshly ground pepper

Stir together tarragon vinegar and mustard in a medium bowl; season with coarse salt. Pour in oil in a slow, steady stream, whisking until emulsified. Stir in sour cream and tarragon. Season with pepper.

green bean, shell bean, and sweet onion fattoush

SERVES 4 TO 6 | PHOTO ON PAGE 217

Coarse salt

¾ cup shelled fresh shell beans, such as cranberry or lima

½ pound haricots verts, trimmed and cut into 1-inch pieces

3 pocket pitas, split open

Extra-virgin olive oil, for brushing

Freshly ground pepper

Lemon-Garlic Vinaigrette (recipe follows)

½ large Vidalia onion, chopped

1 English (hothouse) cucumber, quartered and cut into 1-inch pieces

4 ounces feta cheese, crumbled

½ cup coarsely chopped fresh mint, plus more for garnish

⅓ cup chopped fresh flat-leaf parsley

1 Prepare an ice-water bath; set aside. Bring a medium pot of water to a boil; add 2 tablespoons salt. Simmer shell beans until tender, 18 to 20 minutes. Let cool in ice-water bath. Drain, and pat dry.

2 Prepare another ice-water bath; set aside. Bring another medium pot of water to a boil; add 2 tablespoons salt. Blanch haricots verts until just tender, about 2 minutes. Let cool in ice-water bath. Drain, and pat dry.

3 Heat a grill or grill pan until medium-hot. Brush both sides of pita halves with oil; season with salt and pepper. Grill pita, turning once, until golden and crisp, about 2 minutes; let cool. Tear into 1-inch pieces.

4 Drizzle ½ cup vinaigrette over shelled and green beans, onion, cucumber, feta, herbs, and pita in a bowl; toss well. Season with salt and pepper. Garnish with mint. Let stand 10 minutes before serving.

from Salad Days

lemon-garlic vinaigrette

MAKES ABOUT ¾ CUP

Freshly grated zest of 1 lemon plus juice of 2 lemons

2 garlic cloves, crushed

½ teaspoon coarse salt

½ cup extra-virgin olive oil

Freshly ground pepper

Stir together lemon zest and juice, garlic cloves, and salt in a medium bowl. Pour in oil in a slow, steady stream, whisking until emulsified. Season with pepper. Let stand at least 15 minutes. Discard garlic before serving.

melon bowls with prosciutto and watercress salad

SERVES 4 | PHOTO ON PAGE 216

4 ounces thinly sliced prosciutto

2 Charentais melons or small cantaloupes

Champagne Vinaigrette (page 170)

8 ounces watercress, tough stems discarded

1 small red onion, halved and thinly sliced

½ cup yellow grape or cherry tomatoes, halved

¼ cup fresh basil leaves

Coarse salt and freshly ground pepper

1 Preheat oven to 325°F. Arrange prosciutto slices in one layer on a wire rack set over a rimmed baking sheet. Bake until crisp, about 20 minutes. Let cool. Coarsely chop half the prosciutto, and set aside.

2 Halve melons, and discard seeds. Drizzle 3 tablespoons vinaigrette over watercress, onion, tomatoes, chopped prosciutto, and basil in a bowl. Season with salt and pepper, and toss well. Divide salad among melon halves, and serve with remaining prosciutto slices.

from Salad Days

champagne vinaigrette

MAKES ABOUT ⅓ CUP

1 tablespoon champagne vinegar

¼ teaspoon coarse salt

3 tablespoons extra-virgin olive oil

Freshly ground pepper

Stir together vinegar and salt in a medium bowl. Pour in oil in a slow, steady stream, whisking until emulsified. Season with pepper.

orange and jicama salad

SERVES 6 TO 8

1 jicama (1½ pounds)

2 navel oranges

4 lemon cucumbers

1 snake melon or English (hothouse) cucumber

1 cup nasturtium flowers and leaves

Coarse salt and freshly ground pepper

½ cup Creamy Orange Vinaigrette (recipe follows)

1 Prepare an ice-water bath; set aside. Peel jicama; cut into 4-inch batons (½ inch thick). Let soak in ice-water bath.

2 Cut peel and pith from oranges; cut flesh into ¼-inch-thick rounds; quarter rounds. Quarter lemon cucumbers lengthwise. Cut melon into ¼-inch-thick rounds.

3 Drain jicama, and pat dry. Arrange all ingredients on a platter. Season with salt and pepper. Drizzle with vinaigrette.

from Brunch with Southwestern Style

creamy orange vinaigrette

MAKES 1 CUP

1 teaspoon cumin seeds

1 navel orange

2 teaspoons Dijon mustard

2 teaspoons orange-flower honey or regular honey

3 tablespoons champagne vinegar

Coarse salt

½ cup extra-virgin olive oil

¼ cup heavy cream

Freshly ground pepper

1 Toast cumin in a dry small skillet over high heat until fragrant, about 1 minute. Finely grind with a mortar and pestle or in a spice grinder.

2 Zest orange; set zest aside. Cut pith from orange. Working over a bowl to catch the juices, cut orange segments from membrane, letting them fall into bowl. Squeeze any remaining juice from membrane into bowl. Remove segments, and coarsely chop; return to bowl.

3 Whisk together mustard, honey, vinegar, 1 teaspoon salt, and the cumin. Pour in oil in a slow, steady stream, whisking until emulsified. Whisk in orange flesh, juice, zest, and the cream; whisk until thickened. Season with salt and pepper.

red romaine salad with walnuts and eggs

SERVES 4 TO 6 | **PHOTO ON PAGE 217**

6 large eggs

1 head red-leaf romaine, torn into pieces

1 cup walnut halves, toasted

Shallot Vinaigrette (recipe follows)

Coarse salt and freshly ground pepper

1 Prepare an ice-water bath; set aside. Put eggs in a medium saucepan of water, and bring to a boil. After 2 minutes, cover; turn off heat. Let stand 6 minutes. Let cool in ice-water bath.

2 Drizzle lettuce and walnuts in a bowl with 5 tablespoons vinaigrette (or to taste); toss. Peel eggs, then halve. Serve on top of salad. Season with salt and pepper.

from Salad Days

shallot vinaigrette

MAKES ¾ CUP

1 shallot, chopped

5 oil-packed anchovy fillets

2 tablespoons red-wine vinegar

1 teaspoon Dijon mustard

1½ teaspoons coarse salt

¾ cup extra-virgin olive oil

Freshly ground pepper

Put shallot, anchovy fillets, vinegar, mustard, and salt in a blender. Let stand 10 minutes. With blender running, pour in olive oil in a slow, steady stream, and blend until emulsified. Season with pepper.

spicy chicken salad in lettuce cups

SERVES 4 TO 6 | **PHOTO ON PAGE 217**

Ground, toasted rice adds crunch and a slight nuttiness to this salad. Thai basil, available at gourmet and farmers' markets, has a licorice flavor; you can use regular basil instead.

1 tablespoon jasmine rice or another long-grain rice
Coarse salt
1 pound ground chicken
Lime-Chile Dressing (recipe follows)
¼ cup chopped fresh Thai basil, plus more for garnish
¼ cup chopped cilantro, plus more for garnish
Freshly ground pepper
1 head Boston lettuce, leaves separated
1 carrot, peeled and cut into matchsticks
½ daikon radish, peeled and cut into matchsticks
3 tablespoons salted, roasted peanuts, chopped

1 Toast rice in a dry nonstick skillet over medium-high heat until deep golden, 1 to 2 minutes. Coarsely grind with a mortar and pestle or in a spice grinder.

2 Bring a medium pot of water to a boil; add 1 tablespoon salt. Boil chicken, separating it into pieces with a spoon, until cooked through, 3 to 4 minutes.

3 Transfer chicken to a medium bowl using a slotted spoon; reserve ¼ cup cooking liquid. Add dressing, rice, herbs, and cooking liquid, and toss. Season with salt and pepper.

4 For each serving, put about ¼ cup chicken in a lettuce leaf. Garnish with carrot, daikon, basil, cilantro, and nuts.

from Salad Days

lime-chile dressing

MAKES ⅔ CUP

5 tablespoons fresh lime juice
3 tablespoons Asian fish sauce
2 tablespoons rice-wine vinegar (not seasoned)
1 tablespoon sugar
2 fresh hot red chiles, finely chopped
2 garlic cloves, minced
2 shallots, thinly sliced
2 tablespoons cilantro, finely chopped

Stir together lime juice, fish sauce, vinegar, sugar, chiles, garlic, and shallots. Let stand at least 15 minutes. Stir in cilantro.

tangy corn salad

SERVES 8 TO 10

4 large shallots, thinly sliced
½ cup red-wine vinegar
3 tablespoons sugar
¼ cup extra-virgin olive oil
6 cups fresh corn kernels (about 6 ears)
1 red bell pepper, cut into ¼-inch dice
½ jicama, peeled and cut into ¼-inch dice
2 to 3 tablespoons fresh lime juice
½ cup small fresh basil leaves
Coarse salt and freshly ground pepper

1 Set the shallots aside in a small bowl. Bring the vinegar and sugar to a boil in a small saucepan, stirring until sugar is dissolved. Pour over shallots, and let cool.

2 Heat 2 tablespoons oil in a large skillet over medium heat until hot but not smoking. Cook corn, stirring, until just tender, 3 to 5 minutes. Transfer to a large bowl; add the bell pepper and jicama, and toss.

3 Transfer shallots to the corn mixture with a slotted spoon; reserve vinegar. Add remaining 2 tablespoons oil, lime juice (to taste), and basil. Add reserved vinegar to taste. Season with salt and pepper.

from In the Heartland

wheat-berry salad

SERVES 8 TO 10

1½ cups wheat berries or pearl barley
½ cup fresh lemon juice
2 tablespoons Dijon mustard
2 tablespoons honey
4 teaspoons coarse salt
¼ teaspoon freshly ground pepper
½ cup extra-virgin olive oil
1 small fennel bulb, trimmed and cut into ¼-inch dice
4 medium cucumbers, peeled, seeded, and cut into ¼-inch dice
2 celery stalks, cut into ¼-inch dice
6 scallions, thinly sliced (about 1 cup)
⅓ cup chopped fresh flat-leaf parsley

1 Cover wheat berries with cold water by 2 inches in a large saucepan. Cover; bring to a boil. Uncover; reduce heat, and simmer until tender, about 40 minutes. Drain, then transfer to a serving bowl.

2 Whisk together lemon juice, mustard, honey, salt, and pepper. Pour in oil in a slow, steady stream, whisking until emulsified. Drizzle over wheat berries; toss.

3 Add fennel, cucumbers, celery, scallions, and parsley; toss. Cover, and refrigerate at least 8 hours to allow the flavors to develop. Bring to room temperature before serving.

from In the Heartland

braised baby bok choy
SERVES 4

Baby bok choy is sold at Asian markets and many grocery stores. If you can't find it, substitute one head of regular bok choy; cut it in half lengthwise, then cut into quarters.

1 tablespoon vegetable oil

8 heads baby bok choy, trimmed, and halved lengthwise if large

¼ cup homemade or low-sodium store-bought chicken stock, or water

3 tablespoons soy sauce

1 Heat oil in a large skillet over medium-high heat until hot but not smoking. Add bok choy, and cook, turning once, until just beginning to turn golden, about 2 minutes. Add stock and soy sauce. Cover; reduce heat to medium, and simmer until bok choy is tender, about 5 minutes. Transfer bok choy to a serving platter, reserving cooking liquid in skillet.

2 Cook liquid over medium-high heat until it is reduced by half, 1 to 2 minutes. Pour over bok choy, and serve.

from What's for Dinner?

coconut noodles
SERVES 4 | **PHOTO ON PAGE 215**

Coarse salt

1 package (8 ounces) thin dried rice noodles

1 can (14 ounces) unsweetened coconut milk

1¾ cups homemade or low-sodium store-bought chicken stock

1 cup loosely packed cilantro, plus more for garnish

½ cup loosely packed fresh basil, plus more for garnish

4 garlic cloves

1 piece (2 inches) fresh ginger, peeled, cut into ⅛-inch-thick rounds

2 small fresh red chiles, halved, stems removed

2 tablespoons Asian fish sauce (optional)

1 fresh lemongrass stalk, bottom 4 inches only, crushed

1 tablespoon sugar

1 to 2 tablespoons fresh lime juice

1 Bring a large pot of water to a boil; add salt. Cook noodles until al dente, about 2 minutes. Drain; rinse with cold water.

2 Bring coconut milk and chicken stock to a gentle simmer in a medium saucepan over medium-low heat. Meanwhile, process cilantro, basil, garlic, ginger, and 1 chile in a food processor until coarsely chopped, 5 seconds. Add cilantro mixture, fish sauce (if desired), lemongrass, and sugar to coconut-milk mixture; simmer 6 minutes. Discard lemongrass.

3 Add noodles, and cook until just heated through, about 1 minute. Remove from heat. Stir in lime juice. Finely chop remaining chile. Divide noodles among bowls, and top with cilantro, basil, and chile.

from What's for Dinner?

green poblano-chile rice
SERVES 6 TO 8

1½ cups long-grain rice

1 bunch scallions, white and pale-green parts only

2 fresh poblano chiles, stems, seeds, and ribs discarded, flesh coarsely chopped

3 garlic cloves

12 cilantro sprigs, plus more for garnish

1 tablespoon vegetable oil

3 cups homemade or low-sodium store-bought chicken stock

Coarse salt and freshly ground pepper

1 Soak rice in water 5 minutes; drain. Purée scallions, chiles, garlic, cilantro, and ¼ cup water in a blender.

2 Heat oil in a large nonstick saucepan over medium-high heat until hot but not smoking. Cook rice, stirring, until just golden, 4 to 5 minutes. Add chile purée; cook, stirring, until rice is almost dry, about 3 minutes. Add stock and 1 teaspoon salt; bring to a boil. Reduce heat to medium-low. Cook until nearly all liquid is absorbed, about 10 minutes. Remove from heat. Cover; let stand until all liquid is absorbed, 25 to 30 minutes. Fluff rice with a fork, and season with salt and pepper. Garnish with cilantro.

from Brunch with Southwestern Style

lamb sausages

SERVES 6

1 tablespoon olive oil

6 lamb sausages

Lime wedges, for serving

Heat oil in a large skillet over medium heat until hot but not smoking. Cook sausages, turning occasionally, until well browned but still slightly pink in center, about 12 minutes. Cut sausages on the diagonal into thirds. Serve with lime wedges.

from Brunch with Southwestern Style

smoky pinto beans

SERVES 6 TO 8

1 pound dried pinto beans, picked over

½ white onion, plus more, finely chopped, for garnish

2 garlic cloves, crushed

2 dried avocado leaves

1 teaspoon dried epazote

3 fresh cilantro sprigs

Coarse salt and freshly ground pepper

2 plum tomatoes, seeded and chopped

2 ounces cotija cheese, crumbled

Lime wedges, for serving

1 Cover beans with cold water by 2 inches in a large bowl; refrigerate 8 hours or overnight.

2 Drain beans; transfer to a small stockpot. Add onion, garlic, avocado leaves, epazote, and cilantro; cover with cold water by 2 inches. Bring to a boil; add 1 tablespoon salt. Reduce heat to medium-low; simmer, adding water as needed to cover beans, until beans are tender and liquid is soupy, 2 to 2½ hours. Discard avocado leaves. Season with salt and pepper. Garnish with onion, tomatoes, and cheese. Serve with lime wedges.

from Brunch with Southwestern Style

MAIN COURSES

boiled or steamed lobsters

SERVES 4

If your lobsters are larger than one and a half pounds, add one to two minutes per quarter pound to the cooking time. Let cooked lobsters stand until cool enough to handle, six to eight minutes.

½ cup plus 2 tablespoons coarse or sea salt (for boiling only)

4 lobsters (1½ pounds each)

TO BOIL: Fill a very large (4-gallon) stockpot three-quarters full with cold water. Bring to rolling boil; add salt. Plunge lobsters, one at a time, headfirst into the water. Cook, uncovered, 12 to 14 minutes (from the time lobsters enter pot).

TO STEAM: Fit a very large stockpot with a steaming basket (or use a round wire rack or an inverted metal colander). Fill pot with cold water just to reach bottom of basket. Cover; bring to a boil. Quickly set lobsters in one layer in pot (or cook in batches). Cook, covered, 15 to 17 minutes.

from Lobster 101

lobster rolls

MAKES 8 | **PHOTO ON PAGE 219**

Top-split buns are the time-honored choice for lobster rolls, but side-split buns can be used instead.

1½ pounds cooked, shelled lobster meat (about four 1½-pound lobsters), chopped into ½-inch pieces

2 tablespoons mayonnaise

½ teaspoon finely chopped fresh chives (optional)

½ teaspoon finely chopped fresh tarragon or chervil (optional)

1 teaspoon fresh lemon juice (or to taste)

Coarse or sea salt

Freshly ground pepper

8 top-split hot-dog buns

1½ tablespoons unsalted butter, melted, for rolls

1 Stir together lobster and mayonnaise. Add the herbs (if desired) and lemon juice; season with salt and pepper. Refrigerate, covered, while preparing rolls, or up to 2 hours.

2 Heat a large heavy skillet or a griddle over medium heat until hot. Lightly brush outside of buns with butter; transfer to skillet. Cook, turning once, until golden brown, about 1½ minutes per side. Spoon ½ cup lobster mixture into each bun.

from Lobster 101

chicken scaloppine with arugula, lemon, and Parmesan

SERVES 4

To prevent the arugula from wilting, let the chicken cool slightly before serving.

- 4 boneless, skinless chicken breast halves (about 6 ounces each)
- ½ teaspoon coarse salt
  Freshly ground pepper
  Olive-oil cooking spray
- 4 teaspoons fresh lemon juice
- 2 tablespoons extra-virgin olive oil
- 8 ounces arugula (about 1 bunch)
- 1 ounce Parmesan cheese, such as Parmigiano-Reggiano
- 4 lemon wedges

1 One at a time, place chicken breast halves on a cutting board between two sheets of plastic wrap. Pound with the flat side of a meat pounder or the bottom of a small, heavy skillet until ¼ inch thick. Sprinkle each piece all over with ⅛ teaspoon salt; season with pepper.

2 Coat a 12-inch nonstick skillet with cooking spray, and heat over medium heat until hot but not smoking. Put 2 chicken breast halves, smooth sides down, in pan; they should lie flat without touching. Cook 4 minutes; turn, and cook until no longer pink in the center, 2 to 3 minutes more. Wipe skillet clean; repeat with remaining chicken.

3 Whisk together lemon juice and 4 teaspoons oil in a large bowl. Add arugula; toss to coat. Divide among four plates. Top with a chicken breast half, and drizzle each with ½ teaspoon oil. Shave cheese with a vegetable peeler, and divide shavings evenly among the plates. Serve with lemon wedges.

PER SERVING: 295 CALORIES, 11 G FAT, 103 MG CHOLESTEROL, 6 G CARBOHYDRATE, 480 MG SODIUM, 44 G PROTEIN, 2 G FIBER

from Fit to Eat: Skinless Chicken Breast

grilled burgers with Maytag blue cheese and heirloom tomatoes

MAKES 10 | PHOTO ON PAGE 218

- 3¼ pounds ground sirloin
- ¼ cup chopped fresh flat-leaf parsley
- ¼ cup Worcestershire sauce
- 1 teaspoon paprika
- 1 tablespoon coarse salt
- 1 teaspoon freshly ground pepper
- 20 thick slices Sabrina's Sandwich Bread (recipe follows) or other white bread, toasted, if desired
- 5 ounces Maytag or other blue cheese, thinly sliced
  Sliced heirloom tomatoes, sliced onions, and torn lettuce, for serving

Heat a grill or grill pan until medium hot. Combine meat, parsley, Worcestershire, paprika, salt, and pepper. Shape into ten ½-inch-thick patties. Grill, turning once, 4 to 5 minutes per side for medium-rare. Serve burgers on bread with blue cheese, tomatoes, onions, and lettuce.

from In the Heartland

Sabrina's sandwich bread

MAKES 2 LOAVES

- 2 envelopes active dry yeast
- 2 cups warm water (about 105°F)
- ¼ cup honey or granulated sugar
- 3 tablespoons plus 1 teaspoon melted unsalted butter, plus more for bowl
- 2 tablespoons coarse salt
- 6 to 7 cups all-purpose flour, plus more for dusting

1 Sprinkle yeast over warm water in the bowl of an electric mixer fitted with the paddle attachment. Add honey, butter, and salt; whisk until yeast is dissolved. Let stand until foamy, about 5 minutes.

2 Add 3 cups flour; mix on low speed until smooth, about 3 minutes. Add 3 more cups flour; mix until incorporated.

3 On a lightly floured surface, knead dough, adding up to 1 cup more flour as needed; knead until smooth, elastic, and slightly sticky, about 5 minutes. Let rise in a large buttered bowl covered with plastic wrap in a warm, draft-free spot until doubled in bulk, about 45 minutes.

4 Preheat oven to 400°F. Butter two 4½-by-8½-inch loaf pans. Punch down the dough; transfer to a lightly floured surface. Divide dough in half. Gently knead each piece until

smooth. Shape each piece into a loaf, tucking sides underneath to form a seam down the middle.

5 Place loaves, seam sides down, in buttered pans. Let rise just until dough reaches tops of pans, 15 to 20 minutes. Brush tops of loaves with butter. Bake until golden brown and hollow-sounding when tapped on bottom (briefly turn out loaf to test), 35 to 45 minutes. Let cool slightly in pans on wire racks, then unmold. Let cool until just warm before slicing.

grilled chicken stuffed with basil and tomato

SERVES 4 | **PHOTO ON PAGE 219**

Before grilling, soak the toothpicks or skewers in water for thirty minutes to prevent them from burning.

- 4 boneless, skinless chicken breast halves (about 6 ounces each)
- ½ teaspoon coarse salt
- Freshly ground pepper
- 2 garlic cloves, minced
- 1 tablespoon extra-virgin olive oil
- 12 fresh basil leaves, plus more for garnish
- 2 beefsteak tomatoes, cut into ¼-inch-thick slices

1 Butterfly chicken breasts: Put halves on a cutting board, smooth sides down, with the pointed ends facing you. Starting on one long side, cut breasts almost in half horizontally (stop about ½ inch before reaching the opposite side). Open cut breasts like a book. Sprinkle each piece all over with ⅛ teaspoon salt; season with pepper. Transfer to a plate, and coat both sides with garlic and oil. Let stand 30 minutes.

2 Heat a grill or grill pan until medium-hot. Place 3 basil leaves on the bottom half of each opened chicken breast; top each with 2 slices tomato. Fold over other half of chicken breast, and secure with two toothpicks or short skewers.

3 Grill chicken breasts, turning once, until golden brown on both sides and no longer pink in the center, about 15 minutes. Place on a clean serving platter; garnish with basil. If desired, remove toothpicks or skewers before serving.

PER SERVING: 239 CALORIES, 6 G FAT, 99 MG CHOLESTEROL, 5 G CARBOHYDRATE, 359 MG SODIUM, 40 G PROTEIN, 1 G FIBER

from Fit to Eat: Skinless Chicken Breast

poached chicken with tarragon sauce and peas

SERVES 4

- 4 boneless, skinless chicken breast halves (about 6 ounces each)
- 4 garlic cloves
- 1 bay leaf
- 6 whole black peppercorns
- 3 cups loosely packed fresh flat-leaf parsley, plus a few sprigs
- ½ cup loosely packed fresh tarragon, plus more for garnish
- 3 thin slices white bread, crusts removed, bread torn into large pieces
- 2½ tablespoons drained capers, rinsed
- 2 tablespoons extra-virgin olive oil
- ½ teaspoon coarse salt
- Freshly ground pepper
- 1½ pounds garden peas, shelled (1½ cups), or 1½ cups frozen peas, thawed

1 Put chicken, garlic, bay leaf, peppercorns, and a few parsley sprigs in a Dutch oven. Fill pot almost to the top with cold water, and bring to a boil. Reduce heat to a bare simmer. Cook until chicken is no longer pink in the center, 18 to 20 minutes; transfer to a bowl. Add enough poaching liquid to cover chicken; let cool. Reserve garlic and ½ cup remaining poaching liquid from pot.

2 Process tarragon, bread, capers, reserved poached garlic, and parsley in a food processor until smooth, about 15 seconds. With processor running, add oil and reserved ½ cup poaching liquid. Stir in salt, and season with pepper.

3 Bring a small pot of water to a boil; add peas. Cook fresh peas until bright green and crisp-tender (or frozen peas until heated through), about 2 minutes; drain. Spoon 2 tablespoons sauce onto each of four plates. Cut each breast half into 5 or 6 pieces. Divide among plates; scatter peas on top. Garnish with tarragon; serve with extra sauce on the side.

PER SERVING: 378 CALORIES, 11 G FAT, 99 MG CHOLESTEROL, 23 G CARBOHYDRATE, 460 MG SODIUM, 46 G PROTEIN, 5 G FIBER

from Fit to Eat: Skinless Chicken Breast

rolled chicken breasts with almond-mint pesto and zucchini

SERVES 4

1 ounce whole blanched almonds (about ¼ cup)

1 medium shallot, coarsely chopped

1¼ cups loosely packed fresh mint leaves

½ cup finely grated pecorino cheese (about 1 ounce)

1 tablespoon plus 2 teaspoons extra-virgin olive oil

4 boneless, skinless chicken breast halves (about 6 ounces each)

Coarse salt and freshly ground pepper

Olive-oil cooking spray

3 medium zucchini, cut into 3-by-½-inch strips

2 garlic cloves, smashed

1 tablespoon red-wine vinegar

1 Toast nuts in a skillet over medium heat, tossing often, until golden and fragrant, about 6 minutes. Let cool completely. Process nuts and shallot in a food processor until a coarse paste forms. Pulse in 1 cup mint. Add cheese and oil; pulse until combined. Transfer to a small bowl.

2 One at a time, place chicken breast halves on a cutting board between two sheets of plastic wrap. Pound with the flat side of a meat mallet or the bottom of a small, heavy skillet until ⅛ to ¼ inch thick. Sprinkle each piece all over with ⅛ teaspoon salt; season with pepper.

3 Put breast halves on a cutting board, smooth side down, and spread evenly with pesto. Roll up chicken, starting with the pointed tip of each piece. Secure with two toothpicks, pushing them in sideways at an angle; set aside.

4 Coat a 12-inch nonstick skillet with cooking spray, and heat over medium-high heat until hot but not smoking. Add zucchini and garlic; season with ⅛ teaspoon salt. Cook, stirring occasionally, until zucchini just turns golden brown, about 5 minutes. Reduce heat to medium, and cook, tossing occasionally, 5 minutes. Stir in vinegar; season with pepper. Transfer zucchini to a medium bowl, and cover with foil.

5 Wipe skillet clean. Coat with cooking spray; heat over medium heat until hot but not smoking. Add rolled chicken; cook, turning to brown all sides, about 5 minutes. Reduce heat to medium-low; continue cooking until chicken is no longer pink in the center, 20 to 25 minutes. Let rest 5 minutes; cut each roll into 5 pieces. Toss reserved zucchini with ¼ cup mint. Divide zucchini and chicken among four plates.

PER SERVING: 339 CALORIES, 13 G FAT, 103 MG CHOLESTEROL, 9 G CARBOHYDRATE, 532 MG SODIUM, 45 G PROTEIN, 3 G FIBER

from Fit to Eat: Skinless Chicken Breast

spicy stir-fried shrimp

SERVES 4 | PHOTO ON PAGE 215

1 tablespoon vegetable oil

1 shallot, thinly sliced

1 pound large shrimp (about 16), peeled and deveined, tails left intact

2 tablespoons Asian chili sauce

1 tablespoon sugar

Coarse salt and freshly ground pepper

1 Heat oil in a large skillet over medium-high heat until hot but not smoking. Add shallot, and cook until softened and light golden, 2 to 3 minutes.

2 Add shrimp, chili sauce, and sugar; cook, stirring constantly, until shrimp are pink and opaque, 3 to 4 minutes. Season with salt and pepper.

from What's for Dinner?

DESSERTS

apricot-pistachio tart

MAKES ONE 9-BY-17-INCH TART | PHOTO ON PAGE 226

1 cup plus 1 tablespoon unsalted pistachios, shelled and toasted

½ cup granulated sugar

8 tablespoons (1 stick) cold unsalted butter, cut into ½-inch cubes

1 large egg

1 teaspoon pure vanilla extract

Pinch of salt

All-purpose flour, for dusting

1 box (17¼ ounces) frozen puff pastry, thawed

1¼ pounds apricots (about 6), cut into ¼-inch-thick wedges

1 large egg yolk

1 tablespoon heavy cream

2 tablespoons turbinado or other raw sugar

¼ cup apricot jam

1 Process 1 cup nuts and the granulated sugar in a food processor to combine. Add butter; process until a paste forms. Add egg, vanilla, and salt; process to combine. Set mixture aside.

2 On a lightly floured surface, press edges of both pastry sheets together to form one large sheet. Roll out to a 9-by-17-inch rectangle; transfer to a baking sheet. Spread reserved pistachio mixture over dough, leaving a ¾-inch border.

3 Position rectangle so that a short end is nearest you. Arrange apricots on top in 4 vertical rows, alternating the direction in which the apricots face from row to row. Fold in edges of dough; use your index finger to make a scalloped border. Refrigerate until cold, about 30 minutes.

4 Preheat oven to 400°F. Whisk together yolk and cream; brush egg wash over edges of tart shell. Coarsely chop remaining tablespoon pistachios; sprinkle pistachios and turbinado sugar over apricots. Bake, rotating sheet about halfway through, until crust is deep golden brown and fruit is juicy, about 35 minutes. Let cool on a wire rack.

5 Meanwhile, heat jam along with 1½ tablespoons water in a small saucepan over low heat, stirring, until thinned, about 2 minutes. Pass through a fine sieve into a small bowl. Brush glaze over fruit.

from Artful Tarts

panna cotta tarts with strawberries
MAKES SIX 4-INCH TARTS | **PHOTO ON PAGE 228**

If your strawberries are sweet, you won't need as much sugar— use an amount at the lower end of our range in step five.

2½ teaspoons unflavored gelatin
   Vegetable oil, for brushing
2½ cups heavy cream
 ¾ cup sugar, plus 2 tablespoons, if needed
 ½ cup crème fraîche
 ½ teaspoon pure vanilla extract
   Pâte Sucrée (recipe follows)
   All-purpose flour, for dusting
 1 pound strawberries, hulled and halved lengthwise or quartered if large
 1 teaspoon balsamic vinegar

1 Sprinkle gelatin over 3 tablespoons water; let soften 10 minutes. Brush insides of six 5-ounce ramekins or custard cups (3¼ inches in diameter) with oil.

2 Bring cream and ½ cup plus 2 tablespoons sugar to a simmer in a medium saucepan over medium heat, stirring occasionally. Reduce heat to medium-low; add gelatin mixture. Cook, stirring, until gelatin and sugar are dissolved. Remove from heat. Whisk in crème fraîche and vanilla. Pour into a medium bowl set in an ice-water bath. Let cool completely, stirring occasionally. Divide mixture among ramekins. Refrigerate until set, about 3 hours, or up to 1 day.

3 Line a rimmed baking sheet with parchment, and place six 4-inch tart rings on top. Divide dough into 6 pieces. One at a time, roll out each piece into a 7-inch circle (⅛ inch thick) on a lightly floured surface. Press each into a tart ring; trim flush with top edge of ring. Refrigerate tart shells until cold, about 30 minutes.

4 Preheat oven to 375°F. Prick bottoms of tart shells all over with a fork. Line tart shells with parchment paper, and fill with pie weights or dried beans. Bake until edges are golden, about 18 minutes. Remove parchment and weights; continue baking until surfaces are golden, about 10 minutes. Let cool on a wire rack.

5 Heat berries, remaining 2 to 4 tablespoons sugar (depending on sweetness of berries), and vinegar in a skillet over medium-low heat, stirring, until juicy, about 5 minutes. Let mixture cool slightly.

6 Unmold panna cottas: Dip ramekins in warm water; pat dry. Run a small knife around edge of each panna cotta; gently coax, and invert onto a tart shell. Top with berries and sauce.

from Artful Tarts

pâte sucrée

2½ cups all-purpose flour
 ¼ cup sugar
 ¼ teaspoon salt
 8 ounces (2 sticks) cold unsalted butter, cut into small pieces
 2 large egg yolks, lightly beaten
 2 to 4 tablespoons cold heavy cream or ice water

Pulse flour, sugar, and salt in a food processor until combined, about 4 times. Add butter, and process until mixture resembles coarse meal, about 10 seconds. With processor running, add yolks. Gradually pour in cream; process until dough begins to come together, no more than 30 seconds. Pat dough into a disk, and wrap in plastic. Refrigerate at least 1 hour and up to 2 days, or freeze up to 1 month.

summer fruit tart

MAKES ONE 9-INCH SQUARE TART | **PHOTO ON PAGE 229**

All-purpose flour, for dusting

Pâte Sucrée (page 177)

½ cup cold heavy cream

Buttermilk Pastry Cream (recipe follows)

2 cups blackberries

6 ounces fresh figs (about 6), quartered

1 cup blueberries, picked over

1 cup strawberries, hulled and halved lengthwise

¼ cup red currants

2 tablespoons red-currant jelly

1 On a lightly floured surface, roll out dough to ¼ inch thick. Gently press dough into a 9-inch square tart pan with a removable bottom. Trim dough flush with top edge of pan. Refrigerate until cold, about 30 minutes.

2 Preheat oven to 375°F. Prick bottom of dough all over with a fork. Line with parchment paper; fill with pie weights or dried beans. Bake until edges are golden, 15 to 17 minutes. Remove parchment and weights; continue baking until surface is golden, about 20 minutes. Let cool on a wire rack. Remove tart shell from pan.

3 Beat heavy cream until soft peaks form. Gently fold into pastry cream; spread into tart shell. Arrange fruit on top of cream in concentric squares. Refrigerate.

4 Heat jelly with 2 tablespoons water in a small saucepan over low heat, stirring, until thinned, about 2 minutes. Pass through a fine sieve into a bowl. Brush glaze over figs.

from Artful Tarts

buttermilk pastry cream

MAKES 1 CUP

¼ cup sugar

3 tablespoons all-purpose flour

Pinch of salt

1 cup low-fat buttermilk

2 large egg yolks

¼ teaspoon pure vanilla extract

1 tablespoon freshly grated lemon zest

2 teaspoons fresh lemon juice

1 Prepare an ice-water bath; set aside. Whisk together sugar, flour, and salt; set aside. Put buttermilk and yolks in a small saucepan. Gradually whisk in sugar mixture, and cook over medium heat, whisking constantly, until thick enough to coat the back of a spoon, about 4 minutes. Stir in vanilla, zest, and lemon juice.

2 Pour pastry cream into a bowl; set in ice-water bath. Let cool completely, stirring occasionally. Refrigerate in an airtight container until ready to use, up to 2 days.

sweet cherry galette

MAKES ONE 14-INCH TART | **PHOTO ON PAGE 227**

All-purpose flour, for dusting

Pâte Sucrée (page 177)

¼ cup plus 2 tablespoons sugar

¼ cup unsalted almonds, toasted and cooled

¼ teaspoon freshly grated nutmeg

¼ teaspoon salt

1½ pounds sweet cherries, such as Bing, pitted

2 tablespoons cold unsalted butter, cut into small pieces

1 large egg yolk

1 tablespoon heavy cream

1 On a piece of lightly floured parchment, roll out dough to a 16-inch-long oval (¼ inch thick). Transfer dough and parchment to a baking sheet. Refrigerate 30 minutes.

2 Process ¼ cup sugar, the almonds, nutmeg, and salt in a food processor to combine. Gently toss with cherries.

3 Preheat oven to 375°F. Spoon cherries over dough, leaving a 2-inch border. Dot with butter. Fold in edges, pressing gently. Refrigerate until cold, 30 minutes.

4 Whisk yolk with cream; brush over edges of tart. Sprinkle entire surface of tart with remaining 2 tablespoons sugar (or to taste). Bake until golden, 45 to 50 minutes.

from Artful Tarts

berry tartlets

MAKES SIXTEEN 2½-INCH TARTLETS | **PHOTO ON PAGE 229**

Pâte Sucrée (page 177)

All-purpose flour, for dusting

Orange-Vanilla Pastry Cream (recipe follows)

1¼ **cups mixed berries, such as red and golden raspberries, blueberries, blackberries, red and white currants, gooseberries, and wineberries, picked over**

Blueberry leaves, for garnish (optional)

1 Divide dough in half. On a lightly floured surface, roll out 1 piece to ⅛ inch thick. (Keep remaining dough refrigerated.) Using a 3-inch round cookie cutter, cut out 8 rounds. Gently press into eight 2½-inch round tart pans. Trim dough flush with top edge of pans. Refrigerate until cold, about 30 minutes.

2 Preheat oven to 375°F. Line tart shells with parchment, and fill with pie weights or dried beans. Bake until edges are golden, 12 to 14 minutes. Remove parchment and weights; continue baking until surfaces are golden, about 10 minutes. Let cool on a wire rack. Repeat process with remaining dough.

3 Remove tart shells from pans; spoon 2 teaspoons pastry cream into each. Top with berries. Refrigerate until ready to serve. Top with berry leaves, if desired.

from Artful Tarts

orange-vanilla pastry cream

MAKES ¾ CUP

1 **cup whole milk**

½ **vanilla bean, halved lengthwise and seeds scraped to loosen**

2 **tablespoons freshly grated orange zest**

2 **large egg yolks**

¼ **cup plus 3 tablespoons sugar**

3 **tablespoons all-purpose flour**

1 Bring milk, vanilla bean, and zest to a simmer in a medium saucepan over medium heat. Remove from heat. Cover, and let steep 20 minutes.

2 Put yolks and sugar in the bowl of an electric mixer fitted with the whisk attachment; beat on high speed until pale and fluffy, about 2 minutes. Add flour; mix until incorporated.

3 On low speed, add ½ cup steeped milk. Return milk-yolk mixture to pan; whisk. Heat over medium heat, whisking, until thick enough to coat the back of a wooden spoon, about 4 minutes. Pass through a fine sieve into a bowl set in an ice-water bath. Let cool completely, stirring occasionally. Refrigerate in an airtight container until ready to use, up to 2 days.

blueberry-lemon tart

MAKES ONE 9-INCH TART | **PHOTO ON PAGE 229**

½ **recipe Pâte Sablée (page 180)**

½ **cup sugar**

3 **tablespoons all-purpose flour, plus more for dusting**

2 **pinches of salt**

1 **cup low-fat buttermilk**

2 **large eggs, separated, room temperature**

½ **teaspoon pure vanilla extract**

1 **tablespoon freshly grated lemon zest**

2 **teaspoons fresh lemon juice**

Pinch cream of tartar

2 **cups blueberries, picked over**

1 **tablespoon honey**

1 Preheat oven to 375°F. Place a 9-inch cake ring on a rimmed baking sheet lined with parchment. Roll out dough between sheets of lightly floured parchment to an 11-inch circle (⅛ inch thick). Refrigerate 15 minutes. Peel off parchment; press dough into ring. Trim flush with top edge of ring. Refrigerate until cold, about 30 minutes.

2 Prick dough all over with a fork. Line tart shell with parchment, and fill with pie weights or dried beans. Bake until crust starts to turn golden, 20 to 25 minutes. Remove parchment and weights; continue baking until pale golden, about 5 minutes more. Let cool on a wire rack.

3 Whisk together ¼ cup sugar, the flour, and a pinch of salt; set aside. Whisk buttermilk and yolks in a small saucepan over medium-low heat; gradually whisk in sugar mixture. Cook, whisking constantly, until thickened, 5 to 7 minutes. Stir in vanilla, zest, and juice. Transfer to a medium bowl set in an ice-water bath. Let cool completely, stirring occasionally.

4 Meanwhile, put whites and cream of tartar in the bowl of an electric mixer fitted with the whisk attachment. Add a pinch of salt. Beat on low speed until foamy. With mixer running, gradually add remaining ¼ cup sugar. On medium-high, beat until stiff, glossy peaks form.

5 Gently fold pastry cream and 1 cup berries into meringue. Pour mixture into tart shell, making swirls and peaks. Bake until golden, 40 to 45 minutes. Let cool on a wire rack. Remove cake ring.

6 Meanwhile, heat remaining cup berries and honey in a medium skillet over medium-low heat, stirring gently, until just warm, about 2 minutes. Spoon glazed berries over tart.

from Artful Tarts

pâte sablée

8 ounces (2 sticks) unsalted butter, softened

¾ cup confectioners' sugar

4½ teaspoons pure vanilla extract

2 cups all-purpose flour

1 teaspoon salt

Put butter and sugar in the bowl of an electric mixer fitted with the paddle attachment. Mix on medium speed until pale and fluffy, about 3 minutes; mix in vanilla. Add the flour and the salt, and mix on medium-low speed until just combined and crumbly, about 15 seconds (do not overmix). Pat the dough into a disk, and wrap in plastic. Refrigerate at least 1 hour or up to 2 days, or freeze up to 1 month.

fig and grape tart

MAKES ONE 4-BY-14-INCH TART

Pâte Sablée (recipe above)

1 cup Almond Frangipane (recipe follows)

4 ounces figs (about 4), halved lengthwise or quartered if large

⅓ cup black seedless grapes, halved

1 tablespoon turbinado or other raw sugar

Gorgonzola dolce, for serving

1   Press dough into a 4-by-14-inch rectangular tart pan with a removable bottom. Refrigerate 10 minutes. Trim dough flush with top edge of pan. Refrigerate until cold, about 30 minutes.

2   Preheat oven to 375°F. Line tart shell with parchment, and fill with pie weights or dried beans. Bake until edges are golden, about 15 minutes. Remove parchment and weights; continue baking until surface is golden, about 10 minutes. Let cool on a wire rack.

3   Spread frangipane in tart shell. Arrange figs and grapes on top, pressing gently. Sprinkle with the sugar. Bake until golden, 40 to 45 minutes. Let cool on rack. Serve with Gorgonzola.

from Artful Tarts

almond frangipane

MAKES 2 CUPS

1 cup whole blanched almonds, toasted and cooled

½ cup plus 3 tablespoons sugar

8 tablespoons (1 stick) unsalted butter, softened

1 large egg plus 1 large egg yolk, room temperature

2 teaspoons all-purpose flour

½ vanilla bean, halved lengthwise and seeds scraped to loosen

¼ teaspoon salt

1   Preheat oven to 375°F. Process nuts with 3 tablespoons sugar in a food processor until finely ground.

2   Put butter and remaining ½ cup sugar in the bowl of an electric mixer fitted with the paddle attachment; cream on medium speed until pale and fluffy, about 2 minutes. Add egg and yolk; mix 2 minutes. Add nut mixture, flour, vanilla seeds, and salt; mix on medium-high until pale and fluffy, about 3 minutes. Refrigerate frangipane in an airtight container until ready to use, up to 3 days.

sugar plum tart

MAKES ONE 10-INCH TART | PHOTO ON PAGE 229

Pâte Sablée (recipe above)

Almond Frangipane (recipe above)

1 pound 2 ounces sugar plums or other small plums, halved crosswise and pitted

3 tablespoons turbinado or other raw sugar

Confectioners' sugar, for dusting

1   Press dough into a 10-inch round tart pan with a removable bottom. Refrigerate 10 minutes. Trim dough flush with top edge of pan. Refrigerate until cold, about 30 minutes.

2   Preheat oven to 350°F. Line tart shell with parchment, and fill with pie weights or dried beans. Bake until edges are golden, about 10 minutes. Remove parchment and weights; continue baking until surface is golden, about 10 minutes. Let cool on a wire rack.

3   Spread frangipane in tart shell. Arrange plums, cut sides up, on top in concentric circles, pressing down gently. Sprinkle with turbinado sugar. Bake tart until golden, 45 to 50 minutes. Let cool on a wire rack. Just before serving, dust tart with confectioners' sugar.

from Artful Tarts

plum and piñon coffee cake

MAKES ONE 10-INCH CAKE | **PHOTO ON PAGE 230**

Piñon is Spanish for "pine nut."

FOR THE STREUSEL:

3 tablespoons cold unsalted butter

½ cup packed dark-brown sugar

1 teaspoon ground canela (Mexican cinnamon) or regular cinnamon

½ cup pine nuts, toasted

Pinch of salt

FOR THE CRUMB TOPPING:

1½ cups all-purpose flour

12 tablespoons (1½ sticks) unsalted butter, softened

¾ cup confectioners' sugar, plus more for dusting

¼ teaspoon salt

FOR THE CAKE:

12 tablespoons (1½ sticks) unsalted butter, softened, plus more for pan

2½ cups all-purpose flour, plus more for dusting

2 teaspoons baking powder

1 teaspoon baking soda

½ teaspoon salt

1¼ cups granulated sugar

3 large eggs, lightly beaten

1½ cups sour cream

12 ounces Italian prune plums or other plums, cut into ½-inch pieces

4 teaspoons pure vanilla extract

1 Make streusel: Put all streusel ingredients in a bowl. Using a pastry cutter or two knives, blend until mixture resembles coarse meal. Refrigerate.

2 Make crumb topping: Put all topping ingredients in a bowl. Using a pastry cutter or two knives, blend until mixture resembles coarse meal. Refrigerate.

3 Make cake: Preheat oven to 375°F. Butter and flour a 10-inch tube pan. Sift flour, baking powder, baking soda, and salt together into a medium bowl; set aside.

4 Put butter and granulated sugar in the bowl of an electric mixer fitted with the paddle attachment. Cream on medium-high speed until pale and fluffy, 2 to 3 minutes. Add beaten eggs in two batches, mixing well. Mix in one-third of flour mixture. Mix in half of sour cream. Repeat with remaining flour and sour cream. Stir in plums by hand.

5 Pour half of the batter into prepared pan; sprinkle with streusel. Top with remaining batter. Pour vanilla on top. Bake 20 minutes. Sprinkle with crumb topping; bake until golden brown, 25 to 30 minutes more. Let cool on a wire rack. Unmold cake. Dust with confectioners' sugar.

from Brunch with Southwestern Style

profiteroles with chocolate-macadamia semifreddo

MAKES ABOUT 20

4 tablespoons unsalted butter

½ teaspoon sugar

¼ teaspoon salt

½ cup all-purpose flour

2 large eggs, plus 1 large egg white if needed

Chocolate-Macadamia Semifreddo (page 182)

Chocolate Sauce (page 182)

1 Preheat oven to 350°F. Line a baking sheet with parchment paper, and set aside. Bring butter, sugar, salt, and ½ cup water to a boil in a small saucepan over medium-high heat. Remove from heat, and stir in flour. Return to medium-high heat; stir with a wooden spoon until batter pulls away from sides of pan, about 4 minutes.

2 Transfer batter to the bowl of an electric mixer fitted with the paddle attachment. Mix on low speed until slightly cooled, about 2 minutes. With mixer on medium speed, add eggs, one at a time, mixing well after each addition. Test batter for doneness by dabbing it with your finger; as you pull away, a sticky thread should form. If not, add the extra egg white, 1 teaspoon at a time.

3 Fit a pastry bag with a ½-inch plain round tip, and fill with dough. Pipe 1½-inch-diameter rounds 2 inches apart on lined sheet. Gently smooth peaked tops with a dampened fingertip.

4 Bake until golden brown, 28 to 30 minutes. Let cool completely on a wire rack. If not using immediately, store at room temperature in an airtight container up to 3 days, or freeze up to 1 month.

5 To assemble profiteroles, halve them horizontally, and fill with a 1½-ounce ice-cream scoop (3 tablespoons) of semifreddo. Top profiteroles with chocolate sauce.

from Dessert of the Month

chocolate-macadamia semifreddo

MAKES 5 CUPS

⅔ cup salted macadamia nuts

4 ounces bittersweet chocolate, coarsely chopped

⅔ cup sugar

1⅓ cups heavy cream

3 large egg whites

¼ teaspoon pure vanilla extract

1 Preheat oven to 350°F. Toast nuts on a baking sheet until pale golden brown, about 10 minutes. Let cool completely.

2 Pulse the nuts and chocolate in a food processor until coarsely ground. Add ⅓ cup sugar, and pulse until combined, about 7 times. (Do not overprocess; mixture should not form a paste.) Set aside.

3 Beat cream in the bowl of an electric mixer fitted with the whisk attachment until stiff peaks form. Transfer to a large bowl; cover with plastic wrap, and refrigerate. Meanwhile, beat egg whites in the clean bowl of the mixer fitted with the clean whisk attachment until soft peaks form. Add vanilla and remaining ⅓ cup sugar; beat until stiff peaks form.

4 Fold egg whites into whipped cream; gently fold in nut mixture. Spoon into a glass baking dish, and smooth with a rubber spatula. Press plastic wrap on surface; freeze at least 4 hours, or up to 1 week.

Note: Raw eggs should not be used in food prepared for pregnant women, babies, young children, the elderly, or anyone whose health is compromised.

chocolate sauce

MAKES ABOUT 1 CUP

5 ounces bittersweet chocolate, melted

¼ cup light corn syrup

Whisk chocolate, corn syrup, and ¼ cup hot water in a small bowl until smooth. If not using immediately, refrigerate, covered, up to 3 days; bring to room temperature before using.

sugar cream pie

MAKES ONE 9-INCH PIE | **PHOTO ON PAGE 231**

½ recipe Pâte Brisée (recipe follows)

1 cup sugar

½ cup all-purpose flour

½ teaspoon salt

2 cups heavy cream

2 teaspoons pure vanilla extract

2 tablespoons unsalted butter, cut into small pieces

¼ teaspoon freshly grated nutmeg

Raspberries, for serving

Raspberry Whipped Cream, for serving (recipe follows)

1 Roll out dough to an 11-inch circle (⅛ inch thick). Fit into a 9-inch pie plate; crimp edges. Refrigerate pie shell. Preheat oven to 425°F. Sift sugar, flour, and salt together into a stainless-steel bowl, and set aside.

2 Prepare an ice-water bath; set aside. Heat cream in a small saucepan over medium-high heat until hot but not boiling. Whisk into sugar mixture; whisk until sugar is dissolved. Stir in vanilla. Set in ice-water bath, and let cool completely.

3 Pour filling into pie shell. Dot with butter; sprinkle with nutmeg. Bake 15 minutes. Reduce temperature to 350°F. Cover edges of crust with a foil band. Bake until a thin knife inserted in the center comes out clean, 50 to 55 minutes more. Let cool on a wire rack. Serve pie warm with berries and raspberry whipped cream.

from In the Heartland

pâte brisée

MAKES ENOUGH FOR 2 SUGAR CREAM PIES

2½ cups all-purpose flour

1 teaspoon salt

1 teaspoon sugar

8 ounces (2 sticks) cold unsalted butter, cut into small pieces

Scant ¼ cup ice water

1 Pulse flour, salt, and sugar in a food processor to combine. Add butter; pulse until mixture resembles coarse meal. Drizzle in ice water, processing just until dough comes together.

2 Divide dough in half; turn each half out onto a sheet of plastic. Flatten each into a circle; wrap. Refrigerate until cold, at least 30 minutes and up to 2 days, or freeze up to 1 month.

raspberry whipped cream

MAKES 1 QUART

2 teaspoons sugar

1 cup raspberries

1½ cups cold heavy cream

1   Sprinkle sugar over raspberries in a bowl. Let stand until juices are released, about 30 minutes. Mash gently with a fork until saucy but still chunky.

2   Beat cream until stiff peaks form. Fold raspberry mixture into whipped cream, leaving it slightly swirled.

mini black-and-white cookies

MAKES ABOUT 4 DOZEN | PHOTO ON PAGE 225

1¼ cups all-purpose flour

½ teaspoon baking soda

½ teaspoon salt

6 tablespoons unsalted butter, softened

½ cup granulated sugar

1 large egg

¾ teaspoon pure vanilla extract

⅓ cup low-fat buttermilk

2 cups confectioners' sugar

4 teaspoons light corn syrup

2½ teaspoons fresh lemon juice

1 tablespoon unsweetened cocoa powder

1   Preheat oven to 350°F. Line two baking sheets with parchment paper. Sift flour, baking soda, and salt into a bowl; set aside. In the bowl of an electric mixer fitted with the paddle attachment, mix butter until creamy, about 2 minutes. Add granulated sugar, and mix until fluffy, about 3 minutes. Mix in egg and ½ teaspoon vanilla. Mix in flour mixture in 3 batches, alternating with the buttermilk.

2   Roll tablespoons of dough into balls (or use a ½-ounce capacity ice-cream scoop); place them 2 inches apart on lined sheets. Bake until bottoms turn golden, about 10 minutes. Transfer to wire racks; let cool.

3   Whisk confectioners' sugar, corn syrup, lemon juice, remaining ¼ teaspoon vanilla, and 1 tablespoon water in a small bowl until smooth. If necessary, add more water (icing should be a bit thicker than honey). Transfer half to a small bowl. Stir in cocoa; if necessary, thin with water. Spread white icing on half of each cookie's flat side, and cocoa icing on other half; let set 30 minutes.

from Cookie of the Month

sweet sesame wonton crisps

SERVES 4

Serve these crisp wontons as an alternative to fortune cookies. If you like, use round wrappers instead of square.

8 square wonton wrappers, thawed if frozen

1½ teaspoons sugar

¼ teaspoon ground ginger

Pinch of salt

1 large egg yolk

1 tablespoon heavy cream

4 teaspoons white or black sesame seeds, or a mixture

1 pint sorbet, such as mango, for serving

1   Preheat oven to 350°F. Line a rimmed baking sheet with parchment paper. Arrange wonton wrappers in a single layer on baking sheet, and set aside.

2   Stir together sugar, ginger, and salt in a small bowl; set aside. Whisk together the egg yolk and cream in another small bowl. Brush wontons with egg wash, and sprinkle each with about ½ teaspoon sesame seeds and a scant ¼ teaspoon sugar mixture. Bake until wontons are golden and crisp, 8 to 10 minutes. Let cool on sheet on a wire rack. Serve wonton crisps with sorbet.

from What's for Dinner?

. . . .

DRINKS

. . . .

Bloody Marys with tequila

SERVES 6 | PHOTO ON PAGE 209

3 cups tomato juice

3 tablespoons prepared horseradish (or more to taste)

½ cup tequila

2 teaspoons Worcestershire sauce

Coarse salt

Juice of 1 lime

1 teaspoon freshly ground pepper

Dash of hot sauce, such as Tabasco

Pickled jalapeños, for garnish (page 184)

Stir together juice, horseradish, tequila, Worcestershire, salt, lime juice, pepper, and hot sauce in a pitcher. Pour into ice-filled glasses, and garnish with jalapeños.

from Brunch with Southwestern Style

pickled jalapeños

MAKES 20

2 cups distilled white vinegar
1 tablespoon coarse salt
1 tablespoon sugar
1 teaspoon cumin seeds, lightly toasted
8 garlic cloves
20 fresh jalapeño chiles
2 small red onions, cut into ¼-inch-thick rings

Bring vinegar, 1 cup water, salt, sugar, cumin, and garlic to a boil in a medium saucepan. Add jalapeños and onions; boil 5 minutes. Let cool completely, about 45 minutes. Refrigerate in an airtight container at least 1 week or up to 1 month.

prickly pear aguas frescas

SERVES 6 | PHOTO ON PAGE 209

Prickly pear flesh can stain; wear disposable gloves when working with them.

4 prickly pears, peeled
¼ cup sugar
Juice of 2 limes, plus slices for garnish
¼ teaspoon ground canela (Mexican cinnamon) or regular cinnamon
2 cups ice

Purée pears in a blender. Pass through a fine sieve into a bowl. Purée pear liquid, sugar, lime juice, canela, and ice in blender 1 minute. Pour into glasses, and garnish with limes.

from Brunch with Southwestern Style

sparkling fresh lemonade

SERVES 10 | PHOTO ON PAGE 210

1 cup sugar
2 cups fresh lemon juice (about 10 lemons)
3 cups cold sparkling water
4½ cups ice

1   Bring 1 cup water and the sugar to a boil in a small saucepan, stirring until sugar is dissolved. Let cool completely; refrigerate until ready to use.

2   Put syrup, lemon juice, and sparkling water in a pitcher. Stir in the ice.

from In the Heartland

lobster stock

MAKES ABOUT 3 QUARTS | PHOTO ON PAGE 213

Use this stock as a base for dishes such as seafood chowder, bisque, stew, and risotto.

Shells from 4 cooked lobsters, including carapaces
2 tablespoons olive oil
2 small onions, quartered
2 small carrots, peeled and cut into 1-inch pieces
2 celery stalks, cut into 1-inch pieces
4 garlic cloves
1 small fennel bulb, trimmed and quartered (optional)
1 can (14½ ounces) whole peeled plum tomatoes, chopped, including juice
2 cups dry white wine (optional)
8 whole black peppercorns
6 fresh thyme sprigs
6 fresh flat-leaf parsley sprigs
1 bay leaf

1   Remove head sacs (behind eyes) in carapaces; discard. Remove any green tomalley or red roe; reserve for another use or discard. Wrap shells in a clean kitchen towel. Using a rolling pin, meat pounder, or hammer, break shells (some large pieces might remain).

2   Heat oil in a Dutch oven or stockpot over medium heat until hot but not smoking. Add shells; cook until fragrant (do not let blacken), about 3 minutes.

3   Stir in onions, carrots, celery, garlic, and fennel (if desired). Cook, without stirring, until vegetables begin to brown, about 3 minutes. Add tomatoes, wine (if desired), peppercorns, thyme, parsley, and bay leaf.

4   Fill pot two-thirds with cold water (about 4½ quarts). Bring to a boil. Reduce heat to a simmer. Skim froth from surface with a ladle. Cook until broth is aromatic and flavorful, about 1 hour 45 minutes.

5   Carefully pour stock through a fine sieve set over a large bowl or container. Discard solids; let stock cool completely. If not using immediately, refrigerate in airtight containers up to 3 days, or freeze up to 2 months.

from Lobster 101

August

polenta and spinach soup

SERVES 4

½ cup plus 4 teaspoons extra-virgin olive oil

3 garlic cloves, minced

½ cup yellow cornmeal

½ cup finely grated Parmesan cheese

3 cups coarsely chopped baby spinach (about 2 ounces)

1 teaspoon coarse salt

 Freshly ground pepper

1 lemon, cut into wedges

1 Heat ¼ cup oil and the garlic in a medium saucepan over medium heat until garlic is fragrant, about 1 minute.

2 Add 6 cups water, and bring to a boil. Whisking constantly, add cornmeal in a slow, steady stream. Reduce heat to medium; cook, stirring occasionally, until soup has thickened slightly, about 8 minutes. Add cheese and ¼ cup oil; cook, stirring, until oil is incorporated, about 1 minute. Stir in spinach and salt; cook, stirring, until spinach is bright green and wilted, about 1 minute more.

3 Divide soup among four bowls; drizzle each serving with 1 teaspoon oil. Season soup with pepper; serve with lemon wedges.

PER SERVING: 393 CALORIES, 35 G FAT, 8 MG CHOLESTEROL, 17 G CARBOHYDRATE, 780 MG SODIUM, 6 G PROTEIN, 3 G FIBER

from Fit to Eat: Olive Oil

Southwestern corn chowder

SERVES 4 TO 6 | **PHOTO ON PAGE 212**

4 ounces bacon (5 or 6 slices), cut into ½-inch pieces

1 medium onion, cut into ½-inch pieces

1 large carrot, cut into ½-inch pieces

2 celery stalks, cut into ½-inch pieces

1 small fresh poblano chile, seeded and cut into ¼-inch dice

 Coarse salt

½ teaspoon ground cumin

 Freshly ground pepper

 Pinch of cayenne pepper

1 cup dry white wine

1 pound Yukon gold potatoes, peeled and cut into ½-inch cubes

5 cups homemade or low-sodium store-bought chicken or vegetable stock

3 cups fresh corn kernels (from about 6 ears)

1 cup heavy cream

¼ cup coarsely chopped cilantro, plus more for garnish

 Hot sauce, such as Tabasco (optional)

1 Heat a dry large pot over medium heat. Add bacon pieces, and cook, stirring occasionally, until crisp, about 5 minutes. Transfer with a slotted spoon to paper towels to drain.

2 Add onion to pot, and cook until just softened, about 4 minutes. Add carrot, celery, and poblano; cook until vegetables are just tender, about 5 minutes. Stir in 1 teaspoon salt, the cumin, ¼ teaspoon pepper, and the cayenne. Raise heat to high, and add wine. Cook until most of the liquid has evaporated, 2 to 3 minutes. Add potatoes and stock, and bring to a boil. Reduce heat to medium-low; gently simmer until all vegetables are tender, about 20 minutes.

3 Stir in corn and cream; cook until corn is tender (do not let cream boil), about 5 minutes more. Stir in cilantro. Season with salt and pepper. Garnish with cilantro and reserved bacon pieces; add hot sauce, if desired.

from Sweet on Corn

grilled bread with chimichurri

SERVES 6

Ciabatta, a long, flat Italian bread, is ideal for this recipe, but you could also use a rustic round loaf; instead of splitting it horizontally, cut six one-and-a-quarter-inch-thick slices. You can refrigerate any leftover chimichurri in an airtight container for up to two days.

½ cup plus 2 tablespoons olive oil

1 medium onion, thinly sliced

½ cup packed fresh flat-leaf parsley leaves

½ teaspoon coarse salt

2 tablespoons red-wine vinegar

2 tablespoons packed cilantro leaves

1 tablespoon fresh oregano leaves

1 tablespoon fresh lemon juice

2 garlic cloves, finely chopped

¼ teaspoon freshly ground pepper

½ teaspoon ground cumin

⅛ teaspoon cayenne pepper

1 large ciabatta loaf, halved horizontally

1   Heat 1 tablespoon oil in a medium skillet over medium heat until hot but not smoking. Add onion, and stir to coat. Cook, stirring, until softened, 3 to 4 minutes. Reduce heat to low, and continue to cook, stirring occasionally, until golden brown, 7 to 8 minutes more. Let cool.

2   Make chimichurri: Process onion, parsley, salt, vinegar, cilantro, oregano, lemon juice, garlic, pepper, cumin, cayenne, and 5 tablespoons oil in a food processor until ingredients are finely chopped and mixture comes together, about 15 seconds. Set aside.

3   Preheat a grill to medium-high (if using a charcoal grill, the coals are ready when you can hold your hand 5 inches above the grill for just 3 to 4 seconds). Using remaining ¼ cup oil, brush cut sides of bread. Grill, cut sides down, without turning, until undersides are lightly charred, about 4 minutes. Cut each bread half crosswise into 3 pieces, and spread each piece with chimichurri.

from Lakeside Picnic

spiked clams and oysters

SERVES 6

Using tequila as a steaming liquid enhances the flavor of the clams and oysters, but it's fine to use water instead. Setting the skillet over a grill will give the dish a touch of smokiness, or you can use your stove turned to medium-high heat.

½ cup tequila

12 littleneck clams (about 1¼ pounds), scrubbed well

12 oysters, such as Malpeque or bluepoint (about 2 pounds), scrubbed well

Chipotle Mayonnaise (recipe follows)

Bloody Mary Sauce (recipe follows)

Lime-Mint Sauce (recipe follows)

1   Preheat a grill to medium-high (if using a charcoal grill, the coals are ready when you can hold your hand 5 inches above the grill for just 3 to 4 seconds). Pour tequila into a medium cast-iron skillet. Add clams and oysters, and tightly cover the skillet with foil. Transfer skillet to grill.

2   Cook oysters and clams until they open (check frequently after 8 minutes, lifting corner of foil with tongs). Using tongs, transfer clams and oysters, as they open, to serving bowls; continue to cook until all oysters and clams are open, up to 5 minutes more. (Discard any that remain closed.) Serve with chipotle mayonnaise and sauces.

from Lakeside Picnic

chipotle mayonnaise

MAKES ABOUT 1 CUP

1 garlic clove

¾ cup mayonnaise

1 tablespoon chopped chipotle chiles in adobo

1 teaspoon fresh lime juice

⅛ teaspoon ground cumin

Coarse salt

Process garlic in a food processor until finely chopped. Add mayonnaise, chipotles, lime juice, and cumin, and process until smooth. Season with salt. If not serving immediately, refrigerate in an airtight container up to 4 days.

Bloody Mary sauce

MAKES ABOUT ⅔ CUP

½ pint cherry tomatoes (about 1 cup)

1½ teaspoons Worcestershire sauce

¼ teaspoon hot sauce, such as Tabasco

1½ teaspoons fresh lemon juice

1 small celery stalk, chopped, plus leaves
   for garnish (optional)

Coarse salt

1½ teaspoons finely grated peeled fresh horseradish,
   or prepared horseradish to taste

1 Blend tomatoes, Worcestershire sauce, hot sauce, lemon juice, and celery in a blender until smooth. Transfer tomato purée to a small saucepan, and season with salt.

2 Cook over medium heat, stirring occasionally, until purée is reduced slightly, about 8 minutes.

3 Pass through a fine sieve set over a bowl, pressing on solids to extract liquid; discard solids. Stir in the horseradish. (If not serving immediately, refrigerate in an airtight container up to 1 day.) Just before serving, garnish sauce with celery leaves, if desired.

lime-mint sauce

MAKES 1 CUP

¼ cup fresh lime juice plus 1 tablespoon freshly grated
   lime zest (2 to 3 limes)

½ cup packed fresh mint leaves

3 tablespoons sugar

3 tablespoons tequila

1 Bring lime juice, zest, mint, sugar, and ½ cup water to a boil in a small saucepan. Remove from heat; cover, and let steep until completely cool, 20 to 25 minutes.

2 Pass lime-juice mixture through a fine sieve set over a bowl, pressing on solids to extract liquid; discard solids. (If not serving immediately, refrigerate sauce in an airtight container up to 1 day.) Just before serving, stir in tequila.

SALADS AND SIDE DISHES

black-eyed-pea and jalapeño salad

SERVES 4 | PHOTO ON PAGE 220

Piquant jalapeño chiles complement the earthy flavor of black-eyed peas in this fiber-rich side salad; they, along with the diced red onion, also add crunch.

2 cans (15 ounces each) black-eyed peas, rinsed and
   drained well

2 fresh jalapeño chiles, seeds and ribs discarded,
   flesh cut into ¼-inch dice

1 small red onion, cut into ¼-inch dice

¾ cup sprouts, such as sunflower or alfalfa

¼ cup extra-virgin olive oil

2 tablespoons red-wine vinegar

Coarse salt and freshly ground black pepper

Put the black-eyed peas, jalapeños, onion, and sprouts in a large bowl. Add oil and vinegar, and toss well. Season salad with salt and pepper.

from What's for Dinner?

creamed corn

MAKES 5 CUPS; SERVES 4

We made this dish with white sweet corn, but yellow or bicolor corn would be delicious as well.

2 tablespoons all-purpose flour

1 tablespoon sugar

1½ teaspoons coarse salt

½ teaspoon ground ginger

¼ teaspoon freshly ground white pepper

1 tablespoon unsalted butter

1 small onion, cut into ¼-inch pieces

4 cups fresh corn kernels (about 8 ears)

1½ cups heavy cream

1 Stir together the flour, sugar, salt, ginger, and white pepper in a small bowl.

2 Melt butter in a large saucepan over medium heat; add onion, and cook, stirring occasionally, until tender, 4 to 5 minutes (do not brown). Add corn, and cook, stirring, until just tender, about 2 minutes. Sprinkle with flour mixture, tossing to coat; cook 1 minute. Add cream; cook, stirring, until corn is tender and mixture is thickened, about 3 minutes.

from Sweet on Corn

grilled corn on the cob wrapped with bacon

SERVES 8 | PHOTO ON PAGE 222

8 ears corn

8 slices bacon

Coarse salt and freshly ground pepper

1 Preheat a grill to high (if using a charcoal grill, the coals are ready when you can hold your hand 5 inches above the grill for just 1 to 2 seconds). Pull back husks to stem end (do not remove), exposing corn. Discard silk, using a vegetable brush to remove it completely.

2 Wrap 1 strip of bacon around each ear of corn. Pull corn husks back up, covering bacon and corn. Tie open end of husks with kitchen twine.

3 Grill corn, turning occasionally with tongs, until kernels are tender and bacon is cooked through, 15 to 20 minutes (husks will blacken). Transfer corn to a large bowl or platter; serve with salt and pepper for seasoning.

from Sweet on Corn

steamed corn on the cob with orange-oregano butter

SERVES 8

8 tablespoons (1 stick) unsalted butter, softened

1 teaspoon freshly grated orange zest

1 tablespoon finely chopped fresh chives

1 tablespoon finely chopped fresh oregano

Coarse salt and freshly ground pepper

8 ears corn, shucked

1 Stir together butter, zest, chives, and oregano. Season with ½ teaspoon salt and ¼ teaspoon pepper; set aside.

2 Bring 1 inch of water to a boil over medium-high heat in a large, covered, stockpot. Place corn in pot vertically, stem ends down. Cover; steam corn until just tender, 5 to 7 minutes.

3 Transfer corn to a large bowl. Toss with some of the butter; season with salt and pepper. Serve with remaining butter.

from Sweet on Corn

summer squash, radish, and watercress salad

SERVES 6

Cotija is a crumbly, salty cheese sold in many Latin markets; ricotta salata can be used instead. You can make the salad and vinaigrette one day ahead; refrigerate them separately.

1 bunch watercress, tough stems discarded (about 3 cups)

2 medium yellow summer squash, cut into very thin rounds (about 3½ cups)

6 medium radishes, halved and cut into thin half-moons (about 1 cup)

½ small red onion, halved and cut into thin half-moons (about 1 cup)

¼ cup sherry vinegar

1 tablespoon Dijon mustard

⅛ teaspoon coarse salt

1½ teaspoons honey

6 tablespoons olive oil

2 ounces cotija cheese, crumbled (about ½ cup)

1 Put watercress, yellow squash, radishes, and onion in a large serving bowl.

2 Whisk together the vinegar, mustard, salt, and honey in a small bowl. Whisking constantly, pour in the oil in a slow, steady stream; whisk until emulsified. Dress salad, and sprinkle with cheese. Serve immediately.

from Lakeside Picnic

tomatoes with oregano and lime

SERVES 4 | PHOTO ON PAGE 220

The dressing in this recipe calls for lime juice, rather than lemon juice or vinegar. We used heirloom tomato varieties for their exceptional taste and vivid colors, but you can use any kind or size—from the farmers' market or your own backyard— as long as they are ripe.

1¼ pounds assorted ripe tomatoes in all sizes, cut into wedges if large or halved if small

Coarse salt and freshly ground pepper

3 tablespoons extra-virgin olive oil

Juice of 1 lime (about 2 tablespoons)

2 tablespoons coarsely chopped fresh oregano

Arrange tomatoes on a serving platter; season with salt and pepper. Drizzle with oil and lime juice; sprinkle with oregano.

from What's for Dinner?

corn and zucchini fritters

MAKES 2 DOZEN | **PHOTO ON PAGE 219**

For a wonderful breakfast or brunch, sandwich cheddar cheese, crisp bacon, creamy avocado, and a juicy tomato slice between these fritters. Or serve them plain, drizzled with extra-virgin olive oil and fresh lime juice.

1½ cups all-purpose flour

2 teaspoons baking powder

  Coarse salt and freshly ground pepper

2 tablespoons unsalted butter, melted

2 large eggs

½ cup plus 2 tablespoons milk

½ cup finely chopped cooked ham (optional)

1½ cups grated zucchini (about 8 ounces)

2 cups fresh corn kernels (3 to 4 ears)

  Vegetable oil, for frying

1 Whisk together flour, baking powder, 2 teaspoons salt, and ¼ teaspoon pepper in a large bowl. In a separate bowl, stir together butter, eggs, and milk; add to flour mixture, and stir until just combined. Add ham (if desired), zucchini, and corn, and stir until well blended.

2 Heat 1 inch of oil in a large cast-iron skillet over medium heat until it registers 350°F on a deep-fry thermometer.

3 Working in batches of 4 or 5, gently drop 2 tablespoons batter into skillet for each fritter, pressing gently with a spatula to flatten. Cook, turning once, until golden brown, about 2 minutes per side. Transfer with a spatula or slotted spoon to paper towels to drain. Season fritters with salt and pepper while still hot.

from Sweet on Corn

crispy cheddar cakes with bacon

MAKES ABOUT 12 CAKES; SERVES 4 | **PHOTO ON PAGE 220**

8 slices bacon

1½ cups grated sharp white cheddar cheese (4 ounces)

½ cup sour cream

1 small yellow bell pepper, cut into ¼-inch dice

2 scallions, white and pale-green parts only, thinly sliced

¼ cup all-purpose flour

½ teaspoon dry mustard

  Coarse salt and freshly ground black pepper

  Pinch of cayenne pepper

2 large eggs, separated

2 tablespoons vegetable oil, plus more if necessary (optional)

1 Cook bacon in a large skillet over medium heat until crisp, about 5 minutes per side. Transfer to paper towels to drain. Pour off fat into a bowl. Wipe skillet clean with a paper towel, and set aside.

2 Stir together cheese, sour cream, bell pepper, scallions, flour, mustard, ½ teaspoon salt, ¼ teaspoon pepper, cayenne, and egg yolks in a large bowl; set aside. In another large bowl, beat egg whites until stiff peaks form. Fold beaten egg whites into reserved batter.

3 Heat 2 tablespoons reserved fat (or vegetable oil) in skillet over medium heat until hot but not smoking. Working in batches of 3 or 4, pour 2 tablespoons batter into skillet for each cake; cook, turning once, until crisp, 8 to 10 minutes (add more fat or oil if skillet seems dry). Season with salt and pepper. Serve hot with reserved bacon.

from What's for Dinner?

grilled rib-eye steaks

SERVES 6

Use any leftover spices on grilled vegetables.

2 tablespoons cumin seeds
½ teaspoon whole black peppercorns
¼ cup coarse salt
6 boneless prime rib-eye steaks (each about 1 inch thick; 4½ pounds total)
  Spicy Cherry-Tomato Salsa, for serving (recipe follows)

1 Toast the cumin and peppercorns in a dry small skillet over medium-high heat, stirring often, until fragrant and slightly toasted, 1 to 2 minutes; let cool. Finely grind in a spice grinder; stir into salt.

2 Rub ¾ teaspoon spice mixture over each side of each steak. Let steaks stand at room temperature 30 minutes.

3 Preheat a grill to medium-high (if using a charcoal grill, the coals are ready when you can hold your hand 5 inches above grill for just 3 to 4 seconds). Grill steaks, turning once, about 4 minutes per side for medium-rare. Serve with salsa.

from Lakeside Picnic

spicy cherry-tomato salsa

MAKES ABOUT 1 QUART

2 pints cherry or grape tomatoes
4 fresh jalapeño chiles
1 teaspoon ground cumin
2 tablespoons fresh lime juice
  Coarse salt and freshly ground pepper

1 Heat a dry large cast-iron skillet over high heat. Cook half the tomatoes and half the jalapeños, turning often. Transfer tomatoes to a large bowl as skins split; transfer jalapeños to a plate as skins char.

2 When jalapeños are cool enough to handle, rub off skins with paper towels. Cut them open, and discard ribs and seeds. Finely chop flesh, and add to tomatoes in bowl. Repeat with remaining tomatoes and jalapeños.

3 Stir cumin and lime juice into tomato mixture. Season with salt and pepper; toss. If not serving immediately, refrigerate in an airtight container up to 1 day.

ratatouille

SERVES 6 | **PHOTO ON PAGE 221**

Ratatouille is very versatile. It can be served as a main course or as a side dish—hot, cold, or at room temperature. You can refrigerate it, covered, for up to three days.

1 large eggplant (about 1½ pounds), cut into 1-inch cubes
4 medium zucchini, cut into 1-inch cubes
½ cup plus 2 tablespoons extra-virgin olive oil
2 tablespoons coarsely chopped fresh thyme
  Coarse salt and freshly ground pepper
6 pounds vine-ripened tomatoes (about 10)
2 bell peppers, 1 red and 1 yellow
4 garlic cloves, finely chopped
2 medium onions, halved and cut into half-moons
½ cup coarsely chopped fresh basil
½ cup coarsely chopped fresh flat-leaf parsley

1 Preheat oven to 400°F. Toss together the eggplant, zucchini, ½ cup oil, 1 tablespoon thyme, 1 teaspoon salt, and ½ teaspoon pepper on a large rimmed baking sheet. Roast, tossing occasionally, until vegetables are golden, about 1 hour.

2 Meanwhile, bring a large pot of water to a boil. Prepare an ice-water bath, and set aside. Cut a small, shallow X in the stem end of each tomato; blanch tomatoes until skins begin to loosen, about 30 seconds. Immediately transfer with a slotted spoon to the ice-water bath. Drain tomatoes. Remove skins; cut tomatoes into quarters, discarding seeds.

3 Place one bell pepper at a time on the trivet of a gas-stove burner on high heat; roast, turning occasionally with tongs, until black all over. (Or, broil peppers in a baking pan, turning them occasionally.) Transfer peppers to a large bowl, and cover with plastic wrap. Let steam in bowl until cool enough to handle, about 10 minutes.

4 Remove skins from peppers. Discard tops and seeds. Cut peppers lengthwise into ½-inch-thick strips.

5 When eggplant and zucchini are done roasting, heat the remaining 2 tablespoons oil in a large, deep skillet over medium-high heat until hot but not smoking. Add garlic and onions; cook until soft, about 4 minutes. Add tomatoes and peppers; cook until tomatoes are soft, about 7 minutes. Add eggplant and zucchini, ¼ cup basil, and remaining tablespoon thyme. Season with salt and pepper. Reduce heat to medium-low; simmer, stirring occasionally, until vegetables are very soft, about 30 minutes. Stir in parsley and remaining ¼ cup basil. Cook until heated through, about 1 minute more.

from Ratatouille 101

spicy whole-wheat linguine with red peppers

SERVES 6

1 pound whole-wheat linguine

½ cup extra-virgin olive oil

1 teaspoon crushed red-pepper flakes

4 garlic cloves, minced

4 medium red bell peppers,
cut lengthwise into ¼-inch-thick strips

1 teaspoon coarse salt

1 Bring 6 quarts water to a boil in a large pot. Add the pasta; cook according to package instructions until al dente.

2 Meanwhile, heat oil, red-pepper flakes, and garlic in a medium saucepan over medium heat, stirring occasionally, until oil is hot but not smoking, about 2 minutes. Add bell-pepper strips, and cook until very soft, about 20 minutes. Stir salt into bell-pepper mixture.

3 Drain pasta well. Rinse with warm water; shake out excess. Return pasta to pot. Add pepper mixture to pasta, and toss well to coat.

PER SERVING: 447 CALORIES, 19 G FAT, 0 MG CHOLESTEROL, 63 G CARBOHYDRATE, 396 MG SODIUM, 12 G PROTEIN, 11 G FIBER

from Fit to Eat: Olive Oil

succotash with seared scallops

SERVES 4

3 tablespoons unsalted butter

1 large leek (white and pale-green parts only),
halved lengthwise, cut into ½-inch-thick
half-moons, and rinsed well

1 red bell pepper, cut into ½-inch cubes

1 box (10 ounces) frozen lima beans, thawed

6 ounces okra, trimmed and cut into ½-inch-thick rounds

3 cups fresh corn kernels (about 6 ears)

2 tablespoons finely chopped fresh chives

2 tablespoons finely chopped fresh oregano or marjoram
Coarse salt and freshly ground pepper

1 tablespoon extra-virgin olive oil

24 sea scallops (about 2 pounds), tough muscles removed

1 Melt butter in a large skillet over medium heat. Add leek; cook until softened, 2 to 3 minutes. Add bell pepper, lima beans, and okra; cook, stirring occasionally, until tender, about 6 minutes. Add corn, and cook until just tender, about 2 minutes more. Stir in chives, oregano, 2 teaspoons salt, and ¼ teaspoon pepper. Cover to keep warm.

2 Heat oil in a large nonstick skillet over medium-high heat until hot but not smoking. Add scallops; cook (in batches, if necessary, to avoid crowding skillet), turning once, until golden and just translucent in centers, about 3 minutes per side. Serve scallops on top of succotash; season with salt and pepper.

from Sweet on Corn

....

DESSERTS

....

blackberry-almond shortbread squares

MAKES 1 DOZEN | PHOTO ON PAGE 224

10 tablespoons (1¼ sticks) unsalted butter,
softened, plus more for pan

1¾ cups all-purpose flour, plus more for dusting

½ cup whole blanched almonds (2 ounces)

½ teaspoon salt

½ teaspoon ground cinnamon

¾ cup plus 2 tablespoons confectioners' sugar,
plus more for dusting

¼ teaspoon pure almond extract

1 pound blackberries (about 4 cups)
Freshly grated zest of 1 orange

1 Preheat oven to 350°F. Butter a 9-by-13-inch baking pan. Line with parchment paper; butter lining. Dust with flour, tapping out excess; set aside.

2 Arrange nuts in a single layer on a rimmed baking sheet. Bake until golden, 15 minutes; let cool. Grind in a food processor until fine.

3 Whisk together flour, nuts, salt, and cinnamon in a medium bowl; set aside. Put ¾ cup plus 1 tablespoon sugar and the butter in the bowl of an electric mixer fitted with the paddle attachment; mix until pale and fluffy, about 3 minutes. Mix in almond extract. Add flour mixture in 2 batches; mix until a crumbly dough forms.

4 Press all but 1 cup dough onto bottom of pan. Toss berries with zest; scatter over dough. Sprinkle with remaining tablespoon sugar, then crumble reserved dough on top. Bake until golden, about 30 minutes. Let cool on a wire rack. Cut shortbread into 12 squares; dust with sugar.

from What's for Dinner?

individual fruit crisps with cinnamon-vanilla ice cream

SERVES 6

This recipe makes three peach and three cherry crisps. We call for fresh cherries, but frozen ones will work just as well if you reduce the brown sugar in step three to one-third cup and increase the cornstarch to two tablespoons.

- 2 pints vanilla ice cream, softened slightly
- 1½ teaspoons ground cinnamon
- 3 large peaches (about 1¼ pounds)
- 2 tablespoons fresh lemon juice
- 1 cup packed dark-brown sugar
- ½ teaspoon ground ginger
- 2 tablespoons cornstarch
- 3 cups sour cherries (about 14 ounces), pitted
- ½ cup yellow cornmeal
- 1 cup all-purpose flour
- ½ teaspoon baking powder
- Pinch of salt
- ¼ cup granulated sugar
- 8 tablespoons (1 stick) cold unsalted butter, cut into pieces
- ½ cup sliced blanched almonds (1½ ounces), toasted

1 Make cinnamon-vanilla ice cream: Cover the bottom of an 8-inch square baking dish with one-third of ice cream; smooth into an even layer. Sprinkle with ½ teaspoon cinnamon. Repeat to make two more ice-cream layers, sprinkling each with ½ teaspoon cinnamon. Cover with plastic wrap, and freeze until ready to use, at least 45 minutes.

2 Preheat oven to 350°F. Bring a medium saucepan of water to a boil. Cut a small, shallow X in the bottom of each peach. Blanch peaches until skins begin to loosen, about 30 seconds; drain. Peel and pit peaches, and then cut into ¼-inch-thick wedges. Transfer to a bowl; toss with 1 tablespoon lemon juice, ¼ cup brown sugar, the ginger, and 1 tablespoon cornstarch. Set aside.

3 Put cherries in a bowl; toss with ½ cup brown sugar and remaining 1 tablespoon each lemon juice and cornstarch.

4 Whisk together cornmeal, flour, baking powder, salt, granulated sugar, and the remaining ¼ cup brown sugar in a medium bowl. Blend in butter with a pastry blender or two knives until it resembles coarse meal. Stir in almonds. Squeeze to form a crumbly topping.

5 Fill six mini foil pie plates (each 4½ inches in diameter and 1¼ inches high) with fruit, three with cherry mixture and three with peach mixture. Transfer to rimmed baking sheets; divide topping among pie plates. Bake until juices are bubbling, about 30 minutes. Let crisps cool slightly; serve warm with scoops of cinnamon-vanilla ice cream.

from Lakeside Picnic

lemon poppy-seed cookies

MAKES ABOUT 30

- ¼ cup fresh lemon juice, plus 3½ teaspoons freshly grated lemon zest (2 to 3 lemons)
- 8 ounces (2 sticks) unsalted butter
- 2 cups all-purpose flour
- 1 teaspoon baking powder
- ½ teaspoon salt
- 1½ cups sugar
- 1 large egg
- 2 teaspoons pure vanilla extract
- 1 tablespoon poppy seeds, plus more for sprinkling

1 Preheat oven to 375°F. Bring lemon juice to a simmer in a small saucepan over medium heat; cook until reduced by half. Add 1 stick butter; stir until melted. Let cool completely.

2 Whisk together flour, baking powder, and salt. Cream remaining stick butter and 1 cup sugar on medium speed in the bowl of an electric mixer fitted with the paddle attachment. Mix in egg and lemon butter. Mix until pale, about 3 minutes. Mix in vanilla and 2 teaspoons zest. Mix in flour mixture and poppy seeds.

3 Stir together remaining ½ cup sugar and 1½ teaspoons zest. Roll spoonfuls of dough into 1¼-inch balls; roll them in sugar mixture. Place 2 inches apart on baking sheets. Press each with the flat end of a glass dipped in sugar mixture until ¼ inch thick. Sprinkle with seeds. Bake until just browned around bottom edges, 10 to 11 minutes. Transfer to wire racks; let cool. Store in an airtight container up to 1 week.

from Cookie of the Month

rocky road tart

MAKES ONE 9-INCH TART | **PHOTO ON PAGE 225**

To toast the almonds, spread them out in a single layer on a rimmed baking sheet, and bake at 350 degrees until fragrant, about ten minutes.

FOR THE CRUST:

- 6 ounces graham crackers (about 11 sheets)
- 1 tablespoon sugar
- ⅛ teaspoon salt
- 5 tablespoons unsalted butter, melted

FOR THE GANACHE AND FILLING:

- 15 ounces bittersweet chocolate
- 1¾ cups heavy cream
- 2 large egg yolks, lightly beaten
- 2 cups mini marshmallows
- 1 cup salted almonds with skins, lightly toasted

FOR THE TOPPING:

- ¾ cup mini marshmallows
- ¼ cup salted almonds with skins, lightly toasted and coarsely chopped
- 2 ounces bittersweet chocolate, coarsely chopped (about ⅓ cup)

1 Make crust: Preheat oven to 350°F. Process graham crackers, sugar, and salt in a food processor until finely ground. Transfer to a medium bowl, and stir in melted butter. Mix until combined.

2 Transfer mixture to a 9-inch cake ring or springform pan set on a parchment-lined baking sheet. Press crumbs with your hands or the bottom of a glass to form an even layer on bottom and up sides of pan. Bake until crust just starts to brown, about 15 minutes. Let cool completely on sheet on a wire rack.

3 Make ganache: Melt 10 ounces bittersweet chocolate in a large heatproof bowl set over a pan of simmering water; keep warm. Meanwhile, bring cream just to a simmer in a medium saucepan over high heat; remove from heat. Whisk ¼ cup hot cream into the beaten egg yolks, then whisk the yolk mixture into the remaining cream in saucepan. Whisk cream mixture into the melted chocolate, and set the ganache aside.

4 Coarsely chop remaining 5 ounces bittersweet chocolate, and transfer to a large bowl. Toss in 2 cups mini marshmallows and 1 cup whole toasted almonds. Scatter mixture all over bottom of cooled crust. Reserve 1 cup ganache for topping, and pour the rest evenly on top of the filling (do not overfill the crust). Refrigerate tart, uncovered, until firm,

about 1 hour. Meanwhile, cover reserved ganache with plastic wrap, and set aside at room temperature.

5 Make topping: Toss together ¾ cup mini marshmallows, ¼ cup chopped toasted almonds, and 2 ounces chopped bittersweet chocolate; sprinkle over filling. Drizzle reserved 1 cup ganache over tart, and refrigerate 10 minutes more before cutting into slices. The tart can be refrigerated, covered, for up to 3 days.

from Dessert of the Month

....

DRINKS

....

arctic mint julep

SERVES 2

- 6 teaspoons Mint Syrup (recipe follows)
- ¼ cup bourbon
- 1⅔ cups small ice cubes
- Fresh mint sprigs, for garnish

Pour 2 teaspoons mint syrup into each glass. Blend bourbon and ice in a blender until smooth. Spoon bourbon mixture into each glass. Drizzle another teaspoon of mint syrup on top of each drink, and garnish with mint.

from Refresher Course

mint syrup

MAKES ⅔ CUP

- 2 cups packed fresh mint leaves
- ¾ cup Simple Syrup (recipe follows)

Prepare an ice-water bath, and set aside. Bring a saucepan of water to a boil; add mint. Cook until bright green and wilted, 3 to 5 seconds. Plunge into ice-water bath; drain. Purée syrup and mint in a blender until smooth; let stand 10 minutes. Pour through a fine sieve into a bowl; discard solids. Refrigerate syrup, covered, up to 1 day.

simple syrup

MAKES ABOUT 3 CUPS

- 3 cups sugar

Prepare a large ice-water bath. Put sugar and 1½ cups water in a small saucepan. Cook over medium-high heat, stirring frequently, until sugar is completely dissolved, about 4 minutes. Transfer to a medium bowl, and set in ice-water bath until cold. Syrup can be refrigerated, covered, up to 2 months.

blueberry-mint lemonade

MAKES 4½ CUPS

1 pint blueberries

¾ cup plus 2 tablespoons fresh lemon juice (about 5 lemons)

1⅓ cups Mint Syrup (page 195)

Blueberries, for garnish

Lemon slices, for garnish

Purée berries and lemon juice in a food processor. Pour mixture through a fine sieve into a bowl; discard solids. Transfer to a pitcher. Stir in mint syrup and 2 cups cold water; add ice. Garnish with blueberries and lemon slices.

from Refresher Course

blueberry smoothies

SERVES 2

½ cup blueberries

½ cup low-fat vanilla yogurt

½ cup skim milk

2 tablespoons honey

5 small ice cubes

Mix all ingredients in a blender until smooth.

from Refresher Course

cherry lemonade

MAKES 9½ CUPS

1 pound sweet cherries, pitted

1 cup sugar

1¾ cups fresh lemon juice (about 10 lemons)

Set aside 10 cherries. Stir together sugar and the remaining cherries in a large bowl, and let stand until cherries release juices, about 10 minutes. Add lemon juice; stir until sugar is dissolved and liquid is bright pink. Transfer to a pitcher; stir in 6 cups cold water and reserved cherries. Serve over ice.

from Refresher Course

classic lemonade

MAKES 2 QUARTS

3 cups fresh lemon juice (about 15 lemons)

2 cups superfine sugar

Pour lemon juice through a fine sieve into a pitcher. Add sugar; stir until dissolved. Stir in 1 quart water; add ice.

from Refresher Course

egg creams

SERVES 2

¼ cup chocolate syrup

½ cup milk

1 cup cold seltzer

Put 2 tablespoons syrup into each of two glasses. Add ¼ cup milk to each. Divide seltzer between glasses; stir vigorously.

from Refresher Course

frozen Bloody Marys

SERVES 2

½ cup bottled red tomato juice, or fresh yellow or orange tomato juice extracted with a juicer

1 tablespoon fresh lemon juice

1 cup fresh tomato chunks, frozen until hardened

1 tablespoon plus 1 teaspoon Worcestershire sauce (use just 1 teaspoon with yellow or orange tomatoes)

3 dashes hot sauce

¼ cup vodka

¼ teaspoon salt

1½ cups small ice cubes

Freshly ground pepper

Grape tomatoes, for garnish

Fresh basil, for garnish

Cubes of mozzarella, for garnish

Blend all ingredients through ice in a blender until smooth; season with pepper. Divide mixture between two glasses; garnish each with skewered tomatoes, basil, and mozzarella.

from Refresher Course

frozen white sangria

SERVES 2

½ peach

½ plum

3 strawberries, chopped, and frozen until hardened

1 tablespoon frozen orange juice concentrate

3 tablespoons superfine sugar

½ cup dry white wine

2 tablespoons brandy

1½ cups small ice cubes

Slices of leftover fruit, for garnish

Mix ingredients in a blender until smooth; garnish with fruit.

from Refresher Course

Latin lovers

SERVES 2

¼ cup frozen pineapple-juice concentrate

2 tablespoons frozen orange-juice concentrate

2 tablespoons frozen cranberry-juice concentrate

1 tablespoon fresh lime juice

¼ cup coconut rum

1½ cups small ice cubes

Fresh sugarcane, for garnish

Mix all ingredients through the ice in a blender until smooth. Divide between two glasses, and garnish with sugarcane.

from Refresher Course

mango coolers

SERVES 2

1 cup chopped mango, frozen until hard

3 tablespoons dark rum

2 tablespoons fresh lemon juice

1 tablespoon Simple Syrup (page 195)

1½ cups small ice cubes

Diced mango, for garnish

Shredded fresh mint, for garnish

Mix all ingredients through the ice in a blender until smooth. Divide mixture between two glasses; garnish with mango and mint.

from Refresher Course

orange clouds

SERVES 2

¼ cup frozen orange-juice concentrate

1 tablespoon heavy cream

2 tablespoons Cointreau

2 tablespoons Galliano

1½ cups small ice cubes

Orange-colored sanding sugar, for garnish

Mix all ingredients through the ice in a blender until smooth. Dip moistened rims of two glasses in orange-colored sugar; pour in orange mixture, and serve.

from Refresher Course

peach iced tea

MAKES 2½ QUARTS

3 bags black tea

6 cups boiling water

1 quart peach nectar

1 bunch fresh mint, trimmed

2 lemons, washed and thinly sliced

Steep tea bags in the boiling water to make a strong tea; discard tea bags. Refrigerate tea until well chilled. Stir together tea and peach nectar in a pitcher. Add mint and lemon slices; refrigerate 1 hour. Add ice, and serve.

from Refresher Course

raspberry martinis

SERVES 2

½ cup vodka

2 tablespoons raspberry-flavored syrup

Raspberries, for garnish

Orange peel, for garnish

Mix vodka and raspberry syrup in a cocktail shaker filled with ice. Strain into two chilled martini glasses. Garnish with raspberries and orange peel; serve.

from Refresher Course

raspberry spritzer

MAKES 2 QUARTS

¼ cup raspberry vinegar

6 tablespoons sugar

2 quarts seltzer (about 2 liters)

Raspberries, for garnish

Fresh mint leaves, for garnish

Bring vinegar and sugar to a boil in a small saucepan over medium heat. Boil, stirring occasionally, until sugar is dissolved, about 1 minute. Set syrup aside to cool. Pour syrup into a pitcher; stir in seltzer, and add ice. Divide mixture among glasses, and garnish with raspberries and mint.

from Refresher Course

semifreddo Bellini

SERVES 2

1 cup peeled, chopped peaches, frozen until hard

¼ cup peach schnapps

¾ cup plus 2 tablespoons chilled Champagne
   or sparkling white wine

2 tablespoons superfine sugar

1 cup small ice cubes
   Peach slices, for garnish

Blend peaches, schnapps, 2 tablespoons Champagne, the sugar, and ice in a blender until smooth. Divide mixture between 2 glasses; top off each glass with ¼ cup plus 2 tablespoons Champagne. Garnish with peach slices.

from Refresher Course

sparkling strawberry-rosemary lemonade

MAKES 1½ QUARTS

2 pints strawberries, hulled

1 cup fresh lemon juice (about 5 lemons)

1 cup Rosemary Syrup (recipe follows)

2 cups cold seltzer
   Sliced strawberries, for garnish

Use a juice extractor to make 2 cups juice from berries; discard pulp. Transfer juice to a large pitcher; add lemon juice, rosemary syrup, and seltzer. Stir until combined. Add ice, and divide among glasses. Garnish with strawberries.

from Refresher Course

rosemary syrup

MAKES ABOUT 1¾ CUPS

¾ cup sugar

6 sprigs fresh rosemary

Bring sugar, rosemary sprigs, and 1½ cups water to a boil in a medium saucepan over medium-high heat. Cook, stirring, until sugar is dissolved, about 1 minute. Remove from heat; let syrup stand 20 minutes. Discard rosemary sprigs. Refrigerate, covered, up to 2 months.

watermelon-tequila refreshers

SERVES 6 TO 8

¾ cup sugar

3½ pounds seedless watermelon,
   cut into 2-inch cubes (about 12 cups)

1 cup tequila

1 cup fresh lime juice (6 to 8 limes),
   plus lime slices for garnish

4 cups ice

1 Stir together sugar and ¾ cup water in a medium saucepan. Bring to a boil over medium-high heat, stirring until sugar is dissolved. Let cool completely. Refrigerate until ready to use, up to 1 week.

2 Working in batches, fill blender with watermelon cubes; blend until smooth. Pass purée in batches through a fine sieve set over a large bowl, discarding solids as you work. Refrigerate juice until ready to use, up to 1 day.

3 Stir together tequila, lime and watermelon juices, and sugar syrup in a large pitcher. Stir in ice and lime slices.

from Lakeside Picnic

....

MISCELLANEOUS

....

grapefruit and mint vinaigrette

MAKES ABOUT 1 CUP

Use this tangy vinaigrette to dress up a simple green salad made with spinach, arugula, or mesclun.

½ cup fresh ruby-red grapefruit juice

2 tablespoons white-wine vinegar

2 tablespoons finely chopped fresh mint, plus 1 tablespoon whole leaves

1 teaspoon sugar

1 teaspoon coarse salt

½ cup extra-virgin olive oil

Combine grapefruit juice, vinegar, mint, sugar, and salt in a small bowl. Whisk in olive oil. Let stand 10 minutes.

PER SERVING (ABOUT 2 TABLESPOONS): 129 CALORIES, 14 G FAT, 0 MG CHOLESTEROL, 2 G CARBOHYDRATE, 291 MG SODIUM, 0 G PROTEIN, 0 G FIBER

from Fit to Eat: Olive Oil

rosemary bread

MAKES 2 LOAVES

1½ teaspoons active dry yeast

¼ cup warm water (110°F)

5 tablespoons extra-virgin olive oil,
  plus more for bowl

1 teaspoon sugar

1 teaspoon salt

2 tablespoons finely chopped rosemary,
  plus 1 tablespoon whole leaves

1½ cups plus 1 teaspoon all-purpose flour,
  plus more for dusting

1 cup whole-wheat flour

1 Stir together yeast and the warm water in the bowl of an electric mixer. Let stand until foamy, about 7 minutes.

2 Add ¾ cup water, the oil, sugar, salt, chopped rosemary, 1½ cups all-purpose flour, and the whole-wheat flour to yeast mixture. Fit mixer with dough hook; mix on low speed until dough comes together, about 1 minute. Raise mixer speed to medium-high; mix until dough is smooth and elastic, 8 to 10 minutes.

3 Lightly oil a large bowl. Shape the dough into a ball, and transfer it to the oiled bowl. Loosely cover with plastic wrap. Let dough rise in a warm, draft-free spot until doubled in bulk, about 1 hour.

4 Punch down the dough; let rest, covered, 15 minutes. Turn out dough onto a lightly floured surface, and divide in half.

5 Roll one piece into an 11-inch-long loaf. Gently twist dough to create contours, then tuck ends underneath. Transfer to a baking sheet. Press half the whole rosemary leaves into loaf. Repeat with remaining piece of dough.

6 Loosely cover baking sheet with plastic wrap, and let loaves rise slightly in a warm, draft-free spot 30 minutes. Meanwhile, preheat oven to 400°F.

7 Dust loaves with remaining teaspoon all-purpose flour. Bake until golden, about 30 minutes. Let cool completely on a wire rack before slicing.

PER SERVING (¼ LOAF): 223 CALORIES, 9 G FAT, 0 MG CHOLESTEROL, 31 G CARBOHYDRATE, 291 MG SODIUM, 5 G PROTEIN, 3 G FIBER

from Fit to Eat: Olive Oil

bread-and-butter pickles

MAKES 2 QUARTS | PHOTO ON PAGE 223

Salting the cucumbers and onion helps draw out excess water, ensuring crisp results.

2 pounds kirby cucumbers

1 medium onion

2 tablespoons coarse salt

2 cups cider vinegar

1 cup sugar

1 tablespoon yellow mustard seed

½ teaspoon celery seed

1 Cut cucumbers and onion into ⅛-inch-thick slices, and transfer to a colander set in a bowl. Toss well with the salt. Refrigerate 1 hour. Rinse well, and drain. Pat dry between paper towels. Transfer cucumbers and onion to a large bowl.

2 Bring vinegar, sugar, mustard seed, and celery seed to a boil in a medium saucepan, stirring. Reduce heat; simmer 4 minutes. Let cool slightly, about 10 minutes.

3 Pour brine over vegetables; let cool completely, about 30 minutes. Transfer to airtight containers; refrigerate at least 1 week (pickles will keep 3 weeks more).

from Easy Pickles

dill-pickle chips

MAKES 2 QUARTS

2 pounds kirby cucumbers

3 tablespoons coarse salt

2 cups distilled white vinegar

1 tablespoon dill seed

4 garlic cloves

2 bunches fresh dill, coarsely chopped

1 Cut the cucumbers into ½-inch-thick rounds, and transfer to a colander set in a bowl. Toss well with the salt. Refrigerate cucumber rounds 1 hour.

2 Rinse cucumber rounds well; drain. Pat dry between paper towels. Transfer cucumber rounds to a large bowl.

3 Bring 3 cups water, the vinegar, dill seed, and garlic to a boil in a medium saucepan, stirring. Reduce heat; simmer 4 minutes. Let mixture cool slightly, about 10 minutes.

4 Add chopped dill to cucumber rounds, and toss to combine. Pour in the brine. Let cool completely, about 30 minutes. Transfer mixture to airtight containers, and refrigerate at least 1 week (pickles will keep 3 weeks more).

from Easy Pickles

pickled zucchini ribbons

MAKES 2 QUARTS | **PHOTO ON PAGE 223**

Let the brine cool completely before pouring it over the vegetables. Otherwise, the zucchini and onions will turn soggy and won't retain their shape or texture during pickling.

2 pounds medium zucchini

2 medium onions

2 tablespoons coarse salt

1 quart cider vinegar

2 cups sugar

1 tablespoon dry mustard

1 tablespoon yellow mustard seed

1½ teaspoons turmeric

1 teaspoon ground cumin

1   Using a mandoline or sharp knife, cut zucchini lengthwise into ⅛-inch-thick ribbons. Halve onions lengthwise, and cut into ⅛-inch-thick slices. Transfer vegetables to a colander set in a bowl. Toss well with the salt. Refrigerate 1 hour.

2   Meanwhile, bring vinegar, sugar, and spices to a boil in a medium saucepan, stirring. Reduce heat; simmer 5 minutes. Let cool completely, about 30 minutes.

3   Rinse zucchini and onions well. Drain, and pat dry.

4   Transfer zucchini and onions to a large bowl; pour in brine. Transfer to airtight containers; refrigerate at least 1 week (pickles will keep 3 weeks more).

from Easy Pickles

sweet pickled red onions

MAKES 1 QUART | **PHOTO ON PAGE 223**

2 pounds red onions

1 tablespoon coarse salt

3 cups cider vinegar

1½ cups sugar

15 whole black peppercorns

4 whole cloves

2 whole cinnamon sticks

6 whole allspice

2 dried hot red chiles

2 small bay leaves

1   Cut onions into ¼-inch-thick slices; transfer to a colander set in a bowl. Toss well with the salt. Refrigerate 1 hour. Rinse well; drain. Pat dry between paper towels.

2   Bring vinegar, sugar, and spices to a boil in a medium saucepan, stirring. Let cool completely, about 30 minutes.

3   Add onions; bring to a boil. Transfer onions to a large bowl using a slotted spoon. Let brine cool completely, about 30 minutes; pour over onions. Transfer to airtight containers; refrigerate at least 1 week (pickles will keep 3 weeks more).

from Easy Pickles

tarragon pickled carrots

MAKES 2 QUARTS | **PHOTO ON PAGE 223**

Coarse salt

2 pounds carrots, peeled

2 cups white-wine vinegar

1 bunch fresh tarragon

1 tablespoon coriander seeds

10 whole black peppercorns

1   Bring a large saucepan of water to a boil; add salt. Prepare an ice-water bath; set aside. Quarter carrots lengthwise; cook until just tender, about 3 minutes. Immediately transfer with tongs to ice-water bath. Drain well; transfer to a large bowl.

2   Bring 2 cups water, the vinegar, tarragon, spices, and 2 tablespoons salt to a boil in a medium saucepan. Reduce heat; simmer 4 minutes. Pour brine over carrots; let cool completely, about 30 minutes. Transfer to airtight containers; refrigerate at least 1 week (pickles will keep 3 weeks more).

from Easy Pickles

spicy pickled green and wax beans

MAKES 2 QUARTS | **PHOTO ON PAGE 223**

Coarse salt

1 pound green beans, trimmed

1 pound yellow wax beans, trimmed

3 cups distilled white vinegar

3 garlic cloves

¼ teaspoon cayenne pepper

1   Bring a large saucepan of water to a boil; add salt. Prepare an ice-water bath; set aside. Cook beans until just tender, about 3 minutes. Immediately transfer with tongs to the ice-water bath. Drain well, and transfer to a large bowl.

2   Bring 3 cups water, the vinegar, 3 tablespoons salt, the garlic, and the cayenne to a boil in a medium saucepan. Reduce heat; simmer 4 minutes. Pour brine over beans. Let cool completely, about 30 minutes. Transfer to airtight containers; refrigerate at least 1 week (pickles will keep 3 weeks more).

from Easy Pickles

September

cheese soufflé

SERVES 6 | **PHOTO ON PAGE 223**

4 tablespoons unsalted butter, plus more, melted, for dish

1 cup finely grated Parmesan cheese, plus more for dusting

1 large shallot, finely chopped

6 tablespoons all-purpose flour

1½ cups milk

2 tablespoons chopped fresh rosemary

2 tablespoons chopped fresh thyme

Generous pinch of freshly grated nutmeg

Pinch of cayenne pepper

1 cup grated Gruyère cheese

Coarse salt and freshly ground pepper

6 large egg yolks plus 8 large egg whites, room temperature

Pinch cream of tartar (if not using a copper bowl)

1 Preheat oven to 400°F, with rack in middle. Brush the outer lip of a 2-quart soufflé dish with melted butter. Tie a sheet of parchment around dish with kitchen twine so it extends 3 inches above rim. Brush inside of dish and collar with melted butter. Dust with Parmesan cheese; tap out excess. Chill dish in freezer 15 minutes.

2 Heat butter in a medium saucepan over medium heat. Add shallot; cook until soft, 3 to 4 minutes. Add flour; cook, whisking, 3 minutes. Whisk in milk, herbs, and spices. Bring to a boil. Reduce heat to low; whisk until thick, about 4 minutes. Add cheeses; whisk until melted. Season with 1 teaspoon salt, and pepper to taste. Pour into a bowl; stir in yolks.

3 Using a balloon whisk, beat whites and a pinch of salt in a copper bowl to stiff peaks. (Or beat with an electric mixer in a stainless-steel bowl, adding cream of tartar.)

4 Spoon whites onto egg-yolk mixture, a third at a time, folding in each before adding the next: Cut through center of mixture with a large rubber spatula; gently turn spatula over. Rotate bowl a quarter turn; continue folding whites and turning bowl until mostly combined.

5 Pour mixture into prepared dish. Bake 15 minutes. Reduce temperature to 375°F; bake until set, 16 to 18 minutes. Remove collar, and serve immediately.

from Master Class: Flawless Soufflés

curried chicken turnovers

MAKES 16

Coarse salt

2 boneless, skinless chicken breast halves (about 1 pound total)

2 tablespoons vegetable oil

1 medium onion, coarsely chopped

2 garlic cloves, minced

2 teaspoons minced peeled fresh ginger

4½ teaspoons curry powder

½ teaspoon ground cumin

1 tablespoon all-purpose flour, plus more for dusting

1½ cups homemade or low-sodium store-bought chicken stock

½ cup plain yogurt

4½ teaspoons tomato paste

¼ cup applesauce

½ cup frozen peas (not thawed)

¼ cup heavy cream

2 boxes (17¼ ounces each) frozen puff pastry, thawed

1 large egg, lightly beaten

Cucumber Dipping Sauce (page 204)

1 Preheat oven to 400°F. Bring 1 quart water to a boil in a medium pot; add 1 tablespoon salt and the chicken. Reduce heat; simmer until chicken is cooked through, about 12 minutes. Transfer with a slotted spoon to a bowl; let cool. Shred chicken with a fork into 2-inch pieces.

2 Heat oil in a large low-sided stockpot over medium-high heat until hot but not smoking. Add onion, garlic, and ginger, and cook, stirring occasionally, until pale golden, about 8 minutes. Stir in curry powder, cumin, and flour; cook 1 minute. Add stock, and bring to a boil. Stir in yogurt, tomato paste, and applesauce; boil 1 minute. Reduce heat to medium; simmer, stirring occasionally, until mixture is thickened, about 30 minutes.

3 Stir in chicken and peas, and cook until mixture is thick, about 3 minutes. Stir in cream and 2 teaspoons salt. Let cool.

4 Lay puff pastry sheets on a lightly floured surface, and cut each into 4 squares. Spoon 2 tablespoons chicken mixture onto each square, leaving a 1-inch border. Brush edges with egg, and fold squares to form triangles. Press edges to seal. (The unbaked turnovers can be frozen, wrapped in plastic and foil, 1 month; thaw before baking.)

5 Arrange turnovers on baking sheets. Bake until golden, 20 to 25 minutes. Serve with sauce.

from Packable Lunches

cucumber dipping sauce

MAKES 1½ CUPS

1 cup plain yogurt

¼ cup sour cream

2 tablespoons fresh lemon juice

1 garlic clove, minced

1 teaspoon coarse salt

8 ounces English (hothouse) cucumber (about ¾ cucumber), peeled, grated, and pressed between paper towels

Stir together yogurt, sour cream, lemon juice, garlic, salt, and cucumber. Sauce can be refrigerated, covered, up to 1 day.

cold sesame noodles

SERVES 5

1 package (10½ ounces) dried udon noodles

1 baby bok choy

¼ cup smooth peanut butter

5 tablespoons toasted sesame oil

3 tablespoons soy sauce

¼ cup rice-wine vinegar (not seasoned)

1 large garlic clove, minced

2 teaspoons sugar

½ teaspoon crushed red-pepper flakes

Sesame seeds, for garnish

1 Bring a large pot of water to a boil; cook noodles according to package directions. Drain; let cool completely.

2 Bring 3 cups water to a boil in a saucepan; boil bok choy 30 seconds. Drain; rinse well. Let cool; coarsely chop.

3 Whisk together the peanut butter, oil, soy sauce, vinegar, garlic, sugar, and red-pepper flakes. Put sauce, noodles, and bok choy into a bowl; toss well. Sprinkle with seeds. Refrigerate in an airtight container until ready to serve, up to 2 days.

from Packable Lunches

salmon with honey-coriander glaze

SERVES 4 | **PHOTO ON PAGE 219**

1 tablespoon whole coriander seeds

¼ cup honey

5 tablespoons soy sauce

2 teaspoons fresh lemon juice

4 salmon fillets (5 ounces each), skinned

2 teaspoons vegetable oil

1 Toast the coriander seeds in a dry large nonstick skillet over medium-high heat, stirring constantly, until golden, about 3 minutes. Remove from heat; let cool. Grind seeds in a spice grinder or crush with a mortar and pestle until coarsely ground; reserve skillet.

2 Make glaze: Stir together crushed coriander seeds, honey, soy sauce, and lemon juice in a small bowl.

3 Lightly brush tops of salmon fillets with some of the glaze; reserve remainder. Heat oil in the nonstick skillet over medium heat until hot but not smoking. Cook fillets, glazed sides down, 1 minute; reduce heat to medium-low, and cook 2 minutes more. Turn fillets over, and cook 3 minutes for medium-rare (salmon will still be slightly pink in the middle), or longer if desired. Transfer to a plate; loosely cover salmon with foil to keep warm.

4 Pour remaining glaze into skillet; bring to a boil over medium heat. Cook until glaze has thickened to the consistency of syrup, about 1 minute. Serve salmon with glaze on the side.

from What's for Dinner?

omelet wraps with vegetables

MAKES 4

These wraps are best eaten the day they are made.

8 large eggs

½ teaspoon coarse salt

¼ teaspoon freshly ground pepper

1 teaspoon unsalted butter

4 soft round sandwich wraps

¼ cup mayonnaise

1 avocado, peeled and cut into 1-by-3-inch pieces

1 carrot, cut into 1-by-5-inch sticks

8 fresh basil leaves

1 Lightly whisk together eggs, salt, and pepper in a small bowl. Heat butter in a 12-inch nonstick skillet over medium heat. Add beaten eggs; cook, pulling cooked egg away from sides with a spatula to let raw egg stream underneath. Cook until set, about 5 minutes. (If top is still runny, heat omelet in a 350°F oven until set, about 5 minutes.)

2 Cut omelet into four strips. Spread each wrap with 1 tablespoon mayonnaise; divide omelet, avocado, carrot, and basil among wraps. Roll up wraps, folding in sides. If not serving immediately, halve wraps and wrap in waxed paper. Refrigerate until ready to serve.

from Packable Lunches

steak and onion sandwiches

MAKES 4

4 hanger steaks (each about 6 ounces and 1 inch thick)

1 teaspoon coarse salt

Pinch of freshly ground pepper

4 medium beefsteak tomatoes, cut into ½-inch-thick slices

2 tablespoons vegetable oil

2 teaspoons unsalted butter

2 large onions, cut into ¼-inch-thick rings

1 long baguette (about 22 inches), split horizontally and cut crosswise into 4 pieces

3 tablespoons hot mustard

1 Preheat a grill to medium-high (if using a charcoal grill, the coals are ready when you can hold your hand 5 inches above grill for just 3 to 4 seconds). Alternatively, heat a grill pan over medium-high heat until hot.

2 Season steaks with the salt and pepper. Grill, turning once, 7 minutes total for medium-rare. Transfer steaks to a cutting board, and let rest 5 minutes.

3 Meanwhile, grill tomato slices, turning once, until soft, about 4 minutes total.

4 Heat oil and butter in a large skillet over medium-high heat until hot but not smoking. Add onions, and cook, stirring occasionally, until golden, about 8 minutes.

5 Cut steaks against the grain into ¼-inch-thick slices. Spread each of the 4 baguette bottoms with 2¼ teaspoons hot mustard. Top with steak slices, tomatoes, onions, and the baguette tops. Wrap sandwiches in waxed paper, and refrigerate until ready to serve.

from Packable Lunches

SIDE DISHES

ginger rice

SERVES 4

2 tablespoons grated peeled fresh ginger

1 teaspoon sugar

1 teaspoon coarse salt

2 cups jasmine rice

Bring ginger, sugar, salt, and 2½ cups water to a boil in a medium saucepan; boil 2 minutes. Stir in rice; reduce heat to low. Cover; cook until most of the water is absorbed, 15 to 18 minutes. Remove from heat; let stand, covered, 7 minutes. Fluff rice with a fork before serving.

from What's for Dinner?

sautéed broccoli rabe

SERVES 4 | **PHOTO ON PAGE 223**

1 tablespoon vegetable oil

1¼ pounds broccoli rabe (about 2 bunches), large outer leaves discarded and stems trimmed to 5 inches

1 garlic clove, thinly sliced

1 teaspoon coarse salt

Heat oil in a large nonstick skillet over medium-high heat until hot but not smoking. Add broccoli rabe, and cook 1 minute. Cover; cook, shaking skillet occasionally, until leaves are lightly browned and crisp, about 2 minutes. Add the garlic; cook 1 minute more. Add salt and toss to combine.

from What's for Dinner?

DESSERTS

broiled plums with mascarpone cream

SERVES 4 | **PHOTO ON PAGE 225**

5 medium black or red plums, halved and pitted

3 tablespoons brandy

6 tablespoons packed light-brown sugar

¼ cup mascarpone cheese or crème fraîche

¼ cup heavy cream

1 Preheat broiler. Place plum halves, cut sides up, in a single layer in an 8-inch square baking dish. Pour brandy evenly over plums, and sprinkle with ¼ cup sugar. Broil until plums are soft and sugar is caramelized, 8 to 10 minutes.

2 Meanwhile, put mascarpone, cream, and remaining 2 table-spoons sugar in the bowl of an electric mixer fitted with the whisk attachment; beat until soft peaks form, about 2 minutes. Top broiled plums with mascarpone cream.

from What's for Dinner?

chocolate-cherry crumb bars

MAKES 9 LARGE OR 1 DOZEN SMALL BARS | **PHOTO ON PAGE 225**

1¼ cups dried cherries, coarsely chopped

10 ounces unsalted butter (2½ sticks), all but 2 tablespoons cut into small pieces

1 cup granulated sugar

½ cup unsweetened Dutch-process cocoa powder

1 teaspoon salt

¾ cup packed light-brown sugar

1 cup unsweetened shredded coconut (about 3 ounces), lightly toasted

2 cups plus 7½ teaspoons all-purpose flour

1 large egg

2 tablespoons kirsch or cherry-flavored liqueur (optional)

½ cup semisweet chocolate chunks

1 Preheat oven to 325°F. Line a 9-inch square baking pan with parchment paper so it overhangs on two sides. Bring cherries, 2 tablespoons butter, ¼ cup granulated sugar, and ⅔ cup water to a simmer in a small saucepan over medium heat. Simmer, stirring occasionally, until almost all of the liquid is absorbed, about 10 minutes. Remove from heat; stir in ¼ cup more granulated sugar. Let cool, stirring occasionally, until sugar is dissolved.

2 Stir together cocoa, salt, brown sugar, coconut, and 2 cups flour in a medium bowl. Blend in remaining 2¼ sticks butter with a pastry blender or your fingertips until mixture resembles coarse meal; press 3 lightly packed cups into lined pan. Bake until just set, about 20 minutes.

3 Beat egg, remaining ½ cup granulated sugar, and the kirsch, if desired, on medium-high speed in the bowl of an electric mixer fitted with the whisk attachment until pale, about 4 minutes. Fold in cherry mixture and remaining 7½ teaspoons flour; stir in chocolate. Spread over crust; top with remaining crumb mixture.

4 Bake until a cake tester inserted in center comes out clean, about 50 minutes. Let cool completely. Run a knife around sides; lift out of pan using parchment. Cut into 9 or 12 bars.

from Cookie of the Month

chocolate soufflé

SERVES 6 | **PHOTO ON PAGE 232**

Unsalted butter, melted, for dish

½ cup sugar, plus more for dusting

5 ounces bittersweet chocolate, chopped

2 ounces semisweet chocolate, chopped

1⅓ cups milk

6 large egg yolks plus 8 large egg whites, room temperature

6 tablespoons all-purpose flour

2 tablespoons brandy (optional)

1 teaspoon pure vanilla extract

Salt

Pinch cream of tartar (if not using a copper bowl)

Crème Anglaise (recipe follows)

1 Preheat oven to 400°F, with rack in lower third. Do not open oven door until ready to bake soufflé. Brush the outer lip of a 2-quart soufflé dish with melted butter. Tie a sheet of parchment around dish with kitchen twine so it extends 3 inches above rim. Brush inside of dish and collar with melted butter. Dust with sugar; tap out excess. Chill soufflé dish in freezer 15 minutes.

2 Stir chocolates in a large heatproof bowl set over a saucepan of simmering water until melted and smooth. Heat milk in a saucepan over medium heat until nearly simmering; remove from heat. Using an electric mixer fitted with the whisk attachment, beat 6 tablespoons sugar and the yolks on high speed until pale, about 4 minutes. On low speed, beat in flour. Beat in half the hot milk, in a little at a time.

3 Whisk mixture into pan of hot milk; bring to a boil over medium-high heat, whisking. Reduce heat to low; simmer until thick, about 2 minutes. Pour into chocolate. Stir in brandy (if desired), vanilla, and a pinch of salt. (This mixture can be refrigerated 2 days. Rewarm in a heatproof bowl set over a pan of simmering water.)

4 Using a balloon whisk, beat whites and a pinch of salt in a copper bowl until foamy. (Or beat with an electric mixer in a stainless-steel bowl with cream of tartar.)

5 Add 1 tablespoon sugar; beat until whites almost hold stiff peaks. Add remaining tablespoon sugar, and beat until peaks are stiff.

6 Spoon egg whites onto egg-yolk mixture, a third at a time, folding in each before adding the next: Cut through center of mixture with a large rubber spatula, then gently turn spatula over. Rotate bowl a quarter turn; continue folding whites and turning bowl in same manner until mostly combined.

7 Pour mixture into prepared dish. Place on a rimmed baking sheet. Bake 15 minutes. Reduce oven temperature to 375°F, and bake until set, 20 minutes. Remove collar; serve immediately with crème anglaise, if desired.

from Master Class: Flawless Soufflés

crème anglaise

MAKES ABOUT 2 CUPS

You can make this classic French sauce two days ahead; press plastic wrap directly onto surface, and refrigerate.

- 4 large egg yolks
- ¼ cup sugar
- 1 cup milk
- ¾ cup heavy cream
- ½ vanilla bean, halved lengthwise

1 Whisk together yolks and sugar in a medium bowl until pale, about 4 minutes.

2 Prepare a large ice-water bath; set aside. Pour milk and cream into a medium saucepan. Scrape in vanilla seeds; add bean. Heat over medium heat until just about to simmer. Reduce heat to low; whisk ⅓ cup into egg-yolk mixture. Pour mixture back into saucepan. Cook over medium heat, stirring, until thick enough to coat back of a wooden spoon, about 8 minutes.

3 Pour mixture through a fine sieve into a stainless-steel bowl set in ice-water bath. Discard solids. Chill until cold, stirring occasionally.

Greek yogurt with strawberry compote

SERVES 4

- 10 ounces strawberries, hulled and cut into ¼-inch-thick slices (about 2 cups)
- ¼ cup sugar
- 2 teaspoons fresh lemon juice
- 14 ounces Greek yogurt (about 2 cups)

1 Bring berries, sugar, and 2 tablespoons water to a boil in a small saucepan over medium heat, stirring. Cook until thickened, about 8 minutes. Remove from heat. Stir in lemon juice; let cool. (Compote can be refrigerated up to 3 days.)

2 Divide yogurt among bowls, and top each serving with compote.

from Packable Lunches

honey cake with caramelized pears

MAKES ONE 10-INCH CAKE

This confection would be perfect to serve on Rosh Hashanah, the Jewish holiday when honey cake and honey-dipped fruit represent hope for a sweet year ahead. If you keep kosher and would like to make a dairy-free version, substitute margarine for the butter, soy milk for the regular milk, and nondairy whipped topping for the whipped cream. The cake can be made (without the pears) one day ahead; store in plastic wrap at room temperature.

- Unsalted butter, softened, for pan
- 1¾ cups all-purpose flour, plus more for dusting
- ¾ teaspoon baking powder
- ½ teaspoon baking soda
- 1 teaspoon coarse salt
- ½ teaspoon ground cinnamon
- 2 large eggs
- ½ cup granulated sugar
- ¼ cup packed light-brown sugar
- ½ cup plus 2 tablespoons best-quality honey
- ½ cup milk
- ½ cup vegetable oil
- ½ teaspoon freshly grated lemon zest
- Caramelized Pears (page 208)
- Freshly whipped cream, for serving (optional)

1 Preheat oven to 325°F. Butter a 10-inch springform pan. Dust with flour, and tap out excess. Whisk together the flour, baking powder and soda, salt, and cinnamon in a bowl; set aside. Mix eggs and sugars on high speed in the bowl of an electric mixer fitted with the paddle attachment until pale and thick, about 3 minutes.

2 Whisk together honey, milk, oil, and zest. With mixer on low, add honey mixture to egg mixture; mix until combined, about 1 minute. Add half the flour mixture; mix until smooth. Mix in remaining flour mixture. Pour batter into pan.

3 Bake until dark golden brown and a cake tester inserted in center comes out clean, about 50 minutes. Let cool in pan on a wire rack 15 minutes. Run a thin knife around edges of cake; carefully remove sides of pan. Transfer cake to a platter. Top with pears. Serve with whipped cream, if desired.

from Dessert of the Month

caramelized pears

MAKES ABOUT 2 CUPS

1 tablespoon unsalted butter

¼ cup sugar

1¾ pounds red Anjou pears, cut into ½-inch-thick wedges
  (or ¼-inch-thick wedges if pears are firm)

¼ cup best-quality honey

Heat butter in a large skillet over medium heat. Add sugar;
cook, stirring, until almost dissolved, 1 to 2 minutes. Add
pears; cook, stirring occasionally, until soft and just golden,
12 to 20 minutes. Pour in honey; cook, stirring, until pears
are coated and very soft, 3 to 5 minutes.

mango-papaya salad with mint

SERVES 5

1 mango, cut into ½-inch cubes

1 papaya, cut into ½-inch cubes

1 tablespoon honey

1 tablespoon chopped fresh mint

Stir together all ingredients. Refrigerate, covered, until ready
to serve, up to 2 days.

from Packable Lunches

peanut crisps

MAKES ABOUT 50

1 cup all-purpose flour

¼ teaspoon salt

¼ teaspoon baking soda

4 tablespoons unsalted butter, softened

1¼ cups packed light-brown sugar

1 large egg

1 teaspoon pure vanilla extract

1 cup salted whole peanuts

1 Preheat oven to 350°F. Stir together flour, salt, and baking
soda in a small bowl; set aside. Put butter and sugar in the
bowl of an electric mixer fitted with the paddle attachment;
mix on medium speed until pale, about 2 minutes.

2 Mix in egg and vanilla. Mix in flour mixture a little at a
time. Stir in peanuts by hand.

3 Line baking sheets with parchment paper. Drop dough by
the teaspoonful on sheets, spacing mounds 3 inches apart.
Bake until edges are just golden, about 8 minutes. Let cool on
sheets. Store in an airtight container up to 1 week.

from Packable Lunches

tomato focaccia

MAKES 8 PIECES

If you don't have a mixer, knead the dough by hand on a
lightly floured surface until smooth, for about ten minutes.

2 tablespoons plus ½ teaspoon active dry yeast
  (from 2 envelopes)

4½ teaspoons sugar

2⅓ cups warm water (110°F)

5½ teaspoons extra-virgin olive oil, plus more for bowl
  and plastic wrap

6¼ cups plus 3 tablespoons all-purpose flour

Coarse salt

1 cup grape tomatoes, halved lengthwise

1 tablespoon fresh rosemary

1 Stir together yeast, sugar, and the warm water in the bowl
of an electric mixer fitted with the paddle attachment. Let
stand until foamy, about 5 minutes.

2 Stir in 4½ teaspoons oil. Add flour and 4½ teaspoons
salt; mix on medium-low speed until combined. Fit mixer
with the dough hook; knead dough on medium speed until
smooth, 5 to 7 minutes.

3 Transfer dough to a lightly oiled large bowl. Loosely cover
with plastic wrap; let dough rise in a warm, draft-free spot
until doubled in bulk, about 20 minutes.

4 Preheat oven to 400°F. Generously oil a 12-by-17-inch
rimmed baking sheet. Spread out dough to fill sheet, working
it into corners. Press in tomatoes; sprinkle with rosemary.
Loosely cover with oiled plastic wrap; let rest 30 minutes.

5 Drizzle dough with remaining teaspoon oil, and sprinkle
with salt. Bake 5 minutes. Rotate sheet; bake until golden,
about 15 minutes more.

6 Let cool in sheet; cut into 8 rectangles. If not serving that
day, wrap pieces in plastic wrap and foil; freeze up to 1 month.

from Packable Lunches

PRICKLY PEAR AGUAS FRESCAS | **PAGE 184**

BLOODY MARYS WITH TEQUILA | **PAGE 183**

SPARKLING FRESH LEMONADE | **PAGE 184**
SUMMER-SQUASH SOUP | **PAGE 166**
GREEN GODDESS DIP | **PAGE 168**

CLASSIC BRUSCHETTA | **PAGE 166**

BRUSCHETTA WITH TOMATO AND BASIL | **PAGE 167**

BRUSCHETTA WITH FAVA BEANS AND ARUGULA PESTO | **PAGE 167**

BRUSCHETTA WITH CANNELLINI BEANS AND HERBS | **PAGE 166**

BRUSCHETTA WITH ROASTED PEPPERS AND
HERBED RICOTTA | **PAGE 167**

BRUSCHETTA WITH POACHED TUNA | **PAGE 167**

SOUTHWESTERN CORN CHOWDER | **PAGE 187**

LOBSTER STOCK | **PAGE 184**

FINGERLING POTATO SALAD WITH SUGAR SNAP PEAS | **PAGE 168**

SPICY STIR-FRIED SHRIMP | PAGE 176

COCONUT NOODLES | PAGE 172

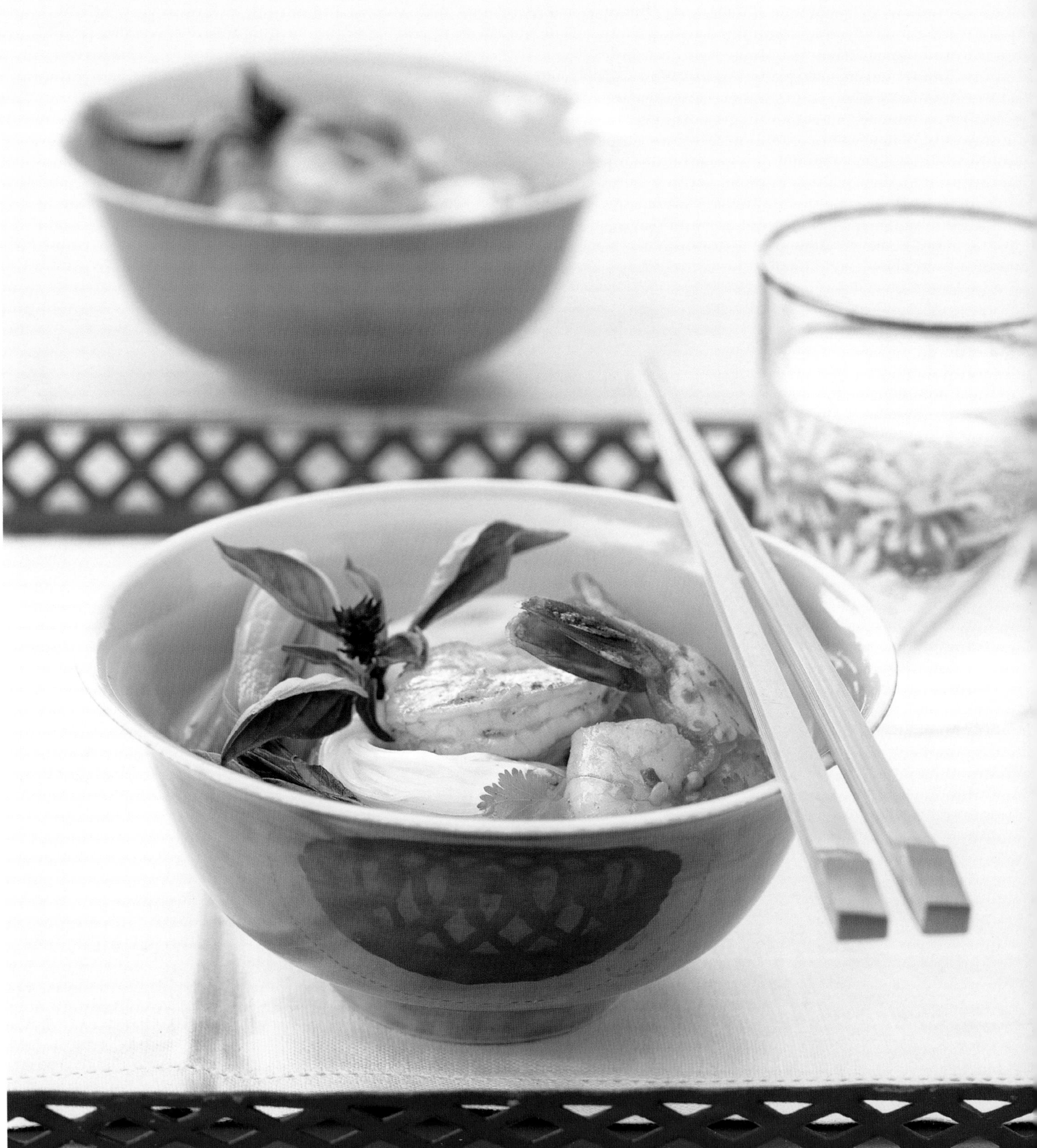

MELON BOWLS WITH PROSCIUTTO
AND WATERCRESS | **PAGE 169**

GREEN BEAN, SHELL BEAN, AND
SWEET ONION FATTOUSH | **PAGE 169**

SPICY CHICKEN SALAD
IN LETTUCE CUPS | **PAGE 171**

RED ROMAINE SALAD WITH
WALNUTS AND EGGS | **PAGE 170**

BEET AND MACHE
SALAD WITH AGED
GOAT CHEESE | **PAGE 168**

GRILLED BURGERS WITH MAYTAG BLUE CHEESE
AND HEIRLOOM TOMATOES | **PAGE 174**

GRILLED CHICKEN STUFFED WITH BASIL AND TOMATO | **PAGE 175**

CORN AND ZUCCHINI FRITTERS | **PAGE 191**

LOBSTER ROLLS | **PAGE 173**

SALMON WITH HONEY-CORIANDER GLAZE | **PAGE 204**

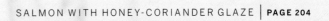

BLACK-EYED-PEA AND JALAPENO SALAD | **PAGE 189**
CRISPY CHEDDAR CAKES WITH BACON | **PAGE 191**
TOMATOES WITH OREGANO AND LIME | **PAGE 190**

RATATOUILLE | **PAGE 192**

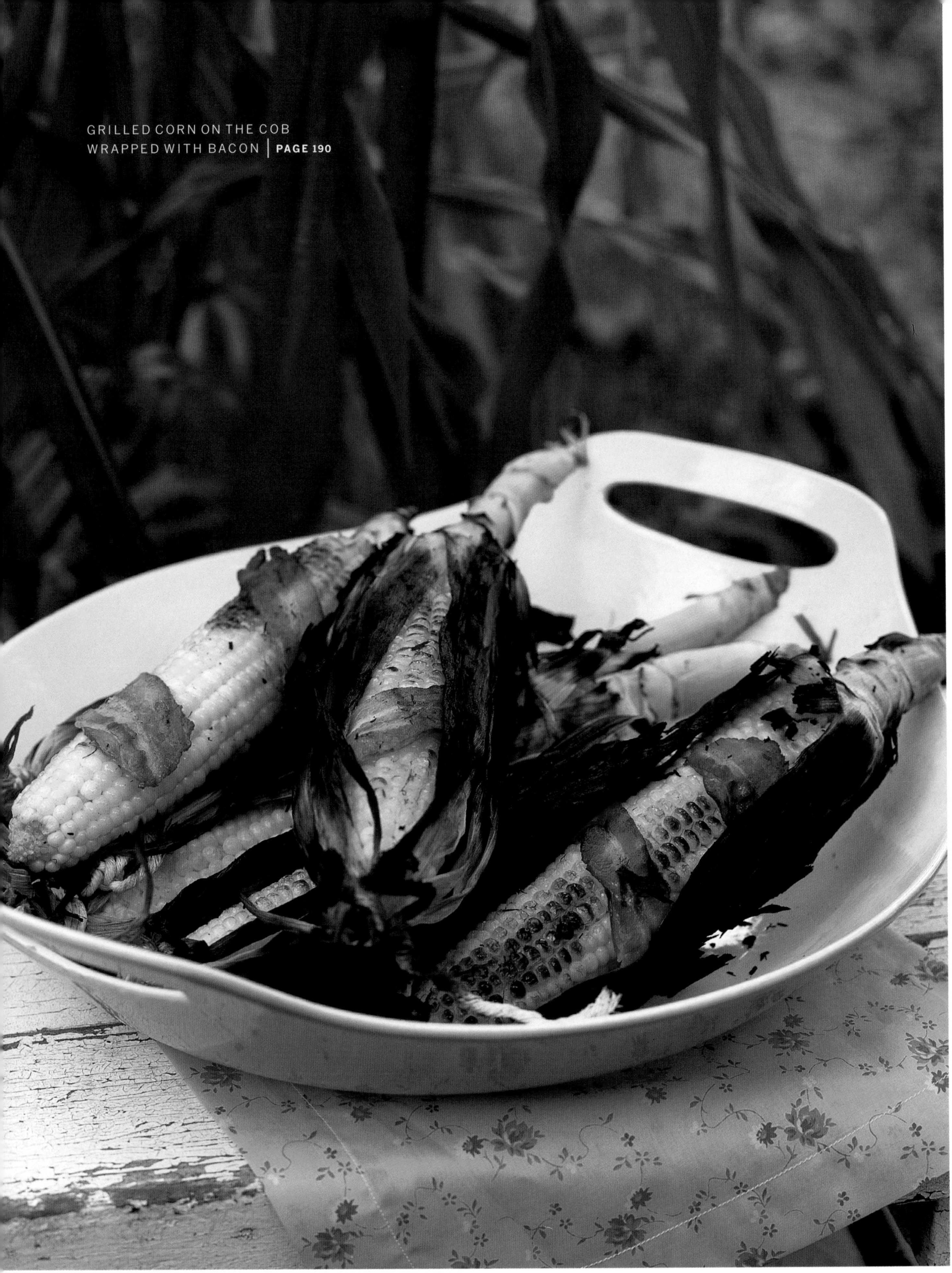

GRILLED CORN ON THE COB WRAPPED WITH BACON | PAGE 190

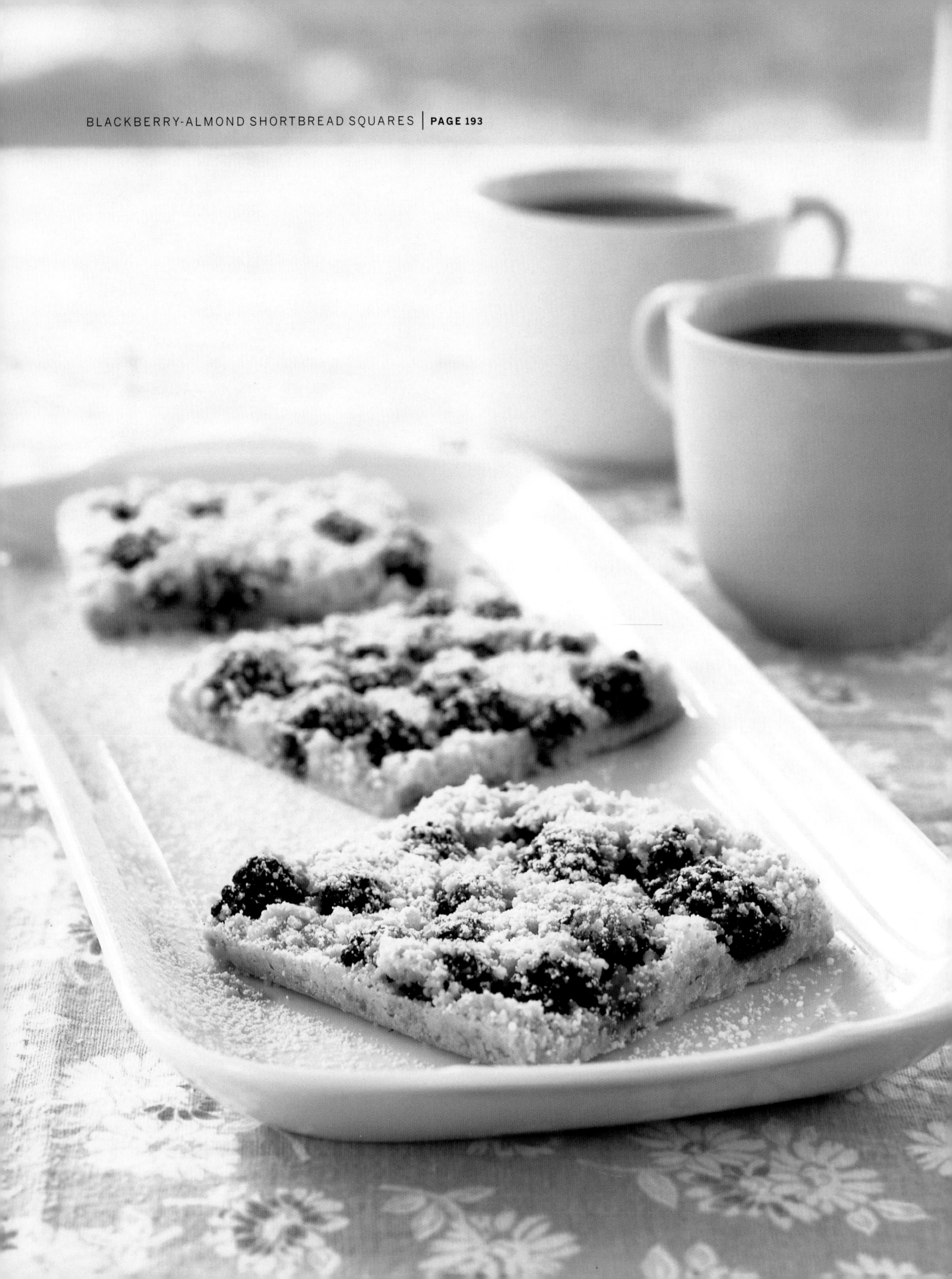

BLACKBERRY-ALMOND SHORTBREAD SQUARES | **PAGE 193**

BROILED PLUMS WITH MASCARPONE CREAM | **PAGE 205**

CHOCOLATE-CHERRY CRUMB BARS | **PAGE 206**

ROCKY ROAD TART | **PAGE 195**

MINI BLACK-AND-WHITE COOKIES | **PAGE 183**

SWEET CHERRY GALETTE | **PAGE 178**

PANNA COTTA TARTS WITH
STRAWBERRIES | PAGE 177

ERRY TARTLETS | **PAGE 179**

SUMMER FRUIT TART | **PAGE 178**

UGAR PLUM TART | **PAGE 180**

BLUEBERRY-LEMON TART | **PAGE 179**

PLUM AND PINON COFFEE CAKE | **PAGE 181**

SUGAR CREAM PIE | **PAGE 182**

Autumn

MANY OF OUR MOST CHERISHED YEAR-END HOLIDAY TRADITIONS remain constant—it's the details that vary. A Thanksgiving meal almost always includes turkey, but salads, stuffings, side dishes, and desserts can change from year to year. Thus we have dozens of recipes that will add variety to your celebrations, and others that can be wrapped up and given as homemade gifts.

October

MAIN COURSES

apricot-Dijon glazed chicken

SERVES 4 | **PHOTO ON PAGE 303**

8 chicken thighs

Coarse salt and freshly ground pepper

1 jar (12 ounces) apricot jam

2 tablespoons honey

2 tablespoons Dijon mustard

1 Preheat oven to 425°F. Rinse chicken thighs; pat dry, and transfer to a baking dish. Season well with salt and pepper; set aside.

2 Bring jam, honey, and mustard to a boil in a small saucepan over medium heat. Reduce heat to medium-low; simmer until thickened and reduced by half, about 15 minutes. Spoon apricot mixture over chicken thighs, spreading with back of spoon to coat evenly.

3 Bake chicken, basting with sauce from bottom of dish every 10 minutes, until juices run clear when chicken is pricked with a fork, about 30 minutes.

from What's for Dinner?

cauliflower, prosciutto, and goat cheese gratin

SERVES 6 TO 8 | **PHOTO ON PAGE 309**

Unsalted butter, for baking dish

2 small heads cauliflower (about 3 pounds total), cut into 1-inch florets

12 ounces soft goat cheese, crumbled

¼ cup fresh orange juice (1 orange)

¼ cup homemade or low-sodium store-bought chicken stock, or water

2 teaspoons chopped fresh thyme

2 tablespoons all-purpose flour

1½ teaspoons coarse salt

½ teaspoon freshly ground pepper

3 ounces thinly sliced prosciutto (about 5 slices), coarsely chopped

1 Preheat oven to 375°F. Butter a 2-quart casserole or an 8-inch square baking dish; set aside. Bring a large pot of water to a boil. Add cauliflower; cook until just tender, 4 to 5 minutes. Drain.

2 Whisk together 8 ounces goat cheese, the orange juice, stock, thyme, flour, salt, and pepper until smooth. Toss in cauliflower and prosciutto. Spoon into buttered dish. Top with remaining 4 ounces goat cheese.

3 Cover with foil; bake 30 minutes. Remove foil; bake until bubbling and just golden, about 30 minutes more. Let cool slightly before serving.

from Gratins

gratinéed macaroni and cheese with tomatoes

SERVES 6 TO 8 | **PHOTO ON PAGE 310**

You can use six two-cup gratin dishes to make individual servings. The baking time will be a bit shorter; look for the tops to be bubbling and golden.

7 tablespoons unsalted butter, plus more for dish

1¼ cups small pieces torn baguette or other crusty bread

1 tablespoon chopped fresh thyme

Coarse salt and freshly ground pepper

1 pound elbow macaroni or other short, tubular pasta

1 quart milk

5 tablespoons all-purpose flour

Pinch of freshly grated nutmeg

4 cups grated sharp white cheddar cheese (about 1 pound)

1 pound red and yellow tomatoes in all sizes, cut into 1-inch pieces if large or halved if small (like cherry, grape, or pear)

1 Preheat oven to 375°F. Butter a 9-by-13-inch baking dish or a 3½-quart casserole dish; set aside. Melt 2 tablespoons butter, and pour over bread in a medium bowl; toss. Add 1 teaspoon thyme, ½ teaspoon salt, and ¼ teaspoon pepper; toss.

2 Bring a large pot of water to a boil; add salt. Cook pasta until just beginning to soften, 2 to 3 minutes (it will not be fully cooked). Drain and rinse.

3 Heat milk in a saucepan over medium heat until warm. Heat remaining 5 tablespoons butter in a high-sided skillet or a pot over medium heat until foaming. Add flour; cook, whisking, 1 minute. Whisk in warm milk a little at a time. Cook, whisking constantly, until bubbling and thickened, 8 to 10 minutes. Remove milk mixture from heat.

4 Add 2 teaspoons salt, ½ teaspoon pepper, remaining 2 teaspoons thyme, the nutmeg, and cheese to milk mixture; stir until cheese is melted.

5 Stir pasta and tomatoes into cheese sauce. Pour into buttered dish; sprinkle with bread mixture. Bake until bubbling and golden, about 30 minutes. Let cool slightly before serving.

from Gratins

salmon, leek, and red potato gratin with horseradish-dill crumbs

SERVES 6

- 4 tablespoons unsalted butter, plus more for baking dish
- 1 cup small pieces torn rye bread (1 to 2 slices)
- ¼ cup chopped fresh dill
- ¼ cup freshly grated horseradish or 3 tablespoons prepared horseradish

  Coarse salt and freshly ground pepper
- 2 medium leeks, white and pale-green parts only, halved lengthwise, cut into half-moons, and rinsed well
- 1½ pounds medium red potatoes, thinly sliced
- 8 ounces sliced smoked salmon
- ¼ cup homemade or low-sodium store-bought chicken stock

  Crème fraîche, for garnish (optional)

1 Preheat oven to 375°F. Butter a 9-inch square baking dish. Stir together bread pieces, 1 tablespoon dill, the horseradish, ¼ teaspoon salt, and a pinch of pepper in a medium bowl. Melt 2 tablespoons butter; stir into bread mixture. Set aside.

2 Melt remaining 2 tablespoons butter in a large skillet over medium heat. Add leeks; cook, stirring occasionally, until very tender, about 5 minutes. Transfer to a bowl, and stir in remaining 3 tablespoons dill; set aside.

3 Toss potatoes with ½ teaspoon salt and ¼ teaspoon pepper in a large bowl. Arrange one-third of potatoes in buttered dish, overlapping slices. Top with half of leek mixture, and then half of the smoked salmon. Add one-third of the potatoes, and one more layer each of remaining leek mixture and smoked salmon. Top with remaining potatoes. Pour stock over layers; gently shake dish back and forth to distribute evenly. Sprinkle with bread mixture.

4 Cover dish with foil; bake 30 minutes. Remove foil; bake until potatoes are very tender and top is golden, 30 to 40 minutes more. Serve gratin warm, garnished with a dollop of crème fraîche, if desired.

from Gratins

sausage, chicken, and white bean gratin

SERVES 10 TO 12

- 1½ cups coarse fresh breadcrumbs
- ¾ cup finely grated Parmesan cheese
- 3 tablespoons chopped fresh flat-leaf parsley
- 4 teaspoons chopped fresh thyme
- 2 teaspoons chopped fresh rosemary
- 1 teaspoon thinly sliced fresh sage leaves

  Coarse salt and freshly ground pepper
- 4 ounces bacon (about 5 slices)
- 2 boneless, skinless chicken breast halves (about 1 pound total), cut into 1-inch cubes
- 1½ pounds sweet Italian sausages (casings removed), cut into ½-inch-thick pieces
- 4 garlic cloves, finely chopped
- 1 medium onion, thinly sliced
- ½ cup dry white wine
- 2 cans (14½ ounces each) navy, great Northern, or cannellini beans, rinsed and drained
- 1 can (14½ ounces) diced tomatoes, with juice
- 1 cup homemade or low-sodium store-bought chicken stock

1 Preheat oven to 375°F. Stir together breadcrumbs, cheese, 1 tablespoon parsley, 1 tablespoon thyme, 1 teaspoon rosemary, ½ teaspoon sage, ¼ teaspoon salt, and a pinch of pepper; set aside.

2 Cook bacon in a 4- to 5-quart Dutch oven over medium heat until browned and crisp, 5 to 7 minutes. Transfer to paper towels to drain.

3 Brown chicken all over in fat in pot, about 6 minutes total. Transfer with a slotted spoon to a plate. Cook sausages in pot, stirring, until browned, about 5 minutes. Transfer to plate.

4 Add garlic and onion to pot; cook, stirring, until softened, about 3 minutes. Add wine, and deglaze pot by scraping up any brown bits from bottom with a wooden spoon; cook until most of the liquid has evaporated, about 2 minutes.

5 Stir in chicken, sausages, beans, tomatoes, and stock; the remaining teaspoon each rosemary and thyme; the remaining ½ teaspoon sage and 2 tablespoons parsley; and ½ teaspoon salt and ¼ teaspoon pepper. Sprinkle breadcrumbs on top; pat down with a wooden spoon.

6 Cover pot, and transfer to oven. Bake until gratin is bubbling, about 20 minutes. Uncover; bake until golden brown, about 15 minutes more. Crumble reserved bacon on top. Let gratin cool slightly before serving.

from Gratins

roast pork loin with apple-cornbread stuffing

SERVES 8 | PHOTO ON PAGE 304

4 ounces bacon (about 5 slices), cut into ¼-inch pieces

2 small onions, chopped (about 1¾ cups)

1 fennel bulb, trimmed and coarsely chopped (about 1¾ cups)

6 firm, tart apples, such as Northern Spy or Cortland: 1 peeled, cored, and chopped (about 1¼ cups); 3 peeled, cored, and cut into 8 wedges each; 2 cored and cut into 8 wedges each

4 sprigs thyme, finely chopped

2 sprigs rosemary, finely chopped

10 fresh sage leaves, finely chopped, plus 6 whole leaves
Coarse salt and freshly ground pepper

12 ounces cornbread, cut into cubes (about 3 cups)

⅓ cup homemade or low-sodium store-bought chicken stock

1 boneless pork loin (4 pounds), butterflied (¾ inch thick)

¼ cup olive oil

2 cups apple cider

1 pound cipollini onions

1 Preheat oven to 350°F. Cook bacon in a large (9-quart) wide, heavy-bottom pot over medium heat until browned and crisp, 5 to 7 minutes. Transfer with a slotted spoon to paper towels to drain.

2 Add onions, fennel, and chopped apple to fat in pot; cook over medium heat, stirring occasionally, until just golden brown, about 8 minutes. Add thyme, rosemary, and chopped sage; cook 2 minutes. Season with salt and pepper. Transfer to a bowl; let cool completely. Keep pot on stove with heat off.

3 Add cornbread, stock, and reserved bacon to bowl. Season stuffing with salt and pepper, and gently stir (do not break up cornbread too much).

4 Generously season cut side of pork with salt and pepper, and then spread with apple–cornbread stuffing, leaving a ½-inch border. Starting from one short side, roll up pork, encasing the stuffing. Tie rolled pork at 1-inch intervals with kitchen twine. Generously season with salt and pepper.

5 Heat oil in pot over high heat until hot but not smoking. Brown pork all over, about 10 minutes total. Transfer pork to a large plate. Pour off fat from pot; blot any fat left in pot with paper towels.

6 Bring cider to a boil in pot, and deglaze pot by scraping up brown bits with a wooden spoon. Return pork to pot; put cipollini onions, peeled apples, and sage leaves around sides. Transfer to oven; cook, uncovered, 30 minutes.

7 Turn pork over; add unpeeled apples. Cook until an instant-read thermometer inserted at least 2 inches into pork registers 140°F, about 15 minutes more.

8 Let pork stand in pot at room temperature 15 minutes; transfer to a carving board. Discard twine. Cut pork into ½-inch-thick slices. Serve with apples, onions, and sauce from pot.

from An Apple a Day

knockwurst with braised cabbage and apples

SERVES 6

4 tablespoons unsalted butter

2 medium onions, thinly sliced

3 pounds green cabbage (about 1 head), cored and thinly sliced

1 large tart green apple, such as Granny Smith, peeled, cored, and chopped

1 cup apple cider

⅓ cup cider vinegar

2 tablespoons packed light-brown sugar

1 tablespoon coarse salt

1 teaspoon freshly ground pepper

9 knockwurst (about 2 pounds)
Whole-grain mustard, for serving

1 Melt butter in a large heavy-bottom pot over medium-low heat. Add onions; cook, stirring occasionally, until very soft and golden brown, about 18 minutes.

2 Stir in cabbage, apple, cider, vinegar, sugar, salt, and pepper. Cover; cook, stirring occasionally, until cabbage is very soft, about 1 hour.

3 Tuck knockwurst into cabbage; cover pot. Cook until heated through, about 20 minutes. Serve with mustard.

from An Apple a Day

quinoa and turkey patties in pita with tahini sauce

SERVES 6 | **PHOTO ON PAGE 303**

1 cup quinoa

1 garlic clove

¼ cup tahini

¼ cup fresh lemon juice

12 ounces ground dark-meat turkey

¼ teaspoon plus 1 pinch ground allspice

½ teaspoon plus 1 pinch ground cumin

Pinch of crushed red-pepper flakes (optional)

2 tablespoons chopped fresh mint

2 scallions, finely chopped

¾ teaspoon coarse salt

Vegetable-oil cooking spray

6 lettuce leaves, torn into large pieces

1 English (hothouse) cucumber, thinly sliced into rounds (10 ounces)

1 small red onion, cut into thin half-moons

6 pita breads

1 Rinse quinoa thoroughly in a sieve; drain. Bring 2 cups water to a boil in a saucepan. Add quinoa; return to a boil. Stir quinoa; cover pan, and reduce heat. Simmer until quinoa is tender but still chewy, about 15 minutes. Fluff quinoa with a fork, and let cool.

2 Meanwhile, process garlic, tahini, lemon juice, and ¼ cup cold water in a food processor until smooth. If necessary, thin with water until pourable. Transfer dressing to a small bowl; cover. Refrigerate until ready to use.

3 Put turkey, spices, mint, scallions, and salt in a clean bowl of the food processor; pulse until a smooth paste forms. Add quinoa; process until mixture clumps around the blade, about 2 minutes. Transfer to a bowl. With dampened hands, roll about 2 tablespoons quinoa mixture into a ball; flatten slightly, and set aside on a plate. Repeat with remaining mixture to make 24 patties total.

4 Heat a dry large cast-iron skillet or grill pan over medium heat until hot. Working in batches, lightly coat both sides of patties with cooking spray. Cook patties in skillet, turning once, until cooked through, about 8 minutes per side. Transfer patties to a clean plate, and loosely cover with foil to keep warm.

5 Divide lettuce, cucumber, and red onion among pita breads; top each with 4 quinoa patties. Drizzle each sandwich with some tahini dressing, and fold pitas over filling.

PER SERVING: 338 CALORIES, 9 G FAT, 39 MG CHOLESTEROL, 44 G CARBOHYDRATE, 498 MG SODIUM, 21 G PROTEIN, 5 G FIBER

from Fit to Eat: Quinoa

---

classic potato gratin

SERVES 6 TO 8

Unsalted butter, for baking dish

1 cup heavy cream

Coarse salt and freshly ground pepper

Pinch of freshly grated nutmeg

2 pounds Yukon gold potatoes, peeled and thinly sliced into rounds

2 cups coarsely grated Gruyère cheese (about 6 ounces)

1 Preheat oven to 350°F. Butter a 9-inch square baking dish, and set aside.

2 Whisk together cream, 1 teaspoon salt, ¼ teaspoon pepper, and the nutmeg in a small bowl, and set aside. Toss potatoes, 1 teaspoon salt, and ¼ teaspoon pepper in a large bowl.

3 Arrange one-third of potatoes in buttered dish, overlapping slices. Sprinkle with one-third of the cheese. Repeat two more times with remaining potatoes and cheese (end with a cheese layer). Pour reserved cream mixture over top layer. Gently shake dish back and forth to distribute evenly.

4 Cover with foil; bake 30 minutes. Remove foil; bake until bubbling and well browned, about 30 minutes more. Let cool slightly before serving.

from Gratins

individual portobello mushroom gratins

MAKES 6

2 tablespoons olive oil, plus more for baking sheet

6 portobello mushrooms, stems removed and reserved

¼ cup finely grated Parmesan cheese (1 ounce)

¼ cup plain dry breadcrumbs

3 tablespoons finely chopped fresh flat-leaf parsley

3 tablespoons chopped fresh chives

2 shallots, thinly sliced

1 pound white or cremini mushrooms, sliced

½ cup dry white wine

½ cup heavy cream

1 teaspoon coarse salt

¼ teaspoon freshly ground pepper

1   Preheat oven to 350°F. Lightly oil a rimmed baking sheet. Arrange portobello caps, gill sides down, on sheet. Bake until tender, 20 to 25 minutes. Transfer portobello caps to a plate to cool. Preheat broiler.

2   Stir together cheese, breadcrumbs, 1 tablespoon parsley, 1 tablespoon chives, and 1 tablespoon oil; set aside.

3   Chop portobello stems into ½-inch pieces. Heat remaining tablespoon oil in a large skillet over medium heat until hot but not smoking. Add shallots; cook, stirring, until softened, about 2 minutes. Add sliced mushrooms and chopped stems; cook, stirring occasionally, until tender, 6 to 7 minutes. Add wine; cook until most of the liquid has evaporated, about 2 minutes. Stir in cream, remaining 2 tablespoons each parsley and chives, and the salt and pepper. Remove from heat.

4   Arrange portobello caps, gill sides up, on a clean baking sheet. Divide mushroom mixture and then breadcrumbs among the caps. Broil until gratins are bubbling and golden brown, about 2 minutes.

from Gratins

Southwestern sweet-potato gratin

SERVES 8 TO 10

Chihuahua, cotija, and Mexican crema give the dish authentic flavor, but Monterey Jack, feta, and sour cream are good substitutes.

Unsalted butter, for baking dish

4   large sweet potatoes (about 4 pounds), peeled and thinly sliced into rounds

1½ teaspoons coarse salt

¼   teaspoon freshly ground pepper

1½ cups grated Chihuahua or Monterey Jack cheese (6 ounces)

1½ cups cotija or feta cheese, crumbled (6 ounces)

1   small onion, thinly sliced

1   teaspoon finely chopped chipotle chile in adobo (optional)

¼   cup plus 2 tablespoons homemade or low-sodium store-bought chicken stock, or water

¼   cup finely chopped cilantro leaves

1   cup crushed tortilla chips

Lime wedges, for garnish

Mexican crema or sour cream, for garnish (optional)

1   Preheat oven to 350°F. Butter a 9-by-13-inch baking dish; set aside. Toss potatoes with the salt and pepper. Arrange half of potatoes in buttered dish, overlapping slices. Sprinkle with half of each cheese. Top with onion.

2   Stir chipotle chile (if desired) into stock; drizzle stock over onion. Sprinkle with half the cilantro. Top with remaining potatoes; sprinkle with remaining cheeses and cilantro. Scatter tortilla chips on top.

3   Cover with foil; bake 30 minutes. Remove foil; bake until very tender and top is well browned, about 30 minutes more. Let cool slightly before serving. Serve with lime wedges, and with crema, if desired.

from Gratins

haricots verts with pecans and lemon

SERVES 4

Coarse salt

1   pound haricots verts or other thin green beans, trimmed

½   cup pecans

3   tablespoons sherry vinegar

1   teaspoon sugar

Freshly ground pepper

¼   cup olive oil

1   teaspoon freshly grated lemon zest

1   Preheat oven to 425°F. Bring a large pot of water to a boil; add salt and haricots verts. Cook beans until bright green and crisp-tender, 3 to 4 minutes; drain. Transfer to a serving dish.

2   Meanwhile, spread pecans in a single layer on a rimmed baking sheet; toast in oven until fragrant, about 5 minutes. Coarsely chop nuts when they are cool enough to handle.

3   Whisk vinegar, sugar, and ¼ teaspoon salt in a small bowl; season with pepper. Whisking constantly, pour in oil in a slow, steady stream; whisk until emulsified. Just before serving, gently toss beans with vinaigrette and chopped nuts; sprinkle with zest. Serve warm.

from What's for Dinner?

red quinoa and mushroom pilaf with dill

SERVES 6

White quinoa will also work here; reduce the cooking time to fifteen minutes.

3½ cups homemade or low-sodium store-bought chicken stock
1 ounce mixed dried mushrooms
2 cups red quinoa
1 tablespoon olive oil
8 ounces cremini or white mushrooms, quartered
2 shallots, coarsely chopped
Coarse salt
1 tablespoon finely chopped fresh thyme
Freshly ground pepper
1 tablespoon unsalted butter
5 tablespoons finely chopped fresh dill
3 tablespoons finely chopped chives
2 Valencia or navel oranges, peel and pith removed, flesh thinly sliced into rounds

1 Bring stock to a boil; pour over dried mushrooms in a small bowl. Soak until soft, about 6 minutes. Using a slotted spoon, lift mushrooms out and set aside. Pour liquid through a fine sieve into a bowl; set aside. Coarsely chop soaked mushrooms; set aside.

2 Rinse quinoa thoroughly in a fine sieve; drain. Heat oil in a large pot over medium-high heat until hot but not smoking; add fresh mushrooms, shallots, and ¼ teaspoon salt. Cook, stirring occasionally, until mushrooms and shallots have released their liquid and are slightly caramelized, about 7 minutes. Add quinoa; cook, stirring, until it begins to pop and crackle, about 5 minutes.

3 Add reserved soaked mushrooms, reserved soaking liquid, and thyme to pot; bring to a boil. Stir; cover, and reduce heat. Simmer until quinoa is tender but still chewy, about 20 minutes. Stir in ¼ teaspoon salt, pepper to taste, and the butter. Just before serving, stir in dill and chives; add oranges, and gently toss.

PER SERVING: 312 CALORIES, 8 G FAT, 6 MG CHOLESTEROL, 51 G CARBOHYDRATE, 583 MG SODIUM, 11 G PROTEIN, 6 G FIBER

from Fit to Eat: Quinoa

quinoa and apple salad with curry dressing

SERVES 4

¼ cup raw whole almonds
1 cup quinoa
1 teaspoon honey
1 tablespoon finely chopped shallot
1 teaspoon curry powder
¼ teaspoon coarse salt
2 tablespoons fresh lemon juice
Freshly ground pepper
2 tablespoons extra-virgin olive oil
2 tablespoons dried currants
1 small McIntosh apple, cut into ⅛-inch-thick wedges
¼ cup loosely packed fresh mint leaves, coarsely chopped, plus more for garnish

1 Preheat oven to 375°F. Spread almonds on a rimmed baking sheet; toast in oven until lightly toasted and fragrant, about 7 minutes. Let cool; coarsely chop nuts.

2 Rinse quinoa thoroughly in a fine sieve; drain. Bring 2 cups water to a boil in a medium saucepan. Add quinoa; return to a boil. Stir quinoa; cover, and reduce heat. Simmer until quinoa is tender but still chewy, about 15 minutes. Fluff quinoa with a fork; let cool.

3 Whisk together honey, shallot, curry powder, salt, and lemon juice in a large bowl. Season with pepper. Whisking constantly, pour in oil in a slow, steady stream; whisk until dressing is emulsified. Add quinoa, currants, apple, mint, and nuts; toss well. Garnish with mint.

PER SERVING: 304 CALORIES, 14 G FAT, 0 MG CHOLESTEROL, 38 G CARBOHYDRATE, 154 MG SODIUM, 8 G PROTEIN, 5 G FIBER

from Fit to Eat: Quinoa

roasted red potatoes

SERVES 4

1½ pounds baby red potatoes, quartered
2 tablespoons olive oil
2 tablespoons coarsely chopped fresh rosemary or thyme
Coarse salt and freshly ground pepper

Preheat oven to 425°F. Toss potatoes, oil, and rosemary on a rimmed baking sheet. Spread out potatoes in a single layer; season with salt and pepper. Roast, stirring once halfway through cooking, until potatoes are golden brown, crisp outside, and tender inside, about 30 minutes.

from What's for Dinner?

classic bread pudding

SERVES 8

For individual bread puddings, divide the mixture among eight buttered six-ounce ramekins; bake for forty minutes.

12 ounces brioche or challah, cut into 1-inch cubes
2 cups milk
3 cups heavy cream
4 large eggs plus 1 large egg yolk
1 cup sugar
½ teaspoon salt
1 tablespoon pure vanilla extract
½ teaspoon ground cinnamon
¼ teaspoon ground nutmeg
½ cup raisins
1 cup boiling water, plus more for pan
2 tablespoons unsalted butter, softened, for baking dish

1 Put bread in a large bowl; set aside. Heat milk and cream in a medium saucepan over medium-high heat until just about to simmer; remove from heat.

2 Whisk together eggs, yolk, sugar, salt, vanilla, cinnamon, and nutmeg in a medium bowl. Whisking constantly, pour cream mixture in a slow, steady stream into egg mixture. Pour over bread; fold to combine. Let stand 30 minutes, tossing and pressing occasionally to submerge bread.

3 Meanwhile, soak raisins in the boiling water for 30 minutes. Butter a 9-by-13-inch baking dish; set aside.

4 Drain raisins; stir into bread mixture. Preheat oven to 350°F. With a slotted spoon, transfer bread to buttered dish; pour liquid in bowl over top. Using spoon, turn top layer of bread crust side up.

5 Set dish in a roasting pan; transfer to oven. Pour boiling water into pan to reach about halfway up sides of dish. Bake until golden brown, about 50 minutes. Let dish cool on a wire rack 10 to 20 minutes before serving.

from The Basics of Bread Pudding

banana, coconut, and rum bread pudding

SERVES 8

For individual bread puddings, divide the mixture among eight buttered six-ounce ramekins; bake for forty minutes.

2 tablespoons unsalted butter, plus 2 tablespoons, softened, for baking dish
12 ounces brioche or challah, cut into 1-inch cubes
2 cups milk
3 cups heavy cream
4 large eggs plus 1 large egg yolk
1 cup granulated sugar
½ teaspoon salt
1 tablespoon pure vanilla extract
3 tablespoons rum
2 tablespoons brown sugar
2 bananas, sliced
¾ cup sweetened flaked coconut
    Boiling water, for pan

1 Butter a 9-by-13-inch baking dish; set aside. Put bread in a large bowl; set aside. Heat milk and cream in a medium saucepan over medium-high heat until just about to simmer; remove from heat.

2 Whisk together eggs, yolk, granulated sugar, salt, vanilla, and rum in a medium bowl. Whisking constantly, pour cream mixture into egg mixture in a slow, steady stream. Pour over bread; fold to combine. Let stand 30 minutes, tossing and pressing occasionally to submerge bread.

3 Heat brown sugar and remaining 2 tablespoons butter in a skillet over medium heat until sugar is dissolved, about 5 minutes. Add bananas; cook 1 to 2 minutes. Fold into soaked bread along with coconut.

4 Preheat oven to 350°F. With a slotted spoon, transfer bread to buttered dish; pour liquid in bowl over top. Using spoon, turn top layer of bread crust side up.

5 Set dish in a roasting pan; transfer to oven. Pour boiling water into pan to reach about halfway up sides of dish. Bake until golden brown, about 50 minutes. Let dish cool on a wire rack 10 to 20 minutes before serving.

from The Basics of Bread Pudding

chai tea bread pudding

SERVES 8

For individual bread puddings, divide the mixture among eight buttered six-ounce ramekins; bake for forty minutes.

12 ounces brioche or challah, cut into 1-inch cubes

 2 cups milk

 3 cups heavy cream

 3 whole cinnamon sticks

 1 piece (2 inches) peeled fresh ginger

 8 whole cloves

10 cardamom pods

 ¼ cup loose black tea

1¼ cups sugar

 4 large eggs plus 1 large egg yolk

 ½ teaspoon salt

 1 tablespoon pure vanilla extract

 2 tablespoons unsalted butter, softened, for baking dish
   Boiling water, for pan

1   Put bread in a large bowl; set aside. Heat milk, cream, cinnamon, ginger, cloves, cardamom, tea, and ¼ cup sugar in a medium saucepan over medium-high heat until just about to simmer; remove from heat. Cover, and let steep 30 minutes.

2   Whisk together eggs, yolk, remaining cup sugar, salt, and vanilla in a medium bowl.

3   Pour cream mixture through a fine sieve; discard solids. Whisking constantly, pour cream mixture into egg mixture in a slow, steady stream. Pour over bread; fold to combine. Let stand 30 minutes, tossing and pressing occasionally to submerge bread.

4   Preheat oven to 350°F. Butter a 9-by-13-inch baking dish; set aside. With a slotted spoon, transfer bread to buttered dish; pour liquid in bowl over top. Using spoon, turn top layer of bread crust side up.

5   Set dish in a roasting pan; transfer to oven. Pour boiling water into pan to reach about halfway up sides of dish. Bake until golden brown, about 50 minutes. Let dish cool on a wire rack 10 to 20 minutes.

from The Basics of Bread Pudding

chocolate bread pudding

SERVES 8

For individual bread puddings, divide the mixture among eight buttered six-ounce ramekins; bake for forty minutes.

 2 tablespoons unsalted butter, softened, for baking dish

12 ounces brioche or challah, cut into 1-inch cubes

 2 cups milk

 3 cups heavy cream

 8 ounces semisweet or bittersweet chocolate, coarsely chopped

 4 large eggs plus 1 large egg yolk

 1 cup sugar

 ½ teaspoon salt

 1 tablespoon pure vanilla extract
   Boiling water, for pan

1   Butter a 9-by-13-inch baking dish; set aside. Put bread in a large bowl; set aside. Heat milk and cream in a medium saucepan over medium-high heat until just about to simmer; remove from heat. Add chocolate; stir until melted and smooth.

2   Whisk together eggs, yolk, sugar, salt, and vanilla in a medium bowl. Whisking constantly, pour chocolate mixture into egg mixture in a slow, steady stream. Pour over bread; fold to combine. Let stand 30 minutes, tossing and pressing occasionally to submerge bread.

3   Preheat oven to 350°F. With a slotted spoon, transfer bread to buttered dish; pour liquid in bowl over top. Using spoon, turn top layer of bread crust side up.

4   Set dish in a roasting pan; transfer to oven. Pour boiling water into pan to reach about halfway up sides of dish. Bake until golden brown, about 50 minutes. Let dish cool on a wire rack 10 to 20 minutes.

from The Basics of Bread Pudding

cranberry, orange, and pecan bread pudding

SERVES 8 | PHOTO ON PAGE 319

For individual bread puddings, divide the mixture among eight buttered six-ounce ramekins; bake for forty minutes.

2 tablespoons unsalted butter, softened, for baking dish

12 ounces brioche or challah, cut into 1-inch cubes

2 cups milk

3 cups heavy cream

4 large eggs plus 1 large egg yolk

1 cup sugar

½ teaspoon salt

1 tablespoon pure vanilla extract

¾ cup dried cranberries

¾ cup fresh orange juice

2 tablespoons freshly grated orange zest

¾ cup chopped toasted pecans

Boiling water, for pan

1 Butter a 9-by-13-inch baking dish; set aside. Put bread in a large bowl; set aside. Heat milk and cream in a medium saucepan over medium-high heat until just about to simmer; remove from heat.

2 Whisk together eggs, yolk, sugar, salt, and vanilla in a medium bowl. Whisking constantly, pour cream mixture into egg mixture in a slow, steady stream. Pour over bread; fold to combine. Let stand 30 minutes, tossing and pressing occasionally to submerge bread.

3 Meanwhile, bring cranberries and orange juice to a simmer in a small saucepan over medium-low heat; simmer until cranberries have plumped, 3 to 5 minutes.

4 Fold cranberries and any juice that remains in pan into bread mixture along with orange zest and pecans. Preheat oven to 350°F. With a slotted spoon, transfer bread to buttered dish; pour liquid in bowl over top. Using spoon, turn top layer of bread crust side up.

5 Set dish in a roasting pan; transfer to oven. Pour boiling water into pan to reach about halfway up sides of dish. Bake until golden brown, about 50 minutes. Let dish cool on a wire rack 10 to 20 minutes.

from The Basics of Bread Pudding

apple pie with cheddar crust

MAKES ONE 10-INCH PIE | PHOTO ON PAGE 319

Cheddar Crust dough (recipe follows)

1½ pounds Granny Smith apples (about 3), peeled, cored, and cut into ¼-inch-thick wedges

2 pounds Cortland apples (about 5), peeled, cored, and cut into ¼-inch-thick wedges

1 cup sugar

½ cup all-purpose flour

2 teaspoons fresh lemon juice

¾ teaspoon ground cinnamon

¼ teaspoon freshly grated nutmeg

¼ teaspoon salt

⅛ teaspoon ground cloves

2 tablespoons unsalted butter, cut into small pieces

1 large egg, beaten

1 Divide dough into two pieces. On a lightly floured work surface, roll out each to a 13-inch circle.

2 Fit one circle into a 10-inch pie plate; transfer plate to a baking sheet. Put other circle on another baking sheet. Refrigerate both pieces of dough until cold, at least 30 minutes.

3 Stir together apples, sugar, flour, lemon juice, cinnamon, nutmeg, salt, and cloves. Spoon into bottom pie crust. Dot filling with butter. Cover with top crust. Fold edges over; crimp decoratively to seal. Cut a steam vent in top. Chill in freezer until firm, about 30 minutes.

4 Preheat oven to 450°F. Brush pie with egg. Bake 10 minutes. Reduce oven temperature to 350°F; bake until golden brown, about 45 minutes. Tent with foil; bake until juices are bubbling, about 45 minutes more. Let cool at least 1½ hours before serving.

from An Apple a Day

cheddar crust

MAKES ENOUGH FOR ONE 10-INCH DOUBLE-CRUST PIE

2½ cups all-purpose flour, plus more for dusting

1 teaspoon sugar

½ teaspoon salt

14 tablespoons (1¾ sticks) cold unsalted butter, cut into small pieces

4 ounces white cheddar cheese, coarsely grated (about 1½ cups)

½ cup ice water

1 Process flour, sugar, and salt in a food processor just to combine. Add butter; pulse until pea-size lumps appear. Pulse in cheese. With processor running, add ice water; process just until dough comes together.

2 Turn dough out; gather into a block. Wrap in plastic wrap. Refrigerate until cold, at least 30 minutes or up to 2 days. Dough can be frozen up to 3 weeks.

applesauce coffee cake

MAKES ONE 10-INCH CAKE | PHOTO ON PAGE 313

Vegetable-oil cooking spray

12 tablespoons (1½ sticks) unsalted butter, softened

½ cup packed dark-brown sugar

¼ cup old-fashioned rolled oats

2¾ teaspoons ground cinnamon

1 teaspoon salt

1½ cups chopped toasted pecans

2 cups all-purpose flour

1 teaspoon baking soda

½ teaspoon freshly grated nutmeg

⅛ teaspoon ground cloves

1 cup granulated sugar

½ cup packed light-brown sugar

4 large eggs

Apple Cider Applesauce (recipe follows) or 1½ cups store-bought applesauce

2 small, juicy apples, such as McIntosh, peeled, cored, and cut into ¼-inch-thick wedges

1 Preheat oven to 350°F. Coat a 10-inch tube pan with cooking spray; set aside. Make crumb topping: Stir together 4 tablespoons butter, the dark-brown sugar, oats, ¾ teaspoon cinnamon, and ¼ teaspoon salt until smooth. Stir in ½ cup pecans; set aside.

2 Make batter: Sift together flour, baking soda, nutmeg, cloves, and the remaining 2 teaspoons cinnamon and ¾ tea-

spoon salt; set aside. Put remaining 8 tablespoons (1 stick) butter, the granulated sugar, and light-brown sugar in the bowl of an electric mixer fitted with the paddle attachment. Cream on medium speed until smooth, about 3 minutes. Mix in the eggs, one at a time. Reduce speed to low; mix in applesauce and then flour mixture. Stir in remaining cup nuts by hand.

3 Pour batter into prepared pan; sprinkle crumb topping over batter. Lay apples on top, tucking some into batter.

4 Bake until a cake tester inserted near center comes out clean, about 1 hour and 10 minutes. Let cool in pan on a wire rack. Cake can be stored at room temperature, covered with plastic wrap, up to 3 days.

from An Apple a Day

apple cider applesauce

MAKES 1½ CUPS

1 pound juicy apples, such as McIntosh, peeled, cored, and quartered

¾ cup apple cider

1 tablespoon sugar, plus more if needed

Pinch of salt

1 Bring apples and cider to a boil in a medium saucepan over medium-high heat. Cover pan; reduce heat. Simmer until apples are very soft, about 12 minutes. Remove lid; stir in sugar and salt.

2 Cook over medium-low heat until apples are broken up and most of the liquid is evaporated, about 15 minutes. Let cool slightly. Blend in a food processor until smooth. Add more sugar, if desired. Applesauce can be stored in an airtight container up to 2 days.

banana chocolate-chunk ice cream

MAKES 1 QUART

Mix your favorite flavors into store-bought vanilla ice cream. You can substitute a combination of whatever you happen to have in your pantry—chopped nuts, chocolate chips, hard candies—for the ingredients in this recipe. The ice cream will need to soften at room temperature for about five minutes before blending in the other ingredients. For a quick, decadent topping, melt some extra chopped chocolate and drizzle it over the top.

6 tablespoons sweetened shredded coconut

2 pints vanilla ice cream, slightly softened

5 ounces best-quality bittersweet chocolate, coarsely chopped

2 small bananas, cut into ½-inch chunks

1 Preheat oven to 350°F. Spread ½ cup coconut evenly on a rimmed baking sheet; toast in oven, tossing about halfway through, until pale golden brown, 3 to 5 minutes. Let cool completely.

2 Mix ice cream, chocolate, bananas, and toasted coconut in the bowl of an electric mixer fitted with the paddle attachment until combined, about 1 minute. Press mixture into a 1-quart airtight container, and freeze until firm, about 50 minutes. Serve scoops of ice cream sprinkled with the remaining 2 tablespoons coconut.

from What's for Dinner?

churros with hot chocolate

MAKES 20

These fluted pieces of deep-fried dough are dusted with cinnamon sugar, which adds pleasing flavor and crunch. They are favorites in Spain and Mexico, where they're often served with rich hot cocoa.

2 tablespoons ground cinnamon

¾ cup sugar

1 cup milk

6 tablespoons unsalted butter

1 teaspoon coarse salt

1 cup all-purpose flour

3 large eggs, lightly beaten

5 to 6 cups vegetable oil, for frying

Hot Chocolate (recipe follows)

1 Stir together cinnamon and sugar in a small bowl; set aside. Bring milk, butter, and salt to a boil in a small saucepan over medium heat. Add flour, and cook, stirring, until mixture forms a ball and pulls away from sides of pan, about 30 seconds. Remove from heat, and let cool 3 minutes. Add eggs, and stir until batter is smooth. Spoon mixture into a pastry bag fitted with a large open-star tip (such as an Ateco #828).

2 Heat 4 to 5 inches oil in a large Dutch oven until it registers 330°F on a deep-fry thermometer. Holding pastry bag a few inches above the oil, squeeze out batter, snipping off 4-inch lengths with a knife or kitchen shears. Fry 6 to 8 churros at a time, turning once, until deep golden brown all over, about 5 minutes; transfer to a paper-towel–lined plate to drain.

3 Roll churros in cinnamon sugar. Serve immediately with hot chocolate.

from Dessert of the Month

hot chocolate

SERVES 4

3 ounces bittersweet chocolate, coarsely chopped

3 cups milk

2 tablespoons sugar

Stir together chocolate, milk, and sugar in a small saucepan. Cook over medium heat, stirring, until chocolate is completely melted and mixture is hot, about 10 minutes. Remove from heat; whisk until frothy.

gratinéed pineapple

SERVES 4

½ cup sweetened shredded coconut

½ cup finely crushed gingersnap cookies

½ cup chopped macadamia nuts

½ cup sweetened condensed milk

2 tablespoons dark rum

1 large ripe pineapple, leaves intact, quartered lengthwise

1 Preheat oven to 350°F. Stir together coconut, cookie crumbs, and nuts; set aside. Whisk together sweetened condensed milk and rum; set aside.

2 Cut core from each pineapple quarter; discard. Cut between skin and flesh of each quarter to separate. Arrange, skin sides down, on a rimmed baking sheet. Drizzle with half of the sweetened-condensed-milk mixture. Sprinkle with coconut mixture; drizzle with the remaining sweetened-condensed-milk mixture. Bake until heated through and golden brown, 10 to 12 minutes. Serve warm.

from Gratins

pumpkin cookies with brown-butter icing

MAKES ABOUT 6 DOZEN

Brown butter, also called beurre noisette, is formed when the milk proteins and sugars in butter caramelize during cooking, giving it a deep, nutty flavor.

2¾ cups all-purpose flour

1 teaspoon baking powder

1 teaspoon baking soda

1¼ teaspoons salt

1½ teaspoons ground cinnamon

1¼ teaspoons ground ginger

¾ teaspoon ground nutmeg

11 ounces (2¾ sticks) unsalted butter, softened

2¼ cups packed light-brown sugar

2 large eggs

1½ cups canned solid-pack pumpkin (14 ounces)

1 cup plus 1 tablespoon evaporated milk, plus more if needed

1 tablespoon pure vanilla extract

4 cups confectioners' sugar, sifted

1 Preheat oven to 375°F. Line baking sheets with parchment paper; set aside. Fit a pastry bag with a large coupler and a ½-inch plain round tip (such as an Ateco #806); set aside.

2 Whisk together flour, baking powder, baking soda, salt, cinnamon, ginger, and nutmeg in a medium bowl; set aside. Cream 12 tablespoons (1½ sticks) butter and the brown sugar on medium speed in the bowl of an electric mixer fitted with the paddle attachment until pale, about 3 minutes. Mix in eggs, scraping down sides of bowl as needed. On low speed, add pumpkin, ¾ cup evaporated milk, and 1 teaspoon vanilla; mix until combined, about 2 minutes. Add flour mixture; mix, scraping down sides and bottom of bowl as needed, until well combined.

3 Transfer 1½ cups batter to pastry bag. Holding tip close to parchment paper, pipe 1½-inch rounds 1 inch apart. Repeat with remaining batter. Bake until tops are springy to the touch, about 12 minutes. Let cool on sheets 5 minutes; transfer to wire racks to cool completely.

4 Meanwhile, put confectioners' sugar in a large bowl; set aside. Melt remaining 10 tablespoons butter in a small saucepan over medium heat. Cook until golden brown, about 3 minutes.

5 Immediately pour butter over confectioners' sugar, scraping any brown bits from sides and bottom of pan. Add remaining 5 tablespoons evaporated milk and remaining 2 teaspoons vanilla; stir until smooth. Spread about 1 teaspoon icing on each cookie. (If icing becomes stiff, stir in a little more evaporated milk until spreadable.) Cookies can be stored in an airtight container up to 3 days.

from Cookie of the Month

vanilla-bean baked apples

MAKES 4 | **PHOTO ON PAGE 313**

4 thick-skinned, mildly sweet apples, such as Rome Beauty

3 tablespoons packed dark-brown sugar

2 tablespoons unsalted butter, softened

2 tablespoons finely chopped toasted pecans, plus more for sprinkling

½ large vanilla bean, halved lengthwise, seeds scraped and reserved

⅛ teaspoon salt

1 Preheat oven to 375°F. Using a cylindrical apple corer, core apples three-quarters of the way down. Fit apples snugly in an ovenproof skillet or a loaf pan.

2 Stir together sugar, butter, nuts, vanilla seeds, and salt in a small bowl. Divide sugar mixture among apples (about 2 teaspoons each). Sprinkle with additional nuts. Bake until apples are soft, about 1 hour. Serve warm with pan syrup spooned on top.

from An Apple a Day

MISCELLANEOUS

applesauce muffins

MAKES 18 | **PHOTO ON PAGE 319**

2 cups all-purpose flour

2 teaspoons ground cinnamon

1 teaspoon baking soda

¾ teaspoon salt

½ teaspoon freshly ground nutmeg

⅛ teaspoon ground cloves

8 ounces (2 sticks) unsalted butter, softened

1 cup granulated sugar

1½ cups packed light-brown sugar

4 large eggs

Apple Cider Applesauce (page 246) or 1½ cups store-bought applesauce

1 cup toasted pecans, chopped

1 package (8 ounces) cream cheese, room temperature

1 Preheat oven to 350°F. Line a 12-cup muffin tin and a 6-cup tin with paper liners. Sift flour, cinnamon, baking soda, salt, nutmeg, and cloves together into a bowl. Set aside.

2 Put 8 tablespoons (1 stick) butter, the granulated sugar, and ½ cup brown sugar in the bowl of an electric mixer fitted with the paddle attachment. Cream on medium speed until mixture is smooth, about 3 minutes. Mix in eggs, one at a time. On low speed, mix in applesauce and then flour mixture. Stir in nuts by hand.

3 Divide batter among muffin cups, filling each about three-quarters full. Bake until a cake tester inserted into centers comes out clean, 18 to 20 minutes. Let muffins cool completely in tins on a wire rack.

4 Meanwhile, in the clean bowl of electric mixer, mix cream cheese with remaining 8 tablespoons (1 stick) butter and 1 cup brown sugar on medium speed until smooth. Spread cream-cheese frosting on muffins. Muffins can be refrigerated in airtight containers up to 2 days.

from An Apple a Day

Bette's chicken liver pâté with sautéed maple-syrup apples

SERVES 8

The pâté can be refrigerated (without the apples) for up to one week.

- 15 tablespoons (1⅞ sticks) unsalted butter
- ¾ pound chicken livers, rinsed and drained
- 8 ounces white mushrooms, sliced
- ⅓ cup chopped scallions (white and pale-green parts only; about 3 scallions)
- 1 tablespoon minced garlic (2 to 3 cloves)
- 1 teaspoon paprika
   Coarse salt
- ⅓ cup white wine
- 1 teaspoon fresh thyme
- 1 loaf crusty bread, for serving
   Sautéed Maple Syrup Apples (recipe follows)

1 Melt 3 tablespoons butter in a large skillet over medium-high heat. Add livers, mushrooms, scallions, garlic, and paprika. Cook, stirring occasionally, until livers are cooked through, about 5 minutes. Stir in 1 teaspoon salt. Add wine and thyme. Reduce heat to low; cover. Cook until mushrooms are very soft, about 10 minutes. Let mixture cool completely.

2 Process mixture and remaining 12 tablespoons butter in a food processor until smooth. Stir in 1½ teaspoons salt. Transfer pâté to an airtight container or a ramekin; cover with plastic wrap directly on surface. Refrigerate until firm, at least 2 hours or overnight. Serve with bread and sautéed apples.

from An Apple a Day

sautéed maple syrup apples

MAKES 2 DOZEN SLICES

- 1 tablespoon unsalted butter
- 2 juicy, sweet-tart apples, such as Jonathan, peeled and cut into 12 wedges each
- 2 tablespoons pure maple syrup
- ¼ teaspoon coarse salt

Melt butter in a medium skillet over medium heat. Add apples; cook, turning once, until golden brown, about 5 minutes total. Stir in syrup and salt; reduce heat to low. Simmer until apples are soft, about 5 minutes. Serve warm.

quinoa, apricot, and nut clusters

MAKES 20

- ¾ cup quinoa
- 1½ cups old-fashioned rolled oats
- ½ cup shelled raw sunflower seeds
- ½ cup shelled raw pistachios, chopped
- 1 cup dried apricots, thinly sliced
- ¼ cup sugar
- ½ teaspoon coarse salt
- ¼ cup honey
- 2 tablespoons vegetable oil
- 1½ teaspoons pure vanilla extract
- 2 large eggs plus 1 large egg white, lightly beaten
   Vegetable-oil cooking spray

1 Preheat oven to 350°F. Rinse quinoa thoroughly in a fine sieve; drain. Bring 1½ cups water to a boil in a small saucepan. Add quinoa; return to a boil. Stir quinoa; cover, and reduce heat. Simmer until most liquid is absorbed and quinoa is slightly undercooked, about 12 minutes; transfer to a rimmed baking sheet. Bake, fluffing with a fork occasionally, until pale golden, 30 to 35 minutes. Let cool in a large bowl.

2 Spread oats on baking sheet; bake until lightly browned, about 15 minutes. Add oats to quinoa. Spread seeds on baking sheet; bake until lightly toasted, about 7 minutes. Add to quinoa mixture; let cool. Reduce oven temperature to 300°F.

3 Toss nuts, apricots, sugar, and salt with quinoa mixture. Beat honey, oil, and vanilla into eggs; stir into quinoa mixture.

4 Line a 12-by-17-inch baking sheet with parchment; lightly coat with cooking spray. Spoon ¼ cup batter onto sheet for each cluster, spaced 3 inches apart. Flatten to ¼ inch thick. Bake, rotating sheet halfway through, until crisp, about 25 minutes. Let cool on a wire rack. Clusters can be stored, loosely covered with foil, up to 2 days.

PER SERVING (2 CLUSTERS): 329 CALORIES, 11 G FAT, 43 MG CHOLESTEROL, 49 G CARBOHYDRATE, 139 MG SODIUM, 10 G PROTEIN, 5 G FIBER

from Fit to Eat: Quinoa

November

French onion soup

MAKES SIXTEEN 1-CUP SERVINGS | **PHOTO ON PAGE 301**

This recipe can be halved. The soup can be refrigerated (without the bread and cheese) in airtight containers for up to three days or frozen for up to one month. To save a little time, heat the stock while you caramelize the onions so that the soup will come to a simmer quickly.

10 tablespoons unsalted butter, plus 6 tablespoons, melted (2 sticks total)

5 pounds onions, halved lengthwise and cut into ¼-inch-thick slices

2 teaspoons sugar

2 tablespoons all-purpose flour

3½ quarts Homemade Beef Stock (recipe follows) or low-sodium store-bought beef stock

1 cup dry white wine

6 tablespoons cognac

3 tablespoons coarse salt (or to taste)
   Freshly ground pepper

1 long baguette, cut into 32 rounds (¾ inch thick each)

12 ounces Gruyère cheese, grated on the large holes of a box grater (4 cups)

1 Melt 10 tablespoons butter in a large (7-quart) Dutch oven over medium-high heat. Add onions, and sprinkle with sugar. Cook onions, stirring only occasionally to prevent sticking, until very soft and translucent, 25 to 30 minutes.

2 Reduce heat to medium; continue to cook onions, stirring frequently to prevent sticking, until caramelized and deep brown, about 1 hour. (Adjust heat if the onions don't change color or if they darken too quickly and stick to the skillet.)

3 Sprinkle flour over onions; stir. Stir in stock, wine, and cognac; bring to a simmer over medium heat. Cook, partially covered, until heated through, 20 to 25 minutes. Add salt, and season with pepper.

4 Preheat broiler. Broil bread on a baking sheet, turning once, until lightly toasted, about 4 minutes (watch carefully so it doesn't burn). With the remaining 6 tablespoons melted butter, brush both sides of each slice.

5 Divide soup among flameproof crocks or bowls. Place 2 slices of bread over soup in each crock, and sprinkle ¼ cup cheese over bread. Broil until the cheese is melted and brown around the edges. Serve immediately.

from French Onion Soup

homemade beef stock

MAKES 4 QUARTS

3 pounds beef bones (such as marrow bones or shin bones)

3 pounds oxtail

2 tablespoons olive oil

2 tablespoons tomato paste

2 pounds unpeeled onions, quartered

2 large leeks, white and pale-green parts only, halved lengthwise, cut into 2-inch pieces, and rinsed well

4 celery stalks, cut into thirds

3 large carrots, peeled, halved lengthwise, and cut into 2-inch pieces

8 garlic cloves, coarsely chopped

6 sprigs fresh flat-leaf parsley

4 sprigs fresh thyme

2 bay leaves

2 teaspoons whole black peppercorns

1 cup red wine

1 Preheat oven to 400°F. Arrange beef bones and oxtail in a single layer in a heavy roasting pan (not glass). Coat with oil. Roast, turning once, until deep brown, about 45 minutes.

2 Add tomato paste, onions, leeks, celery, carrots, and garlic, stirring well. Roast until vegetables are browned and tender, about 40 minutes.

3 Meanwhile, make a bouquet garni by wrapping parsley, thyme, bay leaves, and peppercorns in a square of cheesecloth. Tie bundle with kitchen twine; set aside.

4 Transfer bones and vegetables to a large stockpot, and set aside. Pour off fat from roasting pan. Set pan on stove across two burners. Add wine, and bring to a boil, deglazing pan by scraping up any brown bits from bottom with a wooden spoon; boil until wine is reduced by half, about 3 minutes. Add to stockpot.

5 Add 6 quarts (24 cups) water to stockpot. Bring to a boil. Reduce heat to low, add bouquet garni, and simmer, uncovered, over low heat, 3 hours.

6 Carefully pass stock through a fine sieve into a large bowl or pot; discard solids. Let stock cool completely.

7 Transfer stock to airtight containers. Refrigerate stock at least 8 hours or up to 3 days before using (fat will solidify; discard it before using). The stock can be frozen up to 4 months.

marinated mushrooms

SERVES 4

As an antipasto course, serve these tangy mushrooms with store-bought olives and pickled hot or sweet peppers.

12 ounces cremini mushrooms, or a mix of cremini and oyster mushrooms

2 tablespoons fresh lemon juice

2 tablespoons white-wine vinegar

3 tablespoons coarsely chopped fresh oregano

6 tablespoons extra-virgin olive oil

¾ teaspoon coarse salt

⅛ teaspoon freshly ground pepper

1 Trim stems from the cremini mushrooms (break apart oyster-mushroom clusters, if using). Put mushrooms in a medium bowl, and set aside.

2 Whisk together lemon juice, vinegar, and oregano in a medium bowl. Whisk in oil in a slow, steady stream; whisk until mixture is emulsified. Whisk in the salt and pepper. Pour marinade over mushrooms, and let stand at room temperature, stirring occasionally, at least 20 minutes; if desired, refrigerate mushrooms in an airtight container overnight. Serve at room temperature.

from What's for Dinner?

pinzimonio

SERVES 12

1 pound carrots in assorted varieties, such as regular, yellow, and Thumbelina, peeled (quarter if large)

8 ounces radishes (about 8)

½ head cauliflower, cut into small florets

½ head Romanesca cauliflower (pale-green cauliflower) or broccoli, cut into small florets

1 fennel bulb, trimmed and cut lengthwise into ¼-inch-thick strips

8 ounces haricots verts, trimmed

2 yellow or red bell peppers, cut into strips

6 thin scallions

2 Belgian endives

½ lemon

⅓ cup flaked sea salt or coarse salt

2 teaspoons chopped fresh rosemary

2 teaspoons chopped fresh thyme

Freshly ground pepper

¼ cup extra-virgin olive oil

1 Arrange all vegetables except endives in serving dishes. Just before serving, halve endives lengthwise. Cut out cores, and discard. Separate leaves, and then squeeze lemon over them. Arrange leaves in dishes next to other vegetables.

2 Stir together salt and herbs in a small serving bowl, and season with pepper. Serve vegetables with olive oil for dipping and the seasoned salt for sprinkling.

from Thanksgiving With Italian Flavors

polenta squares with prosciutto

MAKES 48; SERVES 12

Coarse salt

2 cups yellow cornmeal

2 teaspoons extra-virgin olive oil, plus more for pan

6 slices prosciutto, cut into ¼-inch pieces

1 garlic clove, finely chopped

Freshly ground pepper

6 ounces Taleggio cheese, cut into ½-inch cubes (48 pieces)

Fresh marjoram sprigs, for garnish

1 Bring 7 cups water to a boil in a large saucepan; add 4 teaspoons salt. Whisking constantly, add cornmeal a little at a time. Reduce heat to medium-low; cook, stirring frequently with a wooden spoon, until polenta pulls away from sides of pan and is very thick, about 25 minutes.

2 Heat oil in a medium skillet over medium-low heat until hot but not smoking. Add prosciutto and garlic. Cook, stirring, until prosciutto is slightly crisp, about 5 minutes; stir into polenta. Season with salt and pepper, if desired.

3 Pour polenta mixture into a 9-by-13-inch baking pan; smooth with a dampened spatula. Let cool at least 1 hour.

4 If not serving polenta immediately, cover with plastic wrap, and refrigerate until ready to use (or overnight).

5 Trim ¼ inch from all sides. Cut polenta into 48 squares. Preheat broiler with rack 5 inches from heat source. Lightly brush a metal baking pan with oil; heat under broiler 30 seconds. In batches, broil squares in pan, 2 minutes. Place cheese on each square; season with pepper. Broil until cheese is melted, about 1½ minutes. Garnish with herb sprigs.

from Thanksgiving With Italian Flavors

red-and-golden-beet cheese tart

MAKES ONE 9-BY-13-INCH TART | **PHOTO ON PAGE 308**

All-purpose flour, for dusting

1½ disks Pastry Dough (page 269)

1½ pounds (without greens) red, golden, and Chioggia beets

2 tablespoons extra-virgin olive oil, plus more for drizzling

Coarse salt

1 pound soft goat cheese, room temperature

4 ounces fresh ricotta cheese (scant ½ cup)

2 teaspoons finely chopped fresh thyme, plus about 1 teaspoon whole leaves

Freshly ground pepper

½ cup grated fontina cheese

1   Preheat oven to 375°F. On a lightly floured surface, place 1½ disks pastry dough next to each other; roll out to ⅛ inch thick. Press firmly into a 9-by-13-inch rimmed baking sheet, leaving a 1-inch overhang on all sides. Tuck edges of dough under to create a double thickness; press firmly against sides of pan. Prick dough with a fork. Refrigerate 30 minutes.

2   Line shell with parchment or foil; fill with pie weights or dried beans. Bake until golden brown, about 30 minutes. Transfer to a wire rack. Remove weights and parchment. Let shell cool completely. (Leave oven on.)

3   Trim all but ½ inch of stems from beets; rinse. Toss with oil and 1 teaspoon salt. Transfer to a rimmed baking sheet; cover tightly with foil. Roast until beets are tender, 45 to 60 minutes. When cool enough to handle, peel beets with a paring knife. Cut into thin rounds.

4   Raise oven temperature to 425°F. Stir together the goat cheese, ricotta, and chopped thyme until well combined; season with pepper. Spread mixture over tart shell, filling all the way to edges.

5   Arrange beets over cheese mixture, overlapping slices slightly and alternating colors. Lightly season with salt. Sprinkle fontina and whole thyme leaves on top. Lightly drizzle with oil, and then season with pepper. Bake until golden brown, about 25 minutes. Serve warm.

from Earthy Delights

SALADS AND SIDE DISHES

mushroom and celery salad with Parmesan cheese

SERVES 12 | **PHOTO ON PAGE 298**

12 ounces fresh white or cremini mushrooms, thinly sliced

6 ounces fresh chanterelle, porcini, oyster, or yellow oyster mushrooms, thinly sliced

6 celery stalks

7 tablespoons fresh lemon juice (2 to 3 lemons)

3 tablespoons finely chopped shallot

6 tablespoons extra-virgin olive oil

Coarse salt and freshly ground pepper

8 ounces mixed baby lettuces, such as mâche and mesclun

6 ounces Parmigiano-Reggiano cheese

1   Lay mushrooms on sheets of paper towels; cover with clean, damp kitchen towels. Thinly slice celery, and transfer to a bowl; cover with plastic. Refrigerate.

2   Stir together lemon juice and shallot. Let stand at least 15 minutes or up to 2 hours. Whisk in oil until emulsified, and season with salt and pepper. Toss mushrooms and celery with dressing; let stand 10 minutes. Divide lettuce among plates, and top with mushroom mixture. Shave cheese with a vegetable peeler over tops.

from Thanksgiving With Italian Flavors

baked creamed salsify

SERVES 4 TO 6

¼ cup plus 1 teaspoon fresh lemon juice (about 2 lemons)
2 pounds salsify
Coarse salt
1½ tablespoons unsalted butter
½ cup heavy cream
Pinch of freshly grated nutmeg
Freshly ground pepper
¼ cup fresh breadcrumbs, lightly toasted
¼ cup freshly grated Parmesan cheese

1 Preheat oven to 425°F, with rack in highest position. Fill a large bowl two-thirds full with cold water; add ¼ cup lemon juice. Trim salsify, and peel with a vegetable peeler, transferring salsify to lemon water as you work. Cut salsify into 2-inch lengths, and return to bowl. Drain.

2 Cover salsify with cold water by 2 inches in a medium saucepan, and add ½ teaspoon salt. Bring to a boil. Reduce heat to medium-high. Cook until salsify is tender but not mushy, 10 to 15 minutes, and drain.

3 Melt butter in a medium saucepan over medium heat. Stir in salsify. Stir in cream and remaining teaspoon lemon juice. Bring to a bare simmer; remove from heat. Add nutmeg, and season with salt and pepper. Pour the salsify mixture into an 8-inch square baking dish or 8-cup gratin dish. Sprinkle with breadcrumbs and cheese. Bake until golden brown, about 20 minutes.

from Earthy Delights

chestnut and sausage stuffing

SERVES 12; MAKES ABOUT 10 CUPS (ENOUGH FOR ONE 16- TO 18-POUND TURKEY)

1 loaf day-old rustic Italian bread (about 1 pound), trimmed of crust and cut into ¾-inch cubes (about 8 cups)
1 pound fresh chestnuts
1 pound sweet Italian sausages
1 tablespoon extra-virgin olive oil
2 medium onions, finely chopped
4 celery stalks, finely chopped
4 garlic cloves, finely chopped
½ cup dry white wine
½ cup homemade or low-sodium store-bought chicken stock
1 tablespoon chopped fresh thyme
2 tablespoons chopped fresh sage
2 tablespoons chopped fresh flat-leaf parsley
2 teaspoons coarse salt
Freshly ground pepper
2 large eggs, lightly beaten
Unsalted butter, for baking dish

1 Let bread cubes stand on a baking sheet at room temperature 3 hours to dry out.

2 Lay each chestnut flat on a work surface, and cut an X in the pointed tip of shell with a paring or chestnut knife. Bring a medium pot of water to a boil. Boil chestnuts 2 minutes; remove pot from heat. Remove chestnuts with a slotted spoon; peel away shells. Quarter nutmeat; transfer to a large bowl. Add bread.

3 Preheat oven to 350°F. Split sausages; scrape meat into a large sauté pan set over medium heat; crumble with a fork. Cook, stirring occasionally, until cooked through, about 7 minutes. Add oil; swirl pan. Add onions, celery, and garlic. Reduce heat to medium-low. Cook, stirring occasionally, until vegetables are soft, 15 to 17 minutes. Add to bread mixture.

4 Add wine to pan. Scraping up any brown bits from bottom with a wooden spoon, cook over medium heat until wine is reduced by half. Add to bread mixture.

5 Add stock to bread mixture; toss. Add thyme, sage, and parsley. Add the salt, and season with pepper. Stir in eggs.

6 To bake stuffing by itself: Place stuffing in a buttered 9-by-13-inch baking dish; cover with foil. Bake 30 minutes; remove foil. Bake until golden brown, about 25 minutes. To cook in turkey: Stuff turkey as directed on page 261. Place the remaining 5 cups stuffing in a buttered 8-inch square baking dish; bake as directed above.

from Thanksgiving With Italian Flavors

cipollini in agrodolce

SERVES 12 | **PHOTO ON PAGE 307**

- 3 pounds cipollini or pearl onions, root ends trimmed
- 2 tablespoons extra-virgin olive oil
- 1 bay leaf
- 1 sprig fresh thyme
- ⅔ cup red-wine vinegar
- ½ cup dry red wine
- 2 tablespoons plus 2 teaspoons sugar
- 2½ teaspoons coarse salt
- Freshly ground pepper

1 Bring a large pot of water to a boil. Add onions; reduce heat to medium-low. Simmer onions until tender, 25 to 30 minutes. Drain; let cool. Peel onions.

2 Heat oil with bay leaf in a large sauté pan over medium heat until hot but not smoking. Add thyme. Add half of onions; cook, stirring, until deep golden brown in spots, about 5 minutes. Transfer to a bowl with a slotted spoon. Repeat with remaining onions. Add first batch to pan.

3 Stir together vinegar, wine, sugar, and salt; add to pan. Reduce heat to medium-low. Cook, stirring occasionally, until liquid is syrupy and onions are glazed, 20 to 25 minutes. Season with pepper.

from Thanksgiving With Italian Flavors

farro and sausage stuffing

SERVES 8 TO 10; MAKES ABOUT 8 CUPS (ENOUGH FOR ONE 18-POUND TURKEY) | **PHOTO ON PAGE 311**

Farro, also called spelt, is available at health-food stores. If you can't find Tuscan kale, use regular kale instead.

- 3 tablespoons extra-virgin olive oil
- 10 ounces sweet Italian sausages, casings removed, meat crumbled
- 1 fennel bulb, cut into ½-inch cubes, plus ¼ cup chopped fronds
- 1 large onion, cut into ½-inch pieces
- 2 garlic cloves, crushed
- ½ cup dry white wine
- 2½ cups farro
- 10 ounces Tuscan kale, ribs discarded and leaves thinly sliced crosswise (11 cups)
- 1¾ cups homemade or low-sodium store-bought chicken stock
- Narrow strips of zest from 1 large lemon
- 2 tablespoons chopped fresh rosemary
- Coarse salt and freshly ground pepper

1 Heat 1 tablespoon oil in a medium heavy-bottom pot over medium-high heat until hot but not smoking. Add sausage; cook, breaking up meat with a wooden spoon, until deep golden brown, about 7 minutes. Remove meat; set aside.

2 Add 1 tablespoon oil, the fennel, onion, and garlic to pot. Reduce heat to medium; cook, stirring, until fennel and onion are softened, about 5 minutes. Add the wine, and cook until reduced by half.

3 Stir in 2 cups water, the farro, kale, stock, zest, 2 tablespoons fennel fronds, 1 tablespoon each rosemary and oil, and 2 teaspoons salt. Bring to a boil over medium-high heat. Reduce heat; simmer until farro is tender, 15 minutes. Stir in sausage, 1 tablespoon rosemary, and 2 tablespoons fennel fronds. Season with salt and pepper.

4 Serve, or immediately pack loosely in turkey cavity, and cook until an instant-read thermometer inserted into center of stuffing registers 165°F.

from Deliciously Different Stuffings

Israeli couscous and fall-vegetable stuffing

SERVES 8 TO 10; MAKES ABOUT 8 CUPS (ENOUGH FOR ONE 18-POUND TURKEY) | **PHOTO ON PAGE 311**

 1 small acorn squash (about 1½ pounds), halved and seeded
 ¼ cup extra-virgin olive oil
   Coarse salt and freshly ground pepper
 2 small turnips, peeled and cut into ½-inch cubes
 1 celery root (also called celeriac), peeled and cut into ½-inch cubes
 2 tablespoons unsalted butter
 ¾ cup finely chopped shallots
 ½ teaspoon ground coriander
 ¼ teaspoon ground cumin
 ¼ teaspoon hot smoked paprika
 10 ounces Israeli couscous (about 2 cups)
 1¾ cups homemade or low-sodium store-bought chicken stock
 1 fresh bay leaf
 2 tablespoons chopped fresh thyme
 ½ cup golden raisins
 ½ cup sliced almonds with skins, toasted
 ¼ cup chopped fresh flat-leaf parsley

1 Preheat oven to 375°F. Drizzle squash with 1 tablespoon oil; season with salt and pepper. Place, cut sides down, on a rimmed baking sheet; roast 10 minutes.

2 Meanwhile, toss turnips and celery root with 2 tablespoons oil; season with salt and pepper. Place on baking sheet with squash. Continue roasting, stirring once or twice, until vegetables are tender and golden brown, about 30 minutes.

3 Meanwhile, heat butter and remaining tablespoon oil in a medium saucepan over medium heat until butter is melted. Add shallots; cook until softened, about 3 minutes. Stir in coriander, cumin, and paprika; cook until fragrant, about 1 minute. Stir in couscous, stock, bay leaf, 1 tablespoon thyme, and 1 teaspoon salt. Bring to a boil. Cover; reduce heat to low. Cook until couscous is tender but al dente and liquid is absorbed, about 6 minutes. Remove from heat. Let stand, covered, 2 minutes. Fluff with a fork.

4 Peel squash; cut flesh into ½-inch cubes. Stir together couscous, vegetables, raisins, almonds, parsley and remaining tablespoon thyme; season with salt and pepper. Serve, or immediately pack loosely in turkey cavity, and cook until an instant-read thermometer inserted into the center of the stuffing registers 165°F.

from Deliciously Different Stuffings

mashed squash and potatoes with amaretti

SERVES 12 | **PHOTO ON PAGE 307**

 2 pounds russet potatoes, peeled and cut into 1-inch cubes (about 6 cups)
   Coarse salt
 3 pounds buttercup squash (about 1 small), peeled, seeded, and cut into 1-inch cubes (about 8 cups)
 6 tablespoons unsalted butter, plus more for baking dish
 ½ cup heavy cream
 ¼ teaspoon freshly ground nutmeg
   Freshly ground pepper
 ½ cup finely grated Parmigiano-Reggiano cheese
 10 amaretti (Italian almond cookies), crushed into fine crumbs (about ¾ cup)

1 Cover potatoes with cold water in a medium saucepan. Bring to a boil; add salt. Reduce heat to medium-high; cook potatoes until soft, about 25 minutes. In another medium saucepan, cover squash with cold water. Bring to a boil; add salt. Reduce heat to medium-high; cook until soft, 15 to 20 minutes. Drain potatoes and squash thoroughly.

2 Force potatoes through a ricer into a bowl. In a separate bowl, mash squash with a potato masher; stir in potatoes.

3 Bring 4 tablespoons butter and the cream to a simmer in a small saucepan over medium heat. Add ½ teaspoon salt and the nutmeg. Season with pepper. Stir cream mixture and ⅓ cup cheese into potato mixture. Season with salt and pepper, if desired. Spoon into a buttered 10-inch round baking dish.

4 Preheat oven to 350°F. Sprinkle mixture with crushed cookies and remaining cheese. Dot topping with remaining 2 tablespoons butter. Bake until the topping just begins to brown, 20 to 30 minutes.

from Thanksgiving With Italian Flavors

potato and cracker stuffing

SERVES 10 TO 12; MAKES ABOUT 10 CUPS (ENOUGH FOR ONE 20-POUND TURKEY) | PHOTO ON PAGE 311

This stuffing was adapted from a recipe by Dennis and Judy Mareb of Windy Hill Farm in Massachusetts.

- 2 pounds small white boiling potatoes
- ½ cup pine nuts
- 4 tablespoons unsalted butter
- 8 ounces mixed white and shiitake mushrooms, thinly sliced
- 2 medium white onions, coarsely chopped
- 3 celery stalks, thinly sliced
- ¼ teaspoon ground cinnamon
- ½ teaspoon freshly ground pepper
- 2 teaspoons coarse salt
- 7 ounces cream crackers (about 26)

1 Cover potatoes with cold water in a large pot. Bring to a boil. Reduce heat, and simmer until tender but not mushy, about 20 minutes. Drain; set aside.

2 Meanwhile, toast pine nuts in a dry large skillet over medium heat, shaking occasionally, until golden. Set aside. Melt 2 tablespoons butter in skillet over high heat. Add mushrooms, and cook, stirring, until golden brown, about 5 minutes. Remove from skillet; set aside. Melt remaining 2 tablespoons butter in skillet. Add onions and celery; cook, stirring, until soft, about 5 minutes.

3 Peel potatoes, and roughly mash, leaving whole pieces. Add pine nuts, mushrooms, onion mixture, spices, and salt. Break crackers into pieces over top. Stir.

4 To bake stuffing by itself: Cover with foil in a 3-quart baking dish. Bake in a 350°F oven 15 minutes. Remove foil; bake until heated through and golden, about 15 minutes more. To cook in turkey: Immediately pack loosely in turkey cavity; cook until an instant-read thermometer inserted into center of stuffing registers 165°F.

from Deliciously Different Stuffings

roasted radicchio

SERVES 4

- 2 medium heads radicchio, quartered lengthwise
- ¼ cup extra-virgin olive oil
  Coarse salt and freshly ground pepper
- ¼ cup balsamic vinegar
- 1 ounce Parmesan cheese, preferably Parmigiano-Reggiano, shaved (about ⅓ cup)

1 Preheat oven to 400°F. Put radicchio wedges on a rimmed baking sheet. Drizzle with oil, and season with salt and pepper. Toss gently to coat, and turn each wedge so a cut side faces down. Roast, turning once, until leaves are wilted and slightly charred, 12 to 15 minutes. Transfer to a platter.

2 Just before serving, drizzle vinegar over each wedge, and garnish with cheese shavings.

from What's for Dinner?

roasted radishes with capers and anchovies

SERVES 4

- 12 ounces radishes (about 12), halved if large
- 2 teaspoons capers, rinsed and chopped
- 6 anchovy fillets, finely chopped
- 1 garlic clove, minced
- 2 tablespoons extra-virgin olive oil
  Coarse salt and freshly ground pepper
- ½ lemon, for serving

Preheat oven to 375°F, with rack in upper third. Toss together radishes, capers, anchovies, garlic, and oil; season with salt and pepper. Spread out mixture in a small roasting pan. Roast, stirring once, until radishes are shriveled and fragrant, 30 to 35 minutes. Serve warm, and squeeze lemon juice over top.

from Earthy Delights

sautéed spinach with garlic

SERVES 12

- 1 tablespoon minced garlic
- ¼ cup extra-virgin olive oil
- 3 pounds baby or regular spinach, tough stems discarded
- 2 teaspoons coarse salt
- ¼ teaspoon crushed red-pepper flakes
- 1 tablespoon fresh lemon juice

1 Cook half of garlic in 2 tablespoons oil in a large sauté pan over medium heat, stirring, until garlic is fragrant but not browned, about 1 minute. Raise heat to medium-high. Cook half of spinach, adding it little by little, until all of spinach is wilted. Stir in 1 teaspoon salt and ⅛ teaspoon red-pepper flakes. Transfer to a dish; loosely cover with foil.

2 Wipe pan clean with paper towels. Repeat with remaining garlic, oil, spinach, salt, and red-pepper flakes. Add to first batch, and toss with lemon juice.

from Thanksgiving With Italian Flavors

roasted root vegetables with sage and garlic

SERVES 4 TO 6

8 ounces rutabaga, peeled and cut into ½-inch cubes or half-moons

8 ounces turnips, peeled and cut into ½-inch cubes or half-moons

8 ounces carrots, peeled and cut into ½-inch cubes or rounds

8 ounces parsnips, peeled and cut into ½-inch cubes or rounds

8 fresh sage leaves

4 garlic cloves (do not peel)

Coarse salt and freshly ground pepper

4½ teaspoons olive oil

Preheat oven to 375°F. Toss together all ingredients; spread out in a roasting pan. Roast, stirring occasionally, until golden brown and tender, 50 to 60 minutes.

from Earthy Delights

savory cranberry jelly

SERVES 12

2 packages (12 ounces each) fresh or frozen (thawed) cranberries

2 cups sugar

2 teaspoons minced garlic

1 teaspoon grated peeled fresh ginger

½ cup cider vinegar

Large pinch of ground allspice

Large pinch of coarse salt

Freshly ground pepper

4¾ teaspoons unflavored gelatin

1 Bring berries, sugar, and 1 cup water to a simmer in a covered medium saucepan over medium-high heat. Cook until berries are soft, about 10 minutes. Pass through a fine sieve into a bowl, pressing on solids to make a purée.

2 Bring ½ cup water, the garlic, ginger, vinegar, allspice, salt, and a generous amount of pepper to a simmer in a small saucepan over medium-high heat. Cook until reduced by half, about 5 minutes.

3 Pour vinegar mixture into a small bowl. Sprinkle gelatin on top; stir until dissolved. Stir mixture into berry purée.

4 Cover jelly with plastic wrap, and refrigerate at least 2 hours or up to 1 week.

from Thanksgiving With Italian Flavors

sweet potato stuffing with persimmons and plums

SERVES 6; MAKES ABOUT 4 CUPS (ENOUGH FOR ONE 12-POUND TURKEY)

3 sweet potatoes (about 2½ pounds)

2 tablespoons unsalted butter, softened

1 ounce dried red plums (about 6 halves)

2 ripe Fuyu persimmons

2 teaspoons packed light-brown sugar

½ teaspoon freshly grated orange zest

½ teaspoon ground cardamom

¼ vanilla bean, halved lengthwise

½ teaspoon coarse salt

¼ teaspoon freshly ground pepper

1 Preheat oven to 400°F. Bake potatoes until tender, about 1 hour. Let cool; peel. Cut 1 potato into ½-inch cubes. Mash remaining 2 potatoes with butter. Set aside.

2 Bring 4 cups water to a boil in a medium saucepan. Soak plums in 1 cup boiling water until plump, 5 to 7 minutes.

3 Dip persimmons in remaining water for 10 seconds each; rinse in cold water. Stem, peel, and core. Cut persimmons and plums into ¼-inch-thick pieces.

4 Stir together fruit, sugar, zest, and cardamom. Scrape in vanilla seeds. Add salt and pepper. Stir in potatoes.

5 To bake stuffing by itself: Cover with foil in an 8-inch square baking dish. Bake in a 350°F oven 15 minutes. Remove foil; bake until heated through, about 5 minutes more. To cook in turkey: Immediately pack loosely in turkey cavity; cook until an instant-read thermometer inserted into center of stuffing registers 165°F.

from Deliciously Different Stuffings

wild rice and corn stuffing

SERVES 8; MAKES ABOUT 7 CUPS (ENOUGH FOR ONE 18-POUND TURKEY) | **PHOTO ON PAGE 311**

2 cups wild rice

Coarse salt

2 tablespoons corn or vegetable oil

2 small red onions, cut into thin rounds

3 garlic cloves, minced (1 tablespoon)

2 fresh serrano or jalapeño chiles, thinly sliced

1 cup frozen corn kernels, thawed

¼ teaspoon freshly ground pepper

2 tablespoons fresh lime juice

1 Bring 5 cups water to a boil in a medium saucepan; add rice and 1 tablespoon salt. Cover, and reduce heat. Cook rice until al dente, 35 to 40 minutes (not all of the water will be absorbed). Drain rice well.

2 Heat oil in a large skillet over medium-high heat until hot but not smoking. Add onions and garlic; cook, stirring, until soft, about 2 minutes. Add chiles; cook 30 seconds.

3 Stir onion mixture, corn, pepper, and lime juice into rice; season with salt. Serve, or immediately pack loosely in turkey cavity, and cook until an instant-read thermometer inserted into center of stuffing registers 165°F.

from Deliciously Different Stuffings

MAIN COURSES

herb-roasted turkey

SERVES 10 TO 12 | **PHOTO ON PAGE 306**

1 fresh turkey (16 to 18 pounds), giblets removed, turkey brought to room temperature (no more than 2 hours)

8 tablespoons (1 stick) unsalted butter, softened
   Coarse salt and freshly ground pepper

8 small sprigs fresh flat-leaf parsley

12 fresh sage leaves

5 cups Chestnut and Sausage Stuffing (page 256) or other stuffing
   White-Wine Gravy (page 272)

1 Preheat oven to 425°F, with rack in lower third. Rinse turkey inside and out, and pat dry with paper towels. Place on a rack set in a large roasting pan.

2 Blend 4 tablespoons butter with 2 teaspoons salt; season with pepper. Loosen skin of turkey at body-cavity end with your fingers; spread mixture under skin all over (reach as far back as possible).

3 Gently push 3 parsley sprigs under skin on each side of turkey breast (use a table knife to push them as far as possible, keeping leaves flat). Loosen neck skin; slide a parsley sprig on each side of top of breast. Repeat with sage leaves, placing 4 leaves on each side of breast and 2 leaves on each side of top of breast.

4 Rub turkey with remaining 4 tablespoons butter. Sprinkle with 1 teaspoon salt; season with pepper. Loosely stuff body cavity with 4¾ cups stuffing, and neck cavity with ¼ cup. Tie drumsticks together loosely with kitchen twine. Fold neck skin under body, and secure with toothpicks. Tuck wing tips under wings.

5 Roast turkey 30 minutes. Baste turkey; reduce oven temperature to 350°F. Continue to roast until an instant-read thermometer inserted into thickest part of the thigh (avoiding bone) registers 180°F and stuffing registers 165°F, 2 to 3 hours. (If skin darkens too quickly during roasting, tent with foil.)

6 Let turkey rest 20 minutes before carving. Leave juices in roasting pan to make gravy. Serve turkey with gravy.

from Thanksgiving With Italian Flavors

pasta with brussels sprouts and bacon

SERVES 4

6 ounces bacon (about 7 slices), cut into ¾-inch pieces
   Up to ¼ cup extra-virgin olive oil

2 large garlic cloves, minced

4 large shallots, cut into thin rounds

1¼ pounds brussels sprouts, trimmed and halved (quartered if large)

1¼ cups homemade or low-sodium store-bought chicken stock
   Coarse salt and freshly ground pepper

12 ounces rigatoni pasta

½ cup freshly grated Parmesan cheese, plus more for serving

⅓ cup coarsely chopped fresh sage leaves (about 20 leaves)

1 Heat a dry large skillet over medium heat. Add bacon; cook, stirring occasionally, until crisp, 5 to 7 minutes. Using a slotted spoon, transfer to a paper-towel–lined plate to drain. Add enough oil to bacon fat in skillet to total 2 tablespoons. Add garlic, shallots, and sprouts; cook, stirring occasionally, until pale golden, about 3 minutes. Add stock; season with salt and pepper. Cook until most of the liquid has been absorbed and sprouts are tender, 10 to 12 minutes.

2 Meanwhile, bring a large pot of water to a boil; add 1 tablespoon salt and the pasta. Cook according to package directions until al dente. Drain, reserving ½ cup cooking liquid; return pasta to pot.

3 Stir in sprouts mixture, reserved ½ cup cooking liquid, and cheese. Drizzle with 2 tablespoons oil; add sage and bacon. Toss until combined. Serve with more cheese.

from What's for Dinner?

seared scallops
with cabbage and leeks

SERVES 4 | **PHOTO ON PAGE 303**

3 tablespoons olive oil

1 large leek, white and pale-green parts only, halved lengthwise, thinly sliced crosswise, and rinsed well

1 pound green cabbage (about ½ medium head), halved lengthwise, cored, and thinly sliced crosswise

⅓ cup homemade or low-sodium store-bought chicken stock

Coarse salt and freshly ground pepper

12 large sea scallops (about 1 pound), tough side muscles removed

Lemon slices, for garnish

1 Heat 4½ teaspoons oil in a large nonstick sauté pan over medium-high heat until hot but not smoking. Add leek; cook until soft, 1 to 2 minutes. Stir in cabbage, and add stock. Cook, stirring occasionally, until cabbage is slightly soft, about 5 minutes. Stir in ½ teaspoon salt, and season with pepper. Set aside.

2 Sprinkle scallops with ¼ teaspoon salt, and season with pepper. Heat remaining 4½ teaspoons oil in a large nonstick sauté pan over medium-high heat until hot but not smoking. Add scallops; cook, turning once, until dark golden, about 4 minutes per side.

3 Divide cabbage mixture among four plates, and top each serving with 3 scallops. Garnish with lemon.

PER SERVING: 238 CALORIES, 11 G FAT, 37 MG CHOLESTEROL, 14 G CARBOHYDRATE, 461 MG SODIUM, 20 G PROTEIN, 1 G FIBER

from Fit to Eat: Pros of Protein

shiitake mushroom
and cheese frittata

SERVES 6 | **PHOTO ON PAGE 302**

2 tablespoons olive oil

8 ounces shiitake mushrooms, stems discarded, caps cut into ¼-inch slices

1 small onion (about 6 ounces), halved and cut into ¼-inch-thick slices

1½ teaspoons fresh thyme

Coarse salt

10 large eggs

½ cup ricotta cheese

Freshly ground pepper

1 Preheat oven to 350°F. Heat oil in a 9- or 10-inch ovenproof nonstick skillet over medium heat until hot but not smoking. Add mushrooms, onion, and thyme; cook, stirring, until mushrooms and onion are golden brown, about 10 minutes. Stir in ½ teaspoon salt; remove skillet from heat.

2 Whisk eggs in a large bowl until frothy. Stir in the ricotta, 1 teaspoon salt, and ¼ teaspoon pepper. Place reserved skillet over medium heat. Immediately pour in egg mixture, and lightly stir to distribute mushrooms and onion evenly. Reduce heat to medium-low; cook 2 minutes, drawing cooked egg away from sides with a rubber spatula to let uncooked egg flow underneath. Cook until frittata is just starting to set, about 2 minutes more.

3 Transfer skillet to oven. Bake until frittata is just set and top is pale golden, 10 to 12 minutes. Serve frittata in skillet, or slide onto a serving platter.

PER SERVING: 230 CALORIES, 16 G FAT, 365 MG CHOLESTEROL, 9 G CARBOHYDRATE, 408 MG SODIUM, 14 G PROTEIN, 2 G FIBER

from Fit to Eat: Pros of Protein

turkey sausage with
peppers and onions

SERVES 4 | **PHOTO ON PAGE 303**

5 medium Cubanelle peppers (also called Italian frying peppers), seeded and cut into 1-inch-thick strips

2 large red onions, each cut into 6 wedges

2 garlic cloves, finely chopped

1½ teaspoons chopped fresh oregano

2 tablespoons olive oil

1 pound hot turkey sausages, cut on the diagonal into 2-inch pieces

Preheat oven to 400°F. Gently toss peppers, onions, garlic, oregano, oil, and sausages in a large bowl. Transfer to an 11-by-17-inch rimmed baking sheet. Bake, gently tossing about halfway through, until sausages are cooked through and vegetables are tender, 50 to 55 minutes.

PER SERVING: 346 CALORIES, 19 G FAT, 68 MG CHOLESTEROL, 24 G CARBOHYDRATE, 736 MG SODIUM, 22 G PROTEIN, 5 G FIBER

from Fit to Eat: Pros of Protein

Thai beef salad

SERVES 6 | **PHOTO ON PAGE 299**

- 6 tablespoons fresh lime juice (about 3 limes)
- 2½ tablespoons Thai fish sauce (nam pla)
- 1 fresh Thai or serrano chile, seeded and finely chopped (about 1 tablespoon)
- 1 teaspoon sugar
- 2 teaspoons finely chopped cilantro
- 2 teaspoons finely chopped fresh mint
- 4 scallions, white and pale-green parts only, thinly sliced on the diagonal
- 3 shallots, thinly sliced into rings
- 3 kirby cucumbers, peeled, halved lengthwise, and cut into ¼-inch-thick half-moons
- 12 ounces baby arugula (about 5 cups)
- 2 tablespoons olive oil
- 1 boneless sirloin steak (1½ pounds)
- ½ teaspoon coarse salt
- Freshly ground pepper
- ½ cup unsalted peanuts, coarsely chopped (about 2½ ounces)

1 Preheat oven to 400°F. Make dressing: Whisk together lime juice, fish sauce, chile, and sugar in a small bowl until sugar is dissolved. Stir in cilantro and mint. Set aside. Toss together scallions, shallots, cucumbers, and arugula in a large bowl; set aside.

2 Heat oil in a large ovenproof skillet over high heat until hot but not smoking. Sprinkle steak all over with salt; season with pepper. Brown steak, turning once, about 2 minutes per side. Transfer skillet to oven; cook steak to desired doneness, about 6 minutes for medium-rare.

3 Transfer steak to a cutting board, and let stand at least 5 minutes. Cut steak across the grain into ¼-inch-thick slices.

4 Add steak to salad. Drizzle with dressing, and toss. Sprinkle with peanuts.

PER SERVING: 382 CALORIES, 26 G FAT, 63 MG CHOLESTEROL, 12 G CARBOHYDRATE, 712 MG SODIUM, 26 G PROTEIN, 3 G FIBER

from Fit to Eat: Pros of Protein

DESSERTS

amaretto pound cake with flambéed pineapple

SERVES 12 | **PHOTO ON PAGE 312**

- 8 tablespoons (1 stick) unsalted butter, softened, plus more for loaf pan
- 1½ cups all-purpose flour, plus more for dusting
- ½ cup almond flour
- 1 teaspoon baking powder
- 1 teaspoon salt
- 1¼ cups sugar
- 3 large eggs
- 1 teaspoon pure vanilla extract
- ½ teaspoon pure almond extract
- ½ cup milk
- ½ cup amaretto (almond-flavored liqueur)
- Flambéed Pineapple (recipe follows)

1 Preheat oven to 325°F. Butter a 5-by-10-by-2½-inch loaf pan, and line with parchment paper. Butter lining; dust with all-purpose flour, tapping out excess.

2 Whisk together both flours, baking powder, and salt; set aside. Put butter and sugar in the bowl of an electric mixer fitted with the paddle attachment; cream on medium speed until smooth. Add eggs one at a time; mix until smooth. Mix in extracts. With mixer on low speed, add reserved flour mixture in three additions, alternating with two additions of milk; mix until smooth.

3 Pour batter into prepared pan. Bake until a cake tester inserted into center comes out clean, about 1 hour. Transfer cake in pan to a wire rack. Poke holes all over top of cake with a wooden skewer. Pour liqueur on top; let cool completely.

4 Invert cake to unmold; peel off parchment, and reinvert. Just before serving, cut cake into ¾-inch slices, and top with flambéed pineapple and sauce.

from Tipsy Cakes

flambéed pineapple

MAKES 4 CUPS

Never pour alcohol right from the bottle onto food on the stove—any splashes can ignite. On an electric stove, carefully use a long match to ignite the alcohol.

8 rounds (each ¼ inch thick) peeled pineapple (1 small pineapple or ½ large)

½ cup sugar

½ cup amaretto (almond-flavored liqueur)

½ cup heavy cream

2 tablespoons fresh lemon juice

1 vanilla bean, halved lengthwise, seeds scraped and reserved

  Pinch of salt

1 Cut each pineapple round into 4 wedges. Trim core from point of each wedge, and discard; set wedges aside.

2 Heat sugar in a large skillet over medium-high heat, stirring, until sugar melts and turns golden brown, 3 to 4 minutes. Add pineapple; toss to combine.

3 Stand back, and carefully pour in liqueur; immediately tilt skillet slightly, and ignite alcohol. When flames subside and caramel melts, stir in cream, lemon juice, vanilla seeds, and salt. Reduce heat to medium; let sauce boil, stirring occasionally, until thickened, about 5 minutes. Spoon pineapple and sauce over cake slices, and serve immediately.

blood-orange Pavlovas with Grand Marnier

MAKES 1 DOZEN | PHOTO ON PAGE 314

6 blood oranges, peel and pith removed

7 tablespoons Grand Marnier or other orange-flavored liqueur

4 large eggs, separated

1¼ cups sugar

⅛ teaspoon salt, plus a pinch

1 teaspoon distilled white vinegar

1 teaspoon pure vanilla extract

¼ cup orange juice

½ cup heavy cream

1 Preheat oven to 225°F. Cut oranges into segments. Toss with 3 tablespoons liqueur; refrigerate.

2 Make meringue: Put egg whites, 1 cup sugar, and salt in the heatproof bowl of an electric mixer. Set over a saucepan of simmering water; whisk constantly until sugar is melted and mixture is hot.

3 Fit mixer with whisk attachment; beat egg-white mixture on medium speed until soft peaks form. Raise mixer speed to high; beat mixture until cool, and stiff, glossy peaks form. Beat in vinegar and vanilla.

4 Using a rubber spatula, mound meringue into twelve 3-inch-wide rounds on parchment-paper–lined baking sheets. Swirl edges, and make a well in center of each meringue. Bake until crisp and just set in center, 40 to 50 minutes. Let cool on sheet on a wire rack. When meringues are cool enough to handle, peel off parchment. Let cool completely.

5 Make custard: Stir together yolks, juice, remaining ¼ cup each sugar and liqueur, and ⅛ teaspoon salt in a large heat-proof bowl set over a pan of simmering water; whisk until thickened and a spoon leaves a wake, about 4 minutes. Pass mixture through a fine sieve into a bowl; discard solids. Refrigerate until cold, about 1 hour.

6 Beat cream to soft peaks; fold into custard. Refrigerate until ready to serve, up to 4 hours (rewhisk before using).

7 Just before serving, mound custard in each meringue. Top custard mounds with orange segments and their juices.

from Tipsy Cakes

brandied-cherry cassata

SERVES 9 | PHOTO ON PAGE 314

3 cups fresh ricotta cheese

2 cups granulated sugar

1 tablespoon freshly grated orange zest

1 vanilla bean, halved lengthwise

1½ cups drained brandied cherries, plus ¼ cup liquid from jar

  Vegetable-oil cooking spray

1 cup all-purpose flour, plus more for dusting

½ cup milk

4 tablespoons unsalted butter

2 large eggs, room temperature

1 teaspoon pure vanilla extract

1 teaspoon baking powder

¼ teaspoon salt

  Confectioners' sugar, for dusting

1 Put ricotta, ½ cup granulated sugar, and orange zest in a food processor, and scrape in the vanilla seeds. Process until smooth. Transfer mixture to a bowl, and then stir in the drained cherries. Refrigerate.

2 Preheat oven to 350°F. Bring ½ cup water and ½ cup granulated sugar to a boil in a small saucepan, stirring until sugar

is dissolved. Let cool completely. Stir in cherry liquid. Refrigerate. Coat an 8-inch square baking pan with cooking spray. Line with parchment; coat lining with spray. Dust with flour, and tap out any excess.

3 Bring milk and butter to a boil in a small saucepan. Remove from heat. Put eggs in the bowl of an electric mixer fitted with the whisk attachment; beat on medium-high speed until pale and fluffy, about 6 minutes. Beat in remaining cup granulated sugar and the vanilla. On low speed, gradually add flour. Drizzle in hot-milk mixture. Beat in baking powder and salt (do not overmix).

4 Pour into prepared pan. Bake until a cake tester inserted into center comes out clean, about 20 minutes. Let cool on a wire rack 30 minutes. Unmold; remove parchment. Let cool completely.

5 Split cake horizontally into thirds. Brush a cut side of each layer with syrup. Spread half of filling on bottom layer. Top with middle layer, and spread with remaining filling. Top with third layer. Refrigerate until firm, about 2 hours. Dust with confectioners' sugar. Cut into 9 squares.

from Tipsy Cakes

chocolate-almond Marsala cookies

MAKES ABOUT 2 DOZEN

½ cup whole raw almonds with skins
1¼ cups all-purpose flour, plus more for dusting
2 teaspoons baking powder
1¼ teaspoons ground cinnamon
¾ teaspoon coarse salt
2 large eggs
⅓ cup Marsala wine
½ cup finely chopped candied orange peel
4 ounces semisweet chocolate, chopped
3 tablespoons honey

1 Preheat oven to 350°F. Toast whole almonds in oven on a rimmed baking sheet until fragrant and lightly toasted, about 12 minutes. Let cool, and coarsely chop. Reduce the oven temperature to 250°F.

2 Stir together flour, baking powder, cinnamon, and salt. Beat 1 egg with the Marsala wine, and stir into flour mixture. Stir together almonds, orange peel, and chocolate, and stir into flour mixture. Stir in honey.

3 Knead dough on a generously floured work surface just until it holds its shape. Divide dough into 2 pieces; pat each into a 10½-by-1½-by-1-inch rounded log. Refrigerate dough 15 minutes.

4 Cut each log into ¾-inch-thick slices. Gently press down on each slice to flatten bottom. Lightly beat remaining egg. Place cookies, standing vertically, on a parchment-paper–lined baking sheet. Brush tops with beaten egg.

5 Bake 20 minutes. Raise oven temperature to 350°F; bake until cookies are deep golden brown, 10 to 12 minutes. Let cool on sheet on a wire rack.

from Thanksgiving With Italian Flavors

chocolate truffle cakes

MAKES 6 INDIVIDUAL CAKES

For extra fudgy results, make these cakes a day ahead; wrap them well in plastic wrap, and refrigerate. Serve them chilled or at room temperature.

5 tablespoons unsalted butter, plus more for muffin tin
1 tablespoon all-purpose flour, plus more for dusting
14 ounces semisweet chocolate, chopped
2 tablespoons sugar
2 large eggs
¼ teaspoon salt

1 Preheat oven to 375°F. Generously butter a standard 6-cup muffin tin. Dust with flour, tapping out excess; set aside.

2 Put chocolate, butter, and 1 tablespoon sugar in a medium heatproof bowl set over a pan of simmering water; whisk occasionally until smooth. Remove from heat, and let stand until cool and thickened, 3 to 5 minutes. Process eggs and remaining tablespoon sugar in a food processor until pale and doubled in volume, about 2 minutes. Sift flour and salt into egg mixture; pulse to combine. Add the chocolate mixture ¼ cup at a time; pulse each addition until combined, about 10 times. (Batter will be thick.)

3 Spoon mixture into the prepared muffin tin, filling cups three-quarters full; swirl tops with back of spoon. Bake until tops are springy to the touch, 18 to 20 minutes. Immediately turn out onto wire racks; reinvert, and let cool.

from What's for Dinner?

chocolate-espresso Kahlúa tart

SERVES 8 TO 10 | PHOTO ON PAGE 315

FOR THE CRUST:

2 cups hazelnuts (9 ounces)

1⅓ cups finely ground chocolate wafer cookies (about 22)

½ teaspoon instant espresso powder

¼ teaspoon salt

10 tablespoons (1¼ sticks) unsalted butter, melted and cooled slightly

FOR THE MOUSSE:

½ cup Kahlúa (coffee-flavored liqueur)

½ cup unsweetened cocoa powder

2 large eggs, separated

1 teaspoon instant espresso powder

Pinch of salt

4 ounces bittersweet chocolate, chopped

4 tablespoons unsalted butter

1 cup heavy cream

6 tablespoons sugar

1 Make crust: Preheat oven to 375°F. Toast hazelnuts in oven on a rimmed baking sheet until skins split and flesh turns deep golden brown, 10 to 12 minutes. When cool enough to handle, rub nuts in a clean kitchen towel to remove skins (some will remain). Let cool completely. Finely grind in a food processor. Reduce oven temperature to 325°F.

2 Stir together nuts, cookie crumbs, espresso powder, salt, and butter. Press onto bottom and up side of an 11-inch round tart pan with a removable bottom. Refrigerate until firm, about 30 minutes.

3 Bake tart shell on a baking sheet until firm to the touch, about 20 minutes. Let cool completely on a wire rack.

4 Make mousse: Whisk liqueur, cocoa, egg yolks, espresso powder, and salt in a medium bowl until smooth. Melt chocolate and butter in a heatproof bowl set over a pan of simmering water. Whisk in liqueur mixture. Cook, whisking, until mixture is thickened and registers 160°F on an instant-read thermometer. Let cool completely.

5 Beat cream just to stiff peaks; set aside. Whisk egg whites and sugar in the heatproof bowl of an electric mixer set over a pan of simmering water. Cook, whisking, until sugar is dissolved and mixture registers 140°F on thermometer.

6 Fit mixer with the whisk attachment; transfer bowl with meringue to mixer. Starting on medium speed and gradually increasing to high, beat meringue until shiny and cool. Using a rubber spatula, fold chocolate mixture and then whipped cream into meringue. Spread in tart shell. Refrigerate the tart until set, about 1 hour.

from Tipsy Cakes

chocolate-ginger cookies

MAKES 4 DOZEN

2½ cups all-purpose flour, plus more for dusting

½ cup Dutch-process cocoa powder

½ teaspoon ground ginger

1 teaspoon ground cinnamon

½ teaspoon ground nutmeg

¼ teaspoon ground cloves

½ teaspoon salt

½ teaspoon baking powder

½ teaspoon baking soda

12 tablespoons (1½ sticks) unsalted butter, softened

¾ cup packed dark-brown sugar

1 large egg

½ cup dark unsulfured molasses

1 tablespoon grated peeled fresh ginger

Sanding sugar, for sprinkling

1 Preheat oven to 325°F. Line two baking sheets with parchment paper; set aside. Whisk together flour, cocoa, spices, salt, baking powder, and baking soda.

2 Cream butter and brown sugar on medium speed in the bowl of an electric mixer fitted with the paddle attachment until pale and fluffy, about 4 minutes. Add egg, molasses, and grated ginger; mix until combined. Add flour mixture; mix on low speed until just combined.

3 Halve dough; flatten into two disks. Wrap in plastic wrap; refrigerate 1 hour. Transfer disks, one at a time, to a lightly floured surface; roll out to ¼ inch thick. (If dough gets soft, freeze until firm.) Use 3-inch acorn-shaped or leaf-shaped cookie cutters to make shapes; place 1 inch apart on sheets. Refrigerate until firm, about 20 minutes.

4 Score designs with a knife; sprinkle with sanding sugar. Bake, rotating sheets halfway through, until cookies are firm, 11 to 13 minutes. Let cool on a wire rack.

from Cookie of the Month

coconut rum-raisin Bundt cake with rum-caramel glaze

SERVES 12 TO 14 | **PHOTO ON FRONT COVER**

10 ounces (2½ sticks) unsalted butter, softened, plus more for pan

3 cups all-purpose flour, plus more for dusting

1 cup raisins

¾ cup dark rum

1 teaspoon salt

½ teaspoon baking powder

2¾ cups plus 2 tablespoons packed light-brown sugar

6 large eggs

2 teaspoons pure vanilla extract

¾ cup plus 2 tablespoons heavy cream

1 cup sweetened flaked coconut

1 cup granulated sugar

1 Preheat oven to 325°F. Butter a 12-cup Bundt pan; dust with flour, tapping out excess. Soak raisins in ½ cup rum.

2 Whisk together flour, salt, and baking powder; set aside. Put butter and brown sugar in the bowl of an electric mixer fitted with the paddle attachment; cream on medium speed until smooth. Mix in eggs, one at a time. Add vanilla. On low speed, add flour mixture in three additions, alternating with two additions of 6 tablespoons cream each (12 tablespoons total). Blend in raisin mixture and coconut. Transfer batter to prepared pan; smooth top.

3 Bake, rotating about halfway through, until a cake tester inserted near center comes out clean, about 1 hour 55 minutes. Let cool in pan on a wire rack 20 minutes. Run a thin knife around sides of cake; unmold. Let cool.

4 Heat granulated sugar and ¼ cup water in a small saucepan over medium heat, gently stirring occasionally, until sugar is dissolved and syrup is clear. Cook, without stirring, until syrup comes to a boil, washing down sides of pan with a wet pastry brush to prevent crystals from forming. Let boil, gently swirling, until medium amber. Remove from heat. Carefully pour in remaining ¼ cup rum and 2 tablespoons cream. Let cool, stirring, until thickened. Drizzle over cake.

from Tipsy Cakes

coffee crème brûlée

MAKES 5

Wide and shallow nine-ounce molds are perfect for crème brûlée because they provide ample surface area, ensuring a bit of crunchy topping in every bite (you'll need five of them for this recipe). Ten half-cup ramekins can be used instead; reduce the sugar topping for each custard to one and a half teaspoons, and add ten minutes to the baking time.

1 quart heavy cream

1½ cups dark Italian-roast coffee beans

10 large egg yolks

⅔ cup granulated sugar

¼ teaspoon salt

Boiling water, for roasting pan

5 tablespoons superfine sugar

1 Preheat oven to 320°F. Bring cream and coffee beans to a boil in a medium saucepan. Cover, and reduce heat to low; cook at a bare simmer 30 minutes. Pour mixture through a fine sieve into a medium bowl (or use a slotted spoon to remove beans); discard beans.

2 Put yolks, granulated sugar, and salt in a large bowl; whisk until sugar is dissolved and mixture is pale and thick. Gradually add cream in a slow, steady stream, whisking until combined. Pour through a cheesecloth-lined sieve into a large glass measuring cup; skim any foam from surface.

3 Divide custard among molds, filling them almost to the top. Place molds in a roasting pan; put pan on oven rack, and pour boiling water around molds to reach halfway up sides. Bake until custards are set around the edges but still loose in centers, about 30 minutes.

4 Let molds cool in pan 10 minutes; remove from water bath. Cover each with plastic wrap, pressing directly onto surface; refrigerate at least 2 hours or up to 2 days.

5 If using a handheld kitchen torch to caramelize custards, use a fine sieve to sift 1 tablespoon superfine sugar over each just before serving; wipe sugar from edges. Hold torch at a 90-degree angle, 3 to 4 inches from the surface of the custards, and use a steady sweeping motion to caramelize the top of each until golden brown. If you don't have a torch, freeze custards 20 minutes before topping with sugar. Preheat broiler, and place molds on a rimmed baking sheet; surround with ice cubes. Broil, rotating sheet once, until tops are golden brown, 2 to 3 minutes. If molds become warm, refrigerate custards for a few minutes before serving.

from Dessert of the Month

cranberry tart with crème fraîche whipped cream

MAKES ONE 9-INCH TART; SERVES 6 TO 8

4 cups fresh cranberries (about 1 pound)

1½ cups sugar

1 whole cinnamon stick

1 disk Sweet Pastry Dough (recipe follows)

All-purpose flour, for dusting

1 large egg white, lightly beaten

1 cup heavy cream

½ cup crème fraîche

1 Bring ½ cup water, the berries, sugar, and cinnamon to a simmer in a medium saucepan over medium-high heat. Cook, stirring, until berries pop, about 2 minutes. Drain in a sieve set over a bowl. Return strained liquid and cinnamon stick to pan; reserve berries in bowl. Simmer liquid over medium-low heat until thickened, about 15 minutes. Pour over cranberries; let cool. Discard cinnamon.

2 Bring pâte sucrée to room temperature. On a lightly floured surface, roll out dough to ⅛ inch thick. Transfer to a 9-inch square or round tart pan with a removable bottom. Trim edges, leaving a ½-inch overhang. Tuck edges of dough under to create a double thickness, and press firmly against sides of pan. Press bottom of dough firmly into tart pan. Chill in freezer 20 minutes.

3 Preheat oven to 400°F. Line tart shell with parchment or foil, and fill with pie weights or dried beans. Bake until golden brown, about 25 minutes. Transfer to a wire rack. Remove pie weights and parchment. Let cool completely.

4 Reduce oven temperature to 350°F. Brush tart shell with egg white. Fill with cranberry mixture and syrup from bowl. Bake until syrup is slightly runny and berries begin to brown, 45 to 60 minutes (if pastry edges brown too quickly, cover with a band of foil).

5 Meanwhile, beat cream to soft peaks. Beat in crème fraîche; refrigerate.

6 Let tart cool on rack until cool enough to remove from pan. Serve warm, with crème fraîche whipped cream.

from Thanksgiving With Italian Flavors

sweet pastry dough

MAKES 2 DISKS

Our recipe yields enough for two cranberry tarts (you'll need to double the cranberry filling and the whipped cream).

2½ cups all-purpose flour, plus more for dusting

3 tablespoons sugar

8 ounces (2 sticks) cold unsalted butter, cut into small pieces

2 large egg yolks

¼ cup ice water

1 Process the flour and sugar in a food processor just until combined. Add the butter, and process until mixture resembles coarse meal, about 10 seconds.

2 Lightly beat yolks and ice water. With processor running, add yolk mixture in a slow, steady stream; process just until dough holds together (do not process more than 30 seconds).

3 Turn out dough onto a lightly floured work surface. Divide into 2 pieces; place each on a sheet of plastic wrap. Flatten, and shape into disks. Wrap; refrigerate at least 1 hour or overnight, or freeze up to 1 month.

mini carrot-cardamom pies

MAKES EIGHT 4-INCH PIES | PHOTO ON PAGE 316

6 whole green cardamom pods

2 tablespoons unsalted butter

½ cup milk

½ cup heavy cream

1 teaspoon finely grated peeled fresh ginger

12 ounces carrots, peeled and cut into ¼-inch pieces (2½ to 3 cups)

1 cup sugar

⅛ teaspoon coarse salt

4 large eggs, lightly beaten

½ cup finely ground gingersnap cookies

1 disk Pastry Dough (recipe follows; reserve remaining disk for another use)

Freshly whipped cream, for serving

Ground cardamom, for dusting

1 Make filling: Crush cardamom pods with the flat side of a chef's knife just to split. Melt 1 tablespoon butter in a small saucepan over medium heat; add crushed cardamom. Cook until fragrant, about 3 minutes. Add milk, cream, and ginger; bring to a simmer. Reduce heat to medium-low; cook 15 minutes. Remove from heat; let steep 30 minutes.

2 Melt remaining tablespoon butter in a large sauté pan over medium heat. Add carrots; cook, stirring occasionally, 2 minutes. Stir in sugar and salt. Cover pan; cook until carrots are tender, about 8 minutes. Pour steeped milk through a sieve into pan with carrots; discard solids. Remove from heat; let cool slightly, about 5 minutes. Process carrot mixture in a food processor until completely smooth; transfer to a bowl.

3 Temper beaten eggs by whisking in up to ¾ cup carrot mixture, ¼ cup at a time, until eggs are warm to the touch. Pour warmed egg mixture into remaining carrot mixture; whisk until thoroughly combined. Let cool.

4 Make pies: Preheat oven to 375°F. Lightly sprinkle ground gingersnaps on a work surface to form a large circle about 18 inches in diameter. On crumbs, roll out pâte brisée to ⅛ inch thick, turning occasionally to coat both sides.

5 Cut out eight 5-inch rounds from dough. Press rounds into eight 4-inch pie plates; trim excess. With a fork, crimp edges, and then prick bottom of dough all over. Refrigerate pie shells 30 minutes.

6 Line each pie shell with parchment paper or foil, and fill with pie weights or dried beans. Bake until golden brown, about 30 minutes. Transfer to a wire rack. Remove pie weights and parchment. Let shells cool completely.

7 Divide filling among shells. Bake until a cake tester comes out clean, 30 to 35 minutes. Serve pies warm with whipped cream dusted with ground cardamom.

from Earthy Delights

pastry dough

MAKES 2 DISKS

2½ cups all-purpose flour
1 teaspoon coarse salt
1 teaspoon sugar
8 ounces (2 sticks) cold unsalted butter, cut into small pieces
¼ to ½ cup ice water

1 Pulse flour, salt, and sugar in a food processor until just combined. Add butter; process until mixture resembles coarse meal, about 10 seconds. Add ¼ cup ice water, and pulse just until dough holds together (no more than 30 seconds). If dough is dry, pulse in more water, ½ tablespoon at a time, and then test again.

2 Halve dough, and wrap each in plastic. Flatten; shape into disks. Refrigerate dough at least 1 hour or up to 2 days, or freeze up to 1 month.

pear-fig-walnut pie

MAKES ONE 9-INCH PIE; SERVES 8 TO 10

¾ cup Madeira wine
5 ounces soft, dried Black Mission figs (scant ⅔ cup), stemmed and quartered
3 whole star anise
   Perfect Piecrust dough (page 270), almost room temperature
   All-purpose flour, for dusting
3 pounds ripe Anjou pears, peeled, cored, and cut into ¼-inch-thick wedges
3 ounces walnuts, broken into small pieces (about ¾ cup), toasted and cooled
   Juice of 1 lemon
½ cup granulated sugar, plus more for sprinkling (or use sanding sugar)
¼ teaspoon salt
3 tablespoons cornstarch
2 tablespoons cold unsalted butter, cut into small pieces
1 large egg yolk
1 tablespoon heavy cream

1 Preheat oven to 400°F, with rack in lower third. Bring wine, figs, and star anise to a boil in a small saucepan over high heat. Reduce heat to medium-low; simmer until figs are softened, 10 to 12 minutes. Use a slotted spoon to transfer figs to a bowl. Cook liquid over medium-high heat until reduced to a syrup, 3 minutes; discard star anise. Pour syrup over figs.

2 Roll out 1 disk dough on floured parchment paper to make a 13-inch circle; start with pressure in center and ease up just before reaching edges. Drape dough over rolling pin; center over a 9-inch glass pie plate, and unroll. Gently push into the plate. Trim to leave a ¼-inch overhang; refrigerate. Roll out second disk. Cut out a vent with a cookie cutter; chill cutout.

3 Add pears, nuts, lemon juice, sugar, salt, and cornstarch to figs; stir until well combined. Spoon into pie plate (pile high in center). Dot with butter; lightly brush rim of dough with water. Drape second disk over pin; center over filling. Gently press around filling to fit; trim to leave a ½-inch overhang. Fold edge of top crust under bottom one; crimp to seal. Brush water on bottom of cutout; press onto top crust. Beat yolk with cream; brush over crust. Sprinkle with sugar; freeze until very firm, about 30 minutes.

4 Bake on a baking sheet until just golden, 20 to 25 minutes. Reduce heat to 375°F. Bake, rotating halfway through, until bubbling and bottom crust is deep golden brown, 1 hour. (If edges brown too quickly, cover with a foil band.) Let cool.

from How It's Done: Perfect Piecrust Every Time

perfect piecrust dough

MAKES TWO 9-INCH CRUSTS

2¾ cups all-purpose flour

2 teaspoons sugar

1¼ teaspoons salt

9 ounces (2¼ sticks) cold unsalted butter, cut into small pieces

7 tablespoons ice water, plus more if needed

1 Pulse flour, sugar, and salt in a food processor until combined. Add butter; process until mixture has pieces ranging in size from crumbs to ½ inch, about 12 seconds. Add ice water; process until just incorporated but dough is not wet or sticky, no more than 20 seconds. Squeeze a small amount of dough: It should just hold together. If it doesn't, continue to pulse in more ice water, ½ tablespoon at a time, and then test again.

2 Halve dough; wrap each in plastic. Roll to ½ inch thick. Refrigerate 1 hour or up to 2 days, or freeze up to 3 weeks.

pumpkin and ricotta crostata

MAKES ONE 10-INCH CROSTATA; SERVES 6 TO 8

1 disk Pasta Frolla (recipe follows)

All-purpose flour, for dusting

Unsalted butter, softened, for pie plate

1 cup ricotta cheese, drained 30 minutes in a cheesecloth-lined sieve set over a bowl

½ cup mascarpone cheese

1 can (15 ounces) solid-pack pumpkin

5 tablespoons sugar

¼ teaspoon coarse salt

Heaping ¼ teaspoon freshly ground nutmeg

½ teaspoon pure vanilla extract

2 large egg yolks, lightly beaten

2 tablespoons pine nuts

1 large egg white, lightly beaten

1 Preheat oven to 350°F. Bring pasta frolla to room temperature. On a lightly floured surface, roll out dough to ¼ inch thick. Transfer to a lightly buttered 10-inch pie plate. Use your fingertips to press dough against bottom and sides of dish until even. Trim edges; refrigerate scraps in plastic wrap until step 4.

2 Prick bottom of pastry shell all over with a fork. Bake until set and pale golden brown, about 15 minutes. Let cool completely on a wire rack. With a small knife, trim edge of shell where uneven to leave a ¼-inch space between shell and top of dish.

3 Raise oven temperature to 375°F. Process ricotta in a food processor until smooth. Add the mascarpone, pumpkin, sugar, salt, nutmeg, and vanilla; process until well combined, about 30 seconds. Add yolks; process until combined, about 10 seconds. Pour into pastry shell.

4 Tear reserved chilled dough scraps into 1-inch pieces. On a lightly floured surface, gently roll pieces with your hands to make ¼-inch-thick ropes. Gently press one long rope along top edge of shell (patch two ropes together, if necessary). Gently place other pastry ropes on top of filling to create a lattice pattern (ropes of all lengths can be used). Place 3 pine nuts in each square of lattice. Brush latticework with egg white.

5 Bake until crust is golden brown and filling is set, about 40 minutes. Let cool on rack.

from Thanksgiving With Italian Flavors

pasta frolla

MAKES ENOUGH FOR 2 CROSTATAS

Pasta frolla (Italian for "short pastry") is the basic pastry dough of Italy. Our recipe yields enough dough for two desserts (you'll need to double the pumpkin-and-ricotta filling).

2¼ cups all-purpose flour, plus more for dusting

½ cup sugar

⅛ teaspoon salt

14 tablespoons (1¾ sticks) cold unsalted butter, cut into small pieces

1 large egg, lightly beaten

1 large egg yolk, lightly beaten

1 teaspoon pure vanilla extract

1 tablespoon freshly grated lemon zest

1 Pulse flour, sugar, and salt in a food processor until just combined. Add butter; pulse until mixture resembles coarse meal, 6 to 8 times.

2 Whisk together egg, egg yolk, vanilla, and lemon zest. With processor running, add egg mixture; process just until dough begins to come together. Turn out onto a floured work surface; lightly knead to form a ball.

3 Halve dough, and gently press each piece into a flat disk. Wrap tightly in plastic wrap. Refrigerate at least 1 hour or overnight, or freeze up to 1 month.

poire William charlottes

MAKES 6 | PHOTO ON PAGE 313

FOR THE CAKE:

8 tablespoons (1 stick) unsalted butter, softened, plus more for baking pan

1¼ cups plus 2 tablespoons all-purpose flour, plus more for dusting

1 teaspoon baking powder

½ teaspoon salt

1¼ cups sugar

3 large eggs

⅓ cup milk

¾ cup poire William (pear brandy)

1 cup peeled, diced pear

½ cup finely chopped toasted pistachios

FOR THE FILLING:

1 medium pear, peeled and chopped

2 tablespoons poire William (pear brandy)

¾ cup plus 2 tablespoons milk

4 large egg yolks

½ cup sugar

Pinch of salt

1 cup heavy cream

3¼ teaspoons unflavored gelatin

1 Make cake: Preheat oven to 325°F. Butter a 9-by-12-inch baking pan. Line bottom with parchment paper. Butter lining; then flour pan, tapping out excess. Whisk together flour, baking powder, and salt.

2 Put butter and sugar in the bowl of an electric mixer fitted with the paddle attachment; cream on medium speed until pale and fluffy. Mix in eggs, one at a time. Add flour mixture in three additions, alternating with two additions of milk. On low speed, mix in ¼ cup pear brandy and the pear and nuts.

3 Pour batter into prepared pan; spread evenly. Bake until golden brown and springy to the touch, about 40 minutes. Let cool completely on a wire rack.

4 Invert cake to unmold; peel off parchment. Using a long serrated knife, trim off sides of cake. Cut cake crosswise into quarters (each about 2½ inches wide). Split quarters horizontally into 3 strips each (to make 12 strips total).

5 Cut 10 strips crosswise into 6 (1½-by-2½-inch) rectangles. Using a 2-inch round cookie cutter, cut out 6 rounds from remaining 2 strips.

6 Line 6 charlotte molds (4 inches in diameter and 2¼ inches high) or 10-ounce ramekins with overlapping strips, standing them vertically (about 10 strips per mold). Press 1 cake round onto the bottom of each mold. Using remaining ½ cup pear brandy, brush cake in molds.

7 Make filling: Purée chopped pear and pear brandy in a food processor; set aside. Prepare an ice-water bath, and set aside. Heat milk in a medium saucepan over medium heat until just about to simmer.

8 Whisk together yolks, sugar, and salt. Pour half of hot milk into yolk mixture, whisking constantly. Add yolk mixture to the remaining hot milk in pan; whisk. Cook over medium heat, stirring with a wooden spoon, until mixture is thick enough to coat back of spoon. Pour through a fine sieve into a bowl set in ice-water bath. Let cool, stirring occasionally.

9 Beat cream to soft peaks; set aside. Sprinkle gelatin over ¼ cup water in a medium heatproof bowl. Let stand 1 minute to soften. Set bowl over a pan of simmering water; stir until gelatin is dissolved. Stir gelatin mixture into custard in ice-water bath. Stir in pear purée.

10 Whisk mixture in bowl in bath until it thickens to a puddinglike consistency. Whisk in whipped cream. Divide mixture among molds (about ½ cup per mold). Cover with plastic wrap directly on surface; refrigerate until set, about 1 hour. Run a thin knife around edges of charlottes; invert onto plates. Serve cold.

from Tipsy Cakes

sherry trifle with brandy custard

SERVES 10 TO 12 | **PHOTO ON PAGE 313**

This recipe was inspired by a Victorian recipe from *Martha Stewart Living* art director James Dunlinson's Great-Granny Crosthwaite.

9 large egg yolks
¾ cup sugar
4 tablespoons plus 2 teaspoons all-purpose flour
⅛ teaspoon salt
3 cups milk, warmed
1 teaspoon pure vanilla extract
3 tablespoons brandy
1 cup heavy cream
14 ladyfingers, halved lengthwise
¾ cups raspberry jam (9 ounces)
1 cup cream sherry
1 cup sliced almonds, toasted
16 amaretti (Italian almond cookies), broken (about 1¼ cups)

1 Put yolks and sugar in the bowl of an electric mixer fitted with the whisk attachment; beat on medium-high speed until mixture is pale and thick, 2 to 3 minutes. On low speed, beat in flour and salt. Gradually beat in half of warm milk.

2 Pour milk-yolk mixture into remaining milk in pan. Bring to a boil over medium heat, whisking. Cook, stirring, until thickened, about 2 minutes. Pour through a fine sieve into a bowl.

3 Transfer to an ice-water bath; let cool, stirring occasionally. Stir in vanilla and brandy. Place plastic wrap on surface. Refrigerate until ready to use, up to 3 days.

4 Beat cream just until stiff peaks form. Fold into pastry cream. Place 7 ladyfinger halves at bottom of a 12-cup trifle dish or glass bowl; spread with one quarter of jam. Pour in one quarter of sherry. Spoon one quarter pastry cream on top. Sprinkle with one-third each almonds and amaretti. Repeat layering 3 more times (last layer does not need almonds and amaretti). Refrigerate 3 hours or overnight.

from Tipsy Cakes

MISCELLANEOUS

parsnip chips

SERVES 6

1 pound parsnips, peeled
1½ to 2 quarts vegetable oil
Coarse salt

1 Using a vegetable peeler (preferably a swivel peeler), peel each parsnip into long, thin strips until you reach core; discard core. Toss strips by hand to separate.

2 Heat 4 to 5 inches oil in a Dutch oven until oil registers 365°F on a deep-fry thermometer. Add a handful of parsnip strips to oil; cook, stirring with a wire or mesh skimmer, until pale golden and crisp, about 30 seconds. Immediately transfer to a paper-towel–lined baking sheet to drain. Season with salt.

3 Repeat with remaining strips (adjust heat between batches to keep oil at 365°F), transferring cooked chips to a dry section of lined sheet, and seasoning with salt. Serve warm.

from Earthy Delights

white-wine gravy

MAKES ABOUT 1 CUP

¾ cup dry white wine
3 tablespoons all-purpose flour
1¼ cups homemade or low-sodium store-bought turkey or chicken stock
1 teaspoon fresh lemon juice, or to taste
Coarse salt and freshly ground pepper

1 Reserve 3 tablespoons fat from roasting pan used for turkey (page 261); pour off rest of fat. Discard burnt bits on bottom of pan (but reserve brown bits). Place pan on stove across two burners over medium-high heat. Add wine to pan; bring to a boil, scraping up brown bits with a wooden spoon. Pour contents of pan into a measuring cup.

2 Heat reserved 3 tablespoons pan fat in a medium saucepan over medium heat. Add flour, whisking into a paste. Cook, whisking occasionally, 5 minutes.

3 Add reserved deglazing liquid in a slow, steady stream, whisking to combine. Whisk in stock; bring to a boil. Reduce heat; simmer gravy, stirring occasionally, until thickened, about 20 minutes. Stir in lemon juice, and season with salt and pepper. Pour through a sieve into a warmed gravy boat.

from Thanksgiving With Italian Flavors

December

cottage cheese pancakes with lemon

MAKES 2 DOZEN; SERVES 6

6 large eggs, separated and yolks lightly beaten

Pinch cream of tartar

2 cups low-fat (2%) cottage cheese

¼ cup granulated sugar

⅔ cup all-purpose flour

½ teaspoon baking powder

¼ teaspoon coarse salt

¼ teaspoon ground cinnamon

Vegetable-oil cooking spray

Confectioners' sugar, for dusting

2 lemons (1 cut into wedges; 1 zested), for serving

1 Put egg whites in the bowl of an electric mixer fitted with the whisk attachment; beat on medium-high speed until foamy. Add cream of tartar; beat until stiff, glossy peaks form.

2 Heat a griddle or large skillet over medium-high heat until hot. Meanwhile, stir together yolks, cottage cheese, granulated sugar, flour, baking powder, salt, and cinnamon in a bowl. Whisk in one-third of the egg whites. In two batches, gently fold in remaining egg whites with a rubber spatula.

3 Spray griddle with cooking spray; heat until a drop of batter sizzles upon contact. Working in batches, pour ¼ cup batter per pancake onto griddle; cook until surfaces bubble and edges are slightly dry, about 1 minute. Flip pancakes; cook until undersides are golden brown, about 3 minutes more. Dust with confectioners' sugar; serve sprinkled with lemon zest and with lemon wedges on the side.

PER SERVING: 213 CALORIES, 6 G FAT, 216 MG CHOLESTEROL, 22 G CARBOHYDRATE, 152 MG SODIUM, 17 G PROTEIN, 1 G FIBER

from Fit to Eat: Light Breakfasts

hard-boiled egg whites with avocado

SERVES 4

8 large eggs

2 avocados (preferably Hass), halved and pitted

¼ teaspoon coarse salt

Freshly ground pepper

1 tablespoon extra-virgin olive oil

1 Cover eggs with cold water in a large saucepan; bring to a boil. Remove pan from heat; cover. Let eggs stand 8 minutes.

Transfer eggs to an ice-water bath; let cool. Peel eggs. Separate yolks from whites (reserve yolks for another use). Tear whites into 1-inch pieces; divide among four bowls.

2 Using a spoon, scrape avocado to create curls; divide among bowls with egg whites. Divide salt among servings; season with pepper. Drizzle each serving with ¾ teaspoon oil.

PER SERVING: 227 CALORIES, 19 G FAT, 0 CHOLESTEROL, 8 G CARBOHYDRATE, 190 MG SODIUM, 9 G PROTEIN, 5 G FIBER

from Fit to Eat: Light Breakfasts

poached eggs with spinach and pan-roasted tomatoes

SERVES 4

4 large eggs

1 tablespoon olive oil

16 grape tomatoes, halved crosswise

1 teaspoon coarse salt

Freshly ground pepper

8 ounces baby or regular spinach, tough stems discarded

1 garlic clove

2 tablespoons distilled white vinegar

1 tablespoon finely chopped fresh chives

1 Fill a large, shallow, straight-sided pan with 2 inches water. Bring to a boil. Break each egg into a small ramekin.

2 Meanwhile, heat oil in a medium nonstick skillet over medium heat until hot but not smoking. Add tomatoes; cook, stirring occasionally, until starting to break down, about 5 minutes. Add salt; season with pepper. Transfer to a plate; loosely tent with foil. Add spinach and garlic to skillet; cook, stirring occasionally, until spinach is just wilted, 1 to 2 minutes. Discard garlic.

3 When water is boiling, add vinegar; turn off heat. Lower ramekins into pan, and let eggs slide out into water. Cover pan; let eggs stand until whites are opaque and yolks are cooked to desired consistency, 2 to 3 minutes. Transfer eggs with a slotted spoon to paper towels to drain. When cool enough to handle, trim egg whites around edges.

4 Divide spinach among four plates, and lay one poached egg and 8 tomato halves on top. Season with pepper, and sprinkle each serving with ¾ teaspoon chives.

Note: The eggs in this dish are not fully cooked, so it should not be prepared for pregnant women, babies, young children, the elderly, or anyone whose health is compromised.

PER SERVING: 209 CALORIES, 14 G FAT, 425 G CHOLESTEROL, 7 G CARBOHYDRATE, 457 MG SODIUM, 15 G PROTEIN, 2 G FIBER

from Fit to Eat: Light Breakfasts

rye toasts with smoked salmon, cucumber, and red onion

SERVES 4

8 thin slices rye bread

5 tablespoons plus 1 teaspoon low-fat cream cheese

8 thin slices smoked salmon (4 ounces)

½ English (hothouse) cucumber, peeled and thinly sliced diagonally

½ medium red onion, very thinly sliced

1 teaspoon drained capers, rinsed and patted dry

Freshly ground pepper

1 lemon, cut into wedges

1 Preheat oven to 325°F. Toast rye-bread slices in oven on a baking sheet, turning once, until golden, about 10 minutes.

2 Spread 2 teaspoons cream cheese on each toast. Lay 1 salmon slice and 1 cucumber slice on top. Top with onions and capers; season with pepper. Squeeze lemon juice on top.

PER SERVING: 275 CALORIES, 8 G FAT, 17 MG CHOLESTEROL, 39 G CARBOHYDRATE, 873 MG SODIUM, 13 G PROTEIN, 5 G FIBER

from Fit to Eat: Light Breakfasts

carrot and dried-currant muffins

MAKES 6

Unsalted butter, softened, for muffin tin

¾ cup dried currants

1½ cups plus 4½ teaspoons all-purpose flour

1½ teaspoons baking powder

½ teaspoon baking soda

½ teaspoon salt

1 teaspoon ground cardamom

1 teaspoon ground ginger

3 large eggs

½ cup canola or vegetable oil, plus more for wire rack

1 cup sugar

3½ cups finely grated carrots (about 6 carrots)

1 Preheat oven to 350°F. Butter six cups of a large muffin tin (each cup should have a 1-cup capacity). Simmer currants and 1 cup water in a small saucepan over low heat until currants are plump, about 20 minutes. Drain, and let currants cool completely. Set aside.

2 Whisk together flour, baking powder, baking soda, salt, cardamom, and ginger in a medium bowl; set aside.

3 Put eggs, oil, and sugar in the bowl of an electric mixer fitted with the paddle attachment. Mix on medium speed until combined, about 2 minutes. Reduce speed to low. Add flour mixture in three batches; mix until just combined after each addition. Fold in carrots and currants with a rubber spatula.

4 Pour batter into muffin tin, leaving a ½-inch space above batter in each cup. Bake until tops are golden and a cake tester inserted into centers comes out clean, about 30 minutes. Let muffins cool in tin on a wire rack 10 minutes.

5 Remove tin from rack, and lightly oil rack. Run a thin knife around the sides of muffins to loosen, and unmold onto rack. Let cool completely.

from Quick Breads, Easy Presents

chocolate marble bread with ganache

MAKES ONE 8½-INCH LOAF

8 ounces (2 sticks) unsalted butter, softened, plus more for pan

1¼ cups all-purpose flour, plus more for dusting

½ teaspoon salt

¾ teaspoon baking powder

8 ounces semisweet chocolate, coarsely chopped

⅔ cup plus 2 tablespoons sugar

4 large eggs

½ cup whole milk

¼ cup heavy cream

1 Preheat oven to 350°F. Butter a 8½-by-4-by-2½-inch loaf pan; dust with flour, tapping out excess. Sift flour, salt, and baking powder into a medium bowl; set aside.

2 Melt 5 ounces chocolate in a heatproof bowl set over a pan of simmering water, stirring occasionally, until smooth.

3 Put butter in the bowl of an electric mixer fitted with the paddle attachment. Mix on low speed until creamy and smooth, 2 to 3 minutes. Add sugar; raise speed to medium. Cream butter and sugar until pale and fluffy, 3 to 4 minutes. Scrape down sides of bowl. Mix in eggs, one at a time. Reduce speed to low. Add flour mixture in three batches, alternating with two batches of milk. Mix until just combined.

4 Pour half of batter into melted chocolate; stir well. Alternating between remaining plain batter and the chocolate batter, drop large spoonfuls of batter into prepared pan. When pan is filled, run a table knife through mixture to create swirls.

5 Bake until a cake tester inserted into center comes out clean, about 1 hour. (If top of bread browns too quickly, loosely tent with foil.) Let bread cool slightly in pan on a wire

rack, 5 to 10 minutes. Run a thin knife around edges to loosen; unmold onto rack. Let cool completely.

6 Make ganache: Put the remaining 3 ounces chocolate in a bowl. Heat cream in small saucepan over medium heat until just about to simmer. Pour cream over chocolate; stir until mixture is smooth. Let stand 10 minutes to thicken slightly. Using a small offset spatula, spread ganache over cooled cake; let stand until set, about 1 hour. Bread can be stored in an airtight container at room temperature, up to 2 days.

from Quick Breads, Easy Presents

cornmeal rolls

MAKES 1 DOZEN

½ cup milk, warmed to 115°F, plus 1 tablespoon

½ cup water, warmed to 115°F

2 tablespoons packed light-brown sugar

1 envelope active dry yeast (1 scant tablespoon)

4 large egg yolks

1½ teaspoons salt

3 tablespoons unsalted butter, melted, plus more for tin

1 cup yellow cornmeal (preferably stone-ground)

2 cups all-purpose flour, plus more for dusting

   Vegetable oil, for bowl

   Honey Butter (recipe follows), for serving

1 Using a wooden spoon, stir together warm milk, warm water, and sugar in the bowl of an electric mixer. Sprinkle yeast on top; let stand until foamy, about 10 minutes.

2 Fit mixer with the dough hook. Add 3 egg yolks, the salt, butter, cornmeal, and flour to yeast mixture. Mix on low speed until combined. Raise speed to medium; mix until dough is slightly tacky but doesn't stick to your fingers, 6 to 8 minutes.

3 Transfer dough to a large oiled bowl. Loosely cover with plastic wrap, and let dough rise in a warm, draft-free spot until doubled in bulk, about 30 minutes.

4 Preheat oven to 400°F. Butter 12 cups of a standard muffin tin. Turn out dough onto a lightly floured work surface; divide into 12 equal pieces. Roll pieces into smooth balls; transfer to cups in tin. Let rise, loosely covered with plastic wrap, until almost doubled in bulk, about 20 minutes.

5 Whisk together remaining egg yolk and tablespoon milk. Gently brush tops of rolls with egg wash. Bake until rolls are beginning to turn golden, 15 to 20 minutes. Serve rolls warm with honey butter.

from Christmastime in the Country

honey butter

MAKES 1½ CUPS

8 tablespoons (1 stick) unsalted butter, slightly softened

½ cup honey

   Pinch of salt

Put butter in the bowl of an electric mixer fitted with the paddle attachment; mix on medium-high speed until smooth. Add honey; mix on low until combined, scraping down sides of bowl with a spatula as necessary. Mix in salt.

stout spice breads

MAKES 4 BREADS

For safety reasons, don't use enamel-lined cans, and be sure to avoid any sharp edges when buttering the cans and when unmolding the cakes.

2 tablespoons unsalted butter, softened, for cans

3¾ cups all-purpose flour

½ teaspoon plus a pinch of baking soda

1¾ teaspoons baking powder

1¼ teaspoons salt

1 tablespoon ground cinnamon

1¼ teaspoons ground nutmeg

1¼ cups vegetable oil

1¼ cups dark molasses (not blackstrap)

½ cup plus 1 tablespoon packed light-brown sugar

2 large eggs plus 1 large egg yolk

1¼ tablespoons freshly grated orange zest

1¼ cups Guinness or other stout, poured and settled

   Confectioners' sugar, for dusting

1 Preheat oven to 350°F. Using a pastry brush, generously butter insides of four clean 19-ounce bean or soup cans.

2 Sift together flour, baking soda, baking powder, salt, cinnamon, and nutmeg into a bowl. Put oil, molasses, brown sugar, eggs, yolk, zest, and stout in the bowl of an electric mixer fitted with the paddle attachment; mix thoroughly on medium speed. Reduce speed to low; add flour mixture a little at a time, scraping down sides of bowl, until just combined.

3 Pour about 1 cup batter into each buttered can (filling them no more than two-thirds full). Transfer cans to a baking sheet. Bake until a cake tester inserted into centers comes out clean and cakes are pulling away from sides of cans, about 50 minutes. Unmold; let cool completely on a wire rack. Dust with confectioners' sugar.

from Quick Breads, Easy Presents

strawberry-jam yogurt bread

MAKES 1 LOAF | PHOTO ON PAGE 314

8 ounces (2 sticks) unsalted butter,
  softened, plus more for pan

1½ cups all-purpose flour, plus more for pan

¾ teaspoon baking soda

1 teaspoon baking powder

½ teaspoon plus a pinch of salt

2 large eggs, separated

⅔ cup plus 2 tablespoons sugar

2 teaspoons freshly grated lemon zest

1 teaspoon pure vanilla extract

1 tablespoon fresh lemon juice

½ cup plain whole-milk yogurt

½ cup strawberry jam

1 Preheat oven to 350°F. Butter a 9-by-5-by-2½-inch loaf pan, and dust with flour, tapping out excess. Sift flour, baking soda, baking powder, and ½ teaspoon salt together into a medium bowl; set aside.

2 Put egg whites in the bowl of an electric mixer fitted with the whisk attachment; beat on medium speed until soft peaks form. Add ⅓ cup plus 1 tablespoon sugar; beat until stiff, glossy peaks form. Transfer to a large bowl. Clean mixing bowl, and return to mixer.

3 Fit mixer with paddle attachment. Put butter in bowl; mix on medium-high speed until fluffy, 2 to 3 minutes. Add the remaining ⅓ cup plus 1 tablespoon sugar and the zest; beat on medium speed until pale and fluffy, 3 to 4 minutes. Scrape down sides. Reduce speed to low; add egg yolks, one at a time. Add vanilla, lemon juice, and a pinch of salt; beat until just combined. Add flour mixture in three batches, alternating with two additions of yogurt. Beat until just combined.

4 Whisk one-third egg-white mixture into batter. Gently fold in remaining whites with a rubber spatula. Spoon batter into prepared pan; smooth top with an offset spatula.

5 Bake until bread is firm to the touch and surface is browned and crisp, about 55 minutes. (If top of bread browns too quickly, loosely tent with foil.) Let cool slightly in pan on a wire rack, about 10 minutes. Run a thin knife around sides of loaf to loosen; unmold. Let cool completely.

6 Cut cake horizontally into three equal layers. Spread half of jam on bottom layer. Top with middle layer. Spread remaining jam on middle layer. Top with third layer. Refrigerate until set, about 2 hours.

from Quick Breads, Easy Presents

rosemary corn bread

MAKES TWO 5-INCH LOAVES | PHOTO ON PAGE 297

If you don't have heatproof poplar-wood-lined molds with silicone paper (such as Panibois), you can use one 9-by-5-by-2½-inch loaf pan brushed with melted butter.

1 cup yellow cornmeal

1 cup all-purpose flour

1 teaspoon baking powder

½ teaspoon baking soda

½ teaspoon salt

1 tablespoon finely chopped fresh rosemary,
  plus 6 sprigs for garnish

2 large eggs, lightly beaten

5 tablespoons sugar

⅔ cup low-fat buttermilk

⅔ cup olive oil

1 Preheat oven to 425°F. Put cornmeal in a large bowl. Sift flour, baking powder, baking soda, and salt into cornmeal. Stir in chopped rosemary.

2 Put eggs, sugar, buttermilk, and olive oil in the bowl of an electric mixer fitted with the paddle attachment. Mix on medium speed until combined. Reduce speed to low. Mix in flour mixture in two batches, scraping down sides of bowl, until just combined.

3 Divide batter between two 5⅛-by-3¾-by-2 inch wood molds; top each with 3 rosemary sprigs. Bake until a cake tester inserted into centers comes out clean, 20 to 25 minutes. Let cool completely in pans on a wire rack.

from Quick Breads, Easy Presents

SOUPS AND STARTERS

butternut squash and celery-root soup

MAKES 3½ CUPS; SERVES 4

5 cups peeled, cubed butternut squash (about 1½ pounds)

¾ cup peeled, cubed celery root (about 4 ounces)

1 medium onion, quartered

1 tablespoon extra-virgin olive oil

1¼ teaspoons fennel seeds

Coarse salt and freshly ground pepper

¼ cup dry white wine

1 quart homemade or low-sodium
  store-bought chicken stock

1 Preheat oven to 400°F. Put squash, celery root, onion, oil, and ¼ teaspoon fennel seeds on a rimmed baking sheet. Season with salt and pepper, and toss well. Spread mixture out in a single layer. Roast, tossing occasionally, until vegetables are soft and golden brown, about 50 minutes.

2 Transfer mixture to a medium saucepan. Add wine and stock; bring to a boil. Reduce heat to medium-low; simmer, covered, 30 minutes. Remove from heat; uncover. Let mixture cool 10 minutes.

3 Blend stock mixture in a blender (in batches, if necessary, so that blender is never more than halfway full) until smooth. Pass through a sieve into a bowl; discard solids. Return purée to saucepan, and heat over medium heat until warm, about 5 minutes. Season with salt and pepper, if desired.

4 Toast remaining teaspoon fennel seeds in a dry, small skillet over medium-low heat until fragrant and pale golden brown, 2 to 3 minutes. Let cool. Ladle soup into bowls, and garnish with fennel seeds.

from Holiday Classics

brandade

MAKES 3½ CUPS | **PHOTO ON PAGE 300**

The salt cod in this recipe needs to be soaked twice, for a total of sixteen hours, so plan accordingly. The brandade can be refrigerated, covered with plastic wrap, for up to one day.

1 **pound best-quality salt cod**

2 **garlic bulbs, papery outer skins discarded**

7 **tablespoons best-quality extra-virgin olive oil**

1 **large russet potato (about 12 ounces),
  peeled and cut into chunks**

1 **cup heavy cream**

Coarse salt and freshly ground pepper

Caperberries, cut into small wedges, for garnish

Crostini (recipe follows), for serving

1 Rinse cod under cold water. Transfer to a large bowl, and cover with cold water. Cover with plastic wrap, and refrigerate 8 hours or overnight.

2 Drain cod. Return to bowl, and cover with fresh cold water. Refrigerate 8 hours or overnight.

3 Preheat oven to 400°F. Cut a thin slice from top of each bulb to expose cloves. Place bulbs on a sheet of foil. Drizzle with 1 tablespoon oil; wrap in foil. Roast until soft, about 45 minutes. Let stand until cool.

4 Squeeze cloves from bulbs into a bowl, and discard skins. (You should have about 3 tablespoons roasted garlic.)

5 Drain cod; transfer to a medium saucepan. Cover with cold water, and bring to a boil. Reduce heat to low; simmer 20 minutes. Drain cod, and let cool slightly. Transfer to a large bowl; flake into small pieces with a fork. Let cool completely.

6 Cover potato chunks with cold water by 2 inches in a small saucepan. Bring to a boil. Reduce heat; simmer until tender, about 20 minutes. Drain well. When cool enough to handle, force potato through a ricer into a bowl. Let cool completely.

7 Add potato and garlic to cod; stir with a fork. While stirring, pour in cream and remaining 6 tablespoons oil; stir until incorporated. Season with salt and pepper. Garnish with caperberries. Serve with crostini.

from Everybody Loves Dips

crostini

MAKES ABOUT 40

1 **ficelle or other thin baguette,
  cut diagonally into ¼-inch-thick slices**

3 **tablespoons olive oil**

Coarse salt

Preheat oven to 400°F. Arrange bread slices on a rimmed baking sheet in a single layer. Brush one side of each slice with oil, and season with salt. Bake until golden brown on edges, 8 to 12 minutes. Let cool on sheet.

caramelized-onion dip

MAKES 4 CUPS | **PHOTO ON PAGE 300**

4 Spanish or other large onions, for serving (optional)
2 tablespoons extra-virgin olive oil, plus more for drizzling
 Coarse salt
3 pounds yellow onions (about 8 large),
  halved and thinly sliced
¼ cup red-wine vinegar
1 tablespoon coarsely chopped fresh thyme
1 package (8 ounces) cream cheese, room temperature
1 cup sour cream (8 ounces)
 Freshly ground pepper
 Crisp Onions, for garnish (optional; recipe follows)
 Waffle Chips, for serving (optional; recipe follows)

1 To serve dip in Spanish-onion "bowls": Preheat oven to
350°F. Cut top third from each Spanish onion, and discard.
Trim bottoms to level. Transfer to a 9-by-13-inch baking dish.
Drizzle with oil, and season with salt. Bake until soft, 65 to
75 minutes. When cool enough to handle, gently pull out and
discard all but outer 2 or 3 layers of onions. Set onions aside.

2 Heat oil in a medium heavy-bottom pot over medium-high
heat until hot but not smoking. Add sliced onions, and cook,
stirring occasionally, until soft and golden brown, about 15
minutes. Cover; reduce heat to low. Cook onions, stirring occasionally, until caramelized, about 40 minutes more.

3 Raise heat to medium, and season onions with salt. Stir
in vinegar; simmer until absorbed. Stir in thyme; remove from
heat. Let cool completely; coarsely chop.

4 Put cream cheese in the bowl of an electric mixer fitted
with the paddle attachment. Mix on medium speed until
smooth and fluffy, about 1 minute. Fold in onion mixture and
sour cream with a rubber spatula; season with salt and pepper. Divide dip among baked onions, or transfer to a serving
dish. Cover with plastic wrap; refrigerate 1 hour. Garnish with
crisp onions, and serve with waffle chips, if desired.

from Everybody Loves Dips

crisp onions

MAKES 1½ CUPS

5 tablespoons vegetable oil
1 small onion, thinly sliced

Heat oil in a medium skillet over high heat until hot but not
smoking. Working in small batches, fry onion slices until
crisp, about 1 minute. Using a slotted spoon, transfer onion
rings to paper towels to drain.

waffle chips

MAKES 6 CUPS

4 russet potatoes, peeled
2½ quarts vegetable oil
 Coarse salt

1 Using a mandoline fitted with the zigzag blade, slice potatoes ⅛ inch thick, turning them a quarter turn after each slice
to create a waffle pattern. Soak slices in cold water 1 hour.

2 Fill a 6-quart heavy-bottom pot halfway with vegetable oil,
and heat over medium-high heat until oil registers 365°F
on a deep-fry thermometer. Meanwhile, drain potato slices,
and dry thoroughly with paper towels.

3 In batches, fry potato slices until golden brown, 1 to 1½
minutes. Using a slotted spoon, transfer chips to paper
towels to drain. Lightly season with salt. (Adjust heat between
batches, if necessary, to keep temperature at 365°F.)

curried yogurt dip

MAKES 1 CUP

1 cup plain whole-milk yogurt, preferably Greek (8 ounces)
3 tablespoons vegetable oil
½ teaspoon brown mustard seed
10 fresh curry leaves, plus more for garnish
1 teaspoon finely grated peeled fresh ginger
5 fresh small, hot chiles, such as serrano or Thai
  (1 seeded and finely chopped; 4 whole)
½ teaspoon turmeric
1 teaspoon coarse salt
½ teaspoon sugar
 Crudités or store-bought pappadam for serving

1 Put yogurt in a small bowl; set aside. Heat 2 tablespoons
oil in a small skillet over medium-high heat until hot but not
smoking. Add ¼ teaspoon mustard seed. Cook, shaking pan
occasionally, until seeds begin to crackle and pop, about 45
seconds. Add curry leaves, and cook until starting to wilt,
about 1 minute. Add ginger and chopped chile. Cook, stirring,
30 seconds. Stir in turmeric. Pour mixture over yogurt. Stir
in salt and sugar. Transfer to a serving dish.

2 Heat remaining tablespoon oil in a small skillet over
medium-high heat until hot but not smoking. Add remaining
¼ teaspoon mustard seed and the whole chiles. Cook, shaking pan occasionally, until seeds crackle and pop, about 45
seconds. Garnish dip with chile mixture and curry leaves.
Serve with desired accompaniments.

from Everybody Loves Dips

fava bean and sausage dip

MAKES ABOUT 3 CUPS | PHOTO ON PAGE 300

Merguez sausages are available at specialty food stores.

1 cup large, dried, split fava beans (8 ounces)

6 garlic cloves (3 whole; 3 thinly sliced lengthwise)

Coarse salt

12 ounces merguez (spicy Moroccan lamb sausages), casings removed

⅓ cup extra-virgin olive oil, plus more for drizzling

¼ cup tahini

¼ cup fresh lemon juice, plus 1 teaspoon freshly grated lemon zest

Freshly ground pepper

3 tablespoons fresh flat-leaf parsley leaves, for garnish

Flatbread crisps, for serving

1 Bring 5 cups water, the fava beans, whole garlic cloves, and ½ teaspoon salt to a boil in a medium saucepan. Reduce heat; simmer until beans are tender, about 30 minutes. Drain well; let bean mixture stand until cool, about 15 minutes.

2 Crumble sausage into a large skillet. Cook over medium heat, stirring and draining off excess fat occasionally, 6 minutes. Add sliced garlic. Continue to cook, stirring occasionally, until sausage is cooked through and garlic is crisp and brown, about 4 minutes more.

3 Put bean mixture, oil, tahini, lemon juice and zest, ¾ teaspoon salt, a pinch of pepper, and ¼ cup water in a food processor. Process, adding up to ¼ cup more water, until smooth and creamy. Season with salt and pepper, if desired.

4 Transfer dip to a serving platter, and smooth into an even layer. Using a slotted spoon, arrange sausage mixture over top. Sprinkle dip with parsley leaves, and drizzle with oil. Serve with flatbread crisps.

from Everybody Loves Dips

bacon-wrapped chicken livers

MAKES 12 TO 15

12 to 15 rosemary sprigs (about 5 inches each)

8 ounces chicken livers, trimmed

10 ounces bacon (12 to 15 slices)

Extra-virgin olive oil, for drizzling

Coarse salt and freshly ground pepper

1 Remove leaves from bottom two-thirds of each rosemary sprig. Reserve 2 tablespoons leaves, and finely chop. Rinse chicken livers, and pat dry. Wrap a slice of bacon around each liver; thread each liver onto a rosemary sprig. Drizzle with oil, and season with salt and pepper.

2 Heat a grill pan over medium-high heat until hot. Grill bacon-wrapped livers, turning once, until livers are cooked through and bacon is crisp, 4 to 5 minutes per side. Sprinkle with chopped rosemary.

fig and port dip

MAKES 1 CUP

1 tablespoon olive oil

1 tablespoon finely chopped shallot

1 cup dried Black Mission figs, cut into ½-inch-thick pieces

1 whole clove

1 whole cinnamon stick

1½ teaspoons fresh rosemary leaves, plus sprigs for garnish

1 strip orange zest (2 inches long)

¾ cup tawny port

1 tablespoon red-wine vinegar

Coarse salt and freshly ground pepper

Bacon-Wrapped Chicken Livers (recipe above)

1 Heat oil in a small saucepan over medium heat until hot but not smoking. Add shallot, and cook, stirring occasionally, until softened, about 2 minutes. Add figs, clove, cinnamon stick, rosemary, orange zest, port, vinegar, and ¼ cup water. Bring to a boil. Reduce heat to medium-low; simmer until figs are softened, about 5 minutes.

2 Discard clove and cinnamon stick. Transfer fig mixture to a food processor; process until smooth. Transfer dip to a serving bowl, and season with salt and pepper. Garnish with fresh rosemary sprigs. Serve with bacon-wrapped chicken livers.

from Everybody Loves Dips

feta and cucumber dip

MAKES 3½ CUPS

4 medium cucumbers, peeled

Coarse salt

2 cups plain whole-milk yogurt, preferably Greek (16 ounces)

1 cup crumbled feta cheese, preferably French (6 ounces)

½ cup finely chopped fresh mint, plus 1 sprig for garnish

½ cup heavy cream

5 tablespoons fresh lemon juice (about 2 lemons)

Freshly ground pepper

Napa cabbage leaves, for lining bowl (optional)

Crudités (such as carrots; radishes; blanched, chilled asparagus; and ribbons of yellow squash and zucchini), for serving

1 Holding cucumbers lengthwise, grate on the large holes of a box grater down to the seeds. Discard seeds, and continue grating. Transfer grated cucumber to a colander set in the sink. Stir in 2 teaspoons salt; let stand 15 minutes.

2 Rinse cucumber under cold water; shake out excess liquid. Transfer to a clean kitchen towel; squeeze out as much liquid as possible. (You should have about ⅔ cup grated cucumber.)

3 Stir together cucumber, yogurt, feta, mint, cream, and lemon juice in a large bowl. Season with salt and pepper. If desired, transfer to a bowl lined with cabbage leaves. Garnish dip with mint sprig, and serve with crudités.

from Everybody Loves Dips

hot crab dip

MAKES 4 CUPS

1 loaf rustic bread (about 1 pound), trimmed of crust

8 tablespoons (1 stick) unsalted butter

1 medium onion, finely chopped (about 1⅓ cups)

2 garlic cloves, minced

6 tablespoons all-purpose flour

1½ cups milk

¼ teaspoon cayenne pepper

2 teaspoons dry mustard

4 ounces sharp white cheddar cheese, shredded (1 cup)

2 tablespoons fresh lemon juice, plus freshly grated zest of 1 lemon

2 teaspoons Worcestershire sauce

10 ounces lump crabmeat, picked over

2 tablespoons coarsely chopped fresh flat-leaf parsley

Coarse salt and freshly ground pepper

Toasted baguette slices, for serving

1 Preheat oven to 400°F. Tear enough bread into 1-inch pieces to measure 4 to 5 cups.

2 Melt 6 tablespoons butter in a medium saucepan over medium heat. Add onion and garlic, and cook, stirring occasionally, until soft, about 4 minutes. Whisk in flour; cook, whisking constantly, 4 minutes. Whisking constantly, pour in milk in a slow, steady stream. Simmer mixture over medium heat, whisking, until thickened, about 4 minutes. Stir in cayenne and mustard. Whisk in shredded cheese a little at a time; cook, whisking, until melted.

3 Remove cheese mixture from heat. Stir in lemon juice, zest, and Worcestershire sauce. Gently stir in crabmeat and parsley. Season with salt and pepper. Transfer to a 1-quart ovenproof dish or casserole.

4 Melt remaining 2 tablespoons butter; stir into bread pieces. Season with salt and pepper. Arrange bread mixture over crab dip. Bake until heated through and golden brown, 25 to 30 minutes. Let stand at room temperature 10 minutes before serving. Serve with toasted baguette slices.

from Everybody Loves Dips

mushroom and bacon dip

MAKES 4 CUPS | **PHOTO ON PAGE 300**

3 pieces dried porcini mushroom

½ cup boiling water

8 slices thick-cut bacon

1 large or 2 small leeks, white and pale-green parts only, halved lengthwise, thinly sliced crosswise, and rinsed well (about 2 cups)

4 garlic cloves, finely chopped (4 teaspoons)

1 pound fresh cremini, white, or shiitake mushrooms (stems discarded), coarsely chopped, plus sliced mushrooms for garnish (optional)

1 teaspoon coarse salt

¼ teaspoon freshly ground pepper

1½ teaspoons finely chopped fresh thyme

1 package (8 ounces) cream cheese, room temperature

2 cups sour cream (16 ounces)

3 tablespoons thinly sliced scallions (green parts only), plus more for garnish

Roasted Fingerling Potato Chips, for serving (optional; recipe follows)

Pretzels, for serving (optional)

1 Soak dried porcini in boiling water until soft, about 20 minutes. Lift out porcini and drain well, squeezing out liquid. Coarsely chop porcini (you should have about 4 teaspoons). Pour soaking liquid through a fine sieve into a bowl; set aside.

2 Cook bacon in a large nonstick skillet over medium heat until crisp, about 5 minutes per side. Transfer to paper towels to drain. Reserve 4 tablespoons bacon fat. Wipe skillet clean with paper towels. Coarsely chop bacon; set aside.

3 Return 3 tablespoons bacon fat to skillet. Add leek and garlic; cook over medium heat, stirring occasionally, until translucent, about 2 minutes. Add fresh mushrooms and reserved porcini; season with salt and pepper. Raise heat to high; cook, stirring frequently, until mushrooms are tender, 5 to 8 minutes. Add thyme; cook 2 minutes more. Remove mixture from skillet and let cool completely.

4 Put cream cheese in the bowl of an electric mixer fitted with the whisk attachment; beat until smooth. With mixer running, add sour cream a little at a time; beat until smooth. Using a wooden spoon, stir in mushrooms, three-quarters of the bacon, and the sliced scallions. Stir in 2 tablespoons reserved porcini liquid. If necessary, add more porcini liquid to achieve desired consistency.

5 Just before serving, garnish with remaining bacon and sliced scallions. If desired, cook additional sliced mushrooms in remaining tablespoon bacon fat in a medium skillet over medium heat, stirring occasionally, until golden brown, about 2 minutes. Scatter over dip. Serve with roasted fingerling potato chips.

from Everybody Loves Dips

roasted fingerling potato chips

MAKES ABOUT 4 CUPS

1 pound fingerling potatoes, cut lengthwise into ¼-inch-thick slices
1 tablespoon olive oil
Coarse salt and freshly ground pepper

Preheat oven to 400°F. Toss potatoes with oil, and season with salt and pepper. Arrange in a single layer on a rimmed baking sheet. Bake until potato slices are golden brown and crisp, about 25 minutes.

SALADS AND SIDE DISHES

fennel, escarole, and radish salad

SERVES 4

1 fennel bulb, thinly sliced crosswise, fronds reserved
1 head escarole, cut crosswise into 2-inch-wide ribbons
1 bunch small or medium radishes, thinly sliced
1 tablespoon extra-virgin olive oil
2 teaspoons champagne vinegar
Coarse salt and freshly ground pepper

Toss together sliced fennel, escarole, and radishes in a large bowl. Drizzle with oil and vinegar, and season with salt and pepper. Gently toss. Garnish with fennel fronds.

from What's for Dinner?

candied sweet potatoes

SERVES 6 | PHOTO ON PAGE 307

6 small sweet potatoes (about 2¼ pounds), peeled and cut into 1-inch-thick wedges
1½ cups apple cider
½ cup pure maple syrup
Coarse salt
3 sprigs fresh rosemary
3 tablespoons unsalted butter, cut into small pieces

1 Preheat oven to 375°F. Toss together potatoes, cider, and syrup in a large bowl; season with salt.

2 Transfer potato mixture to a large cast-iron or other heavy ovenproof skillet, layering wedges. Tuck rosemary sprigs around wedges. Dot with butter. Transfer skillet to oven. Bake potatoes, tossing carefully about halfway through, until browned on edges and very tender, and until liquid is reduced to a syrup, about 1½ hours. Serve warm.

from Holiday Classics

creamed spinach and pearl onions

SERVES 4 | **PHOTO ON PAGE 307**

1¼ pounds spinach, tough stems discarded, leaves rinsed well (do not pat dry)

10 ounces white pearl onions (about 2½ cups)

5 tablespoons unsalted butter

2 tablespoons all-purpose flour

1¼ cups milk

3 ounces slab bacon, cut into ¼-inch dice (about ¾ cups)

Coarse salt and freshly ground pepper

Generous pinch of freshly grated nutmeg

½ cup heavy cream

2 teaspoons lemon juice

1 Heat a large pot over high heat until hot. Cook spinach (with water still clinging to leaves) in pot, covered, until beginning to wilt, about 1 minute. Stir, and cook, covered, 1 minute more. Uncover; stir spinach until completely wilted.

2 Transfer to a colander; rinse under cold water. Squeeze spinach dry in a clean kitchen towel. Finely chop; set aside.

3 Bring a medium saucepan of water to a boil. Add onions; cook until skins soften, about 3 minutes. Remove onions with a slotted spoon (reserve water in pot); rinse under cold water. Trim root ends, and remove skins. Halve onions if large.

4 Return onions to cooking water. Cook until tender, about 10 minutes. Drain, and rinse under cold water.

5 Melt 4 tablespoons butter in a medium saucepan over medium heat. Add flour, and whisk until smooth. Whisking constantly, pour in milk in a slow, steady stream. Boil, whisking constantly, 1 minute. Remove from heat.

6 Melt remaining tablespoon butter in a large saucepan over medium heat. Add bacon; cook, stirring occasionally, until well browned, about 6 minutes. Stir in onions and spinach. Stir in cream and reserved milk mixture. Add 1 teaspoon salt, ¼ teaspoon pepper, and nutmeg. Cook, stirring occasionally, until heated through and thickened, about 10 minutes (adjust heat if necessary; do not let boil). Stir in lemon juice. Season with salt and pepper, if desired.

from Holiday Classics

mashed potatoes with horseradish

MAKES 6½ CUPS; SERVES 6 TO 8

1½ cups heavy cream

½ cup freshly grated or prepared (drained) horseradish

3 pounds Yukon gold potatoes, peeled and cut into 2-inch chunks

Coarse salt

3 tablespoons unsalted butter

1 Heat cream and horseradish in a small saucepan over medium heat until just about to simmer. Remove from heat.

2 Cover potatoes with cold water in a large saucepan. Bring to a boil, and add salt. Cook until the potatoes are tender, about 8 minutes; drain.

3 Force potatoes through a ricer or pass through a food mill into a bowl. Add butter and the cream mixture. Season potato mixture with salt. Stir until smooth.

from Holiday Classics

....

MAIN COURSES

....

beef Wellington

SERVES 12

3½ pounds whole center-cut beef fillet

Coarse salt and freshly ground pepper

2 tablespoons olive oil

6 ounces foie gras pâté or other liver pâté, room temperature

1½ cups Duxelles (recipe follows)

All-purpose flour, for dusting

1 box (17¼ ounces) frozen puff-pastry sheets, thawed

1 large egg, beaten

1 Preheat oven to 400°F. Set a wire rack on a rimmed baking sheet. Season beef with salt and pepper. Heat oil in a large sauté pan over high heat until hot but not smoking. Add beef, and brown all over, about 5 minutes total. Transfer to wire rack, and let stand until cool to the touch, about 10 minutes. Spread pâté over entire fillet. Cover with duxelles, pressing into pâté; set beef aside.

2 On a lightly floured work surface, place two puff-pastry sheets side by side, overlapping by ½ inch. Roll out to a 12-by-20-inch rectangle. Place duxelles-covered beef lengthwise in middle of rectangle; wrap pastry around beef so long sides overlap. Place beef, seam side down, on a baking sheet, and tuck pastry ends underneath. Brush pastry with egg wash. Refrigerate at least 30 minutes or up to 4 hours.

3 Bake, tenting with foil when pastry is golden brown (after about 30 minutes), until an instant-read thermometer inserted into the center of beef registers 130°F (for medium-rare), about 45 minutes total. Transfer to a clean wire rack set over a rimmed baking sheet. Let stand 20 minutes before slicing.

from Holiday Classics

duxelles

MAKES ABOUT 1½ CUPS

1 pound portobello mushrooms, stem ends trimmed, stems and caps broken into small pieces

2 tablespoons unsalted butter

¼ cup finely chopped shallots (1 large shallot)

¼ cup heavy cream

3 tablespoons sherry or Madeira wine

2 tablespoons finely chopped fresh flat-leaf parsley

2 teaspoons coarsely chopped fresh thyme

½ teaspoon coarse salt

⅛ teaspoon freshly ground pepper

1 Finely chop mushrooms in a food processor. Transfer to a large square of cheesecloth, and squeeze dry.

2 Melt butter in a medium skillet over medium heat. Add shallots, and cook, stirring occasionally, until translucent, 2 to 3 minutes. Add mushrooms, stirring often, until beginning to brown, 5 to 6 minutes. Remove from heat. Stir in cream, sherry, parsley, thyme, salt, and pepper. Let duxelles cool completely before using.

crown roast of pork

SERVES 12 TO 14 | **PHOTO ON PAGE 305**

1 large loaf dense rustic bread, trimmed of crust and torn into small pieces (8 cups)

6 tablespoons unsalted butter

2 cups coarsely chopped onions (about 2 medium onions)

¼ cup minced garlic

12 ounces pancetta, cut into ¼-by-½-inch strips

1½ cups coarsely chopped prunes

1½ cups pine nuts, toasted

3 tablespoons finely chopped fresh rosemary, plus rosemary sprigs (optional) for garnish

1 cup homemade or low-sodium store-bought chicken stock

1 cup dry white wine

Coarse salt and freshly ground pepper

1 crown roast of pork (8 to 10 pounds), frenched

Seckel pears and lady apples, roasted (optional), for garnish

1 Preheat oven to 350°F. Spread out bread pieces on a rimmed baking sheet. Bake until lightly toasted, about 25 minutes. Let bread pieces cool completely. Raise the oven temperature to 400°F.

2 While bread toasts, melt butter in a large sauté pan over medium-low heat. Add onions and garlic; cook, stirring occasionally, until softened and translucent, about 10 minutes. Add pancetta. Raise heat to medium-high; cook, stirring, until browned, about 5 minutes. Remove pan from heat. Stir in prunes, pine nuts, and 1 tablespoon rosemary. Transfer to a large bowl. Let cool completely.

3 Stir reserved bread, the stock, and wine into onion mixture. Season with salt and pepper, and set aside.

4 Rub pork inside and out with salt, pepper, and remaining 2 tablespoons rosemary. Transfer to a roasting pan. Loosely fill cavity with stuffing. Transfer remaining stuffing to a 9-by-13-inch baking pan; set aside. Cover pork with foil. Roast until an instant-read thermometer inserted into thickest part of pork (avoiding bone) registers 160°F, about 2 hours. While pork roasts, bake reserved stuffing in pan, uncovered, until heated through and golden brown, about 45 minutes. Let pork stand 20 minutes before cutting into chops and serving with stuffing. Garnish with pears, apples, and rosemary, if desired.

from Holiday Classics

poached halibut
in lemon-thyme broth

SERVES 4

Sea bass and striped bass can be used in place of halibut.

 3 lemons
3½ cups cold homemade or low-sodium
    store-bought chicken stock
 3 garlic cloves
 8 sprigs fresh thyme
10 whole black peppercorns
 4 halibut fillets (6 ounces each), skinned
   Coarse salt
   Extra-virgin olive oil, for drizzling

1 Using a vegetable peeler, remove zest in strips from 2 lemons. Juice zested lemons. Transfer zest and juice to a 12-inch straight-sided skillet with a tight-fitting lid. Add chicken stock, garlic, 4 sprigs thyme, and the whole black peppercorns to the pan. Bring to a boil.

2 Season each fillet on both sides with salt; carefully add to skillet. Cover skillet, and turn off the heat. Let stand until fish is opaque and firm to the touch, 9 to 12 minutes. Using a slotted spatula, transfer fish to a platter, and tent loosely with foil to keep warm.

3 Pour poaching liquid through a cheesecloth-lined sieve into a bowl; discard solids. Return liquid to pan; bring to a boil, then turn off heat.

4 Divide broth among four wide bowls; gently place a fish fillet in each. Cut remaining lemon into wedges. Garnish each serving with a wedge of lemon and a sprig of thyme, and lightly drizzle with oil.

from What's for Dinner?

vegetable chili

MAKES 10 CUPS; SERVES 8

 ½ cup dried chickpeas
 ¾ cup dried kidney beans
 2 tablespoons olive oil
 1 large onion (12 ounces), cut into ¼-inch pieces (2 cups)
 2 carrots, cut into ¼-inch dice (1 cup)
 2 stalks celery, cut into ¼-inch dice (1 cup)
 1 garlic clove, minced
12 ounces white mushrooms, cut into ¼-inch dice (3½ cups)
 1 red bell pepper, cut into ¼-inch dice (1 cup)
 1 fresh jalapeño chile, seeded and finely chopped
 3 tablespoons tomato paste
 1 teaspoon chili powder
 1 teaspoon ground coriander
 1 tablespoon ground cumin
 2 teaspoons dried oregano
   Coarse salt
 ¼ teaspoon freshly ground pepper
 1 tablespoon Worcestershire sauce
 ⅓ cup dry red wine
 1 can (28 ounces) crushed tomatoes
 ½ cup bulghur
   Grated cheddar cheese, fresh cilantro,
   and sour cream, for serving

1 Put chickpeas and kidney beans in separate bowls, and cover each with 3 cups cold water. Loosely cover with plastic wrap, and let soak overnight at room temperature.

2 Drain beans, and rinse. Transfer to separate medium saucepans, and cover with water by 1½ inches. Bring to a boil. Reduce heat; simmer until tender; about 50 minutes for kidney beans and 1 hour for chickpeas. Drain.

3 Heat oil in a 6-quart stockpot over medium-high heat until hot but not smoking. Add onion, carrots, celery, and garlic. Cook, stirring occasionally, until onion is translucent, about 6 minutes. Add mushrooms, bell pepper, and jalapeño. Cook until pepper and chile are just tender, about 8 minutes. Stir in tomato paste, spices, 2 teaspoons salt, the pepper, Worcestershire sauce, and wine. Add crushed tomatoes, 3½ cups water, the chickpeas, kidney beans, and bulghur.

4 Reduce heat; simmer until slightly thick, about 30 minutes. Season with salt, if desired. Serve with cheddar cheese, cilantro, and sour cream.

from Christmastime in the Country

candy-stripe cookie sticks

MAKES 30

To work with the cookies while they're hot, use a pair of disposable food-handler's gloves. To make a template, fold a sheet of card stock in half; cut a three-by-six-inch rectangle in the center, leaving a border of one inch to one and a half inches. Seal the edges with tape.

- 8 large egg whites
- 2 cups sugar
- 2 cups all-purpose flour
  Pinch of salt
- 10 tablespoons (1¼ sticks) unsalted butter, melted and cooled
- 6 tablespoons heavy cream
- 1 teaspoon pure vanilla extract
  Gel-paste food coloring in red and deep pink

1 Preheat oven to 400°F. Put egg whites and sugar in the bowl of an electric mixer fitted with the whisk attachment. Beat on medium speed until mixture is foamy, about 2 minutes. Beat in flour and salt. Add butter, cream, and vanilla; beat until combined, about 30 seconds.

2 Put ¾ cup batter into each of two small bowls (set remaining batter aside). Tint one portion red, the other deep pink. Transfer colored batters to separate pastry bags fitted with small plain, round tips (such as Ateco #2). Secure ends of pastry bags with rubber bands. Set aside.

3 Spoon a heaping tablespoon of the remaining batter (untinted) onto a baking sheet lined with a nonstick baking mat (such as a Silpat baking mat). Using a small offset spatula, spread it into a 3-by-6-inch rectangle (or use a template). Repeat to make another rectangle. Pipe diagonal stripes in desired colors onto each rectangle.

4 Bake until just turning pale golden, 6 to 8 minutes. Immediately loosen edges of cookies with a small spatula. Using your hands or the spatula, lift one cookie, and flip it over. Starting from one long side, roll cookie into a stick. Transfer to a clean work surface, seam side down, and let cool until set. Quickly repeat with second cookie.

5 Repeat process, tinting and baking 2 or 3 cookies at a time. Cookies will keep in an airtight container at room temperature for up to 1 week.

from Christmastime in the Country

peppermint meringue cookies with chocolate filling

MAKES ABOUT 5 DOZEN | **PHOTO ON PAGE 314**

- 3 large egg whites
- ¾ cup sugar
- ½ teaspoon pure peppermint extract
  Gel-paste food coloring in red
  Ganache (recipe follows)

1 Preheat oven to 175°F. Line two baking sheets with parchment paper, and adhere corners to sheets with masking tape. Fit a pastry bag with a small open-star tip (such as Ateco #22).

2 Put egg whites and sugar in the heatproof bowl of an electric mixer. Set over a pan of simmering water; stir until sugar is dissolved and mixture is warm to the touch, 2 to 3 minutes.

3 Fit mixer with whisk attachment. Beat egg-white mixture on medium-high speed until stiff peaks form. Beat in extract.

4 Fold down edges of a pastry bag. Using a small, new paintbrush, paint two or three stripes of red food coloring inside the bag. Fill bag with 1 to 2 cups meringue. Pipe small (¾-inch-high) star shapes onto parchment. Refill bag as necessary, adding more food coloring each time.

5 Bake meringues until crisp but not brown, about 1 hour 40 minutes. Let cool completely on sheets on wire racks.

6 Fit a clean pastry bag with a small, plain round tip (such as Ateco #5). Fill bag with ganache. Pipe a small amount onto bottom of 1 meringue. Press against bottom of another. Gently place on wire racks. Repeat with remaining meringues. Let stand until set, about 30 minutes.

from Christmastime in the Country

ganache

MAKES 1½ CUPS (ENOUGH FOR 5 DOZEN COOKIES)

- 6 ounces good-quality semisweet chocolate, chopped
- 1 cup heavy cream

1 Set chocolate aside in a heatproof bowl. Heat cream in a small saucepan until just about to simmer. Pour over chocolate. Let stand 5 minutes. Gently stir with a rubber spatula until combined and smooth, about 5 minutes.

2 Let ganache cool, stirring every 5 to 10 minutes, until thick enough to pipe (test by spooning a small amount onto a plate; it should hold its shape), about 45 minutes. If ganache sets before using, gently reheat in a heatproof bowl set over a pan of simmering water, and repeat the cooling process.

chocolate-almond swirl cookies

MAKES 30

- 10 ounces (2½ sticks) unsalted butter, softened
- 1½ cups sugar
- 2 large eggs plus 1 large egg white
- 1 teaspoon salt
- 1 tablespoon pure vanilla extract
- ½ cup milk
- 4 cups all-purpose flour, plus more for dusting
- 1 cup unsweetened cocoa powder

  Almond Dough (recipe follows)

1   Put butter and sugar in the bowl of an electric mixer fitted with the paddle attachment. Cream on medium-high speed until fluffy, 2 to 3 minutes. Mix in eggs and salt. Add vanilla, milk, flour, and cocoa; mix until incorporated.

2   Turn out dough, and wrap in plastic; gently flatten into a rectangle. Refrigerate until firm, about 1 hour, or up to 1 day.

3   Cut out a 12-by-26-inch sheet of parchment paper, and generously flour. On floured parchment, roll out chocolate dough to a 10-by-24-inch rectangle, dusting with flour as needed and occasionally using an offset spatula to lift dough to prevent sticking. Transfer on parchment to refrigerator.

4   Cut out another 12-by-26-inch sheet of parchment, and generously flour. On floured parchment, roll out almond dough to a 9-by-20-inch rectangle, using same technique as above.

5   Brush the chocolate dough with just enough egg white to cover surface. Gently stack almond dough on top of chocolate dough. Starting with one short side, roll doughs together into a log, gently lifting parchment as you roll to help turn dough over. Brush overlap with a small amount of egg white; seal seam by pinching gently and pressing. Wrap log in parchment or waxed paper. Freeze until firm, about 1½ hours.

6   Preheat oven to 350°F. Line baking sheets with parchment paper. Let dough logs stand at room temperature 10 minutes. Using a serrated knife, cut logs into ¼-inch-thick rounds, rotating log after each cut to help keep it round. Transfer rounds to lined sheets. Bake until set (do not let brown), 18 to 20 minutes. Let cookies cool on parchment on wire racks.

from Christmastime in the Country

almond dough

MAKES ENOUGH FOR 30 COOKIES

- 1 cup whole blanched almonds (5 ounces)
- ½ cup sugar
- ⅔ cup almond paste (7 ounces)
- 1½ cups all-purpose flour
- ½ teaspoon salt
- 8 tablespoons (1 stick) unsalted butter, cut into small pieces
- 2 large eggs
- ½ teaspoon pure vanilla extract

1   Preheat oven to 350°F. Toast almonds on a baking sheet, shaking occasionally, until lightly toasted, 13 to 15 minutes. Let cool completely.

2   Pulse sugar, almond paste, flour, and salt in a food processor until very fine. Add toasted nuts; process until finely ground. Add butter, eggs, and vanilla; pulse until combined. Turn out dough onto a sheet of plastic wrap, and pat into a rectangle; wrap. Refrigerate at least 1 hour or up to 1 day.

chocolate waffle cookies

MAKES ABOUT 45

- 3 ounces unsweetened chocolate, coarsely chopped
- 9 ounces (2¼ sticks) unsalted butter
- 4 large eggs
- 1 teaspoon pure vanilla extract
- 1½ cups granulated sugar
- ½ teaspoon salt
- 1½ teaspoons ground cinnamon
- ½ cup plus 2 tablespoons unsweetened cocoa powder
- 1½ cups all-purpose flour

  Vegetable-oil cooking spray

- ¼ cup confectioners' sugar, plus more for dusting
- 4½ teaspoons milk

1   Heat chocolate and 2 sticks butter in a small saucepan over medium-high heat, stirring occasionally, until melted. Let mixture cool slightly.

2   Put eggs, vanilla, and granulated sugar in the bowl of an electric mixer fitted with the paddle attachment. Mix on medium speed until very pale, 4 to 5 minutes. Mix in melted chocolate. Add salt, cinnamon, ½ cup cocoa, and the flour; mix until just combined.

3   Lightly coat the grids of a waffle iron with cooking spray, and heat until hot. Using a very small ice-cream scoop or a

spoon, drop batter in centers of each waffle-iron square (rounds should be about 1½ inches in diameter). Close cover; cook until waffles are completely set, about 1½ minutes. Remove cookies with a fork, and let cool, bottom sides up, on a wire rack. Continue to cook batter, lightly coating grids with cooking spray between batches.

4   When cookies are cool, melt remaining 2 tablespoons butter in a small saucepan. Add confectioners' sugar and remaining 2 tablespoons cocoa; stir until smooth. Stir in milk.

5   Gently dip top side of each cookie in icing so it just coats waffle lines (not gaps). Let stand until icing is set, about 10 minutes. Using a small fine sieve, dust cookies with confectioners' sugar. Cookies can be stored in an airtight container in a cool, dry spot up to 2 days.

from Christmastime in the Country

cream cheese-walnut cookies

MAKES ABOUT 4 DOZEN

4   cups all-purpose flour
1¼ teaspoons salt
1   pound (4 sticks) unsalted butter, softened
6   ounces cream cheese (not whipped), room temperature
1¼ cups sugar
2   tablespoons plus ½ teaspoon pure vanilla extract
2½ cups walnut halves (1½ cups toasted and chopped; 1 cup finely chopped)

1   Line two baking sheets with parchment paper; set aside. Whisk together flour and salt in a large bowl; set aside.

2   Put butter and cream cheese in the bowl of an electric mixer fitted with the paddle. Mix on medium speed until pale and fluffy, about 2 minutes. Mix in sugar and vanilla. Reduce speed to low. Add the flour mixture, and mix until just combined (do not overmix). Mix in 1½ cups toasted walnuts.

3   Transfer dough to a work surface. Divide in half; shape each into an 8½-inch-long log (about 2 inches in diameter). Wrap each log in parchment. Freeze until firm, 30 minutes.

4   Preheat oven to 350°F, with racks in upper and lower thirds. Remove one log from freezer. Roll in ½ cup finely chopped walnuts, coating completely. Cut log into ¼-inch-thick rounds; transfer rounds to parchment-lined sheet.

5   Bake, rotating and switching positions of sheets halfway through, until cookies are golden around the edges, 18 to 20 minutes. Transfer to wire racks; let cool completely. Repeat with remaining dough and nuts once baking sheets are cool.

from Cookie of the Month

fruitcake

SERVES 12 | PHOTO ON PAGE 318

1   cup golden raisins (5 ounces)
1   cup dried Calimyrna figs, chopped (5 ounces)
1   cup dried apricots, chopped (6 ounces)
1   cup dried pears, chopped (5¼ ounces)
⅓ cup candied ginger, chopped (1¾ ounces)
¼ cup candied orange peel, chopped
½ cup Cointreau or other orange-flavored liqueur, plus more (optional) for brushing cake
    Vegetable-oil cooking spray
3   cups all-purpose flour, plus more for dusting
1½ teaspoons baking powder
1   teaspoon ground cinnamon
½ teaspoon ground ginger
½ teaspoon ground cloves
½ teaspoon salt
8   ounces (2 sticks) unsalted butter, melted
1½ cups granulated sugar
¾ cup packed dark-brown sugar
4   large eggs
2   tablespoons unsulfured molasses
1   tablespoon pure vanilla extract
1   cup chopped toasted walnuts
1   cup sweetened flaked coconut

1   Stir together dried fruit, ginger, peel, and liqueur. Let macerate at room temperature at least 3 hours or overnight.

2   Cut a round of parchment paper to line the bottom of a 7-inch round cake pan (3 inches deep) or a 9-inch round cake pan (2 inches deep). Coat pan with cooking spray; line with parchment. Spray lining, then flour pan, tapping out excess.

3   Preheat oven to 325°F. Whisk together flour, baking powder, cinnamon, ginger, cloves, and salt in a medium bowl; set aside. Put butter and sugars in the bowl of an electric mixer fitted with the paddle attachment; mix on medium speed until smooth. Mix in eggs, one at a time. Mix in molasses and vanilla. Add flour mixture a little at a time; mix until smooth. Mix in macerated fruits, the walnuts, and coconut.

4   Pour batter into prepared pan. Bake until a cake tester inserted into center comes out clean, about 45 minutes for 7-inch cake and 2½ hours for 9-inch cake.

5   Transfer cake in pan to a rack. If desired, brush warm cake with up to ½ cup liqueur. Let cool completely. Cake can be refrigerated, wrapped well in plastic, up to 1 month.

from Holiday Classics

gingercake house

SERVES 10 TO 12 | **PHOTO ON PAGE 320**

Gingerbread Cakes (recipe follows)

Chocolate Swiss Meringue Buttercream (recipe follows)

Gingerbread Cookies (recipe follows)

Clean, thin, nontoxic tree branches

About 1 ounce chocolate, melted, for brushing branches

Cornstarch, for dusting

5 ounces rolled fondant

Gel-paste food coloring in red and orange

Chocolate sprinkles, for decorating

Black licorice gumdrops, for decorating

½ recipe Royal Icing (recipe follows), room temperature

Sanding sugar

1 Quarter 1 cake diagonally to make 4 triangles. Halve the remaining cake to make 2 rectangles. Place 1 rectangle on a cake board or plate. Using a small offset spatula, frost top with buttercream. Place remaining rectangle on top; frost top.

2 On a work surface, stack 3 triangles, frosting between layers. Set stacked "roof" on cake. Refrigerate cake 15 minutes.

3 Using a small offset spatula, frost exterior of house with a thin layer of buttercream to make a crumb coat. Chill cake in refrigerator until set, about 20 minutes. Frost the house with a thicker layer of buttercream, smoothing the sides and front. Make a log pattern by running a decorating triangle with scalloped edge along the front, back, and sides. Transfer cake to a serving platter using two large spatulas. Refrigerate.

4 Press scalloped cookie borders onto edges of roof, trimming with a paring knife as needed and matching up corners. Press shingles onto roof, starting at bottom and overlapping as you work up; add top border.

5 Press large windows and door into place; press a shingle into place for attic window. Press scalloped cookie borders along house's base; trim as necessary. Refrigerate cake at least 20 minutes or up to 5 hours.

6 Cut a miniature house shape for doghouse from remaining cake triangle. Frost and comb; add roof and door. With a small brush, cover tree branches with melted chocolate. Place on parchment. Refrigerate until set, about 20 minutes.

7 Lightly dust a work surface with cornstarch. Roll balls of white fondant to form a snowman, gluing them together with royal icing, if necessary. Tint a very small amount of fondant orange, and shape into a carrot nose. Tint a small amount of fondant red, and make a scarf. Make toothpick holes for nose, eyes, and buttons; put carrot and sprinkles in place. Wrap

scarf around neck; top with licorice hat. Display cake house, doghouse, and scenery on a platter that's been "snowed" on with sanding sugar, if desired.

8 Just before serving, fit a pastry bag with a small, round tip (such as Ateco #3), and fill with royal icing. Pipe icicles around roof edge.

from Building a Gingercake House

gingerbread cakes

MAKES TWO 9-INCH SQUARE CAKES

10 tablespoons (1¼ sticks) unsalted butter, softened, plus more for pans

3¾ cups all-purpose flour, plus more for dusting

1½ teaspoons baking soda

1½ cups boiling water

4 teaspoons ground ginger

2 teaspoons ground cinnamon

¾ teaspoon ground cloves

¾ teaspoon ground nutmeg

1 teaspoon salt

1 tablespoon baking powder

1 cup packed dark-brown sugar

1½ cups unsulfured molasses

3 large eggs, room temperature

1 Preheat oven to 350°F. Cut two 9-inch squares of parchment paper to line the bottoms of two 9-inch square baking pans. Butter pans; line with squares of parchment. Butter linings, then flour pans, tapping out excess. Set pans aside.

2 Stir together baking soda and boiling water; set aside. Whisk together flour, ginger, cinnamon, cloves, nutmeg, salt, and baking powder in a medium bowl. Set aside.

3 Put butter and brown sugar in the bowl of an electric mixer fitted with the paddle attachment. Cream on medium speed until fluffy, about 4 minutes. Mix in molasses and eggs, scraping down sides of bowl as needed, until mixture is creamy, about 4 minutes. Add the flour mixture in three batches, alternating with two batches of the baking soda mixture. Reduce speed to low; mix until flour is incorporated. Raise speed to high; mix until well combined, about 15 seconds. Stir well with a rubber spatula, scraping bottom of bowl.

4 Divide batter between prepared pans. Bake until a cake tester inserted into centers comes out clean, about 40 minutes. Let cool in pans on wire racks, 20 minutes. Run a thin knife around sides of cakes to loosen. Turn cakes out onto racks, and peel off parchment. Reinvert; let cool completely.

chocolate Swiss meringue buttercream

MAKES 5½ CUPS

The buttercream will keep for up to three days in an airtight container in the refrigerator. Before using, bring it to room temperature and mix with the paddle attachment until smooth. Given that the buttercream isn't fully cooked, we used store-bought pasteurized egg whites. You'll find them in the dairy section of the supermarket.

1½ cups sugar

6 ounces whipping-quality pasteurized egg whites (6 large egg whites)

1 pound (4 sticks) unsalted butter, softened

1 teaspoon pure vanilla extract

5½ ounces semisweet chocolate, melted and cooled

1 Put sugar and egg whites in the heatproof bowl of an electric mixer. Set bowl over a pan of simmering water; whisk until sugar is dissolved, about 5 minutes.

2 Fit mixer with the whisk attachment. Beat egg-white mixture on medium speed until stiff peaks form and mixture is completely cooled, about 10 minutes.

3 Beat in butter a few tablespoons at a time. Reduce speed to low; add vanilla and melted chocolate. Beat until mixture is smooth, about 5 minutes.

gingerbread cookies

MAKES ENOUGH FOR ONE GINGERBREAD HOUSE

Once the icing is dry, cookies can be stacked in two layers (separated by a sheet of parchment paper) and stored in a large airtight container for up to two days.

3 cups all-purpose flour, plus more for dusting

½ teaspoon baking soda

¼ teaspoon baking powder

2 teaspoons ground ginger

2 teaspoons ground cinnamon

¾ teaspoon ground cloves

¾ teaspoon salt

8 tablespoons (1 stick) unsalted butter, softened

½ cup packed dark-brown sugar

1 large egg

½ cup unsulfured molasses

½ recipe Royal Icing (recipe follows)

   Sanding sugar, for sprinkling

1 Whisk together flour, baking soda, baking powder, ginger, cinnamon, cloves, and salt in a large bowl; set aside.

2 Put butter and sugar in the bowl of an electric mixer fitted with the paddle attachment; cream on high speed until fluffy, about 3 minutes. Add egg and molasses; mix 2 minutes. Reduce speed to low. Add flour mixture a little at a time, mixing until combined. Divide dough in half; wrap each piece in plastic wrap. Refrigerate at least 1 hour or up to 3 days.

3 Preheat oven to 350°F. Line baking sheets with parchment paper; set aside. On a lightly floured work surface, roll dough out to slightly thicker than ⅛ inch. Using a 1¼-inch scalloped cutter, make 80 squares for roof, walkway, and small window; use a 1½-inch cutter to make 2 large windows. Using a scalloped pastry wheel, cut out 8 pieces of trim (9 by ½ inch each), 1 door (3 by 2 inches), 2 large squares for doghouse roof (2 inches square each), and 1 arched door for doghouse (1 inch at base). Transfer to lined sheets; refrigerate 30 minutes.

4 Use a wooden skewer to make decorative holes along edges of trim, doors, and windows. Bake until the cookies are set and just beginning to darken around edges, 11 to 12 minutes. Transfer the cookies on parchment paper to a wire rack, and let cool completely.

5 Decorate cookies as desired with icing; sprinkle with sanding sugar. Let cookies stand until icing sets, about 3 hours.

royal icing

MAKES 1 CUP

Royal icing can be stored in an airtight container at room temperature for up to one day or in the refrigerator for up to three days.

2 cups confectioners' sugar

2 tablespoons meringue powder or powdered egg whites

1 Put sugar and meringue powder in the bowl of an electric mixer fitted with the paddle attachment. Mix on low speed until combined. With mixer running, add 3 tablespoons water. Raise speed to medium; mix, scraping down sides of bowl once, until icing is white and a ribbon forms when a spoon is lifted, about 4 minutes. (If necessary, add more water, 1 tablespoon at a time, until the right consistency is reached.)

2 Just before using, stir icing. Fit a pastry big with a small, round plain tip (such as Ateco #2), and fill with royal icing. Twist top of bag; seal with a rubber band. To keep icing from drying out, put a damp paper towel in the bottom of a tall glass; stand bag inside, tip side down.

lemon-oatmeal lacies

MAKES ABOUT 65

Vegetable-oil cooking spray

1 tablespoon unsalted butter

1 cup sugar

2 large eggs

½ teaspoon pure vanilla extract

Freshly grated zest of 1 lemon

¼ teaspoon salt

2 teaspoons baking powder

1 cup old-fashioned rolled oats

1 Preheat oven to 350°F. Line baking sheets with parchment paper, and lightly coat with cooking spray.

2 Put butter and sugar in the bowl of an electric mixer fitted with the paddle attachment. Mix on medium speed until crumbly. Add eggs, vanilla, lemon zest, and salt. Mix until pale, about 1 minute. Mix in baking powder and then oats. Let batter stand 10 minutes to thicken.

3 Drop batter on prepared sheets, using 1 teaspoon per cookie and spacing rounds about 3 inches apart. Using the back of a spoon, gently press each round into a circle.

4 Bake until golden and lacy, about 9 minutes. Slide parchment with cookies off sheets onto a work surface. Let cookies cool completely. Gently remove cookies from parchment. Cookies can be stored in an airtight container up to 3 days.

from Christmastime in the Country

cherry-vanilla snowdrop cookies

MAKES ABOUT 30

8 ounces (2 sticks) cold unsalted butter, cut into small pieces

1 cup confectioners' sugar

¼ cup cornstarch

¼ teaspoon salt

1½ teaspoons pure vanilla extract

1 vanilla bean, halved lengthwise

1½ cups all-purpose flour

¾ cup dried cherries, coarsely chopped

1 Preheat oven to 325°F. Put butter, ½ cup confectioners' sugar, the cornstarch, and salt in the bowl of an electric mixer fitted with the paddle attachment; mix on medium speed until smooth. Add extract, and scrape in vanilla seeds; reserve bean. Mix until combined. Mix in flour and cherries. Let dough rest 5 minutes.

2 Roll dough into 1-inch balls, and transfer balls to baking sheets, spacing about 1 inch apart. Bake until bottom edges are just beginning to brown, 20 to 25 minutes, rotating sheets halfway through. Let cool completely on a wire rack.

3 Meanwhile, toss remaining ½ cup confectioners' sugar with reserved vanilla bean in a medium bowl.

4 Up to an hour before serving, discard vanilla bean, and roll cooled cookies in vanilla sugar.

from Christmastime in the Country

pecan pie

MAKES ONE 9-INCH PIE | PHOTO ON PAGE 317

This pie can also be made in a nine-inch tart pan with a removable bottom or a nine-inch pie plate. Place it on a rimmed baking sheet before baking. If using a pie plate, the baking time will be about ten minutes longer.

All-purpose flour, for dusting

Tart Shell Dough (recipe follows)

6 large eggs

1¼ cups light corn syrup

1¼ cups packed dark-brown sugar

5 tablespoons unsalted butter, melted and cooled

1 tablespoon pure vanilla extract

2 teaspoons fresh lemon juice

¼ teaspoon salt

2½ cups coarsely chopped toasted pecans (about 10 ounces)

2 cups pecan halves (about 8 ounces), lightly toasted, for decorating

Freshly whipped cream, for serving

1 Set a 9-inch cake ring (with 1½-inch sides) on a baking sheet lined with parchment paper; set aside. On a lightly floured work surface, roll out dough to a 13-inch circle. Fit dough into cake ring; trim edges flush with top edge of ring. Transfer to freezer. Chill until firm, about 30 minutes.

2 Preheat oven to 400°F. Whisk together eggs, syrup, and sugar in a medium bowl until smooth. Whisk in butter, vanilla, lemon juice, and salt. Stir in chopped pecans. Pour filling into tart shell. Arrange pecan halves on top in concentric circles.

3 Bake, covering with foil after 15 minutes, until filling is no longer wobbly in center, about 1 hour. Transfer to a wire rack, and let cool at least 2 hours. Serve with whipped cream.

from Holiday Classics

tart shell dough

MAKES ENOUGH FOR ONE 9-INCH PIE

1¼ cups all-purpose flour

½ teaspoon salt

½ teaspoon sugar

8 tablespoons (1 stick) cold unsalted butter, cut into small pieces

¼ cup ice water

1 Process flour, salt, sugar, and butter in a food processor just until mixture resembles coarse meal, about 10 seconds.

2 With machine running, add ice water. Process just until dough starts to come together (no more than 15 seconds). Turn out dough onto a work surface, and immediately gather together. Wrap in plastic wrap, and press into a flat circle. Refrigerate at least 30 minutes or up to 2 days.

pistachio dacquoise

SERVES 8

1 cup shelled roasted, salted pistachios (4 ounces)

½ cup confectioners' sugar

6 large egg whites

1 cup granulated sugar

Pinch of salt

Pinch cream of tartar

2 cups raspberries (about 9 ounces)

Pastry Cream (recipe page 294)

1½ cups heavy cream

1 Preheat oven to 200°F, with racks in upper and lower thirds. Rub pistachios in a clean kitchen towel to remove skins. Coarsely chop nuts; transfer to a sieve, and shake over a paper towel (if desired, reserve dust for garnish); set aside. Draw three 8-inch circles on parchment paper; place paper, marked sides down, on two baking sheets.

2 Stir together nuts and confectioners' sugar in a bowl.

3 Put egg whites, granulated sugar, salt, and cream of tartar in the heatproof bowl of an electric mixer; set over a pan of simmering water. Whisk until sugar is dissolved and whites are warm to the touch, about 3 minutes (test by rubbing mixture between your fingers). Transfer bowl to mixer fitted with the whisk attachment; beat, starting on medium speed and increasing to high when soft peaks form; continue until stiff, glossy peaks form, 5 to 8 minutes.

4 Fold pistachio mixture into egg-white mixture. Spread one-third of the meringue onto each parchment circle (do not smooth the tops of the meringues).

5 Bake meringues 1 hour. Switch positions of sheets; reduce temperature to 175°F. Bake, switching positions of sheets after 45 minutes, until meringues are dry and crisp on the outside and can be lifted easily from parchment, 1 to 2 hours more. Turn off oven; let meringues cool in oven 45 minutes. Remove from oven; let cool completely on baking sheets. Store in airtight containers, up to 1 day.

6 Purée ⅔ cup raspberries in a food processor. Pass through a fine sieve into a bowl; discard seeds. (Purée can be refrigerated up to 1 day.) Beat pastry cream until smooth; set aside. Beat ½ cup heavy cream with electric mixer until soft peaks form. Gently fold into pastry cream; set aside.

7 Line a baking sheet with parchment paper. Put one meringue on sheet; spread half of pastry cream on top. Spoon 4½ teaspoons purée in a spiral over pastry cream; swirl with a knife. Top with another meringue. Set aside a few berries for garnish. Scatter remaining 1⅓ cup berries over meringue; spread remaining pastry cream on top, leaving a 1½-inch border. Spoon remaining purée in a spiral over pastry cream; drag a knife through purée to swirl. Top with last meringue; gently press to spread filling to edges. Freeze until filling is solid but not completely frozen, 2 to 3 hours.

8 Beat remaining cup heavy cream with electric mixer until soft peaks form. Top dacquoise with whipped cream; garnish with reserved berries, and pistachio dust, if desired. Using a serrated knife, cut into wedges and serve.

from Dessert of the Month

pastry cream

MAKES ABOUT 1¾ CUPS

½ cup sugar

2 large egg yolks

¼ teaspoon salt

¼ cup cornstarch

2 cups milk

1 Whisk together ¼ cup sugar, the yolks, and salt in a medium bowl. Whisk in cornstarch, 1 tablespoon at a time.

2 Bring milk and remaining ¼ cup sugar to a simmer in a medium saucepan over medium heat. Whisk a little milk mixture into egg-yolk mixture. Whisking constantly, gradually add remaining milk mixture. Return mixture to pan; bring to a boil, whisking constantly.

3 Cook, whisking, until very thick, 2 to 3 minutes. Pour through a fine sieve into a bowl; discard solids. Press plastic wrap directly onto surface of cream; refrigerate until completely chilled, at least 1 hour or up to 3 days.

mascarpone-stuffed dates with clementines and almonds

SERVES 4

½ cup mascarpone cheese (about 4 ounces)

¼ teaspoon ground cinnamon

1 tablespoon sugar

8 Medjool dates

½ cup whole raw almonds, skin on

¼ teaspoon olive oil

Pinch of coarse salt

3 clementines or tangerines, peeled and separated into segments

1 Preheat oven to 425°F. Stir together mascarpone, cinnamon, and sugar in a small bowl. Cut a slit lengthwise in each date, and remove pit. Fill each date with 1 tablespoon cheese mixture. Refrigerate dates until ready to serve, up to 2 hours.

2 Toss almonds with oil on a rimmed baking sheet. Toast in oven, shaking sheet occasionally, until fragrant and deep golden brown, about 10 minutes; sprinkle with salt. Arrange toasted almonds, stuffed dates, and clementine segments together on a serving platter.

from What's for Dinner?

snowy coconut cake

MAKES ONE 10-INCH CAKE | **PHOTO ON PAGE 314**

To avoid having yolks left over, you can make this cake with whipping-quality pasteurized egg whites.

1 cup sifted cake flour (not self-rising)

1½ cups granulated sugar

12 large egg whites (about 1½ cups)

1 teaspoon cream of tartar

1 tablespoon fresh lemon juice

¼ teaspoon salt

¼ teaspoon pure coconut extract

Coconut Crème Chantilly (recipe follows)

1½ cups dried unsweetened coconut shavings (about 2¼ ounces)

1 Preheat oven to 325°F, with rack in the lower third. Line a 10-inch tube pan with a parchment-paper ring: Cut a 10-inch circle from parchment paper, leaving a hole in the center to fit over tube. Set pan aside. Sift flour and ½ cup sugar onto another piece of parchment paper. Bring edges of paper up, and pour mixture into a fine sieve set over a bowl; sift mixture into bowl, and set aside.

2 Put egg whites in the bowl of an electric mixer fitted with the whisk attachment, and beat on medium speed until frothy. Add cream of tartar, lemon juice, salt, and coconut extract; beat until soft peaks form. With the mixer running, gradually add remaining cup sugar. Raise speed to medium-high; beat until stiff peaks form.

3 Gently transfer egg-white mixture to a large, shallow bowl; sprinkle one-third of the flour mixture over top. Using a large whisk, gently fold flour mixture into batter, letting batter fall through the whisk as you fold. Sprinkle remaining flour mixture over whites in two more batches; fold in until combined (do not overmix). Transfer batter to lined pan; gently run a knife through batter to remove any large air bubbles. Smooth top with the knife or an offset spatula.

4 Bake until a cake tester inserted near center comes out clean and top is springy to the touch, 45 to 50 minutes. Invert pan, and place tube over the neck of a large, heavy, narrow-necked bottle. Let suspended cake cool completely, 1½ to 2 hours. Run a knife around edges of cake; press removable bottom up and out of pan. Lift cake off pan bottom; remove paper. Cut cake in half horizontally; place bottom on a serving platter. Spread 2 cups coconut crème chantilly on bottom layer; set top layer on top, and coat filled cake with remaining crème chantilly. Spread coconut shavings on top of cake. Chill cake at least 1 hour and up to 3 hours before serving.

from Christmastime in the Country

coconut crème chantilly

MAKES 6 CUPS

1 cup milk

⅔ cup sugar

3 tablespoons cornstarch

¼ teaspoon salt

2 large eggs

2 cups heavy cream

¾ teaspoon pure coconut extract

2 tablespoons unsalted butter

1 Prepare an ice-water bath; set aside. Heat milk in a small saucepan over medium-high heat until just about to simmer. Meanwhile, whisk together sugar, cornstarch, and salt in a medium saucepan over medium heat. Whisking constantly, add eggs and 1 cup cream. Whisking constantly, gradually add hot milk; whisk until bubbling. Remove from heat, and whisk in extract and butter. Set pan in ice-water bath; let mixture cool, stirring occasionally. Cover with plastic wrap, and refrigerate until set, about 30 minutes.

2 Beat remaining cup heavy cream in the bowl of an electric mixer fitted with the whisk attachment until stiff peaks are just about to form. Add the chilled coconut-cream mixture, and beat until combined.

Note: The eggs in this dish are not fully cooked, so it should not be prepared for pregnant women, babies, young children, the elderly, or anyone whose health is compromised.

DRINKS

eggnog

SERVES 12 | **PHOTO ON PAGE 319**

9 eggs, separated, room temperature

1¼ cups sugar

½ vanilla bean, halved lengthwise, seeds scraped and reserved

Pinch of salt

4½ cups milk

½ cup bourbon

¼ cup dark rum

1½ cups heavy cream

Freshly grated nutmeg, for serving

1 Put egg yolks, ¾ cup sugar, vanilla bean scrapings, and salt in a large heatproof bowl. Set bowl over a pan of simmering water, and whisk constantly until mixture is pale and thick, about 5 minutes. Whisk in milk, bourbon, and rum until combined; remove from heat.

2 Beat egg whites and remaining ½ cup sugar in the bowl of an electric mixer fitted with the whisk until soft peaks form; whisk into milk mixture. In a clean bowl, beat cream until soft peaks form; whisk into milk mixture. Refrigerate eggnog until ready to serve, up to 1 day; whisk to combine before serving. Ladle into cups; sprinkle grated nutmeg over top of each.

Note: The eggs in this dish are not fully cooked, so it should not be prepared for pregnant women, babies, young children, the elderly, or anyone whose health is compromised.

from Holiday Classics

spiced pear-and-apple cider

MAKES 11 CUPS

6 cups apple cider

6 cups pear nectar

1 piece (2 inches) peeled fresh ginger, cut into thin rounds

3 whole cinnamon sticks

¼ teaspoon ground nutmeg

10 whole cloves

1 tablespoon fennel seeds

Stir together apple cider and pear nectar in a 4-quart saucepan. Add ginger, cinnamon sticks, nutmeg, cloves, and fennel seeds; bring to a boil. Reduce heat to low, and simmer, stirring occasionally, 20 to 25 minutes. Serve hot.

from Christmastime in the Country

macadamia butter-crunch popcorn

MAKES ABOUT 30 CUPS

25 cups popped popcorn (from about 1 cup kernels)

4 cups raw, whole macadamia nuts, toasted (about 1 pound)

1¼ cups packed light-brown sugar

5 tablespoons light corn syrup

10 tablespoons (1¼ sticks) unsalted butter

1¼ teaspoons coarse salt

¾ teaspoon baking soda

1 Preheat oven to 200°F. Put popcorn in a large bowl. Add nuts, and set aside. Put sugar, corn syrup, butter, and salt in a medium saucepan over medium heat. Cook, stirring, until mixture comes to a gentle simmer, about 4 minutes. Stop stirring, and continue cooking until mixture turns pale, 5 minutes more. Remove from heat, and stir in baking soda.

2 Pour sugar mixture over popcorn and nuts; toss to coat. Transfer to rimmed baking sheets; bake, stirring every 20 minutes, until almost dry, about 1 hour. Let cool completely on sheets on wire racks.

from Making Gifts by the Dozen

chocolate-almond popcorn

MAKES ABOUT 30 CUPS

25 cups popped popcorn (from about 1 cup kernels)

3 cups whole raw almonds, skin on, toasted (about 1 pound)

1 cup sugar

1 cup light corn syrup

8 tablespoons (1 stick) unsalted butter

¼ cup unsweetened cocoa powder

2 teaspoons coarse salt

1 Preheat oven to 200°F. Put popcorn in a large bowl. Add nuts; set aside. Put sugar, corn syrup, butter, cocoa, and salt in a medium saucepan over medium heat. Cook, stirring, until mixture comes to a gentle simmer, about 5 minutes.

2 Pour sugar mixture over popcorn and nuts; toss to coat. Transfer to rimmed baking sheets; bake, stirring every 20 minutes, until almost dry, about 1 hour. Let cool completely on sheets on wire racks.

from Making Gifts by the Dozen

peppermint marshmallows

MAKES SIXTEEN 2-INCH SQUARES

Vegetable oil cooking spray

4 packages (¼ ounce each) unflavored gelatin

¾ teaspoon peppermint extract

2 cups sugar

1 tablespoon light corn syrup

2 large egg whites

2 teaspoons red food coloring

1 Cut an 8-inch square of parchment paper to line the bottom of an 8-inch square baking pan. Coat baking pan with cooking spray. Line pan with parchment paper, and coat lining with cooking spray. Set pan aside.

2 Sprinkle gelatin over ¾ cup water in a heatproof bowl; let soften, about 5 minutes. Set bowl with gelatin mixture over a pan of simmering water; cook, whisking constantly until gelatin is dissolved. Remove from heat, and stir in peppermint extract; set aside.

3 Put sugar, corn syrup, and ¾ cup water in a saucepan over medium heat. Cook, stirring, until sugar is dissolved. Stop stirring; let mixture reach a boil. Raise heat to medium-high; cook until mixture reaches 260°F on a candy thermometer.

4 Meanwhile, beat egg whites in the bowl of an electric mixer fitted with the whisk attachment until stiff (but not dry) peaks form, about 4 minutes. Whisk gelatin mixture into sugar mixture; with mixer running, gradually add to egg whites. Mix on high speed until mixture is very thick, 12 to 15 minutes.

5 Pour mixture into lined pan. Working quickly, drop dots of red food coloring across surface of marshmallow. Using a toothpick, swirl food coloring into marshmallow to create a marbleized effect. Let mixture in pan stand, uncovered, at room temperature until firm, at least 3 hours or overnight. Remove from pan and cut into squares.

from Making Gifts by the Dozen

lavash crisps

SERVES 4

2 pieces lavash, each about 10 by 9 inches

2 teaspoons extra-virgin olive oil

Freshly ground pepper

Preheat oven to 425°F. Put lavash on a baking sheet; brush each with 1 teaspoon oil, and generously season with pepper. Toast in oven until crisp and golden, about 10 minutes. Let cool completely on sheet. Break each piece in two.

from What's for Dinner?

ROSEMARY CORNBREAD | PAGE 278

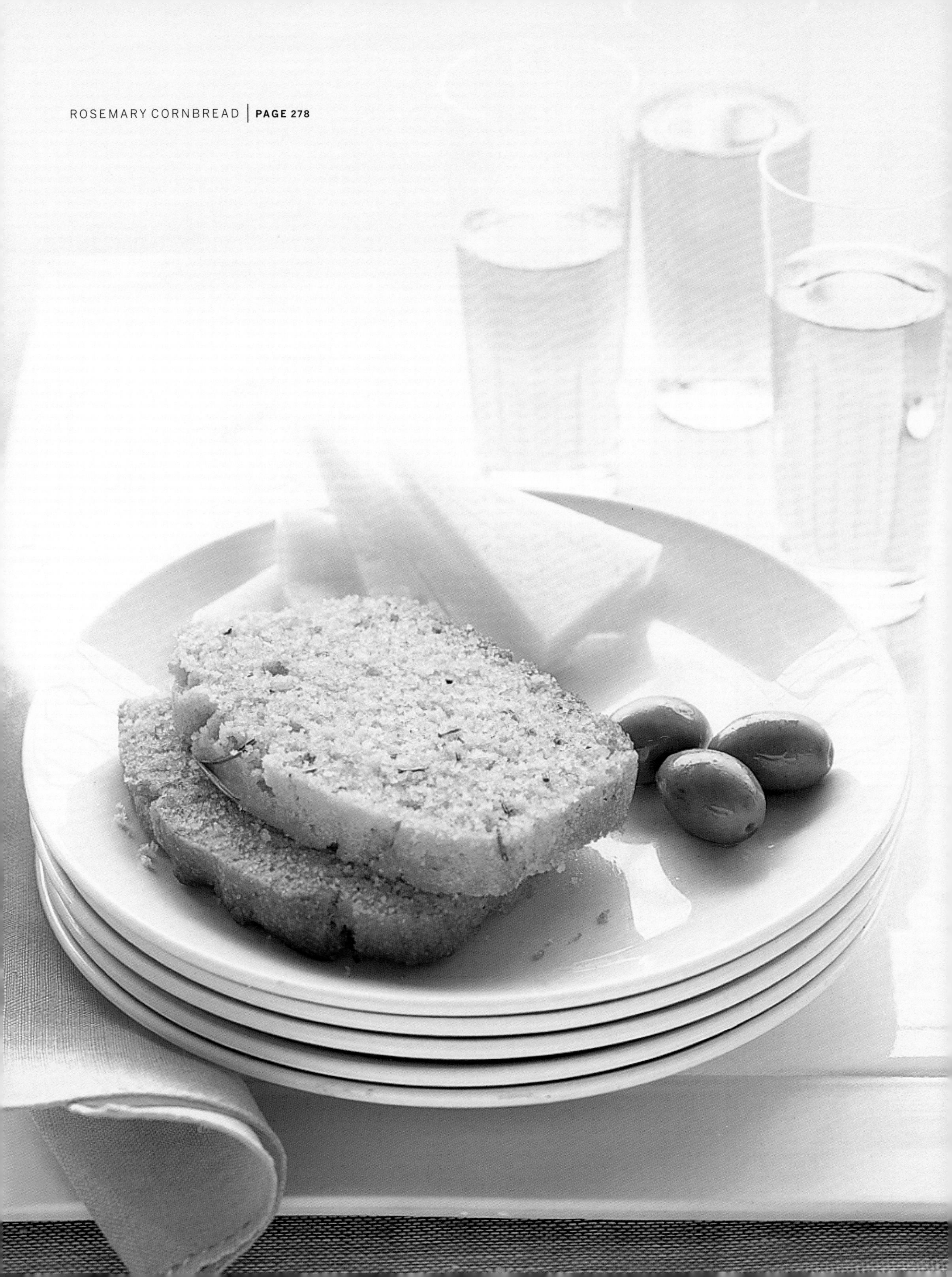

MUSHROOM AND CELERY SALAD
WITH PARMESAN CHEESE | **PAGE 255**

THAI BEEF SALAD | PAGE 263

BRANDADE | **PAGE 279**

CARAMELIZED-ONION DIP | **PAGE 280**

FAVA BEAN AND SAUSAGE DIP | **PAGE 281**

MUSHROOM AND BACON DIP | **PAGE 282**

FRENCH ONION SOUP | PAGE 253

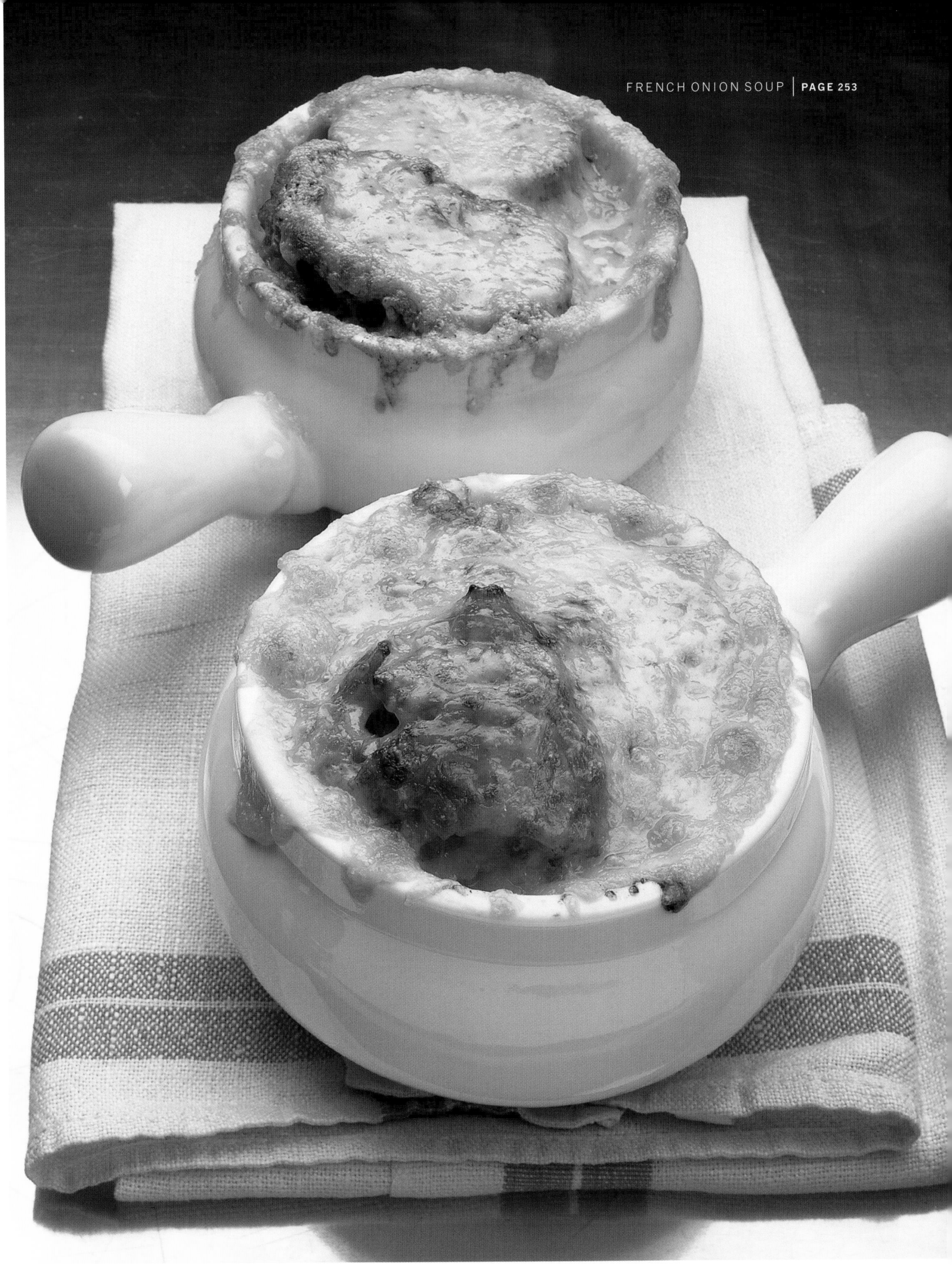

SHIITAKE MUSHROOM AND
CHEESE FRITTATA | **PAGE 262**

APRICOT-DIJON GLAZED CHICKEN | **PAGE 237**

SEARED SCALLOPS WITH
CABBAGE AND LEEKS | **PAGE 262**

QUINOA AND TURKEY PATTIES
IN PITA WITH TAHINI SAUCE | **PAGE 240**

TURKEY SAUSAGE WITH
PEPPERS AND ONIONS | **PAGE 262**

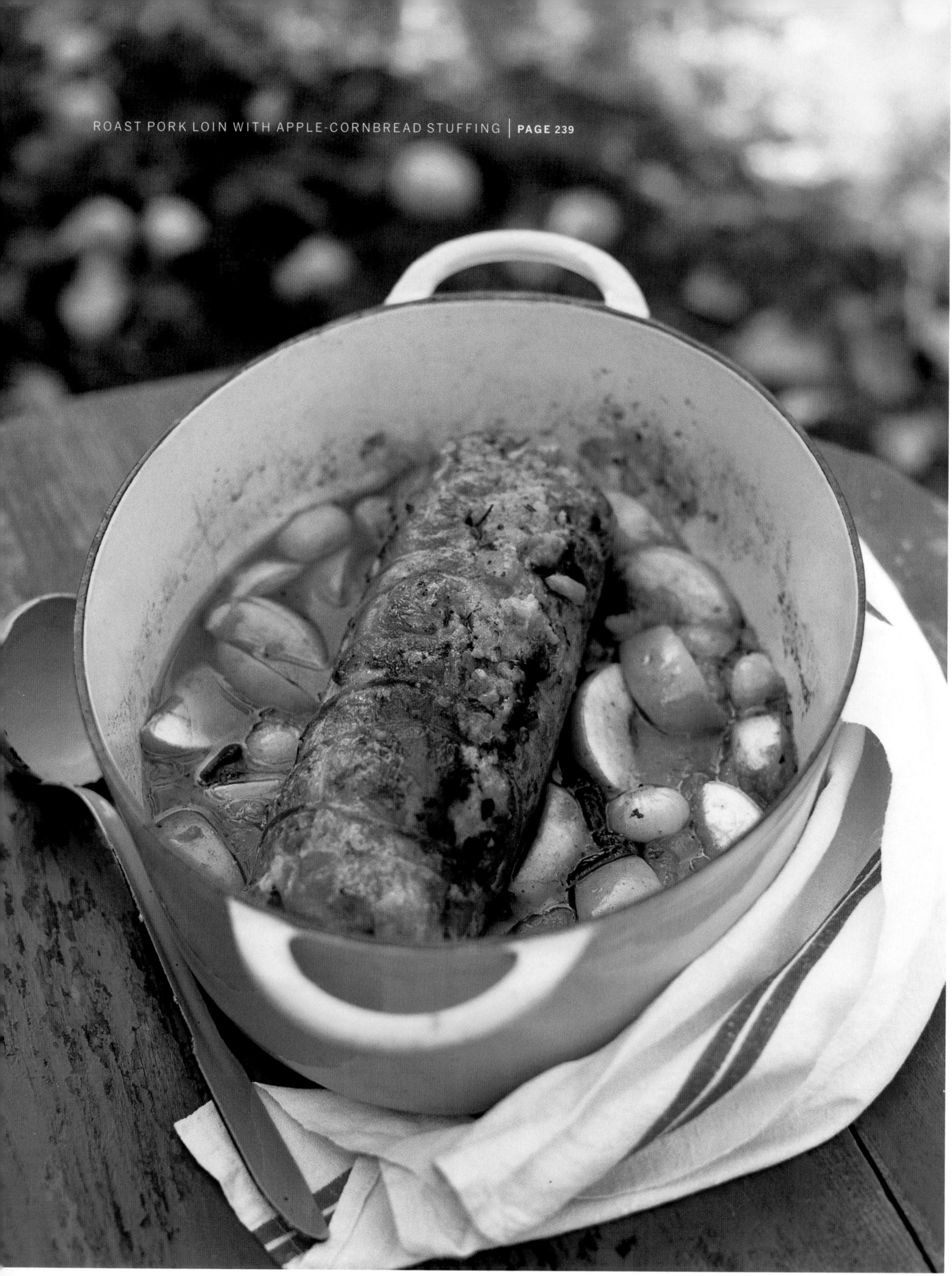

ROAST PORK LOIN WITH APPLE-CORNBREAD STUFFING | **PAGE 239**

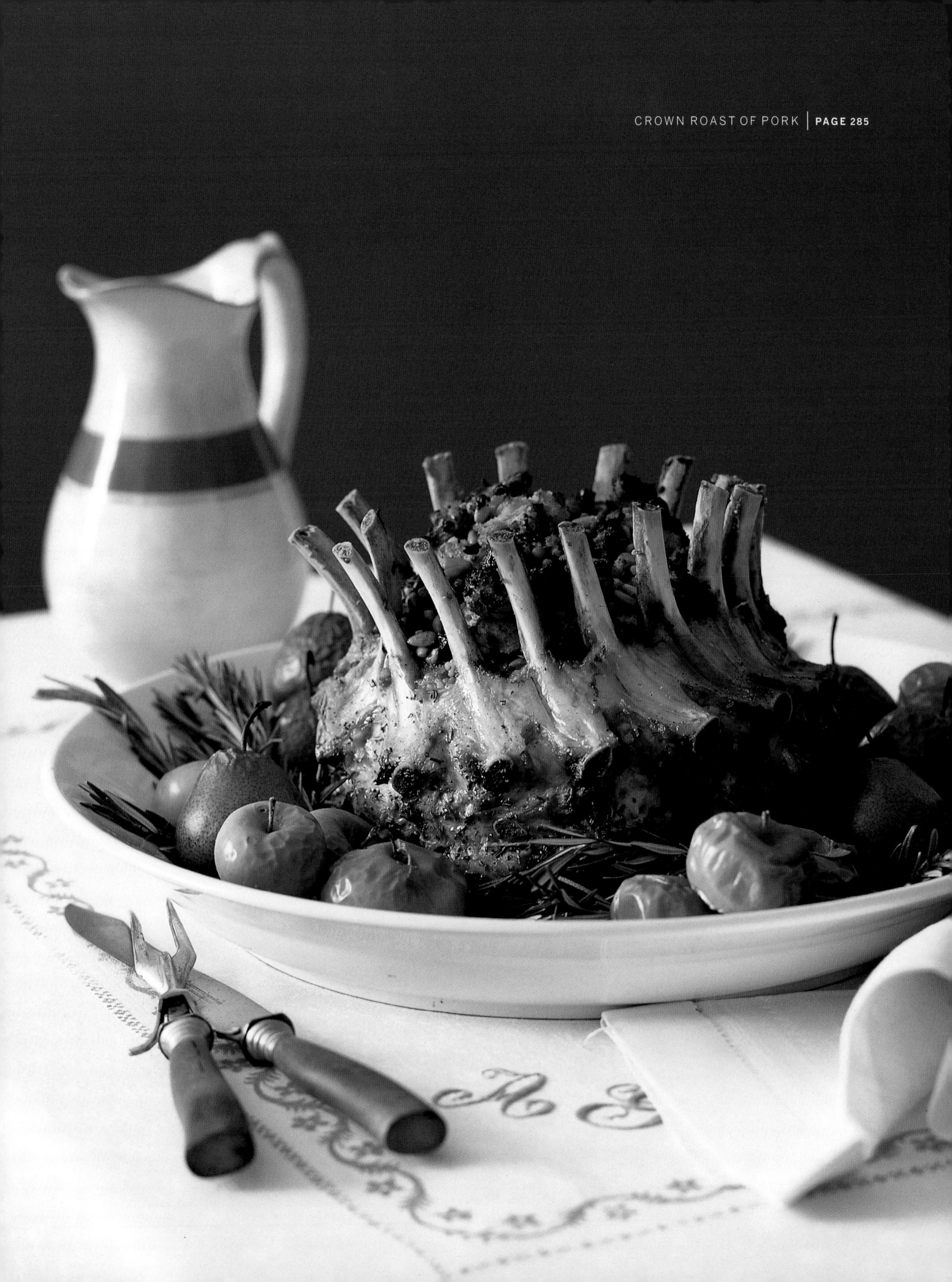

CROWN ROAST OF PORK | **PAGE 285**

HERB-ROASTED TURKEY | **PAGE 261**

MASHED SQUASH AND POTATOES WITH AMARETTI | **PAGE 258**

CREAMED SPINACH AND PEARL ONIONS | **PAGE 284**

CANDIED SWEET POTATOES | **PAGE 283**

CIPOLLINI IN AGRODOLCE | **PAGE 257**

RED-AND-GOLDEN-BEET CHEESE TART | **PAGE 255**

CAULIFLOWER, PROSCIUTTO, AND
GOAT CHEESE GRATIN | **PAGE 237**

GRATINEED MACARONI AND
CHEESE WITH TOMATOES | PAGE 237

WILD RICE AND CORN STUFFING | **PAGE 260**

ISRAELI COUSCOUS AND
FALL-VEGETABLE STUFFING | **PAGE 258**

POTATO AND CRACKER STUFFING | **PAGE 259**

FARRO AND SAUSAGE STUFFING | **PAGE 257**

AMARETTO POUND CAKE WITH
FLAMBEED PINEAPPLE | **PAGE 263**

PPLESAUCE COFFEE CAKE | **PAGE 246**

SHERRY TRIFLE WITH BRANDY CUSTARD | **PAGE 272**

OIRE WILLIAM CHARLOTTES | **PAGE 271**

VANILLA-BEAN BAKED APPLES | **PAGE 249**

STRAWBERRY-JAM YOGURT BREAD | **PAGE 278**

BRANDIED-CHERRY CASSATA | **PAGE 264**

BLOOD-ORANGE PAVLOVAS WITH
GRAND MARNIER | **PAGE 264**

PEPPERMINT MERINGUE COOKIES
WITH CHOCOLATE FILLING | **PAGE 287**

SNOWY COCONUT CAKE | **PAGE 294**

CHOCOLATE-ESPRESSO KAHLUA TART | **PAGE 266**

MINI CARROT-CARDAMOM PIES | **PAGE 26**

PECAN PIE | **PAGE 292**

FRUITCAKE | **PAGE 289**

EGGNOG | **PAGE 295**

APPLESAUCE MUFFINS | **PAGE 249**

APPLE PIE WITH CHEDDAR CRUST | **PAGE 245**

CRANBERRY, ORANGE, AND PECAN
BREAD PUDDING | **PAGE 245**

GINGERCAKE HOUSE | **PAGE 290**

V

Menus

Sources

AIDELLS SAUSAGES *Gourmet Garage*

AMARETTI DI SARONNO COOKIES
Dean & DeLuca

ASIAN CHILI PASTE *Pacific Rim Gourmet*

ASIAN GREENS *Diamond Organics*

ATECO TIPS *Sweet Celebrations*

AUREUS DE SAUTERNES WINE
Beekman Liquors and Wines

AVOCADO LEAVES *Kitchen/Market*

BABY BOK CHOY *Diamond Organics*

BABY TATSOI GREENS
Diamond Organics

BLACK MISSION FIGS *Kalustyan's*

BLANCHED ALMOND FLOUR
A.O. Bazzini

BOCCONCINI *Eli's Manhattan*

BROWN FLAXSEED, WHOLE
Eli's Manhattan

BROWN FLAXSEED, GROUND
Whole Foods Market

BULGHUR WHEAT *Whole Foods Market*

CAJUN SEASONING *Kalustyan's*

CAKE RING, 8-BY-2 INCHES (M570-8)
J.B. Prince

CALIMYRNA FIGS *Kalustyan's*

CANAPE BAKING SHELLS (#6421)
Fante's Kitchen Wares Shop

CAPTAIN MORGAN'S SILVER SPICED
LIGHT RUM *Beekman Liquors and Wines*

CARDAMOM PODS *Kalustyan's*

CAST-IRON SAUCEPAN (L2919-20)
IN WHITE *Le Creuset*

CHALLAH BREAD *Eli's Manhattan*

CHERRIES, TART, INDIVIDUALLY QUICK-
FROZEN *Friske Orchards*

CHERVIL *Whole Foods Market*

CHIHUAHUA CHEESE *Kitchen/Market*

'CHIOGGIA' BEETS *Diamond Organics*

CHIPOTLE CHILES IN ADOBO
Kitchen/Market

CHOCOLATE JIMMY SPRINKLES
Sweet Celebrations

CHOCOLATE ROCKS *Sweet Celebrations*

CHORIZO *igourmet.com*

CHRYSANTHEMUM SEEDS
Kitazawa Seed

CIPOLLINI ONIONS *Greenleaf Produce*

COCONUT CHIPS, UNSWEETENED
Kalustyan's

COOKIE CUTTERS *Sweet Celebrations,
Bridge Kitchenware*

CORIANDER SEEDS *Kitchen/Market*

COTIJA CHEESE *Kitchen/Market*

CRANBERRY BEANS *Eli's Manhattan*

CRYSTAL SUGAR (#45284)
Sweet Celebrations

CRYSTALLIZED GINGER
Russ & Daughters

DRIED CANNELLINI BEANS
Eli's Manhattan

DRIED EPAZOTE *Kitchen/Market*

DRIED GUAJILLO CHILES
Kitchen/Market

DRIED MEXICAN OREGANO
Kitchen/Market

DRIED PEARS *Russ & Daughters*

ENTREMET RINGS, 4-BY-1⅓ INCHES
(M246-4) *J.B. Prince*

EXCALIBUR NONSTICK WOK WITH LID
Williams-Sonoma

FAVA BEANS *Kalustyan's*

FISH SAUCE *Pacific Rim Gourmet*

FLAXSEED OIL *Eli's Manhattan*

FLUTED TART PAN, NONSTICK, WITH
REMOVABLE BOTTOM, 11-BY-1 INCH
(#408980) *Broadway Panhandler*

FOIE GRAS PATE *D'Artagnan*

FRANKFURTER ROLLS, TOP-SLICED
Pepperidge Farm

FRESH CHESTNUTS *Diamond Organics*

FRESH CURRY LEAVES *Kalustyan's*

FONTINA VAL D'AOSTA CHEESE
Murray's Cheese Shop

GAETA OLIVES *Whole Foods*

GAI CHOI CHINESE MUSTARD SEEDS
Kitazawa Seed

GAI LAN (CHINESE BROCCOLI) SEEDS
Kitazawa Seed

GARAM MASALA *Kalustyan's*

GEL PASTE, DEEP PINK AND RED
Sweet Celebrations

GERHARD'S NAPA VALLEY SAUSAGES
Trader Joe's

GOLDEN FLAXSEED
Whole Foods Market

GORGONZOLA DOLCE
Murray's Cheese Shop

GREEK YOGURT *Whole Foods Market*

GROUND CANELA *Kitchen/Market*

HATCH WHOLE GREEN CHILES
Kitchen/Market

HOT SOPPRESSATA
Murray's Cheese Shop

ICE-CREAM SCOOP, HALF-OUNCE
(U573-100) *J. B. Prince*

INSTANT TAPIOCA *Eli's Manhattan*

JELLY ROLL PAN, ALUMINUM, 12-BY-17
INCHES (#22391) *Sur La Table*

KEY LIME JUICE *Famous Florida*

LAVASH *Kalustyan's*

LEMON VERBENA *Greenleaf Produce*

LES PARISIENNES CHERRIES IN BRANDY
S.O.S. Chefs of New York

LOAF PAN, 8½-BY-4½ INCHES
Williams-Sonoma

MACHE LETTUCE *Whole Foods Market*

MADURO PLANTAINS
Greenleaf Produce

MASCARPONE CHEESE
Murray's Cheese Shop

MAYTAG BLUE CHEESE
Murray's Cheese Shop

MEDJOOL DATES *Dean & DeLuca*

MERGUEZ SAUSAGE *D'Artagnan*

MIZUNA GREENS *Diamond Organics*

MIZUNA SEEDS *Kitazawa Seed*

MOLCAJETE Y TEJOLOTE (MEXICAN
MORTAR AND PESTLE)
GourmetSleuth.com

MOREL MUSHROOMS, FRESH
Whole Foods Market

MOSCATO D'ASTI *Beekman Liquors
and Wines*

MUSCAT DE BEAUMES DE VENISE,
BY PAUL JABOULET AINE
Beekman Liquors and Wines

MUSCATEL WINE VINEGAR
Whole Foods Market

NASTURTIUM FLOWERS AND LEAVES
The Herb Lady

NEW MEXICAN CHILI POWDER
Kitchen/Market

NEW MEXICAN CHILES
Kitchen/Market

NONSTICK TART PANS WITH
REMOVABLE BOTTOMS
Bridge Kitchenware

OKRA *Whole Foods Market*

ORANGE-COLORED SUGAR
The Baker's Catalogue

PANIBOIS MOLDS (#BP2393),
5⅛-BY-3¾ INCHES *Kitchen Krafts*

PANETTONE *Buon Italia*

PASSION-FRUIT JUICE
Whole Foods Market

PASTRY CUTTER *Sweet Celebrations*

PEA SHOOTS *Diamond Organics*

PEARL TAPIOCA, LARGE *Kalustyan's*

PICHOLINE OLIVES *Whole Foods Market*

PILLIVUYT RECTANGULAR
ROASTING PAN *Broadway Panhandler*

PITU AQUARDENTE CACHAÇA RUM
BevMo.com

POIRE WILLIAM (PEAR EAU-DE-VIE),
BY MASSENEZ *Beekman Liquors
and Wines*

POLISH BOROWIK MUSHROOMS, DRIED
Polish Art Center

POPOVER PAN, NONSTICK (#114547)
Broadway Panhandler

PRICKLY PEARS *Dean & DeLuca*

QUICHE PAN WITH REMOVABLE
BOTTOM, 8-BY-11-BY-1¼ INCHES
(#780246) *Broadway Panhandler*

QUINOA, RED AND WHITE *Kalustyan's*

RAMEKINS, 5-OZ. *Broadway Panhandler*

RICE NOODLES *Pacific Rim Gourmet*

RICE WINE *Pacific Rim Gourmet*

ROUND CAKE PAN, 7-BY-3 INCHES
Pfeil & Holing

RYE FLOUR *The Baker's Catalogue*

SALSIFY *Greenleaf Produce*

SALT COD *Gorton's Fresh Seafood*

SANDEMAN MADEIRA *Beekman Liquors
and Wines*

SANDING SUGAR, CLEAR
Sweet Celebrations

SCALLOPED PASTRY COMB
Wilton Industries

SCALLOPED PASTRY CRIMPER
Bridge Kitchenware

SHELLFISH POT *Sur La Table*

SKILLET GRILL, SQUARE, 10-BY-10
INCHES (L2021-26) *Le Creuset*

SOUFFLE DISH, 2-QT. *Crate & Barrel*

SOUFFLE DISH, DEEP, 1 QT
Broadway Panhandler

SPECK, DOMESTIC *Dean & DeLuca*

SPRINGFORM PAN, 10 INCHES
(#2017903) *Will0ms-Sonoma*

STAINLESS-STEEL CAKE RING,
8¾-BY-2¼ INCHES (#7121) *Sur La Table*

STAR PASTRY TIP *Bridge Kitchenware*

SUNFLOWER SPROUTS
Whole Foods Market

SWISS GRUYERE CHEESE
Murray's Cheese Shop

TAHINI *Whole Foods Market*

TALEGGIO CHEESE
Murray's Cheese Shop

TARTLET MOLDS *Bridge Kitchenware*

TATSOI SEEDS *Kitazawa Seed*

THAI FISH SAUCE *Pacific Rim Gourmet*

THAI GREEN-CURRY PASTE
Pacific Rim Gourmet

TERRA-COTTA FLOWERPOTS,
2¾ INCHES, UNGLAZED AND UNTREATED
Arizona Pottery

TORANI RASPBERRY SYRUP
Chew Brokers

TORRONE *Whole Foods Market*

TURMERIC *Kitchen/Market*

UDON NOODLES *Whole Foods Market*

WHEAT BERRIES, ORGANIC
Whole Foods Market

WHEAT GERM *Eli's Manhattan*

WHITE NONPAREILS *Sweet Celebrations*

WHOLE-WHEAT GRAHAM FLOUR
Hodgson Mill

WILTON FONDANT *Sweet Celebrations*

Directory

Addresses and telephone numbers of sources may change prior to or following publication of this book, as may the availability of any item.

A.O. BAZZINI
339 Greenwich Street
New York, NY 10013
212-334-1280
www.bazzininuts.com

ARIZONA POTTERY
15681 North Cave Creek Road
Suite #2
Phoenix, AZ 85032
800-420-1808
www.arizonapottery.com

THE BAKER'S CATALOGUE
800-827-6836
www.bakerscatalogue.com

BEEKMAN LIQUORS AND WINES
500 Lexington Avenue
New York, NY 10017
212-759-5857
www.beekmanliquors.com

BEVMO.COM
877-772-3866
www.bevmo.com

BRIDGE KITCHENWARE
214 East 52nd Street
New York, NY 10022
800-274-3435
www.bridgekitchenware.com

BROADWAY PANHANDLER
477 Broome Street
New York, NY 10013
866-266-5927
www.broadwaypanhandler.com

BUON ITALIA
75 Ninth Avenue
New York, NY 10011
212-633-9090
www.buonitalia.com

CHEW BROKERS
800-311-7692
www.chewbrokers.com

CRATE & BARREL
800-967-6696
www.crateandbarrel.com

D'ARTAGNAN
280 Wilson Avenue
Newark, NJ 07105
800-327-8246
www.dartagnan.com

DEAN & DELUCA
560 Broadway
New York, NY 10012
212-226-6800

DIAMOND ORGANICS
1272 Highway 1
Moss Landing, CA 95039
888-674-2642
www.diamondorganics.com

ELI'S MANHATTAN
1411 Third Avenue
New York, NY 10028
212-717-8100
www.elizabar.com

FAMOUS FLORIDA
888-352-2665
www.famousflorida.com

FANTE'S KITCHEN WARES SHOP
1006 South 9th Street
Philadelphia, PA 19147
800-443-2683
www.fantes.com

FRISKE ORCHARDS
10743 North U.S. 31
Ellsworth, MI 49729
888-968-3554
www.friske.com

GORTON'S FRESH SEAFOOD
800-335-3674
www.gortonsfreshseafood.com

GOURMET GARAGE
453 Broome Street
New York, NY 10013
212-941-5850
www.gourmetgarage.com

GOURMETSLEUTH.COM
408-354-8281
www.gourmetsleuth.com

GREENLEAF PRODUCE
1955 Jerrold Avenue
San Francisco, CA 94132
415-647-2991
www.greenleafsf.com

THE HERB LADY
52792 42nd Avenue
Lawrence, MI 49064
269-674-3879

HODGSON MILL
800-347-0105
www.hodgsonmill.com

IGOURMET.COM
877-446-8763
www.igourmet.com

J.B. PRINCE
36 East 31st Street
New York, NY 10016
800-473-0577
www.jbprince.com
($25 minimum on website)

KALUSTYAN'S
123 Lexington Avenue
New York, NY 10016
212-685-3451 (in New York City)
800-352-3451
www.kalustyans.com

KITAZAWA SEED
P.O. Box 13220
Oakland, CA 94661
510-595-1188
www.kitazawaseed.com

KITCHEN KRAFTS
P.O. Box 442-ORD
Waukon, IA 52172
800-776-0575
www.kitchenkrafts.com

KITCHEN/MARKET
218 Eighth Avenue
New York, NY 10011
888-468-4433
www.kitchenmarket.com

LE CREUSET
877-273-8738
www.lecreuset.com for locations

MURRAY'S CHEESE SHOP
257 Bleecker Street
New York, NY 10014
888-692-4339
www.murrayscheese.com

PACIFIC RIM GOURMET
800-910-9657
www.pacificrim-gourmet.com

PEPPERIDGE FARM
888-737-7374 for locations
www.pepperidgefarm.com

PFEIL & HOLING
58-15 Northern Boulevard
Woodside, NY 11377
800-247-7955
www.cakedeco.com

POLISH ART CENTER
9539 Joseph Campau
Hamtramck, MI 48212
888-619-9771

RUSS & DAUGHTERS
179 East Houston Street
New York, NY 10002
800-787-7229
www.russanddaughters.com

S.O.S. CHEFS OF NEW YORK
212-505-5813

SUR LA TABLE
800-243-0852
www.surlatable.com

SWEET CELEBRATIONS
P.O. Box 39426
Edina, MN 55439
800-328-6722
www.sweetc.com

TRADER JOE'S
555 9th Street
San Francisco, CA 94103
415-863-1292
www.traderjoes.com

WILLIAMS-SONOMA
110 Seventh Avenue
New York, NY 10001
877-812-6235
www.williams-sonoma.com

WILTON INDUSTRIES
800-794-5866
www.wilton.com

WHOLE FOODS MARKET
250 Seventh Avenue
New York, NY 10001
212-924-5969
www.wholefoods.com

Index

Page numbers in italics indicate color photographs

Photography Credits

CONVERSION CHART *Equivalent Imperial and Metric Measurements*

American cooks use standard containers, the 8-ounce cup and a tablespoon that takes exactly 16 level fillings to fill that cup level. Measuring by cup makes it very difficult to give weight equivalents, as a cup of densely packed butter will weigh considerably more than a cup of flour. The easiest way, therefore, to deal with cup measurements in recipes is to take the amount by volume rather than by weight. Thus the equation reads: 1 cup = 225 ml = 8 fl. oz.; ½ cup = 110 ml = 4 fl. oz. It is possible to buy a set of American cup measures in major stores around the world. In the States, butter is often measured in sticks. One stick is the equivalent of 8 tablespoons. One tablespoon of butter is therefore the equivalent to ½ ounce/15 grams.

SOLID MEASURES

U.S./IMPERIAL MEASURES		METRIC MEASURES	
ounces	pounds	grams	kilos
1		28	
2		56	
3½		100	
4	¼	112	
5		140	
6		168	
8	½	225	
9		150	¼
12	¾	340	
16	1	450	
18		500	½
20	1¼	560	
24	1½	675	
27		750	¾
28	1¾	780	
32	2	900	
36	2¼	1000	1
40	2½	1100	
48	3	1350	
54		1500	1½
64	4	1800	
72	4½	2000	2

LIQUID MEASURES

FLUID OUNCES	U.S.	IMPERIAL	MILLILITERS
	1 teaspoon	1 teaspoon	5
¼	2 teaspoons	1 dessert spoon	7
½	1 tablespoon	1 tablespoon	15
1	2 tablespoons	2 tablespoons	28
2	¼ cup	4 tablespoons	56
4	½ cup or ¼ pint		110
5		¼ pint or 1 gill	140
6	¾ cup		170
8	1 cup or ½ pint		225
9			250, ¼ liter
10	1¼ cups	½ pint	280
12	1½ cups	¾ pint	340
15	¾ pint		420
16	2 cups or 1 pint		450
18	2¼ cups		500, ½ liter
20	2½ cups	1 pint	560
24	3 cups or 1½ pints		675
25		1¼ pints	700
27	3½ cups		750, ¾ liter
30	3¾ cups	1½ pints	840
32	4 cups or 2 pints or 1 quart		900

OVEN TEMPERATURE EQUIVALENTS

FAHRENHEIT	CELSIUS	GAS MARK	DESCRIPTION
225	110	¼	cool
250	130	½	
275	140	1	very slow
300	150	2	
325	170	3	slow
350	180	4	moderate
375	190	5	
400	200	6	moderately hot
425	220	7	fairly hot
450	230	8	hot
475	240	9	very hot
500	250	10	extremely hot

LINEAR AND AREA MEASURES

1 inch	2.54 centimeters

EQUIVALENTS FOR INGREDIENTS

all-purpose flour	plain flour
arugula	rocket
buttermilk	ordinary milk
confectioners' sugar	icing sugar
cornstarch	cornflour
eggplant	aubergine
granulated sugar	caster sugar
half-and-half	12% fat milk
heavy cream	double cream
light cream	single cream
lima beans	broad beans
scallion	spring onion
squash	courgettes or marrow
unbleached flour	strong, white flour
zest	rind
zucchini	courgettes

REAKFAST ENCHILADAS, *bruschetta with fava beans*

ND ARUGULA PESTO, BRUSCHETTA WITH POACHED TUNA, BRUSCHETTA WITH

OASTED PEPPERS AND HERBED RICOTTA, GREEN GODDESS DIP, BEET AND

ÂCHE SALAD WITH AGED GOAT CHEESE, FINGERLING POTATO SALAD WITH

UGAR SNAP PEAS, GREEN BEAN, SHELL BEAN, AND SWEET ONION FATTOUSH,

melon bowls with prosciutto AND WATERCRESS SALAD,

ED ROMAINE SALAD WITH WALNUTS AND EGGS, TANGY CORN SALAD, SPICY

HICKEN SALAD IN LETTUCE CUPS, COCONUT NOODLES, GREEN POBLANO-

HILE RICE, SMOKY PINTO BEANS, ROLLED CHICKEN BREASTS WITH ALMOND-

INT PESTO AND ZUCCHINI, LAMB SAUSAGES, CHICKEN SCALOPPINE WITH

RUGULA, LEMON, AND PARMESAN, GRILLED BURGERS WITH MAYTAG BLUE

HEESE AND HEIRLOOM TOMATOES, GRILLED CHICKEN STUFFED WITH BASIL

ND TOMATO, LOBSTER ROLLS, *spicy stir-fried shrimp,*

ANNA COTTA TARTS WITH STRAWBERRIES, APRICOT-PISTACHIO TART, SWEET

HERRY GALETTE, FIG AND GRAPE TART, SUGAR PLUM TART, PROFITEROLES

ITH CHOCOLATE-MACADAMIA SEMIFREDDO, MINI BLACK-AND-WHITE COOKIES,

LOODY MARYS WITH TEQUILA, PRICKLY PEAR AGUAS FRESCAS, SPARKLING

RESH LEMONADE, SOUTHWESTERN *corn chowder,* SPIKED CLAMS

ND OYSTERS, BLACK-EYED-PEA AND JALAPEÑO SALAD, GRILLED CORN ON

HE COB WRAPPED WITH BACON, CREAMED CORN, CRISPY CHEDDAR CAKES

ITH BACON, *grilled rib-eye steaks,* SUCCOTASH WITH SEARED

CALLOPS, RATATOUILLE, BLACKBERRY-ALMOND SHORTBREAD SQUARES,

ROCKY ROAD TART, LEMON POPPY-SEED COOKIES, ARCTIC MINT JULEP, EG

CREAMS, FROZEN WHITE SANGRIA, PEACH ICED TEA, SPARKLING STRAWBERR

ROSEMARY LEMONADE, WATERMELON-TEQUILA REFRESHERS, ROSEMAR

BREAD, *sweet pickled red onions,* PICKLED ZUCCHIN

RIBBONS, BREAD-AND-BUTTER PICKLES, SPICY PICKLED GREEN AND WAX BEAN

CURRIED CHICKEN TURNOVERS, COLD SESAME NOODLES, SALMON WIT

HONEY-CORIANDER GLAZE, STEAK AND ONION SANDWICHES, OMELET WRAP

WITH VEGETABLES, *broiled plums* WITH MASCARPONE CREAM

CHOCOLATE SOUFFLÉ, CHOCOLATE-CHERRY CRUMB BARS, HONEY CAKE WIT

CARAMELIZED PEARS, MANGO-PAPAYA SALAD WITH MINT, PEANUT CRISP

TOMATO FOCACCIA, GRATINÉED *macaroni and cheese* WIT

TOMATOES, ROAST PORK LOIN WITH APPLE-CORNBREAD STUFFING, APRICOT

DIJON GLAZED CHICKEN, CAULIFLOWER, PROSCIUTTO, AND GOAT CHEES

GRATIN, KNOCKWURST WITH BRAISED CABBAGE AND APPLES, CLASSIC POTAT

GRATIN, INDIVIDUAL PORTOBELLO MUSHROOM GRATINS, SOUTHWESTER

SWEET-POTATO GRATIN, *chocolate bread pudding*

APPLESAUCE COFFEE CAKE, BANANA CHOCOLATE-CHUNK ICE CREAM, PUMPKI

COOKIES WITH BROWN-BUTTER ICING, APPLE PIE WITH CHEDDAR CRUST

BETTE'S CHICKEN LIVER PÂTÉ WITH SAUTEED MAPLE-SYRUP APPLES, FRENC

ONION SOUP, POLENTA SQUARES WITH PROSCIUTTO, RED-AND-GOLDEN-BEE

CHEESE TART, MUSHROOM AND CELERY SALAD WITH PARMESAN CHEES

savory cranberry jelly, ISRAELI COUSCOUS AND FALL